Securing Employer-Based Pensions: An International Perspective

Pension Research Council Publications

A complete listing of PRC publications appears in the back of this volume.

Securing Employer-Based Pensions

An International Perspective

Edited by Zvi Bodie, Olivia S. Mitchell, and John A. Turner

Published by

The Pension Research Council
The Wharton School of the University of Pennsylvania

and

University of Pennsylvania Press
Philadelphia

The chapters in this volume are based on papers presented at the May 5 and 6, 1994 Pension Research Council Symposium entitled "Securing Employer-Based Pensions: An International Perspective."

Library of Congress Cataloging-in-Publication Data
Securing employer-based pensions: an international perspective /
edited by Zvi Bodie, Olivia S. Mitchell, and John Turner.
    p. cm.
   Earlier versions of these papers presented at a conference in May
1994.
   Includes bibliographical references and index.
   ISBN 0–8122–3334–4
   1. Pensions — Congresses.   2. Old age pensions — Congresses.
3. Pension trusts — Congresses.   4. Social security — Congresses.
I. Bodie, Zvi.   II. Mitchell, Olivia S.   III. Turner, John A. (John
Andrew), 1949 July 9–   IV. Wharton School. Pension Research
Council.
HD7090.S36   1996
331.25'2 — dc20   95-37311
                                 CIP

Pension Research Council

Pension Research Council

The Pension Research Council of The Wharton School of the University of Pennsylvania is an organization committed to generating debate on key policy issues affecting pensions and other employee benefits. The Council sponsors interdisciplinary research on the entire range of private and social retirement security and related benefit plans in the United States and around the world and seeks to broaden public understanding of these complex arrangements through basic research into their social, economic, legal, actuarial, and financial foundations. Members of the Executive Board of Council, appointed by the Dean of The Wharton School, are leaders in the employee benefits field, and though they recognize the essential role of social security and other public sector income maintenance programs, they share a strong desire to strengthen private sector approaches to economic security.

Contents

Preface   xi

1. Pension Security in an Aging World   1
Zvi Bodie and Olivia S. Mitchell
    Glossary of Terms   29

I. Pensions in Developed Nations   31

2. Occupational Pension Provision in the United Kingdom   33
Christopher D. Daykin
    Comments by Anthony M. Santomero   69

3. Pension Financial Security in Germany   73
Peter Ahrend
    Comments by Lucy apRoberts   105
    Comments by Marc M. Twinney   114

4. Private Pension Plans in Japan   121
Noriyasu Watanabe
    Comments by Robert L. Clark   143

II. Pensions in Emerging Economies   149

5. Mandatory Saving Schemes: Are They an Answer to the
Old Age Security Problem?   151
Estelle James and Dimitri Vittas
    Comments by Alan J. Auerbach   183
    Comments by Donald S. Grubbs, Jr.   187

6. Private Pension Systems in Transition Economies   193
John A. Turner and David M. Rajnes

III. Instruments of Pension Policy   211

7. The Taxation of Private Pensions   213
Andrew Dilnot
   Comments by Angela E. Chang   232
   Comments by Sylvester J. Schieber   235

8. An International Comparison of the Financing of
Occupational Pensions   244
E. Philip Davis
   Comments by Marshall E. Blume   282

9. The Government's Role in Insuring Pensions   286
James E. Pesando
   Comments by Carolyn L. Weaver   306
   Comments by Dallas L. Salisbury   312

Contributors   317
Index   325

Preface

As the world's population ages, pensions will be sought by millions as the mainstay of old age retirement income. This is a book about how to increase pension security in the international context. The contributors to this volume take a serious look at both public and private pensions, evaluating what they do well and what they do poorly in both developed and developing nations. This volume also seeks to help policymakers and practitioners look ahead, offering numerous suggestions for better pension designs in the future.

As shown in this book, sensible tax, insurance and funding policy, and investment management and actuarial oversight are central to building and maintaining a successful pension system. The ways in which these factors interact are traced across a variety of institutional environments, each of which generates its own pension system. Contributors to the volume illustrate the range of options as they vary across cultures, from Japan to Germany, and the United Kingdom to Canada. In addition, pensions in emerging economies offer both opportunities and cautionary lessons about how to secure retirement income in the new global economic order.

The most important contribution of this book is that it offers new perspectives and evaluation tools, which readers may then employ to examine their own as well as other pension systems. Views from government actuaries, lawyers, corporate benefits managers, economists, and policymakers make it an invaluable collection of international and inter-disciplinary insights, supplying an unusually rich combination of facts and observations about pensions around the world. The book should be required reading for all managers and policymakers designing pension systems for a global workforce.

This volume owes its existence to the Pension Research Council Executive Board, who enthusiastically supported the concept of an international pension security theme for its May 1994 conference, at which earlier versions of these papers and discussions were presented. Sponsorship for the conference was generously provided by the United States Department of Labor and the World Bank, as well as the Institutional Members of the Pension Research Council. On behalf of the Pension Research Council at The Wharton School, I thank the many contributors and the various institutions supporting the high-quality research leading to this volume.

OLIVIA S. MITCHELL
Executive Director
Pension Research Council

Chapter 1
Pension Security in an Aging World

Zvi Bodie and Olivia S. Mitchell

Providing adequate retirement income for the aged population is a serious concern confronting policymakers around the world. There is much that countries can learn from each other as they explore alternative ways to design retirement benefit programs using a wide range of financing methods. This volume encourages the sharing of cross-national experiences by making available to a wide audience the lessons learned by practitioners and analysts as they assess public and private pensions around the world. By evaluating what pensions can do well and what they have done poorly in both developed and developing nations, this volume also seeks to help policy experts assess numerous suggestions for constructing better pension institutions now and in the future.

In this introductory chapter we offer a conceptual framework for understanding the different country experiences and policy issues addressed in this book. This framework requires evaluating the roles of the government, employers, and individuals in providing retirement income, and asking why some employers voluntarily sponsor pension plans for their employees. In addition it is important to determine whether a defined benefit or a defined contribution plan offers greater security to employees, which in turn depends on employer funding and pension investment policy. To this end we offer some thoughts on how government regulatory policy affects pensions, focusing on tax as well as pension insurance. A brief description of the book's sections and themes rounds out the chapter, followed by a Glossary of Terms to clarify the pension terminology used in this chapter and throughout the volume.

Retirement Income Systems

In developed nations, the primary function of a retirement income system is to provide people with adequate income in their old age. Prior

TABLE 1   An International Comparison of Social Security Replacement Rates and Pension Coverage

Country	Social Security Retirement Benefit as a Percentage of Final Earnings	Percentage of Labor Force Covered by a Pension Plan
Australia	28 to 11	92 (compulsory)
Canada	34	41
Denmark	83 to 33	50
France	67 to 45	100 (compulsory)
Germany	70 to 59	42
Italy	77 to 73	5
Japan	54	50
Netherlands	66 to 26	83
Sweden	69 to 49	90
Switzerland	82 to 47	90 (compulsory)
United Kingdom	50 to 26	50
United States	65 to 40	46

Source: Davis (Chapter 8, this volume), Table 3.
Note: Replacement rates given for 1992 and based on final salaries of US$ 20,000–US$ 50,000.

to the Industrial Revolution, the extended family was the primary institution that performed this function. Elderly family members lived and worked with offspring on a family-owned farm, and all drew a common livelihood from it. In many of today's less developed countries, this family-based pattern for old age support still holds true.

Over time, urbanization and other fundamental economic and social changes gave rise to new institutional structures for the care and support of the elderly in much of the industrialized world. An often-used metaphor for describing developed countries' retirement income systems is that of the "three-legged stool." The first leg consists of government-provided old age assistance and insurance programs, the second is comprised of employer- or labor union-provided pensions, and the third is individual and family support (James and Vittas, this volume).

There is substantial variation across households and countries in the mix of these three components of retirement income. For instance, government-provided social security benefit generosity varies widely for the countries included in Table 1. That table reports the social security replacement rate, which is defined here as the annual government pension benefit as a fraction of final salary. At one extreme is Italy, where the government-run social security system provides a replacement rate greater than 70 percent for workers earning a wide range of pay. Table 1 also shows the proportion of the labor force covered by an occupational or privately sponsored pension plan, and in light of the generous social payments it is not surprising to see that in Italy only 5 percent of the labor force is covered by a voluntarily provided occupational pension. At the other extreme is Australia, where the social security replacement rate is quite low but 92 percent of workers are covered by a compulsory employer-based pension plan (Davis, this volume).

A Conceptual Framework: The Life Cycle Model

Retirement income security and employer-based pensions are often described in the context of a life cycle model of saving. In this framework, people are posited to save during their working years so that they can afford to consume in their non-working retirement period.[1] As we shall see, pensions are only one of the many ways in which forward-looking workers can save effectively.

Some simplifying assumptions are useful in quickly conveying the essence of the lifecycle approach. Assume for the sake of illustration that an individual enters the labor force at age 20, works until retiring at age 65, and dies at age 80. During the working years, this person earns a constant real labor earnings, a portion of which is saved for retirement. These savings are deposited in a fund that earns a zero real rate of interest. At retirement, a constant real retirement benefit is paid, structured such that at death the retirement fund is completely depleted. We further assume that the individual saves an amount during the working years sufficient to provide the same level of real consumption before and after retirement.

Figure 1 depicts the profiles of earnings and consumption just described. The two shaded areas represent, respectively, total accumulated savings during the working years and total accumulated retirement benefits. Absent any net subsidies to the household (and assuming away any bequest motive for the moment), these two areas must be equal for the lifetime consumption plan to be feasible. The equality of these two areas implies that the ratio of consumption over earnings must equal the ratio of years of work to total years of work and retirement. In other words if we define the replacement rate as the ratio of consumption to earnings, this can be derived as follows:

Years of work ∗ (Earnings − Consumption) = Years of retirement ∗ Consumption

Years of work ∗ Earnings = (Years of work + Years of retirement) ∗ Consumption

$$\frac{\text{Replacement}}{\text{rate}} = \frac{\text{Consumption}}{\text{Earnings}} = \frac{\text{Years of work}}{\text{Years of work} + \text{Years of retirement}}$$

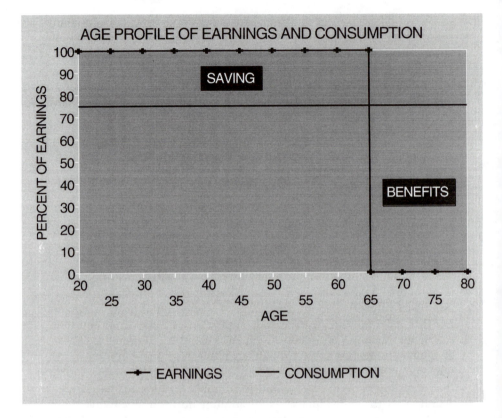

Figure 1. Life cycle earnings and consumption profiles.

In this example, there are 45 years of work and 15 years of retirement, so the replacement rate is equal to 45/60 or 75 percent.

In this example the individual's total or "gross" saving during his or her working years, and the benefits thus generated during retirement, may be divided into three components depending on the institution or provider controlling the fund: government, employer, and individual. The government component of gross saving consists of social security taxes paid by the individual and the employer. The pension component of gross saving that goes to the employer's pension plan is the employee's own contribution, plus the employer's contribution, which is also thought of as the cash compensation foregone to qualify for the future pension benefits. Any residual saving needs must be met by the individual accumulating private assets (e.g., housing, equities).

In the next few sections we explain why these three different components of retirement savings arise, and what the role of each may be in the life cycle savings plan.

The Role of the Government in Retirement Income Provision

The role of the government in retirement income provision varies considerably across countries.[2] Despite obvious cross-national differences in the government's role, many of which are outlined in the chapter by Estelle James and Dimitri Vittas, there remains a common theme: in virtually every country the government provides a "floor" of income protection for the elderly, with the aged population's needs met by some mix of national insurance and national welfare systems, in the form of cash and medical insurance. This floor (or "safety net") is usually mandatory and non-assignable.

Several economic justifications are offered for government provision of a layer of retirement benefits for everyone. These include the following[3]:

Informational Inefficiencies

It is costly to acquire the knowledge necessary to prepare and carry out long-run plans for income provision. Although people's lifetime financial plans depend on their individual preferences and opportunities, their goals may be similar enough such that a standard retirement savings plan can prove suitable to many. By providing a basic plan that supplies at least a minimum level of old age support, the government is likely to help everyone save more efficiently than they could on their own.

Adverse Selection Problems

Because one's date of death is not known with certainty, there is considerable risk that people will outlive their retirement savings in contrast to the simplest version of the life cycle model. One way to insure against the risk of exhausting one's savings during retirement is by purchasing a life annuity contract. But the private market for life annuities suffers from adverse selection, since people with a higher than average life expectancy have a high demand for this kind of insurance. As a consequence, an average individual will find the equilibrium price for privately purchased life annuities unattractive, and will tend to self-insure against longevity risk by providing an extra reserve of retirement savings.[4] Universal and mandatory social security is one way of overcoming this adverse selection problem. By making participation in the national plan mandatory, and by restricting benefit payouts to the form of life annuities, the social cost of adverse selection is greatly reduced.

Free-Rider Problems

An alternative rationale for a government-mandated universal retirement income system is to address the free rider problem, which arises when the citizenry collectively feels an obligation to offer a "safety net" for everyone living in the society. As a consequence, there emerges a de facto promise to provide a tax-funded "safety net" or minimum benefit even when no formal provision is made for one. If this collective commitment is well understood by all, some people might avoid saving for their own retirement, intending instead to rely on tax-funded benefits when old. Similarly, some might take on more risk in investing their retirement savings than they would in the absence of a safety net. In such an environment, mandating universal participation simply forces people to pre-pay for benefits they ultimately will receive from the system. Therefore the purpose of a mandatory system is to protect society against free riders.

While these arguments offer a rationale for why governments might believe it important to mandate a minimum level of universal participation in a national retirement program, they are silent about what the particular level of government benefits should be. These arguments are also silent on whether the government might stop after mandating a plan, leaving it to the private sector to manage the plan once it is mandated. For example, in several countries the other two legs of the retirement income stool are encouraged by government regulation as an alternative to government provision. As Andrew Dilnot shows (this volume), governments often use tax policy to provide incentives for employers and unions to sponsor pension plans that — like the government-run plan — are mandatory and non-assignable. In some of those countries, tax incentives are also given to self-employed individuals and households (who are not otherwise covered) to create a retirement fund for themselves. Use of such funds for other purposes is discouraged by imposing penalties on early withdrawal of money from the fund.

The Role of Employers in Retirement Saving

Pension plans sponsored by employers or unions are often integrated with the government-run plan, either explicitly or implicitly.[5] When combined with the government-provided retirement benefit, these plans are usually designed to replace 70 to 100 percent of pre-retirement earnings of lower and middle income employees in developed nations. Benefits are usually lower for higher-income workers, who must rely on direct personal savings for a larger part of their retirement income. In this section we examine the motivations for and effects of employer-based pension plans.

Why are employers and / or trade unions logical sponsors of retirement plans for their employees? There are at least four good reasons:

Efficient Labor Contracting

Pension plans are an important incentive device in labor contracts, affecting employee hiring and turnover patterns, work effort, and the timing of retirement.

Informational Efficiencies

Employment-based plan sponsors often have better access than the plan beneficiaries to information needed for preparing long-run financial plans tailored to the needs of the employees. In particular, sponsors may have better knowledge of the probable path of future labor income for their employees. By providing a basic plan that saves enough to provide for replacement of anticipated future labor earnings, the corporate sponsor can potentially save more efficiently than each employee acting individually. In order for the sponsor to provide efficiently for future wage and salary replacement of employees, it is enough to have accurate forecasts of the earnings of the group as a whole and not the individual earnings of each member of the group. It is probably easier (although by no means simple) to forecast group earnings than it is to forecast an individual's future earnings.

Principal-Agent Problems

While plan sponsors and beneficiaries may have conflicting economic interests, in many respects their interests coincide. Employers who acquire a reputation for taking care of their employees' retirement needs may find it easier to recruit and retain higher quality employees. If employees' trust and good will toward the employer develop, then motivation and labor productivity may be enhanced. Employers therefore have some economic incentive to act in the best interests of their employees.

Other possible providers of retirement planning services may be less suitable as beneficial agents of the employee. Insurance agents, stock brokers, and others who are often engaged in providing these services to individual households may be less trustworthy than an employer because they may be interested in selling the individual some product or service that the individual might not choose were he or she well-informed. These other agents may be motivated to persuade the individual to save too much for retirement or to invest in inappropriate ways. Anyone who has ever tried to find competent and impartial personal financial planning or investment advice is aware of the difficulties.

Access to Capital Markets

Plan sponsors often have access to capital markets that is unavailable to their employees acting as individual savers. A risk faced by an individual employee may be uninsurable directly through the capital markets, but it may be insurable through the employer. In addition, scale economies can be gleaned by large investors where small savers cannot. Of course, financial intermediaries such as insurance companies often can provide a suitable vehicle for the insurance needs of employees. But often a financial intermediary will not be willing to provide enough of the insurance desired by the individual at an efficient price because of problems of adverse selection and moral hazard.

Longevity insurance is an important example of this. In principle, longevity risk is to a large extent diversifiable and can be largely eliminated through risk pooling and sharing. But, as described earlier, the problem of adverse selection can make the private insurance market for life annuities inefficient. Group insurance through pension plans is often seen as a solution to this problem.

Defined Benefit and Defined Contribution Pension Plans

In order to investigate aspects of pension plans more fully it is useful to define a few terms. Pension plans are then described in terms of "who," "when," and "how much" is promised in benefits and how much in the way of contributions is required to sustain the plans.

In the nations that are the focus of analysis in this book, we follow convention in describing two polar types of pension plans: defined contribution and defined benefit plans. In a defined contribution plan, a formula specifies the amount of money that must be contributed to the plan, but not benefit payouts. Contribution rules usually are a predetermined fraction of salary (e.g., the employer contributes 10 percent of the employee's annual wages to the plan), although that fraction need not be constant over an employee's career. The pension fund consists of a set of individual investment accounts, one for each covered employee. Pension benefits are not specified, other than that at retirement the employee gains access to the total accumulated value of contributions and earnings on those contributions. These funds can be used to purchase an annuity, or become accessible as a lump sum.

In a defined contribution plan, the participating employee frequently has some choice over both the level of contributions and the way the account is invested. In principle, contributions could be invested in any security, although in practice most plans limit investment choices to bond, stock, and money market funds. The employee bears all the investment risk; the retirement account is, by definition, fully funded by the contributions, and the employer has no legal obligation beyond making its periodic contributions. Investment policy for defined contribution assets is essentially the same as for any tax-qualified individual retirement account. Indeed, the main providers of investment products for these plans are the mutual funds and insurance companies that also serve the general investment needs of individuals. Therefore in a defined contribution plan much of the task of setting and achieving retirement income replacement goals falls on the employee.

In a defined benefit plan, by contrast, the pension plan specifies formulas for the cash benefits to be paid after retirement. The benefit formula typically takes into account years of service for the employer and level of wages or salary (e.g., the employer pays a retired worker an annuity from retirement to death, the amount of which might be equal to one percent of the employee's final annual earnings multiplied by years of service). Contribution amounts are not specified, and the employer (called the "plan sponsor") or an insurance company hired by the sponsor guarantees the benefits and thus absorbs the investment risk. The obligation of the plan sponsor to pay the promised benefits is similar to a long-term debt liability of the employer.

As measured either by number of plan participants or total assets, the defined benefit form of pensions dominates in most countries around the world. This is so in the United States, although the trend since the mid-1970s is for sponsors to select the defined contribution form when starting new plans. But the two plan types are not mutually exclusive. Many sponsors adopt defined benefit plans as a "primary" plan, in which participation is mandatory, and supplement them with voluntary defined contribution plans. Moreover, there are some plan designs that are "hybrids" combining features of both plan types. For example, in a "cash balance" plan each employee has an individual account that accumulates interest. Each year, employees are told how much they have accumulated in their account, and if they leave the firm, they can take that amount with them. If they stay until retirement age, however, they receive an annuity determined by the plan's benefit formula. A variation on this design is a "floor" plan, which is a defined contribution plan with a guaranteed minimum retirement annuity determined by a defined benefit formula. These plan designs usually take into account the benefits provided by the government-run system.

From the employee perspective, the major advantage of the defined benefit approach is that it offers plan participants who stay with the same employer a guaranteed benefit designed to replace their pre-retirement labor income. The main defect of private defined benefit plans in most countries is that they do not currently offer explicit inflation insurance. The major advantages of the defined contribution approach are that it offers participants a more portable and flexible retirement savings vehicle whose value during the pre-retirement years is easier to understand and measure. In addition some employees see the cash-out access to the defined contribution plan's lump sum accumulation to be attractive. Hybrid pension plans, such as cash-balance or floor plans, are often designed to combine the best features of both "pure" types.

When Are Private Pension Plans Funded?

In the present context, we use the term "pension fund" to represent the cumulation of assets created from contributions and the investment earnings on those contributions, less any payments of benefits from the fund.[6] The pension plan is the contractual arrangement setting out the rights and obligations of all parties; the fund is a separate pool of assets set aside to provide collateral for the promised benefits. In defined contribution plans, the value of the benefits equals that of the assets and so the plan is always exactly fully funded. But in defined benefit plans, there is a continuum of possibilities. There may be no assets dedicated to the pension plan in a separate fund, in which case the plan is said to be unfunded. When a separate fund exists but assets are worth less than the present value of the promised benefits, the plan is underfunded. And if the plan's assets have a market value that exceeds the present value of the plan's liabilities, it is said to be overfunded.

Why and how does funding matter? The assets in a pension fund provide collateral for the benefits promised to the pension plan beneficiaries. A useful analogy is that of an equipment trust. In an equipment trust, such as one set up by an airline to finance the purchase of airplanes, the trust assets serve as specific collateral for the associated debt obligation. The borrowing firm's legal liability, however, is not limited to the value of the collateral. By the same token, if the value of the assets serving as collateral exceeds the amount required to settle the debt obligation, any excess reverts to the borrowing firm's shareholders. So, for instance, if the market value of the equipment were to double, this would greatly increase the security of the promised payments, but it would not increase their size. The residual increase in value accrues to the share-holders of the borrowing firm.

The relation among the shareholders of the firm sponsoring a pension plan, the pension fund, and the plan beneficiaries is similar to the rela-tion among the shareholders of the borrowing firm in an equipment trust, the equipment serving as collateral, and the equipment-trust lend-ers. In both cases, the assets serving as collateral are "encumbered" (i.e., the firm is not free to use them for any other purpose as long as that liability remains outstanding), and the liability of the firm is not limited to the specific collateral. Any residual or "excess" of assets over promised payments belongs to the shareholders of the sponsoring firm. Thus, the greater the funding, the more secure the promised benefits. However, whether the plan is underfunded, fully funded, or overfunded, the size of the promised benefits does not change.

Why do employers fund their defined benefit plans? Reasons appear to vary across countries. First, funding offers benefit security if there is no government insurance of pension benefits, or only partial insurance. Employees may demand that the future pension promises made to them by their employer be collateralized through a pension fund (Mitchell and Smith, 1994). In the United Kingdom, for example, there is no govern-ment pension insurance beyond the minimum guaranteed pension of the State Earnings Related Pension scheme (SERPs). Pension funding in this case provides an important cushion of safety for retirement income (Daykin this volume).

Second, some countries impose minimum funding standards by law. These standards seek to insure that promised pension benefits are paid even in the event of default by the corporate sponsor, and also aim to protect the government (and the taxpayer) from abuse of government-supplied pension insurance. In the United States, for example, a govern-ment pension insurance group called the Pension Benefit Guaranty Cor-poration (PBGC) must continue pension payments offered by defined benefit pension plans even if their sponsoring corporations become bankrupt with an underfunded pension plan. Recent changes in United States pension law have required that the PBGC insurance premium must depend on the plan's extent of underfunding, and have also elimi-nated the possibility of voluntary termination of an underfunded pen-sion plan (Ippolito 1989; Utgoff 1992). In Canada, pension insurance was offered only by a single province for a limited number of years (Pesando, this volume).

Third, there may be tax incentives for plan sponsors to fund their defined benefit plans. As Dilnot (this volume) notes, the tax advantage to pension funding in the United States and the United Kingdom stems from the ability of the sponsor to earn the pre-tax interest rate on pension investments. It is no accident that in Germany, where employers face a tax disadvantage if they fund their pension plan, pensions are predominantly unfunded (Ahrend, this volume).

Finally, funding a pension plan may provide the sponsoring firm with financial "slack" that can be used in case of financial difficulties the firm may face in the future (Bodie et al. 1987). In the United States, pension law allows plan sponsors facing financial distress to draw upon excess pension assets by reduced funding or, in the extreme case, voluntary plan termination. The pension fund therefore effectively serves as a tax-sheltered contingency fund for the firm.

Inflation and the Adequacy of Pension Funding

For the purposes of measuring funding adequacy, it is critical to consider the extent to which defined benefit pension promises are protected against inflation. There is considerable controversy among pension professionals in the academic and business worlds about whether it is appropriate to view pension promises as fixed in nominal or real terms. The resolution of this issue determines one's view of the adequacy of pension funding and of the appropriate way for a plan sponsor to hedge the liability.

As previously described, in a defined benefit plan a retiree's pension benefit amount is determined by a formula that takes into account the employee's history of service and wages or salary. Under the terms of the defined benefit promise, the plan sponsor is required to provide this benefit regardless of the investment performance of the pension fund assets. As a consequence, the benefit annuity promised to the employee is the employer's liability. What is the nature of this liability?

To answer this question, one matter that must be confronted is whether promised benefits are protected from inflation at least until the worker retires. Many believe that final-pay retirement benefit formulas, for instance, offer indexation inasmuch as earnings track inflation. But this is a misperception in many countries. In the United States, for instance, social security benefit payments at retirement are indexed to a general wage series, but pension benefits even in final-pay private sector plans are "indexed" only to the extent that (1) the employee continues to work for the same employer; (2) the employee's own wage or salary keeps pace with the general index; and (3) the employer continues to maintain the same plan. In the past few decades these three conditions have not generally held: turnover and plant downsizing have been significant for older workers; real wages have fallen on average; and pension plans have been altered quite frequently over time.[7]

A related concern is that few private sector defined benefit pension plans offer an explicitly inflation-protected benefit under the plan's formula. However, many plan sponsors in the United States have from time to time provided voluntary increases in benefits to their retired employees, depending on the financial condition of the sponsor and the increase in the living costs of retirees (Clark 1990; Gustman and Steinmeier 1993). Some observers have interpreted such increases as evidence of implicit cost of living indexation (Ippolito 1986). These voluntary ad hoc benefit increases, however, are very different from a formal COLA (cost of living adjustment).

The difference between indexed and non-indexed benefits emerges quite clearly in comparing the way inflation protection of accrued pension benefits is treated in different countries. In the United States, the plan sponsor is under no legal obligation to pay more than the amount explicitly accrued under the plan's benefit formula. Since very few U.S. employers offer pension benefits automatically indexed for inflation, this lack of inflation indexation gives rise to the portability problem. Workers who change jobs wind up with lower pension benefits at retirement than otherwise identical workers who stay with the same employer, even if the employers have DB (defined benefit) plans with the same final-pay benefit formula. In the United Kingdom, by contrast, accrued benefits are indexed to the cost of living up to the age of retirement (subject to a 5 percent per year cap). Thus even a terminated employee has indexation for general inflation up to retirement age, as long as his or her benefit is vested (Daykin, this volume).

Insuring Private Pensions

A major putative advantage of a defined benefit pension plan over a defined contribution plan is that it protects the employee against investment risk.[8] The economic efficiency of this protection against investment risk is enhanced by the provision of guarantees against default risk. To understand the social welfare gains from guarantees of pension annuities, it is critical to distinguish between employees and investors (stockholders and bondholders) in firms that provide pension annuities. The distinction is that, unlike the firm's investors, the employees holding the sponsor's pension liabilities strictly prefer to have the payoffs on their contracts as insensitive as possible to the default risk of the firm itself. The function served by a pension annuity is for the beneficiaries to receive a specified benefit upon retirement. That function is less efficiently performed if the contract instead calls for the benefit to be paid in the joint event that the employee retires and the firm is still solvent.[9]

Even if the sponsoring firm offers an actuarially fair increase in the employee's cash wages to reflect the risk of insolvency, it is still likely that an employee might prefer a pension annuity with the least default risk. Employees typically have a large non-diversified stake in the firm already.[10] They may have invested in firm-specific human capital, which loses value if the firm does poorly. Thus, few employees would consciously agree to accept default risk on their pension benefits in order to increase their expected cash wages. This is true even when the employee has all the relevant information necessary to assess the default risk of the firm. In most cases, the employees do not have the relevant information, and this fact makes the welfare loss even greater.

For example, consider the profile of a "typical" defined benefit plan beneficiary. The vast majority of those covered by PBGC guarantees in the United States are blue collar and white collar workers for whom pension benefits constitute a large portion of total retirement savings. These employees are very unlikely to have asset portfolios of sufficient size or the investment expertise necessary to hedge the non-diversifiable risks of their defined benefit pension asset. Only the most highly compensated managerial employees of the firm might have the financial wealth and knowledge required to diversify away the risks of their defined benefit pension claims. But to hedge this risk, they would effectively have to take a short position in the sponsoring firm's equity. Typically, managers and employees are prohibited from shortselling the firm's securities by the provisions of their incentive compensation package.

In contrast, an investor in the stocks or bonds issued by the sponsoring firm is explicitly taking an interest in the fortunes of the firm itself. The function of these securities is to allow investors to participate in the risk and return prospects of the firm. Investors can diversify away much of the default risk associated with any one specific firm as part of their total portfolios. Employees with a substantial part of their wealth in firm-specific defined benefit pension annuities usually cannot achieve such optimal diversification. They are like investors who are constrained to hold a large fraction of their wealth in the form of long-term bonds issued by a single firm, which is also their employer.[11] Thus, both their tangible and human capital are significantly exposed to the fortunes of a single firm.

The above reasoning establishes a rationale for insuring defined benefit pensions against the risk that the plan sponsor will default on its promise to provide benefits. It does not establish a rationale for the government to provide such insurance. Indeed, James Pesando's analysis (this volume) of the pension systems in several developed countries reveals that the number of governments that provide such insurance is remarkably limited.

Whether or not a national government offers pension insurance, there is a case for government oversight. If a significant part of the private pension system failed to deliver the benefits promised to millions of people who had relied on those benefits for their retirement security, the government would surely step in to provide at least some of those benefits. Thus, even in the absence of a formal system of pension insurance, the government is the de facto "guarantor of last resort."

Pension Investment Policy and Benefit Security

As already stated, in a defined contribution pension plan the beneficiary's retirement income depends directly on the performance of the assets in the fund.[12] The employee bears the entire investment risk; the retirement account is, by definition, fully funded by the contributions, and the employer has no legal obligation beyond making its periodic contributions. For defined contribution plans, investment policy considerations are essentially the same as for a tax-qualified individual retirement account: a trade-off between risk and expected return.

In a defined benefit plan, the sponsor's investment policy does not, in general, affect the retirement benefits received by the plan's beneficiaries. For well-funded plans or for plans sponsored by financially healthy employers, the promised benefits are paid regardless of the pension fund's investment performance. Nevertheless, investment performance in defined benefit plans can affect benefit payments if the plan sponsor defaults with inadequate assets to cover promised benefits, and government insurance is insufficient to cover all the resulting shortfall (i.e., the insured benefits are capped at some level).

Even for defined benefit plans that have fully funded the entire benefit promise, investment policy can matter if the sponsor pursues any policy other than strict "matching" of assets to the plan's liabilities to the beneficiaries. For example, for pension funds that invest heavily in equity securities, a funding shortfall can quickly develop if interest rates decline (thus increasing the present value of promised benefits) or if stock prices fall precipitously. If a funding shortfall is not subsequently covered by either the plan sponsor or the government insurer, then some of the promised benefits will not be paid.

Funding of Pensions in the Public Sector

In a strictly unfunded pay-as-you-go government-operated pension system, retirees' benefits depend entirely on the stream of revenue generated by taxes levied on currently active workers. If this were exactly true, benefits would fluctuate with changes in economic fortunes, rising when tax collections rise and falling in recessions. In practice this does not happen in lock-step, since most government pensions are of the defined benefit variety and promise to deliver retirement benefits according to a specified benefit formula. Nevertheless, without funding, benefit payouts are susceptible to cuts when the public sector experiences a rising ratio of retired to active workers and/or large government deficits. In this event benefits accrued under that formula may be altered as a way of reducing this form of government debt.

As a case in point, consider the 1983 reform of the United States social security system. A changing demographic structure for workers led many to become concerned that there could be dramatically reduced benefits in the future in a pure pay-as-you-go system. Hence, a key provision of that reform was to require substantial pre-funding of future benefits. To do this, the social security payroll tax rate was raised and the excess of current revenues over current benefit payments was invested in government bonds held in a trust fund.

While this reform apparently funds the plan, some are less sure about the result. In a private plan, funding is used to insure against default by the plan sponsor. Under social security, the promise to pay benefits seemingly has the same level of full faith and credit of the government as the bonds used to fund the plan. Yet there seems to be a belief that pre-funding will ensure that, when workers reach retirement, they will indeed receive benefits approximating those promised under the current benefit formula (i.e., the one in effect when they were active in the labor force).

A problem with this view is that there remains a potential risk associated with benefits promised under a government-run retirement income system. Even if those currently in the government are committed to maintaining the current schedule of promised benefits, they cannot credibly fully bind future governments to do so. This arises from a paradox of power: the government is too powerful to bind itself credibly to any set of existing rules (Diamond 1993). Indeed, it has become evident in many countries that that benefit formula and the method of financing those benefits can be and often is changed. In the United States, for example, the Congress has changed both in the past and it can surely do so again in the future. In Europe benefit promises have been eroded by inflation to the same end (Turner and Rajnes, this volume), and perhaps more strikingly, public pensions in Chile were recently radically restructured, replacing the defined benefit public social security system with a mainly private defined contribution plan (Myers 1992).

Another example that highlights the importance of funding in securing promised pension benefits in government-run plans is the case of underfunded state and local government retirement plans in the United States (Mitchell and Smith 1994). In more than one instance, firefighters, police officers, and other public employees have been required to defer or even forgo a portion of the retirement benefits they had been promised because taxpayers were unwilling to shoulder the financial burden they impose. Had these plans been fully funded as pension benefits were accruing, it is doubtful that these public employees would now be asked to forego any of their pension benefits.[13]

These examples bring out an important difference between government and private sector obligations. A private sector plan sponsor cannot unilaterally repudiate its legal liability to make promised payments. It can default because of inability to pay, but it cannot repudiate its legal obligations without penalty. On the other hand, a government — because it has the power to legislate changes in the law — can sometimes find ways to repudiate such obligations without immediate and obvious penalty. Indeed, an integrated system in which private plan sponsors supplement government-provided pension benefits to achieve a promised "replacement ratio" of pre-retirement earnings can be seen as a type of private-sector insurance against the political risks of the government-run system (Merton, Bodie, and Marcus 1987; Myers 1977).

In sum, a mixed public-private system of retirement income provision is a way of reducing the risks of each separate component through diversification across providers. Public sector pension plans can change the law to reduce promised benefit levels. Private sector pension plan sponsors are committed by law (and perhaps reputation) to pay promised benefits, but they may default. And sometimes, as an additional linkage reinforcing the first two legs of the retirement income stool, the government may insure private pension benefits against the risk of default.

Overview of the Volume

Before turning to this book's individual contributions, the reader may find useful an overview of the volume and its parts. The chapters are divided into three sections, with the first set of studies devoted to pensions in developed nations; the second focusing on pension issues in developing countries; and the final section unifying the discussion by concentrating on regulatory issues affecting pensions the world over. We discuss each in turn.

Policymakers in developed countries sense rising concern about old-age retirement income security, particularly in the light of aging trends and overstressed government budgets which undermine retirement income programs. Nowhere is this more evident than in the United Kingdom, where a pension investment scandal focused awareness on severe British pension problems. In Chapter 2, the United Kingdom's Chief Actuary Christopher Daykin begins with an unusually clear statement of the complex British multiple-tier pension system. For the first tier the national government guarantees a modest flat rate indexed benefit, on top of which employees may join either a state-provided earnings-based pension system or a private system. The private system includes two options, either an employer-sponsored pension (if a firm has "contracted out" from the government second-tier), or a personal pension plan. Most of the private pensions are of the defined benefit variety.

As Daykin shows, coverage by group pensions is very high among employees of large organizations, and contracting out is extremely popular. Nevertheless, there is no common regulatory framework governing these pensions, there are few legal requirements concerning the responsibilities and authority of trustees, and funding as well as reporting requirements are rather relaxed by United States standards. In addition, pension plan liabilities in Britain are not formally insured, though in the event of company bankruptcy, a pension plan has the option to buy back workers' rights in the state-guaranteed earnings-based system. While this multiple-pillar arrangement has some strengths, it also suffers from some important vulnerabilities. Many of these are the subject of current efforts to reform the British pension system identified by Daykin, but as he points out, some of the important risks remain less than fully insured. Daykin also raises other salient issues in this chapter regarding the future of pensions, including mobile employees' desires to maintain pension membership as the European Community relaxes migration barriers. In his commentary on this work, Anthony M. Santomero raises additional questions about whether current redesign efforts will go far enough to secure private pensions in that nation.

Common themes are sounded in a companion chapter about occupational pensions in Germany by Peter Ahrend, a German benefits attorney. As in the United Kingdom, in Germany a national social security system underlies an employer-sponsored second tier. Most unusual to pension experts from other nations is the German practice of holding only "book reserves" in a pension fund, which means that retiree benefit payments depend entirely on the sponsoring company's assets. Since there is no separate trust fund established for pension accumulations, the pension promise represents a long-term claim against the corporate balance sheet, and the sponsoring company is allowed to defer its taxes by virtue of these book reserves.

Ahrend goes on to describe a German mutual insurance arrangement covering guaranteed vested benefits and retiree benefits after age 60 in the event of company bankruptcy; this arrangement, first established in 1974, is operated on a pay-as-you-go basis and is backstopped by a federal bank. While the arrangement has apparently worked fairly well thus far, the pension system is facing new threats of late, including the fact that employment has not grown quickly in the last decade, the population is aging, and many pension plans are "closed" to new entrants. In addition, recent European Court of Justice cases have held that men must be permitted to retire as early as women. All these changes may further challenge the plans' health.

In her assessment of the German pension system, Lucy apRoberts argues that differences in tax structures as well as labor-management relations may explain why German pensions are completely invested in the sponsoring company, while United States pensions are more diversified. In Germany as well as in France, employees frequently have a stronger say in corporate management than in the United States. Marc Twinney discusses factors militating change in pensions worldwide, and finds some lessons for German pensions as well as those in North America. In particular he argues that pre-funding pension obligations is likely to become more common, particularly as international companies are judged in terms of their credit ratings. He also warns that pension accounting practices for many German firms do not meet accounting and valuation standards demanded by international capital markets.

In the final chapter on developed country pensions, the state of pensions in Japan is discussed by Noriyasu Watanabe, a Japanese pension expert. He notes that social security in Japan was recently restructured into two components, a flat benefit plus an earnings-related segment and a supplementary private plan. Nevertheless, the rapid aging of Japan's population has prompted the government to predict payroll tax rates of 35 percent by the year 2025, in order to preserve promised (pay-as-you-go) benefits payable at age 60. Private defined benefit pension plans developed after World War II under a regulatory structure allowing book reserves as in Germany; in these plans, most benefits are payable as sizable lump sum benefits (about US$ 200,000 at retirement).

Three interrelated and very deep-seated challenges are identified as key to the future development of pensions in Japan. First, as Watanabe says, "good accounting rules for pension systems have not yet been established." This leads to the second problem: employees fail to understand their exposure to pension risk and their lack of legal recourse in the event of company failure. Finally, financial and insurance markets are facing deregulation in Japan, leading to increased competition among institutions managing the funds. In his commentary on this chapter, Robert Clark broadens the discussion to include challenges to the Japanese retirement system wrought by rapid population aging and low mandatory retirement ages. Indeed, many developed nations would be well served by studying how the Japanese adapt their pensions to the new social and economic environment, inasmuch as that nation's population is aging more rapidly than the population in most other OECD countries.

The second section of this volume carries on some of the themes developed in the first, and shows clearly that retirement policy in emerging economies confronts many of the same problems as in developed nations. This is somewhat ironic, because development specialists for the past several decades have sought to solve the most immediate problems facing poor countries — widespread morbidity and mortality, insufficient food production, and inadequate jobs for the working-age population — only to find that their successes imply the burden of an increasingly aging population.

These phenomena, and how pensions can respond to such massive socioeconomic changes, are taken up in the chapter by Estelle James and Dimitri Vittas from the World Bank. These authors review a range of nationally mandated provident funds beginning with Malaysia's, established in 1951, and others in Asia and Africa. Most recently, in 1981, Chile replaced its national, unfunded, social security system with a mandated privately managed, defined contribution plan into which 10 percent of pay must be contributed. Many development experts attribute at least some of Chile's economic boom over the last fifteen years to the rapid growth of the pension system, including the rapid deepening of the capital market and excellent rates of return. Nevertheless this purely private system potentially limits the flexibility with which governments can exercise fiscal and monetary policy, tends to produce high administrative costs, and does not guarantee a minimum income to retirees. Partial answers to these issues are offered by the authors.

Two sets of commentaries provide an interesting counterpoint to this chapter. Alan Auerbach emphasizes the risks associated with mandated savings schemes and is skeptical that they can be used either to redistribute income or to generate "cheap capital." Donald S. Grubbs agrees that forced savings systems are needed when employees are too shortsighted to make provision for themselves, but argues that a government-run system that invests in private assets may potentially be more cost effective than the Chilean model. In any event, he holds that a universal defined benefit plan is needed to guarantee a floor of retirement income, a floor that a defined benefit contribution plan does not promise.

Conditions are somewhat more primitive elsewhere in the developing world. As John A. Turner, pension specialist from the United States Department of Labor, points out, the countries of central and eastern Europe confront a particularly difficult set of issues in contemplating retirement policy and the role pensions can play. Turner and colleague David M. Rajnes review several economic preconditions needed to set up pensions, and point out that both Hungary and the Czech Republic have experienced grave difficulties investing in foreign securities inasmuch as they lack foreign exchange. Ownership of domestic assets is made difficult by the slow pace of privatization, though in Slovakia, for instance, workers have gained shares in jointly held Investment Privatization Funds. Of course inflation is an ever present worry threatening real returns, made worse by bankrupt social security systems, confusion over property rights, and lack of regulation regarding financial malfeasance. Lessons of the British, the German, and of course the Chilean models are assessed with regards to the feasibility of their applicability in these European nations.

The third and final section of this volume examines the main ways in which governments mold the private pension environment. The policies deemed most important in the present context are (1) taxation of pension contributions and benefits, (2) regulation of pension financing, and (3) pension insurance. Many countries make a formal stance on these policy issues, often explicitly as part of a coordinated approach to encouraging retirement saving, while other times they act implicitly. But as the analysis chapters demonstrate, these three government policies profoundly influence the shape and strength of the pension institution in all nations.

In a very useful analysis Andrew Dilnot of the Institute for Fiscal Studies offers a taxonomy to be used in thinking about how governments tax pension plans. He notes that taxes may be levied at one of three points: when contributions are made, when plan assets earn income, and when benefits are received. In the United States, for instance, the government (more or less) allows tax-protected contributions and inside buildup but taxes pension benefits at payout. As the discussion notes, this yields a quite different outcome than a system that taxes inflows but exempts payouts, particularly during inflationary times.

Of special interest to pension tax experts is the situation of pension taxation in New Zealand and Australia, described in some detail. While both countries recently simplified their tax structure for pensions somewhat, Dilnot still holds that there is no feasible tax system that both raises revenues and is fiscally neutral. On the other hand, he does point out that available statistical evidence on the likely effects of taxes on pension savings suggests that the behavioral responses are likely to be small. The discussion concludes with a critical analysis of the concept of tax expenditures, which he concludes makes little sense theoretically or practically.

In her comments on this chapter, Angela Chang emphasizes that curtailing the favorable tax treatment of pensions may undermine their contribution to old age saving. She then goes on to outline additional research questions that require analysis, including the matter of how and whether to permit pension participants to take lump-sum distributions from their pensions and, if so, how much to tax them. Sylvester Schieber sketches exactly how inflation affects real pension returns under different scenarios and emphasizes that, in the United States at least, government tax policy toward pensions often conflicts directly with the goal of increasing retirement income.

While policy experts discuss pension taxation, those interested in the role of pensions in corporate finance emphasize pension funds' investments, as well as the risks and returns they bring to sponsoring companies. Just how widely these differ across the Organization for Economic Cooperation and Development (OECD) nations is the subject of E. Philip Davis's chapter, seen from his international vantage point at the European Monetary Institute. Davis finds dramatic variability in the ways in which pensions are financed across the OECD nations, beginning with different practices as between funded versus pay-as-you-go or unfunded plans. Looking across a dozen developed nations, he shows that countries with smaller social security systems tend to have larger private funded plans, while nations that have "generous" tax provisions have larger private funded plans, and that pensions are larger where contracting out is available.

How pension assets are invested, conditional on there being some sort of funding, also varies widely across nations. This is in part due to widespread regulation of portfolio composition — as in Japan, where equities and foreign assets may not exceed a threshold level; in Germany, where foreign asset holdings are limited to 4 percent and equities held at 20 percent; and in France, where at least 34 percent of mutual societies' funds for pensions must be deposited in state bonds. These regulations are apparently quite effective in influencing what pension plans hold: in Sweden, for instance, pensions held only one percent in equity, but more than half the funds in mortgages and mortgage-related bonds, while equity made up over 60 percent of pension holdings in the United Kingdom. Davis documents wide variation in fund performance resulting from these vastly different holdings.

In his provocative comments on this chapter, Marshall Blume offers several caveats to Davis's arguments. He questions whether funded plans can solve the problems with which pay-as-you-go systems cannot cope. Blume's answer is "perhaps not," particularly if the preferred solution is to lower pension benefits offered to today's retirees. He goes on to critique the author's views that unfunded plans crowd out private saving and that pensions should invest in equities. Based on his own reading of the data, neither conclusion is persuasive.

Plan termination insurance is the subject of James Pesando's work. This Canadian economist and long-time pension expert asks why governments sometimes insure pensions, and comes to the conclusion that no country has yet determined the economically sensible risk-adjusted premium needed to pay for this type of bankruptcy coverage. He notes that of 11 Canadian jurisdictions (10 provinces and the national government) only one, the Province of Ontario, adopted a form of pension insurance in 1980, which it is now pulling back from by halting the offering of inflation-indexed pension coverage. The author also delves into pension guarantee funds in the United States, Germany, and the United Kingdom, and concludes that these cross-subsidize less profitable firms by taxing more productive ones. In his view, some of the coverage is associated with redistribution toward certain firms or industries, rather than inefficiencies in the market for insurance.

Pesando's chapter is discussed by two commentators who disagree with each other to a very substantial degree. On the one hand, Dallas Salisbury salutes the transfer function of pension insurance mechanisms, believing as he does that pension insurance can only be operated by the government precisely because the strong would not be willing voluntarily to subsidize the weak. On the other hand, Carolyn Weaver believes that moral hazard makes pension insurance unworkable as insurance, and notes that few countries have quantified the risk governments carry when guaranteeing private pension benefits. These problems deserve additional research, and will certainly receive more debate.

Conclusions

The conceptual framework for understanding cross-national experiences and policy issues addressed in this book may be summarized by providing brief answers to the key questions mentioned at the outset.

What are the roles of the government, employers, and individuals in providing retirement income?

In most developed nations, and increasingly in emerging economies, the retirement income system can be viewed as a three-legged stool. The first leg is government-provided pension and welfare programs for the aged; the second is employer- or labor union-provided pensions, and the third is individual and family support. This volume demonstrates substantial variation in the mix of the three sources of retirement income, across households and regions of the world.

One can view a mixed public-private system of retirement income provision as a way of reducing the risks of each separate component through diversification across providers. Private sector pension plan sponsors are committed by law (and perhaps reputation) to pay promised benefits, but they may default. Public sector pension promises are backed by the government's taxing authority, but governments sometimes alter benefit promises by changing the legislated benefit formulas after the fact. As an additional linkage reinforcing the first two legs of the retirement income stool, there may be government insurance of private pension benefits.

Why do some employers voluntarily sponsor pension plans for their employees?

Companies find that pensions achieve many useful labor force objectives. Pension plans are an important incentive device in labor contracts, affecting employee turnover, work effort, and the timing of retirement. Employers who acquire a reputation for taking care of their employees' retirement needs may find it easier to recruit and retain higher quality employees. Workers desire pensions when their companies can help them tailor their long-run financial plans to their needs, and may find that employers are more suitable beneficial agents of the employee than are other potential providers of retirement planning services. Additionally, plan sponsors often have access to capital markets that may be unavailable to employees acting individually, permitting them to insure risks that are uninsurable privately through group provision.

Which type of pension plan offers greater security to employees — defined benefit or defined contribution?

The major advantage of a defined benefit pension is that it offers plan participants who remain with the same employer a specified benefit designed to replace a portion of their pre-retirement labor income. The main defect of a private defined benefit plan in most countries is that it does not usually offer explicit inflation insurance, and benefit payments are subject to default in the event of corporate bankruptcy. In contrast, the major advantage of a defined contribution pension is that it offers participants a more portable and flexible retirement savings vehicle whose accumulation value prior to retirement is easier to understand and measure. Hybrid plans, such as cash-balance plans, combine features of both "pure" pension types.

Why do some employers fund their defined benefit pension plans while others do not?

Funding in private plans offers benefit security when there is no government insurance of pension benefits, a factor that is recognized in some countries by requiring minimum legal funding standards and by supplying tax incentives for plan sponsors to fund their defined benefit plans. In public pension plans, funding can offer some protection against changes in benefit formulas in times of fiscal stress. In addition, funding a pension plan may provide the sponsor with financial "slack" useful should the firm face future financial difficulties.

What effect does a pension fund's investment policy have on benefit security?

In a defined contribution pension plan, a beneficiary's retirement income depends directly on the investment performance of the fund assets, and as with any investment, performance will depend on the assets' risk and expected return patterns. In a defined benefit plan, the plan sponsor's investment policy can affect benefit payments if the plan sponsor defaults with inadequate assets to cover promised benefits and if there is insufficient government insurance to cover all the resulting shortfall (i.e., if no government insurance is available, or if insured benefits are capped at some level).

What form of government regulation of employer-provided pensions is desirable?

In some countries, the government provides explicit insurance against default risk on private-sector defined benefit pension promises. But whether or not the government offers pension insurance, there is a case for government oversight. If a significant part of the private pension system fails to deliver the benefits promised to millions of people who had relied on those benefits for their retirement security, governments are asked to step in to provide at least a minimum old-age income benefit. Thus, even in the absence of a formal system of pension insurance, governments often become the de facto "guarantor of last resort."

Notes

[1]See Friedman (1957) and Modigliani and Brumberg (1954).

[2]This section draws on Bodie (1990a) and Bodie and Merton (1993).

[3]See Bodie (1989), Diamond (1977), Kotlikoff (1987), McGill (1977), Merton (1983), and Wachter (1988).

[4]Rothschild and Stiglitz (1976) analyze theoretical models of adverse selection in an insurance setting. Friedman and Warshawsky (1988) study the private annuities market empirically, and conclude the annuities are priced unattractively for the average individual.

[5]This section draws on Bodie (1990a), Gustman and Mitchell (1992), and Gustman, Mitchell and Steinmeier (1994).

[6]For a survey of pension funding practices in various countries, see Bodie (1990c), Davis (Chapter 8, this volume), and Turner and Dailey (1990).

[7]Hutchens (1993) discusses problems of job loss and displacement of older workers; earnings patterns are discussed by Katz and Murphy (1992); and Luzadis and Mitchell (1991) show that defined benefit pension plan formulas have changed rapidly over time.

[8]For a further discussion of pension insurance, see Bodie and Merton (1993) and Pesando (Chapter 9, this volume). For a more general discussion of the role of the government and private sectors in providing guarantees against default risk, see Merton and Bodie (1992).

[9]Ippolito (1986) argues that, when workers are represented by a union, they accept default risk of the sponsoring firm (through the pension plan) as a way of binding the union to bargain more cooperatively with management. Under his assumptions, therefore, a defined benefit plan with default risk is efficient. Pesando (Chapter 9, this volume) offers additional arguments to support this view.

[10]The risk exposure is especially large for a lifetime employee of a single firm, as is quite common in Japan (Watanabe, this volume). Even if the employee is willing to bear risk, we know from portfolio theory that efficient risk bearing calls for broad diversification across various firms and asset classes. Here, the employee's entire pension benefit is tied to the fortunes of a single firm.

[11]Should employees wish to invest in their company's securities, they often can do so through a variety of special employee stock ownership programs. These investment programs are usually voluntary. By contrast, participation in an employer's defined benefit plan is usually a condition of employment. See Bodie and Munnell (1992).

[12]This section draws heavily on Bodie (1990b, 1991).

[13]If pension benefits were funded as they accrued, local governments would have to recognize the cost of providing them in their current budgets. In the past, promising more pension benefits without funding them was a way for local government to offer increases in compensation without public accountability. The cost of actually paying the benefits when they came due would then become a problem for later generations of politicians. This may help explain why there is a reluctance to fully fund these benefits; see Mitchell and Smith (1994).

References

Ahrend, Peter. "Pension Financial Security in Germany." This volume.

Bodie, Zvi. "Enhancing the Efficiency of Pension Plans." *What is the Future for Defined Benefit Pension Plans?* ERBI-ERF roundtable. Washington, DC: EBRI, 1989: 101–111.

——. "Pensions as Retirement Income Insurance." *Journal of Economic Literature* 28 (March 1990): 28–49. (1990a).

——. "Managing Pension and Retirement Assets." *Journal of Financial Services Research* 4 (December 1990): 419–60. (1990b).

——. "Pension Funding Policy in Five Countries." In John Turner and Lorna Dailey, eds., *Pension Policy: An International Perspective*, Washington, DC: U.S. GPO, 1990 (1990c): 59–72.

——. "Shortfall Risk and Pension Asset Allocation." *Financial Analysts Journal* 47, 3 (May/June 1991): 57–61.

Bodie, Zvi, Jay O. Light, Randall Morck, and Robert A. Taggart, Jr. "Funding and Asset Allocation in Corporate Pension Plans: An Empirical Investigation." In Zvi Bodie, John Shoven, and David Wise, eds., *Issues in Pension Economics*. Chicago: University of Chicago Press, 1987: 15–44.

Bodie, Zvi and Robert C. Merton. "Pension Benefit Guarantees in the United States: A Functional Analysis." In Ray Schmitt, ed., *The Future of Pensions in the United States*. Philadelphia: Pension Research Council and University of Pennsylvania Press, 1993: 194–246.

Bodie, Zvi and Alicia Munnell, eds. *Pensions and the Economy: Sources, Uses, and Limitations of Data*. Philadelphia: Pension Research Council and University of Pennsylvania Press, 1992.

Clark, Robert L. "Inflation Protection of Retiree Benefits." In John A. Turner and Lorna Dailey, eds., *Pension Policy: An International Perspective*. Washington, DC: U.S. GPO, 1990: 53–58.

Davis, E. Philip. "An International Comparison of the Financing of Occupational Pensions." This volume.

Daykin, Christopher D. "Occupational Pension Provision in the United Kingdom." This volume.

Diamond, Peter A. "A Framework for Social Security Analysis." *Journal of Public Economics* 8 (1977): 275–98.

———. "Privatization of Social Security: Lessons from Chile." NBER Working Paper 4510, October 1993.

Dilnot, Andrew. "The Taxation of Private Pensions." This volume.

Friedman, B. M. and Marc Warshawsky. "Annuity Prices and Saving Behavior in the United States." In Zvi Bodie, John Shoven, and David Wise, eds., *Pensions in the U.S. Economy*. Chicago: University of Chicago Press, 1988: 53–84.

Friedman, Martin. *A Theory of the Consumption Function*. Princeton, NJ: Princeton University.

Gustman, Alan and Olivia S. Mitchell. "Pensions and Labor Market Activity." In Zvi Bodie and Alicia Munnell, eds., *Pensions and the Economy: Sources, Uses, and Limitations of Data*. Philadelphia: Pension Research Council and University of Pennsylvania Press, 1992: 39–113.

Gustman, Alan S., Olivia S. Mitchell, and Thomas Steinmeier. "The Role of Pensions in the Labor Market." *Industrial and Labor Relations Review* 47, 3 (1994): 417–438.

Gustman, Alan S. and Thomas Steinmeier. "Cost of Living Adjustments in Pensions." In Olivia Mitchell, ed., *As the Workforce Ages: Costs, Benefits and Policy Challenges*. Ithaca, NY: ILR Press, 1993: 147–180.

Hutchens, Robert. "Restricted Job Opportunities and the Older Worker." In Olivia Mitchell, ed., *As the Workforce Ages: Costs, Benefits and Policy Challenges*. Ithaca, NY: ILR Press, 1993: 81–102.

Ippolito, Richard A. *Pensions, Economics and Public Policy*. Homewood, IL: Pension Research Council and Dow Jones-Irwin, 1986.

———. *The Economics of Pension Insurance*. Homewood, IL: Pension Research Council and Richard D. Irwin, 1989.

James, Estelle and Dmitri Vittas. "Mandatory Savings Schemes: Are They an Answer to the Old Age Security Problem?" This volume.

Katz, Lawrence and Kevin Murphy. "Changes in Relative Wages: Supply and Demand Factors." *Quarterly Journal of Economics* 46 (October 1992): 35–78.

Kotlikoff, Laurence J. "Justifying Public Provision of Social Security." *Journal of Policy Analysis and Management* 6, 4 (1987): 674–696.

Luzadis, Rebecca and Olivia S. Mitchell. "Explaining Pension Dynamics." *Journal of Human Resources* 26 (Fall 1991): 679–703.

McGill, Dan M., ed. *Social Security and Private Pensions: Competitive or Complementary*. Homewood, IL.: Pension Research Council and Richard D. Irwin.

Merton, Robert C. "On Consumption-Indexed Public Pension Plans." In Zvi Bodie and John Shoven, eds., *Financial Aspects of the U.S. Pension System*. Chicago: University of Chicago Press, 1983.

Merton, Robert C. and Zvi Bodie. "On the Management of Financial Guarantees." *Financial Management* 21, 4 (Winter 1992): 87–109.

Merton, Robert C., Zvi Bodie, and Alan Marcus. "Pension Plan Integration as Insurance Against Social Security Risk." In Zvi Bodie, John Shoven, and David

Wise, eds., *Issues in Pension Economics*. Chicago: University of Chicago Press, 1987: 147–172.

Mitchell, Olivia S. "Retirement Systems in the Developed and Developing World: Institutional Structure, Economic Effects, and Lessons for Economies in Transition." In Avril Van Adams, Elizabeth King, and Zafiris Tzannatos, eds., *Labor Market Policies for Managing the Social Cost of Economic Adjustment*. Washington, DC: World Bank, forthcoming.

Mitchell, Olivia S. and Robert S. Smith. "Pension Funding in the Private Sector." *Review of Economics and Statistics* (May 1994): 278–290.

Modigliani, Franco and Richard Brumberg. "Utility Analysis and the Consumption Function: An Interpretation of Cross-Section Data." In Kenneth K. Kurihara, ed., *Post-Keynesian Economics*. New Brunswick, NJ: Rutgers University Press, 1954: 388–436.

Myers, Robert J. "Concepts of Balance Between OASDI and Private Pension Benefits." In Dan McGill, ed., *Social Security and Private Pension Plans: Competitive or Complementary?* Homewood, IL: Pension Research Council and Richard D. Irwin, 1977: 94–109.

——. "Chile's Social Security Reform After Ten Years." *Benefits Quarterly* 1 (Third Quarter 1992): 41–55.

——. *Social Security*. Fourth edition. Philadelphia: Pension Research Council and University of Pennsylvania Press, 1993.

Pesando, James E. "The Government's Role in Insuring Pensions." This volume.

Rothschild, Michael and J. E. Stiglitz. "Equilibrium and Competitive Insurance Markets: An Essay on the Economics of Imperfect Information." *Quarterly Journal of Economics* 90 (1976): 629–650.

Turner, John A. and Lorna M. Dailey, eds. *Pension Policy: An International Perspective*. Washington DC: U.S. GPO, 1990.

Turner, John A. and David M. Rajnes. "Private Pension Systems in Eastern Europe." This volume.

Utgoff, Kathleen P. "The PBGC: A Costly Lesson in the Economics of Federal Insurance." In M. S. Sniderman, ed., *Government Risk-Bearing*. Cleveland, OH: Federal Reserve Bank of Cleveland, 1992.

Wachter, S. *Social Security and Private Pensions*. Lexington, MA: Lexington Books, 1988.

Watanabe, Noriyasu. "Private Pension Plans in Japan." This volume.

Glossary of Terms

Defined Benefit and Defined Contribution Pension Plans

Pension plans are classified into two types: defined contribution (DC) and defined benefit (DB). As the names suggest, in a DC plan a formula determines contributions (e.g., 10 percent of annual wages), whereas in a DB plan a formula defines benefits (e.g., one percent of final pay per year of service). In a defined contribution plan, the employee receives at retirement a benefit whose size depends on the accumulated value of the funds in the retirement account. The employee bears all the investment risk, and the plan sponsor has no obligation beyond making its periodic contribution. In a defined benefit plan the plan sponsor or an insurance company guarantees the formula benefits and thus absorbs the investment risk. In some countries governments insure a portion of defined benefit pension promises in the event of corporate sponsor bankruptcy; defined contribution benefits are not, however, insured by governments.

Pension Funding

With defined benefit plans, there is an important distinction between the pension plan and the pension fund. The plan is the contractual arrangement setting out the rights and obligations of all parties; the fund is a separate pool of assets set aside in a trust to provide collateral for the promised benefits. In defined contribution plans, the value of the benefits and the assets are equal by definition, so the plan is always exactly fully funded. But in defined benefit plans there need not be a separate fund, in which case the plan is said to be unfunded. In an unfunded plan, the sponsor's own assets back the pension claims.

Vesting and Portability

Employees are vested in their pension plan if they retain their pension benefits even if they stop working for the employer sponsoring the pension plan. Vested benefits are not necessarily portable, where portability refers to the ability of a vested worker to take pension benefits from one employer to another. In the United States, employees who have accrued benefits under one employer's defined benefit plan usually cannot transfer those accruals to another employer, even if they are vested. The result is that benefits of employees who change jobs are not protected against inflation. In the United Kingdom, occupational pensions permit greater portability.

Pension Indexing

There are two types of indexing: market indexing and inflation indexing. Market indexing consists of managing an investment portfolio so as to match the performance of some broad market index of stocks, bonds, or a combination of both. Inflation indexing consists of tying benefits to an index of the cost of living. Market indexing became a common investment strategy of pension funds during the 1980s in the United States, but automatic inflation indexing of private pensions is still rare.

I
Pensions in Developed Nations

Chapter 2
Occupational Pension Provision in the United Kingdom

Christopher D. Daykin

This chapter examines the variety of occupational pension provision within the United Kingdom, including the interaction of the pension system with the social security system.[1]

In the United Kingdom all employed and self-employed workers earning more than a low threshold income pay contributions to the social security system to earn entitlement to a basic pension. The amount of the basic pension depends on the individual's contribution record but not on the level of earnings. A second tier of provision is available to all employees through State Earnings Related Pension Plans (SERPs). However, it is possible to contract out of this part of the social security system through membership in a suitable occupational pension plan or by means of an appropriate personal pension.

Occupational pension plans usually provide additional benefits over and above those required for contracting out of SERPs. Some plans only provide such additional benefits, and their members remain contracted in to SERPs. Employers are free to set up an occupational pension plan (or not), and, even where the employer has set up a plan, employees can choose whether or not to join. Employees who do not join a contracted-out occupational pension plan, or who do not own a personal pension designed for the purposes of contracting out, will automatically be covered by SERPs.

All members of occupational pension plans are free to make additional personal pension provision, as are those who are covered by SERPs, although upper limits are imposed by the tax authorities on contributions to tax-efficient personal pension contracts.

About 50 percent of employees are members of an occupational pension plan. Some 90 percent of these are contracted out of SERPs. Nearly

25 percent of employees are contracted out of SERPs by means of an appropriate personal pension.

Social Security in the United Kingdom

Basic Pension (First Tier)

All employed and self-employed workers in the United Kingdom earning more than a low threshold income — about 18 percent of national average earnings — are required to pay National Insurance Contributions to gain entitlement to the basic social security pension.[2]

The social security system provides a flat rate basic pension (i.e., not dependent on earnings) from state pension age (currently 65 for males and 60 for females, although the female pension age will be increased to 65 between the years 2010 and 2020, with the intention of achieving equal retirement ages for males and females). The maximum amount is payable only if contributions have been paid (or credited) for 90 percent of the working lifetime, from age 16 to state pension age, but proportionately reduced pensions are payable to those with incomplete contribution records, provided that contributions have been paid or credited for 25 percent of the working lifetime.

The maximum flat rate pension for a single person in 1994/95 is equivalent to some US$ 86 a week. A married couple can qualify for a maximum pension of about US$ 138 a week on the basis of the husband's contribution record. Pensions are revalued in April of each year at least in line with the movement of the Retail Price Index (the United Kingdom's consumer price index) over a specified previous 12-month period. Social security pensions are not reduced if the pensioner has other earnings or income.

Additional Pension (Second Tier)

In addition to the flat rate pension, earnings-related pensions are payable from state pension age to those who have contributed as employed persons. The main benefit is an additional pension that is based on earnings between the lower and the upper earnings limits, revalued to the level appropriate at the time of retirement. It was planned to build up over the first 20 years of the scheme to 25 percent of the individual's average earnings between the limits (i.e., excluding earnings below the lower earnings limit). Once the scheme had been in place for more than 20 years, the average was to have been taken over the best 20 (revalued) years of the individual's career. Additional pension does not accrue in respect of periods of self-employment.

The lower earnings limit corresponds fairly closely to the amount of the basic pension (about 18 percent of national average earnings). The upper earnings limit is 7½ times the lower earnings limit (currently 135 percent of national average earnings). Following changes made in 1988, the proportion of revalued earnings that will be paid to those who retire will fall for new awards after 1998, until a long-term figure of 20 percent of average revalued total career earnings is achieved (the best 20 years provision has also been dropped). Revaluation of relevant career earnings is in line with the general movement of earnings over the period. The upper and lower earnings limits are revalued in line with the basic state pension, that is, usually in line with the retail price index.

Contracting Out of the Second Tier

Employers are permitted to contract out (from the additional earnings-related pension) employees who are members of an adequate defined benefit occupational pension plan. The plan must undertake to provide members and their surviving spouses with guaranteed minimum pensions that are broadly equivalent, although not identical, to the earnings-related additional pension to which they would have been entitled if they had not been contracted out.

Those who are contracted out are entitled to a rebate in their National Insurance Contributions in respect of earnings between the lower and the upper earnings limits. This is set for each five-year period on the basis of a recommendation from the Government Actuary regarding the cost to the average occupational plan of funding the accruing liability for guaranteed minimum pensions. The rebate was set at 4.8 percent of earnings for the period commencing in April 1993.

The effect of this form of contracting out is to substitute earnings-related benefits provided by occupational pension plans, on a fully funded basis, for the earnings-related benefits that would otherwise have been payable through the social security system on a pay-as-you-go basis. Almost half the workforce is contracted out through membership in such defined benefit occupational pension plans.

In 1987 the possibility of contracting out was extended to those with an appropriate personal pension. The minimum contribution, which was initially set as equal to the rebate for contracted-out defined benefit occupational pension plans, is paid directly into the personal pension arrangement by the Department of Social Security. There are certain restrictions on the form in which the benefit may be paid, so that appropriate personal pensions always have to be distinguished from other types of personal pension contract.

Since the minimum contribution is the same for all, regardless of age and sex, but the cost of providing a given level of benefit increases with age, contracting out by means of an appropriate personal pension is particularly attractive to younger employed persons. About a quarter of the employed workforce (nearly 5 million people) is now contracted out on the basis of appropriate personal pensions.

Contracting out is now also possible for employers with money purchase (defined contribution) plans (COMPs). The employer's obligation extends only to paying the minimum contribution into the plan and no guarantees have to be given concerning the minimum level of pension. Additional contributions may be made by the employer and by the employees. About 300,000 employees are now thought to be members of COMPs.

An individual who has been contracted out may still receive an earnings-related additional pension from the social security system. The amounts of any guaranteed minimum pensions payable from occupational pension plans are simply deducted from the total entitlement to additional pension that would have existed if the individual had not been contracted out; the balance is payable from social security.

In 1994/95 contributions to social security will fall by about US$ 11 billion, or some 17 percent of gross contribution income, as a result of contracting out. Gross earnings-related additional pension from the social security system would have been around US$ 6 billion in 1994/95, but the net amount payable, once account is taken of contracting out, is at about half this level. The proportionate reduction will increase further as the scheme matures, so that in 2035/36 the net payments are expected to be US$ 18 billion (in terms of 1994/95 levels of benefit) as compared to potential gross expenditure of around US$ 45 billion.

Major changes to the contracting out arrangements were introduced through a pensions bill in the 1994/95 session of Parliament, which involve the abolition of the guaranteed minimum pension concept from April 1997. Instead, contracted out defined benefit plans will have to satisfy certain overall benefit requirements. Those who are contracted out will in future be totally contracted out and will not be entitled to any additional pension from the social security system in respect of that period. The contracted out contribution reduction will reflect the full value of earnings-related social security benefit forgone.

The minimum contribution for appropriate personal pensions (and for COMPs) will be made age-related (although the same for men and women at any particular age) and designed to cover the cost of replicating the earnings-related social security benefit forgone through an individual pensions contract. Greater flexibility will be introduced in the way in which appropriate personal pension benefits can be taken, including flexibility regarding retirement age.

Private Pension Plans

Private pension plans play a vitally important role in the overall structure of provision for retirement in the United Kingdom.[3] Until 1987 private pension plans were mainly sponsored by individual employers, although a few plans existed on an industry-wide basis. Personal pensions were considered suitable for the self-employed and for some senior executives with individually tailored pension arrangements. The introduction in 1987 of appropriate personal pensions as a vehicle for contracting out of the State Earnings Related Pension led to a rapid growth in personal pension coverage, mainly among the 50 percent or so of employed workers who were not previously members of any occupational pension plan.

Concern in the 1970s and 1980s about some of the apparent inequities of many private sector occupational pension plans, particularly in regard to the treatment of early leavers and the absence of full indexation of pension benefits, led to a proliferation of legislative requirements for pension plans. The effect of these, together with the complexities of contracting out, has been to dampen enthusiasm, at least among employers, for defined benefit occupational pension plans. Nevertheless, there is little evidence so far of employers discontinuing defined benefit plans or of any significant switch to group money purchase plans, although some employers setting up new schemes may be attracted to the defined contribution route.

Small employers are more likely to operate an insured plan. There has been a reduction in the number of insurance companies willing to operate such plans on a defined benefit basis, largely because of the administrative burden involved. It is thought that a number of smaller employers have switched from defined benefits to money purchase arrangements.

Money purchase, whether on a group basis or in the form of personal pensions, has come back into fashion, having been badly discredited in the 1950s and 1960s because of inadequate payouts. Results for individual pensioners are bound to be variable. Investment performance will have to be very good to overcome the inherent cost disadvantages of individual pension policies, as compared to the relatively efficient cost structure of occupational pension plans and the very low administrative costs of the social security system.

Money purchase plans may have the effect of stimulating more widespread interest in the value of the pension promise and the importance of one's accumulated pension rights as a major personal asset. The effect of the emphasis on personal pensions in recent years has certainly been to goad occupational pension plans (and employers) into much more

TABLE 1   Members of Pension Plans as Percentage of Number of Employees, by Sector and by Sex, United Kingdom, 1975–1991

	Private Sector		Public Sector		Both Sectors		
Year	Men	Women	Men	Women	Men	Women	All
1975	52	17	86	59	63	30	49
1979	48	24	88	55	62	35	50
1983	52	24	94	59	64	37	52
1987	49	22	90	61	60	35	49
1991	48	27	85	61	57	37	48

Source: Government Actuary (1994a), Tables 2.1 and 2.4, and earlier surveys.
Note: Excludes employees who have some pension rights but are not accruing benefits in respect of current employment.

TABLE 2   Occupational Pension Plan Coverage, United Kingdom, 1991   (millions)

	Men		Women		Total	
Sector	Employees	Members	Employees	Members	Employees	Members
Civil Employment						
Private Sector	9.3	4.5	7.4	2.0	16.7	6.5
Public Sector						
Public Corporations	0.5	0.45	0.2	0.15	0.7	0.6
Central Government	0.6	0.6	1.25	0.85	1.85	1.45
Local Authorities	1.3	0.95	1.65	0.9	2.95	1.85
Total Public Sector	2.4	2.0	3.1	1.9	5.5	3.9
Total Civilians	11.7	6.5	10.5	3.9	22.2	10.4
Armed Forces,						
Central Government	0.3	0.3	—	—	0.3	0.3
Total	12.0	6.8	10.5	3.9	22.5	10.7

Source: Government Actuary (1991), Table 2.4.
Note: Employees are single-counted, i.e., those with two jobs are counted once only.

active marketing to employees of the benefits of the pension plan, and hence to a heightened awareness of what pensions are all about.

Coverage

Table 1 shows the development of membership of occupational pension plans in the public and private sectors in the United Kingdom since 1975, based on regular surveys carried out by the Government Actuary. Table 2 shows in more detail the coverage in different types of employment, while Table 3 shows the coverage by size of membership for private sector

TABLE 3 Self-Administered and Insured Private Sector Pension Plans by Membership Size, United Kingdom, 1991

Number of Active Members[1]	Self-Administered		Insured		Total	
	Plans	Members (thousands)	Plans	Members (thousands)	Plans	Members (thousands)
1 to 11[2]	18,000	120	77,500	210	95,500	330
12 to 99	11,820	460	14,930	360	26,750	820
100 to 999	4,390	1,190	560	90	4,950	1,280
1,000 to 4,999	610	1,200	9	10	619	1,210
5,000 to 9,999	95	670	—	—	95	670
10,000 & over	85	2,160	1	30	86	2,190
Totals	35,000	5,800	93,000	700	128,000	6,500

Source: Government Actuary (1991), Table 4.2.
Note: [1]Plans with no members accruing benefits in respect of current service are excluded from the table.
[2]The number of plans with 11 or fewer members is subject to a wide margin of uncertainty because of the limitations of the sampling method used.

plans. Further data from the Government Actuary's Ninth Survey of Occupational Pension Schemes are given in Tables 4, 5, 8, 9, and 10.

In the private sector, coverage is generally very high among large organizations and relatively low among small firms. These figures do not, however, include personal pensions, which can be expected to be more common among employees of small organizations. Of the 10.7 million members of occupational pension plans in 1991, 9.7 million were contracted out of the SERPs. All of the one million members of schemes not contracted out were in the private sector, so that 100 percent of public sector pension plan members and 78 percent of private sector pension plan members were contracted out.

Framework for Occupational Pension Plans

There is no general legislative framework for occupational pension plans in the United Kingdom. The main constraint on the form of such schemes is the need to obtain approval from the Inland Revenue (the taxation authority) in order to qualify for beneficial taxation treatment. This tax treatment is not available for plan membership for earnings above about US$ 115,000 per year.

In order to qualify for tax privileges, a plan must be established under an irrevocable trust, with the administration and financial management of the plan in the hands of trustees. The trust fund has to be maintained quite separately from the assets of the sponsoring employer, and money

TABLE 4   Members of Pension Plans Paying Contributions of Various Types, United Kingdom, 1991 (thousands)

	Private Sector		Public Sector	
	Contracted	Not Contracted		
Percentage of Salary	Out	Out	All	Total
Defined Benefit Plans				
Under 2%	20	5	650	675
2% and under 3%	150	25	—	175
3% and under 4%	275	105	—	380
4% and under 5%	730	30	5	765
5% and under 6%	1,690	85	240	2,015
6% and under 7%	1,125	70	2,805	4,000
7% and over	105	35	210	350
Total Paying Percentages	4,095	355	3,910	8,360
Non-Contributory or Other Basis	945	205	290	1,440
Total	5,040	560	4,200	9,800
Money Purchase Plans				
Under 2%	—	25	—	25
2% and under 3%	65	60	—	125
3% and under 4%	45	65	—	110
4% and under 5%	40	45	—	85
5% and under 6%	50	60	—	110
6% and under 7%	10	10	—	20
7% and over	20	10	—	30
Employee's Share of National Insurance Contracted-Out Rebate	170	—	—	170
Total Paying Percentages	400	275	—	675
Non-Contributory or Other Basis[1]	30	195	—	225
Totals	430	470	—	900
Combined Totals	5,470	1,030	4,200	10,700

Source: Government Actuary (1991), Table 6.5.
Note: [1] Includes members whose contributions are purely voluntary.

can only be lawfully returned to the employer in special circumstances. This applies to plans in both the private and public sectors, apart from a few public service plans that are established under their own legislation and do not require separate Inland Revenue approval (e.g., the civil service, the armed forces, teachers, and health service workers). With the exception of the scheme for local authority workers, these statutory public service plans are not funded.

Pension plans are usually established by individual firms or companies

TABLE 5   Number of Active Members of Final Salary Plans by Pension Accrual Fraction (thousands)

Pension Accrual Fraction	Private Sector		Public Sector	Total
	Contracted Out	Not Contracted Out		
Plans giving benefit on retirement of pension only, possibly part commutable to a lump sum				
Better than 60ths (if service less than 40 years)	755	120	190	1,065
60ths	3,405	245	170	3,820
Between 60ths and 80ths	95	25	—	120
80ths	120	45	—	165
Less than 80ths	5	25	—	30
Totals	4,380	460	360	5,200
Plans giving benefit on retirement expressed as pension and separate lump sum				
Better than 60ths (if service less than 40 years)	20	—	5	25
60ths	45	—	130	175
Between 60ths and 80ths	10	10	285	305
80ths	585	70	3,405	4,060
Less than 80ths	—	—	15	15
Totals	660	80	3,840	4,580

Source: Government Actuary (1991), Table 7.8.

for their employees (or for certain categories of employees). A single pension plan may be established in respect of the employees of a group of related companies. There are also a few industry-wide pension plans established for all the employees in a particular industry. The employer must contribute to the plan for it to be approved for tax purposes (or must contribute to another plan of which the employee is also a member).

Trustees

Pension plans operate as trusts under the general provisions of trust law, which lays the responsibility for good conduct of the trust on the trustees. There are no legal requirements regarding the composition of the trustees. In practice about 60 percent of members of private sector plans are in plans where at least some of the trustees are elected or nominated as representatives of the members. The employer usually has the power to appoint the trustees.

TABLE 6   Percentage Distribution of Investments of Self-Administered Pension
Funds, United Kingdom, as of December 31, 1992

United Kingdom Investments		
Cash, Deposits and Other Short Term Assets		
(Net of Short Term Liabilities and Borrowing)	3.3	
Government Fixed Interest Securities	3.8	
Company Fixed Interest Securities (Including Convertibles)	1.6	
Loans and Mortgages	0.1	
All Fixed Interest		8.7
Government Index-Linked Securities		2.8
Ordinary Shares	52.9	
Unit Trust Units	2.2	
All Equity Shares		55.2
Land, Property and Ground Rents	5.2	
Property Unit Trust Units	0.5	
All Real Estate		5.7
Other Investments		7.5
Total United Kingdom Investments		79.9
Investments Outside the United Kingdom		
Cash, Deposits and Other Short-Term Assets	0.3	
Government Securities	2.8	
Ordinary Shares	16.5	
Other	0.5	
Total Investments Outside the United Kingdom		20.1
Total Investments		100.0

Source: Government Actuary (1994b).

TABLE 7   Average Percentage Distribution of Income of Pensioner Units
by Source, United Kingdom, 1980–88

Source of Income	1980	1984	1988
State Pension	61	61	51
Occupational Pension	16	18	23
Savings Income	11	13	17
Earnings	11	8	8
Total Gross Income	100	100	100
Total Net Income	93	92	90

Source: Family Expenditure Survey (1980, 1984, 1988).

With one exception, there are no formal requirements for consultation with members or employers. The exception is the obligation to con-
sult relevant trade unions on the decision whether to contract out of the
social security second tier. In practice pension plan issues will often form
part of negotiations between the employer and employee associations
(or trade unions) on remuneration and conditions of service. Changes to
the pension plan rules, including benefit improvements, are normally a

TABLE 8   Number of Pensions in Payment from Defined Benefit Plans
According to Increases Promised by Plan Rules, United Kingdom,
1991 (thousands)

Amount of Promised Increase	Private Sector	Public Sector	Total
Fixed Increase of:			
5.00% or greater	100	—	100
4.00 to 4.99%	70	—	70
3.00 to 3.99%	440	—	440
Less than 3.00%	90	—	90
Percentage of RPI	30	—	30
Full RPI Linking	460	2,830	3,290
Index-Linking with RPI			
to a maximum of 5%	1,220	100	1,320
Other	390	270	660
None	600	—	600
Totals	3,400	3,200	6,600

Source: Government Actuary (1991), Table 9.5.
Note: RPI is the official Retail Price Index (Consumer Price Index).

TABLE 9   Numbers of Plans and of Members in Plans in the Private Sector by Type of Plan,
United Kingdom, 1991

Private Sector (by Number of Members in Plan)	Contracted Out		Not Contracted Out		Total	
	Plans	Members (thousands)	Plans	Members (thousands)	Plans	Members (thousands)
Defined Benefit						
1–11[1]	9,600	40	10,200	45	19,800	85
12–99	8,900	350	3,600	100	12,500	450
100–999	3,660	970	570	165	4,230	1,135
1,000–4,999	530	1,045	50	100	580	1,145
5,000–9,999	90	625	1	10	91	635
10,000+	80	2,010	4	140	84	2,150
Totals[1]	22,860	5,040	14,425	560	37,285	5,600
Defined Contribution						
1–11[1]	10,300	50	65,700	185	76,000	235
12–99	6,800	185	7,200	195	14,000	380
100–999	400	90	270	55	670	145
1,000–4,999	30	50	7	15	37	65
5,000–9,999	5	30	1	5	6	35
10,000+	1	25	1	15	2	40
Totals[1]	17,536	430	73,179	470	90,715	900
Totals, Both Types[1]	40,396	5,470	87,604	1,030	128,000	6,500

Source: Government Actuary (1991), Table 5.2.
Note: [1]The number of plans with 11 or fewer members is subject to a wide margin of uncertainty because
of the limitations of the sampling method.

TABLE 10   Self-Administered Private Sector Pension Plans by Market Value
of Assets, 1991

Market Value of Assets (US$ million)	Plans	Members (thousands)	Total Value of Assets (US$ billion)
Under 1.5	24,300	340	12
1.5–10	8,000	830	35
15–75	2,080	1,020	73
75–150	260	390	27
150–375	185	610	45
375–750	90	660	45
750–1,500	50	590	51
1,500+	35	1,360	162
Totals	35,000	5,800	450

Source: Government Actuary (1991), Table 4.3.

matter for the employer. Even if the trustees do not have the power to change the rules, their consent is usually required. These provisions are set down in the trust deed that establishes the plan. Unless the deed contains a power of alteration, the law does not permit changes except where approved by the Occupational Pensions Board.

Once trustees have been appointed, they are not expected to behave as representatives of any particular sectional interest. It is their responsibility to administer the trust deed in accordance with the rules of the plan. The responsibilities of trustees are laid down in general trust law, which is of ancient origin and does not provide specifically for pension aspects. The trustees have a personal and fiduciary responsibility to invest the scheme moneys in a prudent way, in compliance with the trust deed and rules. The trustees can delegate the tasks of administration and investment to employed staff or to external experts, but they retain ultimate responsibility for the sound management of the affairs of the pension plan.

Contributions

As mentioned above, the employer must contribute to the plan. The plan may indeed be financed entirely by contributions from the employer. However, it is common for the rules to specify an employee contribution rate, usually defined as a percentage of salary. Table 4 summarizes the distribution of different employee contribution percentages for both public and private sector plans.

The employer's rate of contribution is occasionally specified in the rules of the plan, with appropriate provision for dealing with emerging surpluses or deficits. However, the most common arrangement is for the employer to meet the balance of cost. The employer contribution rate from time to time is then agreed upon in the light of regular actuarial valuations, taking into account the adequacy of the assets already held by the fund in relation to the value of accrued rights, the expected cost of providing the benefits that will be accruing in the future, and the estimated value of future contributions by employees.

Benefit Design

By far the majority of members of occupational pension plans in the United Kingdom belong to defined benefit schemes. Most of these provide benefits based on salary at or near to retirement. The commonest arrangement is for pension to build up as a fraction of final salary, with a pension of $\frac{1}{60}$th payable per year of service. However, other fractions are also sometimes used (see Table 5). Final pensionable salary is defined in the rules of the plan and may be the earnings in the last year before retirement or an average over several years. Where an average is used, the earlier years may be revalued to the level at retirement using an index, usually the Retail Price Index.

In order to qualify for tax approval it is also necessary to comply with certain rules regarding maximum benefits. The maximum permissible pension at normal retirement age is two-thirds of final salary, subject to a limit on pensionable earnings for persons who have changed jobs or entered new pension arrangements since 1989. Although this maximum pension would usually only be attained by those with 40 or more years of service, some plans offer accelerated accrual of benefits for late entrants. The maximum two-thirds pension may be paid provided that there has been at least 20 years' service.

Part of the pension can be commuted (converted) into a lump sum on retirement, subject to limits laid down by the tax authorities. This lump sum is payable free of all taxes, whereas pensions are taxable as earned income.

Many public sector plans provide a pension of $\frac{1}{80}$th of final pensionable salary for each year of service, together with a lump sum equivalent to three years of pension. These are shown in the second half of Table 5 as a pension of $\frac{1}{80}$th of final pensionable salary for each year of service. With pension increases in line with the Retail Price Index, as is the case in the public sector, and corresponding survivors' benefits, a $\frac{1}{60}$th pension is more valuable than a $\frac{1}{80}$th pension and $\frac{3}{80}$th lump sum. The table shows how many members of final salary plans, in the public and private sectors, have various different pension fractions.

Normal retirement age is defined for each plan within the plan rules.

Until recently it was common for plans to follow the state pension ages, although some adopted a different approach, such as age 60 for both males and females, or age 65 for both. The European Court of Justice on May 17, 1990, in the case of *Barber v. Guardian Royal Exchange,* stipulated that it was unlawful, on the basis of Article 119 of the Treaty of Rome, to have inequalities in pension plans between men and women. In the light of this, most plans have now equalized the pension age for men and women, at least for service from the date of the judgment, in spite of the fact that state pension ages in the United Kingdom will not be fully equalized until 2020.

Most defined benefit pension plans also provide pension benefits on ill-health retirement and lump sum benefits on death in service, as well as pensions to surviving widows, widowers, and children. Ill-health retirement benefits are usually based on final pensionable salary, but they often take into account a longer period of service than that actually worked, for example by adding a fixed number of years or by, say, doubling the actual period of service. Many plans now provide a pension on ill-health retirement based on the total potential service that could have been completed up to normal retirement age. Part of the ill-health pension may be taken in lump sum form, as for retirement pension. Ill-health awards are usually subject to a fairly strict definition of inability to continue working because of ill health or incapacity. Most plans can provide early retirement pensions without enhancement where ill-health retirement criteria are met.

Widows' and widowers' benefits are also normally related to final pensionable salary, defined as at the date of death of the member, or at the date of retirement if death occurs after the normal pension has come into payment. Widows' and widowers' pensions are usually at the level of one-half (or occasionally two-thirds) the equivalent member's pension. When the spouse's benefit arises from death in service, it is common for the full potential service to normal retirement age to be taken into account. Many plans increase the payment to the widow or widower if there are dependent children and pay orphans' pensions if there is no surviving spouse. A lump sum benefit is also usually payable on death in service, regardless of family status and whether or not there are surviving family members. This can be up to four years' salary, but two years' salary is the commonest formula.

Vesting and Early Leavers

Anyone who leaves employment (or the pension plan) before normal retirement age, with two or more years' pensionable service, must be granted entitlement to the accrued benefit, although the benefit is not

usually payable until retirement age (or prior death). The accrued benefit is defined according to the usual pension formula, treating the date of
leaving as the date of retirement. Accrued rights deferred to normal
retirement age in this way are required by law to be revalued at 5 percent
a year, or in line with the Retail Price Index if this increases at less than 5
percent a year over the period of deferment. A different formula applies
to accrued rights to guaranteed minimum pension under the contracting-out arrangements. In this case revaluation is in line with an earnings
index, but pension plans can limit their liability to a fixed rate of increase, which is currently set at 7 percent a year. Early leavers with less
than two years' service can be given a simple refund of their own contributions. As an alternative to retaining accrued rights in the pension plan
that they are leaving, those with more than two years' service may have
the cash equivalent of their accrued rights (i.e., a transfer value) paid to
another occupational pension plan or into a personal pension arrangement. Where a transfer value is paid to another occupational plan, it will
be used to provide credited years of pensionable service to be added to
the years of actual future membership in the new plan, or credits on a
money purchase (defined contribution) basis.

The rules of the occupational plan usually provide for the amount of
any transfer value payment to be determined by the plan actuary, and
similarly any credit given to a member in respect of an incoming transfer value. In calculating the transfer value payment, or the credit to be
awarded in the receiving plan, the actuary is required to comply with
the mandatory guidance note "GN11: Retirement Benefit Schemes—
Transfer Values" issued by the Institute of Actuaries and the Faculty of
Actuaries.

GN11 requires the transfer value to be a fair representation of the
actuarial value of the benefits otherwise available on withdrawal, having
regard to market rates of interest. Consistent methods and assumptions
must be used for outgoing and incoming transfers (to discourage bias in
the assumptions). The actuary is required to advise the trustees of a
reduced transfer value if the assets of the plan are not sufficient to cover
the accrued liabilities.

Increases of Pensions in Payment

The pension (and other) benefits are defined in the rules of the plan.
The rules often provide for pensions in payment to be increased by a
fixed percentage each year (say 3 percent or 5 percent), but with discretion to the trustees to award additional increments as the finances of the
pension fund permit, with a view to maintaining more nearly the real
value of the pension at the time of award. Most public sector pension

plans currently provide automatic or near-automatic indexation of pensions in line with movements in the Retail Price Index.

Member Protection

The main protection for pension plan members is provided by the trust fund and the role of the trustees. In principle the assets of the trust fund should be maintained at a level sufficient to ensure that accrued liabilities — that is, liabilities in respect of past service (and salary to date, although allowing for any provisions in the rules or in the law for increases of benefits in deferment or in payment) — can be met.

If the assets should at any time be shown by an actuarial valuation to be insufficient to meet the accrued liabilities, it is the responsibility of the trustees to seek to rectify the situation, usually by means of additional contributions from the employer over a future period. Employee contributions may also be increased in some cases. If the employer is unable or unwilling to increase contributions, it may be necessary for the trustees to wind up the scheme (or apply to the Court for directions) and secure benefits for past service.

In the event of insolvency of the employer, or a decision by the employer to cease contributing to the plan, it is the responsibility of the trustees to ensure that the assets of the trust fund are applied to meet the accrued liabilities, insofar as is possible, in accordance with the rules of the plan. The assets of the plan cannot be called upon by the liquidator of the employer's business. The trustees will usually seek to purchase annuities and deferred annuities for individual members from an insurance company to correspond to the accrued liabilities under the plan.

If there is a deficiency in the assets of the plan when they are applied to meet the discontinuance liabilities, as described in the previous paragraph, the balance is treated as a debt on the employer. In the case of insolvency of the employer, this debt will rank with other creditors in the liquidation (it does not have any priority as a debt, although creditors automatically rank above the interests of equity shareholders). If the debt is not paid, the trustees must reduce the benefits payable. This will be done in accordance with the priorities laid down in the trust deed and rules.

There is no requirement for insurance of pension plan liabilities against the risk of employer insolvency, since the separation of the assets in the trust fund is deemed to provide adequate protection. Protection against the risk that the trust fund might be inadequate to meet the accrued liabilities is provided by the role of the actuary and the disclosure to members of the current funding level.

Limited protection is offered in respect of the guaranteed minimum pensions (GMPs) for contracted-out defined benefit plans. In the event of discontinuance, such plans can buy back the liabilities for GMPs into the State Earnings Related Pension scheme. The GMP rights will be restored in full in the social security system, even if the assets available are inadequate to meet the stipulated buy-back terms. Over the 16 years since this system was introduced, around 750 pension plans have had recourse to the "deemed buy-back" arrangements as a result of winding up with inadequate funds to fulfill promises to members. For all these plans the total buy-back premiums received amount to some US\$ 4.5 million, and approximately US\$ 150 million was treated as having been paid. Some US\$ 145 million of this related to Maxwell companies in 1992/93 and 1993/94. The total amount represents some 0.05 percent of the current assets of funded pension plans.

Insurance companies are subject to an intensive regulatory regime, which covers both financial strength and the marketing of products. In the light of this, insurance company insolvency is regarded as a fairly remote contingency. However, insured pension plans can be inadequately funded relative to the benefits promised, for example because contributions have not been set high enough, or because money has not been passed over to the insurer.

Self-administered plans are not subject to any formal solvency requirement or supervision. However, the investments must be managed by an investment manager with an appropriate authorization under the Financial Services Act 1986, and will as a result be subject to supervision by one of the regulatory bodies, for example the Investment Managers Regulatory Organization (IMRO).

A surplus can only be removed from a continuing plan with the approval of the Inland Revenue and, in the case of some plans, the Occupational Pensions Board, and will be subject to a 40 percent self-standing tax charge on any repayment to the employer. Surpluses can, however, be used to relieve future contributions that the employer might otherwise have expected to pay.

Although the regulatory regime is not comprehensive, there appear to have been relatively few problems and the controls provided by the trust fund structure have been quite robust. However, in the well-known Maxwell case it appears that, without the knowledge of most of the trustees, and in defiance of trust law, a determined employer may have diverted the pension plan assets to purposes unconnected with the pension plan, through a complex web of transactions between connected companies. This appears to have been facilitated because Maxwell also controlled the principal investment manager. As a result, a serious position of underfunding has arisen in some of the plans, although guaranteed minimum pensions in contracted-out plans are protected by the SERPs deemed buy-back arrangements. Some of the lost moneys have been recovered, some voluntary contributions have been made by London firms, and in some plans the deficiency may be rectified in due course by the continuing employer.

In the wake of these problems, the government established the Pension Law Review Committee (1993), under the chairmanship of Professor Roy Goode, to report on the security of pension scheme rights and to recommend any changes to the law that might be desirable to improve such security.

In September 1993 the Report of the Pension Law Review Committee was presented to the Secretary of State for Social Security. The report contained 218 recommendations, covering a broad range of aspects of occupational pension provision in the United Kingdom, having particular regard to the importance of strengthening the security of the rights of members of pension plans. The Report recommended the creation of a post of Pensions Regulator with adequate staffing to supervise the operation of occupational pension plans and with powers to intervene in their affairs in order to safeguard the interests of members. It was further proposed that the trustees of each plan should have an "appointed scheme actuary" with responsibility for monitoring the financial affairs of the plan, for reporting annually on the solvency status of the plan, and for advising the trustees on the level of funding necessary to ensure a satisfactory continuing financial condition.

Pension plans would be required to meet a minimum solvency requirement based on 100 percent of the present value of benefits promised active members and former vested members, together with 100 percent of the cost of purchasing annuities to buy out retirees receiving benefits (and contingent pensions payable to the dependents of such pensioners). Cash equivalents are already used in the context of transfers between pension plans and represent the present value of the vested accrued rights to which an early leaver would be entitled.

Pension plans falling below the minimum solvency standard of 100 percent of cash equivalents would be required to present a proposal to demonstrate how the solvency position was to be restored. Should solvency fall below a "base level" of 90 percent of cash equivalents, the Pensions Regulator would require an immediate injection of cash into the plan or, failing that, consider whether to wind up the plan and invoke the "debt on the employer" provisions.

The Committee recommended that a compensation arrangement should be established to handle the problem of shortfalls in pension plan assets, restricted, however, to shortfalls arising from fraud, theft, and misappropriation. The compensation arrangement would be funded by means of a post-event levy on all occupational pension plans that might be covered by the compensation arrangements.

No fundamental change was proposed in the basic legal structure of pension funds, relying as it does on the precepts of trust law. However, the Committee did propose that there be a consolidated Pensions Act and that the Pensions Regulator should be responsible for administering it.

Some tightening up was proposed in the requirements relating to trustees. For earnings-related plans the active members should be entitled to appoint from among their number at least one-third of the trustees, whereas at present it is left entirely to individual pension plans (and more particularly to the employer) to determine the composition of the trustees. Pensioner trustees should also be encouraged, since the interests of active members, pensioners, and deferred pensioners may often be different and sometimes in conflict. The Pensions Regulator would have the power to disqualify individuals from acting as pension plan trustees.

Employers should retain the right to wind up a pension plan, with or without the consent of members, or to change the benefits of the plan in respect of future service accruals. In the event of a plan winding up, active members should be entitled to 100 percent of the cash equivalents of their early leaver rights. Any shortfall in scheme assets relative to this standard should be made good by the employer. The amount of any such shortfall should be a debt on the assets of the employer, ranking with other creditors in the event of the employer's bankruptcy.

Trustees should be required to satisfy a "prudent man" investment standard. Detailed investment decisions should continue to be made only by individuals authorized under the Financial Services Act 1986 in their conduct of investment business. Self-investment should not exceed 5 percent of the assets of the scheme, as is currently the case for contracted-out plans, and any self-investment above this level should be disregarded in determining compliance with the minimum solvency requirement. Pension plans should not, however, be required to place the assets with an independent custodian. The provision of information for members should be improved, both in content and in clarity and presentation.

Other recommendations related to the importance of taking the value of pension rights into account on divorce, the simplification of Inland Revenue requirements for tax approval of pension funds, the simplification of the contracting-out regime, the use of plan surpluses, and the structure of future pension plan regulation.

These recommendations were accepted by the government almost in their entirety, in a June 1994 White Paper. Follow-on bills introduced in the 1994/95 session of Parliament will implement the proposals, including a minimum solvency standard based on cash equivalents, a compensation fund limited to cases of fraud, theft, and misappropriation of assets, a compulsory requirement for one-third of trustees to be appointed by members and pensioners, whistle-blowing roles for actuaries and auditors, and a Pensions Regulator with fairly wide-ranging powers. The issue of pension rights in divorce settlements is not, however, to be resolved at this stage.

The minimum solvency requirement will apply to all defined benefit plans, apart from those that are not approved for tax purposes because they offer benefits above Inland Revenue limits and those that are backed by a guarantee that offers protection at least as good as that provided by the minimum solvency requirement (for example, unfunded public service plans).

The cash equivalent concept, which is to form the basis for the minimum solvency requirement, is the same as that already used for transferability of pension rights (and for defining any debt on the employer when a scheme is wound up). It represents the present value of the vested accrued early leaver rights or the present value of the pension in payment or deferred pension rights already granted. For the purposes of the solvency test it may be extended to equivalent notional early leaver rights in respect of those with less than two years' service whose benefits have not yet vested.

Cash equivalents will be required to comply with minimum requirements laid down in mandatory professional guidance by the Institute of Actuaries and the Faculty of Actuaries. Discussions are continuing on this but the intention is that pensions in payment should be valued assuming matched investment in government bonds or index-linked bonds. However, deferred pension rights in respect of early leavers or active members will be assumed, at the younger ages, to be invested in equities, with some blending at ages in between.

The solvency position will be reported every three years in the actuarial valuation, but actuaries may be required to disclose material changes to the solvency position on an annual basis. The Pensions Regulator will be responsible for ensuring that action is taken by the trustees of plans that do not meet 100 percent of the minimum solvency requirement. Plans reporting under 90 percent solvency will be expected to take immediate action by means of a cash injection of some other measure of equivalent value. This might be by means of a guarantee from a recognized bank, or possibly by providing some form of cash reserve, if the trustees are satisfied that the reserve is adequately ring-fenced in the event of employer insolvency.

The new legislation will override existing priority rules in pension plan trust deeds so that, in the event of the plan winding up, each member will in principle be entitled to the value of the cash equivalent of his or her accrued rights.

Pension rights accruing after April 1997, whether in respect of defined benefit plans or contracted-out money purchase plans (including appropriate personal pensions), will be required to be revalued in line with price movements up to 5 percent a year (with the limit applied on an annual basis) once they come into payment. Deferred pension rights in respect of early leavers from defined benefit plans will be revalued in line with prices, with an overall cap of 5 percent a year throughout the full period of deferment. This corresponds to the existing arrangements for deferred pension rights in excess of any guaranteed minimum pension.

Disclosure to Plan Members

Trustees are required to make regular disclosure to plan members of certain prescribed documented information. It is sufficient for some to be made available on request, for example the trust deed and rules, but members must receive written notification that the annual report and accounts are available. A large volume of basic information about the plan must be supplied to members. This obligation can be met by issuing a plan booklet, together with an update in the annual report. The information includes the following: tax approval and contracted-out status; eligibility and conditions for membership; how contributions are calculated; whether contributions have been paid in accordance with the rules and the recommendations of the actuary; benefit information; rights of early leavers; treatment of discretionary benefits; awards of pension increases; names of trustees; names of actuary, auditors, solicitors, banks, investment managers, and other advisers; investment policy; investment performance review; extent of any employer-related investments; review of financial development of the scheme.

A statement by the actuary must be included in the annual report, referring to the latest valuation and the recommended rates of contribution. A full copy of the actuary's valuation report must be made available to any member on request.

Actuarial Control

A full actuarial valuation must be carried out at least every three and a half years (to be reduced to three years from 1997). The actuary must comment on the funding position in relation to accrued rights had the plan been wound up on the valuation date, and must also advise on the contributions necessary in the future to support the benefits.

There are several alternative approaches to funding, but the most common in current usage is the projected unit method. Under this method a standard contribution rate is assessed to cover, over the period to the next valuation (or some other control period), the cost of the additional pension rights that may be expected to accrue. The existing assets are then compared with the liabilities in respect of pension rights already accrued up to the valuation date, allowing for expected increases in salaries up to retirement age. Any surplus (or deficit) is dealt with by reducing (or increasing) the standard contribution rate, usually for a fixed period of years. Other funding methods in use include the attained age method, the entry age method and the aggregate funding method.

In the past, there have been no specific funding requirements laid down in regulations, other than an obligation that contracted-out plans demonstrate that they have the resources to meet guaranteed minimum pensions. This is changing with new pension legislation implementing the recommendations of the Pension Law Review Committee.

At present the actuary is required by mandatory professional guidance on actuarial valuations ("GN9: Retirement Benefit Schemes — Actuarial Reports") to report on the "current funding level," which represents the ratio of assets to the value of accrued rights. However, although this is disclosed in the actuarial valuation report, which is made available to members on request, at the moment plans are not obligated to remedy a current funding level of less than 100 percent. This will also change under the new legislative requirements.

Defined Contribution Plans

In recent years some employers have become concerned about the apparently open-ended cost of defined benefit plans and alarmed about the increasing complexity of regulations affecting the running of such plans. An alternative arrangement, which has the merit of simplicity, as well as effectively limiting the employer's liability, is to establish a defined contribution plan. Some employees also appreciate this approach, since it enables them to see more clearly how their "investment" — their own share of the fund — is growing.

The contributions of employees and employer can be invested with an insurance company, either in individual policies or in a managed fund, or can be invested in an autonomous pension fund under the control of the trustees, with suitable investment managers. The interests of individual members will be represented by the value of the insurance policies under the individual approach, or in other cases by the value of units in the fund that have been attributed to them. The main risk, from the point of view of employees, is that the resulting benefit will not bear any reasonable relationship to their final salary level at retirement, particularly after a period of high inflation. This problem can be to some extent alleviated by targeted defined contribution plans, where the contributions can be adjusted in order to target the benefit on a particular level relative to final salary.

Personal Pensions

Employees cannot be forced to join a pension plan operated by their employer. Self-employed persons or employees who are not members of a pension plan can set up their own personal pension arrangement with an authorized pension provider, such as an insurance company, a building society, or a bank. On reaching retirement age, the proceeds of the pension investment must be used to purchase an annuity from an insurance company, although one-quarter may usually be taken in lump sum form. Dependents' benefits can also be purchased. There are limits on the amount of earnings that can be invested in a personal pension, ranging from 17½ percent of earnings at most ages to more than double that level at ages close to normal retirement.

As mentioned earlier, personal pensions can now also be used as a vehicle for contracting out of the state earnings-related additional pension. The contracted-out contribution rebate (referred to in this context as the minimum contribution) is paid by the Department of Social Security directly to the personal pension provider chosen by the individual. The amount is a flat percentage of earnings in the relevant band, regardless of the age or sex of the individual. This is attractive only to younger employees, in particular those who are likely to change jobs frequently. As individuals get older they will be best advised to contract back in to the state additional pension, although they may continue to make contributions to a top-up personal pension.

Appropriate personal pensions for contracting-out purposes (i.e., purchased with minimum contributions) must be taken in pension form, with 3 percent a year pension increases, and a benefit to a surviving spouse of half the member's pension, but additional contributions can be applied for other chosen benefits.

Supervision and Regulation

Pension plans in the United Kingdom are subject to a great deal of regulation, including requirements of the Inland Revenue, rules for contracting out, and provisions for the protection of members. Requirements are laid down regarding authorized investment managers, actuarial valuations, and the disclosure of information to members, but the enforcement of these and other provisions relies upon the integrity of trustees and the legal rights of members in the Courts (or before the Ombudsman). There is no general system of supervision of pension plans and no single pensions regulator.

Plans that are contracted out of the state earnings-related additional pension are monitored by the Occupational Pensions Board, an independent statutory body, to ensure that they have, and are likely to continue to have, adequate resources to meet accrued liabilities in respect of guaranteed minimum pensions. The actuary has to provide a regular certificate to this effect and the supervision relies heavily on this certification process. However, no specific funding standards have been laid down up to now.

Tax Advantages

Tax privileges are given to occupational pension plans to encourage employers to set them up and to maintain them. The four main benefits for a tax-approved occupational pension plan are (1) that employers' contributions are an allowable expense against profits; (2) that employees' contributions are tax-deductible (i.e., tax is assessed only on the net income after the deduction of pension plan contributions); (3) that employers' contributions to the plan are not treated as taxable remuneration in the hands of the employee; and (4) that no tax is payable on investment income or capital gains within the pension fund.

In order to qualify for tax approval, the plan must be established under an irrevocable trust and the employer must contribute. Employee contributions must be limited to a maximum of 15 percent of earnings and the plan must comply with certain maximum benefit requirements. These include a maximum pension (after 20 or more years service) of two-thirds final remuneration (defined in one of several approved ways) and a variety of constraints on other benefits, including invalidity pensions, survivors' pensions, and lump sums.

A lump sum of up to four years' salary may be paid on death in service. This is free of tax provided it does not pass automatically to the member's estate. In practice the trustees generally have complete discretion concerning the choice of recipient. A lump sum of up to one and one-half years' salary may be paid to the member on retirement, subject to 20 or more years service and a corresponding reduction in the members' pension benefit. This is also free of tax. All other benefits are taxable as earned income in the hands of the recipient.

The tax privileges of belonging to a tax-approved occupational pension plan are not available in respect of earnings in excess of about four and a half times national average earnings, except for those individuals who remain in the pension scheme of which they were a member prior to June 1989.

The tax authorities have defined a maximum funding level that qualifies for tax-free treatment of the investments of the fund. The total amount of assets that may be held tax-free is 105 percent of the value of the accrued liabilities on the projected unit method of funding, with prescribed principal assumptions. For the purposes of this comparison the assets are valued on a discounted cash flow basis using prescribed assumptions. If the fund is above the prescribed level at an actuarial valuation, action must be taken, by increasing benefits or reducing contributions, to enable the fund to comply. Otherwise tax is levied on the excess assets. Assets may be returned to the employer to bring the funding level down, subject to Inland Revenue requirements and there being power in the trust deed. If there is no power in the trust deed, the Occupational Pensions Board can be asked to issue a modification order to amend the deed. Any refund to the employer is subject to a self-standing tax charge of 40 percent.

All contributions by the sponsoring employer are tax-deductible, including both regular contributions and contributions to fund a deficiency, provided the plan complies with the rules for tax approval. Although the investment income and capital gains of the investments of approved pension plans are in principle free of all taxes, some Advanced Corporation Tax payable by companies cannot be recovered against dividend payments to pension scheme shareholders.

Contributions to personal pension arrangements approved by the Inland Revenue may be made out of gross income by employed individuals who are not members of occupational pension plans and out of profits by the self-employed. Individuals who are members of an occupational pension plan may make additional contributions to a free-standing additional voluntary contribution (FSAVC) scheme. However, for employees in an occupational plan the overall limitation on contributions of 15 percent of earnings applies. Rather higher limits are applied where the provision is solely through a personal pension, ranging from 17½ percent of earnings at younger ages (35 and under), up to 40 percent of earnings at age 61 and above.

Investment of Funds

The trustees are responsible for investing the assets of the pension fund. Some of the largest schemes employ their own investment managers. Medium to large schemes mostly use the services of stockbrokers or merchant banks for the management of investments, sometimes apportioning the fund between two or more such managers. Investment managers must be authorized under the Financial Services Act of 1986 to carry on investment business. Insurance companies may also offer investment management services of this type.

Smaller schemes often hand over the funds to an insurance company to manage. This can be through the purchase of policies on the lives of individual scheme members, but is now more usually a straight investment contract. This may be unit-linked, where the results depend directly on the behavior of the underlying assets, or deposit administration, where the capital that has been invested is guaranteed and a variable amount of interest is added each year at the discretion of the insurer. The distinguishing feature of an insured arrangement, as compared to a self-administered one, is that the underlying assets are owned by the insurance company. The asset of the pension plan is the insurance contract. However, it is possible (and not uncommon) for plans to be partly insured and partly self-administered.

The investments of self-administered pension funds were estimated at the end of 1990 to account for some US$ 450 billion, equivalent to 55 percent of the gross domestic product in 1990, and a little in excess of the total net assets of all United Kingdom insurance companies (including life insurance, property/casualty insurance, and pensions business) of US$ 415 billion million at the same date.

Since the major part of the liabilities of most pension funds depends on future earnings inflation during the period up to retirement and on future price inflation for pensions in payment, fixed interest assets such as bonds and mortgages are not in general thought to be suitable investments. The emphasis in recent years has been on investment in real assets, such as equities, property, and index-linked government securities. It is not common practice to match price-linked liabilities with index-linked government securities, except in some plans that no longer have any active members and are running off their liabilities. Some 70 percent of the assets of self-administered funds are now invested in equity shares, with about a quarter of these equity holdings in shares quoted on exchanges outside the United Kingdom, in particular in the United States, Japan, various countries of the European Community, and some countries of the Pacific rim. About 6 percent is invested in real estate. Table 6 shows the 1992 estimated distribution of assets into major categories. Self-administered pension funds own just over 30 percent of United Kingdom equities quoted on the London Stock Exchange.

Pension fund trustees are required under trust law to invest the assets of the fund in the best interests of the members. This is usually regarded as precluding investment in the employing company, or in related organizations, unless the terms are fully competitive with those available in the market. Any significant equity investment in the employing company is regarded as unsound, since it reduces the security of members' pension rights. Insolvency of the employer would affect not only their jobs but the value of their accrued pension rights. Regulations have been introduced to restrict self-investment of this type, for contracted-out defined benefit plans, generally to a maximum of 5 percent of total assets. Contracted-out money purchase plans are required to invest in a prescribed list of assets (including insurance policies), some within certain limits, but these requirements are not unduly restrictive and are mainly for the purpose of ensuring appropriateness of investment and adequate diversification. Apart from this there are no regulations or laws constraining the investment policy of pension funds or affecting the value that may be placed on the assets for funding or solvency purposes.

Trustees often use portfolio performance measurement services to monitor the investment performance achieved by the managers. Some of these services compare the fund's performance with that of other funds, so that conclusions can be drawn as to whether the fund's performance is above the median, in the upper quartile, and so on. Other services compare performance sector by sector with a suitable index and overall against a benchmark asset distribution set by the trustees.

Some pension funds are managed on a fully discretionary basis. In other cases the trustees establish a benchmark distribution, for example 60 percent United Kingdom equities, 20 percent overseas equities, and 20 percent index-linked government securities. The investment manager is then monitored against the performance of such a portfolio. They can deviate from the benchmark to achieve improved returns, but will need to be able to justify to the trustees the more "risky" profile adopted.

Over the ten years 1982 to 1991 the median return of all pension funds participating in a major performance measurement service was just over 16 percent a year. This may be compared with average price increases of 5.6 percent a year over the same period and earnings increases of 8.2 percent a year.

Replacement Rates

The basic social security pension aims to provide 100 percent replacement of income up to the lower earnings limits. This represents some 18 percent of national average earnings. Since the benefit is flat-rate, the replacement ratio clearly falls as earnings increase above this level. Replacement ratios may also be less for those with an incomplete contribution record.

The earnings-related additional pension is still not mature. Those reaching state pension age in 1993–1994 can receive an additional pension of around 18 percent of revalued career average earnings in the band between the lower and upper earnings limits. This proportion rises to 25 percent for those reaching state pension age in 1998, before falling gradually to 20 percent for those reaching state pension age in 2001 and later.

Retirement Income

Table 7 shows the average distribution of retirement income by source at a recent date for all those over retirement age, together with corresponding information for selected earlier years. This shows the growth of the role of occupational pension provision, which can be expected to play an even greater role in the future with increased maturity of occupational pension arrangements and with improvements in the facilities for transferring pension rights on change of employment and for preserving up to retirement age accrued pension rights in respect of early leavers.

Public Policy

Government policy for more than a decade has been to restrict the growth of public provision for retirement and to encourage the growth of private provision. The basic pension is intended to provide a low level of guaranteed retirement income for the majority of members of the population, financed according to ability to pay by earnings-related contributions from employees, employers, and the self-employed.

The second tier of retirement income should ideally be provided by occupational pensions or personal pensions. In recognition of the fact that the coverage of such arrangements is not universal and is unlikely to become so in the foreseeable future, an additional earnings-related pension facility is provided by the social security system. This is clearly envisaged as a back-up, or safety net, and every encouragement is provided to employers and to individuals to replace this additional level of social security by occupational or personal pension provision.

Social security for retirement is operated on a contributory basis and is clearly redistributive, with the major part of the benefit expenditure being flat rate, but contributions earnings-related, albeit with an upper earnings limit for employees' contributions. The system incorporates incentives to encourage private provision, particularly by means of appropriate personal pensions. Tax incentives are given to encourage both occupational and personal pensions. The main value of these consists of the deferment of tax, tax-free lump sums, and the possibility of restricting the tax payments to a lower percentage of income since total income is likely to be lower in retirement than at the working ages.

The self-employed are covered by the basic pension and are encouraged to make further provision through tax-efficient personal pensions.

Private pension plans play an important role, covering about 50 percent of employees as active members and another 20 percent of employees with vested accrued rights to a pension at retirement age. About 60 percent of those over the age of 60 are in receipt of an occupational pension, but the proportion is higher for those newly attaining retirement age. The average occupational pension in payment is over US$ 90 a week and for those retiring now it is around US$ 120 a week.

Personal pensions have grown in popularity since they became available as a vehicle for contracting out of the State Earnings Related Pension. The financial incentives in the contracting-out arrangements have meant that most appropriate personal pensions have been taken out by people under the age of 40, with older people remaining fully in the state scheme.

An investigation by the National Audit Office in 1990 estimated that the gross cost of the contracted-out contribution rebate and incentive for personal pension optants might be around US$ 14 billion in the six years from April 1988 to March 1994. The estimated present value of savings in future costs of earnings-related pensions was US$ 5 billion.

Although public policy is to encourage employers to provide occupational pension plans and employees to have private pension provision, it is thought right that individuals should have freedom of choice and not be required to join their employer's plan. Anyone who wishes to can opt instead for a personal pension, or remain in the state earnings-related pension scheme.

In the absence of centralized supervision of occupational pension schemes, disclosure requirements have been developed. These are now quite elaborate and add significantly to the burden on scheme administrators. It is not known how useful this disclosure is to members in general, although in principle it should act as a deterrent to bad practice on the part of employers and scheme administrators. The deterrent effect may be rather weak in the absence of a supervisory body and strong sanctions.

Legislation following the Report of the Pension Law Review Committee is likely to lead to significant changes in the regulatory framework, to a pensions supervisory authority, minimum funding standards, and strengthened roles for scheme administrators, actuaries, auditors and investment managers

It is unlikely that there will be any change in the basic policy of encouraging complementary pension plan provision or, in the next few years at least, any attempt to build up the role of state provision. If anything, the process of privatization of pensions might be expected to go further. There will be moves to simplify the contracting-out arrangements, as part of the process of equalizing state pension age for men and women.

There will be age-related rebates for contracting out by means of money purchase plans. This should make personal pensions and COMPs attractive for contracting out at all ages, and thereby lead to a further growth of complementary provision and a further diminution of the role of the state in providing retirement income.

Personal pensions at the minimum level for contracting out are unlikely to provide a very adequate income in retirement. A major challenge for education (and marketing) is, therefore, to persuade people that they must make additional voluntary contributions and that the responsibility for ensuring an adequate retirement is theirs. The state will not provide more than the basic flat-rate pension to those who have been contracted out. Of course, there will still be the possibility of means-tested income support, but the whole thrust of encouraging private provision for pensions is to lessen the dependence on state benefits.

Views differ as to the likely success of these objectives. Trade unions and staff associations in general remain very suspicious of personal pensions, which they see as putting too much of the risk (particularly of investment performance relative to inflation) on the individual and too much money (commission, profit, etc.) into the hands of financial intermediaries, insurance companies, and other financial institutions. The preferred option of organized labor is the final salary occupational pension plan, if possible with full price indexation of pensions, both in payment and in deferment.

Most large employers remain satisfied with their existing defined benefit occupational pension plan arrangements, although many complain bitterly about the complexity of the many different requirements and threaten to discontinue the plan if any more regulations are introduced. A new employer might, however, be more inclined to set up a money purchase plan.

There are problems associated with the selling of personal pensions. It is a difficult choice for individuals to make to leave the state earnings-related pension scheme for an appropriate personal pension, or to forgo membership of a final salary occupational pension plan for a personal pension. The choice is far from straightforward, because the nature of the benefits is very different. The individual needs to understand that certain types of guarantees are being given up, relating to the level of pension and the extent of indexation. In return there is greater personal control over pension assets and the possibility of good results if the investment policy is successful.

The selling of financial products in the United Kingdom is governed by the Financial Services Act 1986 (FSA), administered by the Securities and Investment Board (SIB), and the various self-regulatory (i.e., industry-led rather than government) bodies. The FSA requires the financial intermediary to "know the customer" and to offer "best advice." There are also requirements regarding documentation of the advice, projections of future benefits, disclosure of commission, and so on.

Of course, there are many reasons why an individual might take out a personal pension. The public policy concern is whether many (or some) such individuals have been badly advised, or even misled, by eager salespersons and have not properly understood the nature of the choice being made.

Since membership of an occupational pension plan is voluntary, it is always possible for an individual to opt out, either just for future service or also by taking a transfer value in respect of past service pension rights to a personal pension. The determination of the transfer value is in the hands of the pension scheme actuary, operating under the requirements of professional Guidance Note 11 (GN11), as for ordinary plan transfers. There is some concern that this gives too great a level of discretion to the actuary and that, as a result, transfer values, although defined as the cash equivalent of the vested accrued rights forgone, may vary too much from plan to plan.

These concerns about transfers, opting out, and personal pensions are of more widespread significance than the higher profile issues of the shortfalls in the Maxwell pension plans. Pensions in payment have so far continued to be paid from the plans and the future prognosis is not looking too bad, since money is being recovered from various sources and guaranteed minimum pensions for the contracted-out plans are in any case underwritten by social security.

However, the publicity surrounding the affair has created concern in the minds of a lot of pension plan members, and many trustees have taken steps to improve controls in order to reduce any risk there might be to pension fund assets. Recent legislation may address this problem with a variety of provisions, including minimum solvency standards, an appointed scheme actuary requirement, member representation on the trustees, an effective pensions regulatory system, and a limited compensation scheme.

Equal Treatment of Men and Women

In 1986 the European Community Directive on equal treatment of men and women in occupational social security schemes was approved. Although requiring equality of treatment, there was a temporary exemption for retirement age and for benefits to surviving spouses, pending equalization of retirement age in social security systems.

Actuarial factors that differed by sex could still be used for individual calculations, such as converting pension to lump sum, and for defined contribution plans. Some of these exemptions have been challenged in the courts, and a very important landmark judgment was given in the European Court of Justice on May 17, 1990 in the case of *Barber v. Guardian Royal Exchange*. The Court took the view in this case that the principle of equal pay for men and women, which is enshrined in Article 119 of the Treaty of Rome establishing the European Community, applied also to equal pensions for men and women (and to other benefits). It followed that the age at which there was entitlement to a pension had to be the same for men and women, and should have been so from 1957 onward.

In the judgment on the *Barber* case the Court sought to limit the retrospective impact on pension plans, but considerable uncertainty remained about the interpretation of these provisions. It was clear, however, that, at the least, pension rights accruing in respect of periods of pension plan membership after May 17, 1990 should comply fully with the principle of equal treatment. Very many United Kingdom plans took action to implement equal pension ages for benefits accruing from that date, but most sought to avoid making the changes in respect of any past service.

There was also uncertainty about whether it was permissible under European Community law to implement equal pension ages by raising women's retirement age. Was it necessary to level up benefits when implementing equal treatment? Did an increase in retirement age constitute a worsening?

Further problems arose in the United Kingdom with regard to bridging pensions (higher pensions paid to men between 60 and 65 to compensate for the fact that the state pension age for men is still 65, while that for women is 60, with the aim of providing an equal pension in total). There was also a continuing debate over whether some types of actuarial calculation should be based on unisex tables.

In December 1991 the government issued a consultation paper on equalization of the state pension age for men and women. Following a period of consultation the government announced a decision to equalize at 65 from 2020, with a phasing in of the higher pension age for women from 2010 to 2020. The system of contracting out of the earnings-related additional pension is also to be equalized from 1997.

Pension Funds Directive

In 1992 the European Commission proposed a pension fund directive that was intended to provide freedom of cross-border investment for pension funds and freedom to choose an investment manager from another European Community country. These proposals were in general welcomed in the United Kingdom. However, a measure intended to liberalize the investment scene for pension funds was modified in the negotiations and might have imposed restrictions that do not exist at present for United Kingdom pension funds.

The original intention of the directive was that relaxing investment constraints throughout the European Community would allow large companies with several subsidiaries in different member states to achieve real savings. These would be available from the potential improvement of investment yields (due to greater investment choice between countries and among asset categories) and the reduction of costs arising from consolidation. There would also be greater competition between asset managers as the market for new business increased.

The proposed directive has now been dropped, as unresolved disagreements arose on matters such as the extent of control on currency matching of assets and liabilities.

Cross-Border Membership

The original intention of the European Commission (1992) had been to include in the pension funds directive some provisions to facilitate cross-border membership of pension plans within the European Community. However, this proved to be too difficult.

Current impediments to the free movement of workers within the European Community include differing social security regimes, differing levels of benefits provided in different countries, different tax regulations applicable to employer and employee contributions to complementary plans, unwillingness to permit transfer values to other countries, and lack of consensus on minimum vesting requirements, ranging from one-year vesting in the Netherlands to no minimum vesting requirements in several member states.

Although social security systems differ substantially, both in structure and in matters such as pension age, some progress was made in 1971 toward reducing obstacles to cross-border movement through a regulation that requires periods of contribution to different social security systems to be aggregated in determining entitlement. Occupational pension plans are not, however, covered by these arrangements.

Probably the biggest obstacle to an effective solution is posed by the rules and regulations relating to tax approval of pension plans. In order to prevent abuse of the tax advantages available to occupational pension plans, transfer payments other than to another approved pension plan in that country may be restricted.

When a member leaves a United Kingdom occupational pension plan after more than two years' membership, he or she has the right to vested accrued benefits, payable in due course at retirement age. This applies whether the member is changing employment within the United Kingdom or moving to another country. Possible loss of pension rights cannot, therefore, be considered to be an obstacle to such moves from the United Kingdom to other countries. When someone changes employment within the United Kingdom, a cash equivalent transfer value to another approved scheme (or to a personal pension) is available as an alternative to the deferred vested benefits. There are some restrictions on such transfers being made outside the United Kingdom. Transfers cannot be made to pay-as-you-go social security systems such as the French "régimes complémentaires" or to internal book reserve schemes such as occur in Germany and to a lesser extent elsewhere. Subject to certain conditions imposed by the Inland Revenue, transfers may be made to independent pension funds (including insured plans) in other member states of the European Community and elsewhere. The relevant conditions are: (1) the move to the other country must be permanent; (2) the member must have requested the transfer or given written consent; and (3) the receiving scheme must be a tax-approved bona fide arrangement. Guaranteed minimum pension (GMP) benefits are not usually transferable, but must be left as an entitlement from the United Kingdom ceding scheme.

Notwithstanding the possibility of making transfers as above, the relevant receiving fund in another country may not be willing to accept a transfer of funds with immediate vesting of accrued rights. Transfer payments from pension schemes in other countries can be accepted by a United Kingdom approved fund with the agreement of the Inland Revenue. The resulting benefit rights to the member, when combined with subsequent entitlements, would, however, be subject to the usual overall benefit limits. Benefits accrued in an occupational pension plan in another country (but not transferred by means of a transfer value) are usually ignored in relation to maximum benefit entitlement in the United Kingdom. An expatriate worker coming to the United Kingdom may have the choice of remaining covered by a home country pension arrangement, joining a United Kingdom plan, or participating in an offshore arrangement.

Because of the two-year vesting requirement and the availability of partially inflation-protected vested accrued benefits, occupational pension plans do not present as great an obstacle to cross-border movement to and from the United Kingdom as in many other countries. There are still obstacles, however, to remaining a member of a plan in one country while working, on a relatively temporary basis, in another. An increased level of mutual recognition of tax-approved pension arrangements would be welcome as a means of lessening these obstacles. Discussions continue within the European Community to see if this problem can be alleviated.

Conclusion

Apart from these direct effects of European Union legislation and Commission initiatives, the development of further economic integration could have an impact on the investment opportunities for pension funds in the United Kingdom. There is already an increasing interest in investing in other European Union markets. There does not seem to be any immediate (or even presently foreseeable) intention of seeking convergence of the form or structure of complementary pension arrangements (or national social security), so we can expect continuation of the current wide variety of arrangements in different countries.

Attention will continue to focus on improving the possibilities for cross-border membership of pension funds, to permit companies operating in several countries of the European Union to offer a common pension arrangement and to overcome obstacles to mobility of labor, such as penal vesting of entitlements.

From a purely United Kingdom perspective there is likely to be continuing debate about contracting out, indexation, and personal pensions. A number of important changes are expected as a result of the recent legislation, but it is unlikely that this will be the end of a continuous process of evolution and change.

Notes

[1]This chapter draws heavily on Government Actuary (1994a, b).

[2]For further reading on Social Security in the United Kingdom see Daykin (1989), Dilnot and Walker (1989), and Government Actuary (1990, 1991, 1992, 1994, b). See also Secretary of State for Social Security (1992, 1993).

[3]For further reading on private pension in the United Kingdom see Arthur and Randall (1990), Collins (1992), Davies (1991), Daykin (1990), and Department of Social Security (1981, 1982, 1989, 1994c), as well as Government Actuary (1994) and McLeish and Stewart (1993).

References

Arthur, Terry G. and Peter A. Randall. "Actuaries, Pension Funds and Investment." *Journal of the Institute of Actuaries* 117 (1990): 1–27.

Collins, Andrew. *Funding and Solvency Levels for Pension Schemes.* London: Staple Inn Actuarial Society, March, 1992.

Davies, Bryn. *Pension Scheme Surpluses.* London: Staple Inn Actuarial Society, October, 1991.

Daykin, Christopher D. *Demography and Financing of Social Security.* Geneva: International Social Security Association Committee on Statistical, Actuarial and Financial Studies, 1989.

――. "Analysis of Methods of Financing Income for Retirement." *Studies and Research No. 3: Quantitative Analysis and the Planning of Social Protection.* Geneva: International Social Security Association, 1990.

Department of Social Security. "Improved Protection for the Occupational Pension Rights and Expectations of Early Leavers." *Report,* Cmnd 8271. London: HMSO, 1981.

――. "Greater Security for the Rights and Expectations of Members of Occupational Pension Schemes." *Report,* Cmnd 8649. London: HMSO, 1982.

――. "Protecting Pensions: Safeguarding Benefits in a Changing Environment." *Report,* Cmnd 573. London: HMSO, 1989.

――. "Security, Equality, Choice: The Future for Pensions." *Report,* Cmnd 2594. London: HMSO, 1994.

Dilnot, Andrew W. and Ian Walker. *The Economics of Social Security.* Oxford: Oxford University Press, 1989.

European Commission. "The Application of Social Security Schemes to Employed Persons, to Self-Employed Persons and to Members of Their Families Moving Within the Community." *Official Journal of the European Communities* 92/C 325/01 (1992).

Government Actuary. "Occupational Pension Schemes." London: HMSO, 1991.

――. "Occupational Pension Schemes 1991." London: HMSO, 1994. (1994a)

――. "Pension Provision in Britain: A Report to the European Commission." London: HMSO, 1994. (1994b).

――. "National Insurance Fund Long Term Financial Estimates." *Report,* HC582. London: HMSO, 1990

――. "Occupational Pension Schemes." *Review,* Cm 1850. London: HMSO, 1992.

――. "Social Security Benefits Up-Rating Order 1994 and the Social Security (Contributions)." *Report,* Cmnd 2445. London: HMSO, 1994.

McLeish, David J. D. and Colin M. Stewart. "The Supervision and Control of Pension Funding in the United Kingdom." *Journal of the Institute of Actuaries* 120 (1993): 67–129.

Pension Law Review Committee. "Pension Law Reforms." *Report,* Cmnd 2342. London: HMSO, 1993.

Secretary of State for Social Security. "Options for Equality in State Pension Age." *Report.* Cmnd 1723. London: HMSO, 1992.

――. "Equality in State Pension Age." *Report,* Cmnd 2420. London: HMSO, 1993.

Comments by Anthony M. Santomero

Christopher Daykin has offered the reader a cogent review of the pension system in the United Kingdom and its evolution during the past couple of decades. The author should be praised for a picture that permits an outsider a clear understanding of the structure, financial position, and public policy issues facing the British pension system.

His review is sufficiently lucid to make any recapitulation redundant. Accordingly, my comments here will focus on three points that Mr. Daykin discusses but that warrant further attention. These are: (1) the stability of the government system in light of the "opt out" option to the private system; (2) the overwhelming dependence of the system on the defined benefits structure; and (3) EEC transferability. In each of these cases the author's description of the current state makes this reader somewhat less comfortable with the *status quo* than the writer. Allow me to discuss each point in turn.

System Stability

As the author would readily admit, pension programs are types of special-purpose financial institutions. The health and stability of these plans depend upon the balancing of income and expenses, in short, maintaining a non-negative present value. Changes in their environment, caused by shocks in the external economy or public policy perspective, will improve the health of these institutions only if they do not adversely affect the balance between the present value of both income and expenses.

Over the last decade, however, the changes affecting public sector pension plans have not all been stabilizing. As Daykin notes, since 1987 individuals could contract out of the state's earnings-related pension plan in favor of one of the private sector alternatives. Indeed, there is an overwhelming movement in the United Kingdom away from the state-run system, toward private sector alternatives.

Extreme care must be taken during this transition, as the residual system could become vulnerable as individual members "opt out" only when it is advantageous to do so. We see this opportunistic behavior in the United Kingdom today. As the author notes, the contract-out rebate is a flat percentage of earnings and is unrelated to the actuarial liability associated with it. Accordingly, younger employees find it attractive to contract out, only to enter the system in older age. Obviously, such behavior is not sustainable unless the benefits are adjusted downward to offset the lost revenue from wage earners reducing their contributions to the program in early years. In this case, the system will exploit the uninformed or low-income earners who have not contracted out of the system. Alternatively, if all become informed players, the system becomes a specialized old-age pension plan viable for elderly workers only.

The resolution to the problem is mentioned by Daykin himself. Contract-out rebates must be made age dependent. Then, the system upon which a large number of workers depends will not possess this adverse selection feature. While it is laudable that this feature is being discussed, it is necessary that such a measure be passed to prevent the movement to private pensions from becoming a long-term public drain.

The Defined Benefit Structure

As the author notes, the United Kingdom pension system is predominantly a defined benefit structure. The public sector system clearly is a defined benefit scheme, and the occupational pension plans are mostly of this type as well. In this respect, the United Kingdom is behind the trend that has been prevalent elsewhere for some time, namely the move toward defined contribution plans. It is obvious that unions prefer defined benefit plans and a greater say in pension fund decisions. Equally obvious is the fact that the employers are increasingly unwilling to absorb the risk of defined (virtually indexed) benefits. Accordingly, firms have been pushing toward limits on both contributions and recourse to firm resources by pension plan trustees.

There is significant evidence of a trend in the United Kingdom toward defined contribution plans as well, although Daykin understates it. He notes that there is little evidence of conversions thus far in the United Kingdom from defined benefits plans to defined contributions plans. However, he goes on to say that newly established schemes have moved toward the defined contribution model. This should be expected. While large firms and/or large unions are reluctant to demand "give-backs" if only because of the employee morale issues, new plans will adapt to the new economic realities that have led others to defined contribution plans. As the international economy becomes more competitive, firms have tried to limit their exposure to long-term, open-ended labor contracts in favor of short-term ones. Multi-year commitments to employment have long given way to layoffs and cyclical employment contracts. It should come as no surprise that management will seek the same short-term focus on pension contributions and commitments.

Of course, labor will object and protest. This is natural as the firm sector sheds its role as insurer of real income in retirement. However, global competition will make this trend as inevitable in the United Kingdom as it has been in the United States and as it is becoming in Japan.

But all is not lost. As the author mentions, a shift toward defined contribution plans increases the employee's involvement in his or her savings decisions and in the capital markets themselves. There is a silver lining to every cloud.

EEC Transferability

The European economy is no longer a set of distinct economic markets. Increasingly, it is an interconnected entity with firms and products crossing borders at will. Labor, of course, has been the slowest commodity to migrate. Even here, however, over time the labor market of Europe will become transnational. In this context, the portability of pensions becomes a serious issue. Yet until recently it has been underdeveloped as an area of harmonization.

Recent policy directives appear to be changing this situation. However, substantial barriers remain. As the author notes, current impediments in the pension area include: (1) differing benefits; (2) different social security regimes; (3) differing tax schemes; and (4) differing vesting rules. While subsequent directives and enabling legislation at the national level will erode away these differences, the status quo is simply not acceptable. Tax differences may be the most difficult politically, but they are the least important. Differential regulation, government guarantees, and public funding of the social system retard cross-border labor movement. They adversely affect both workers and the social objectives of government policy.

If the Second Banking Directorate is any indication, these differences will be worked out, with some combination of cross-border membership and reciprocity. Over time, national origin may well define pension rights, and standardization may well replace the patchwork of systems currently in place. But differences remain in some other areas of financial harmonization because of the sheer complexity of the issues involved. The problems should not be underestimated.

There is, however, a way out. Most problems of pension rights and responsibilities flow from public systems and defined benefits programs. Defined contributions programs more easily lend themselves to financial harmonization, with some exceptions. The trend toward private sector programs and defined contributions programs indicated above, therefore, enhances Europe's ability to offer its workers portability. It does so without the need to reconcile tax legislation, funding differentials, and national origin issues that arise from the public defined benefit systems that are being replaced.

In essence, the forces of change are enhancing workers' rights, while they are transforming the pension fund system in the United Kingdom, as well as elsewhere in the EEC. As a major participant in the United Kingdom system, Daykin will oversee this transformation on behalf of the British workers he represents. Based upon his grasp of the issues relevant to the current British system, and his significant contributions to that system during his stellar career, they are in good hands.

Chapter 3
Pension Financial Security in Germany

Peter Ahrend

Importance of Occupational Pensions

The provision of retirement income in Germany is principally based on three sources: social security, company-sponsored pensions, and private retirement accounts. However, 80 percent of the working population draw the main part of their retirement, disability, or survivors' income from social security.

The financing of Germany's social security system is shared equally between the employer and the employee. The actual contribution rate for each is 9.6 percent of income up to the social security contribution ceiling of US$ 4,606 per month, in 1994.[1] Social security is based on a pay-as-you-go system, often referred to as the "contract between the generations," since the working population finances the current pension payments (principle of solidarity). Because society is aging and contribution volumes are becoming insufficient, the social security system will face severe problems in the future. At present, German social security insurance can rely on a relationship of contributors to retirees of 100 to 44. However, by the year 2040 this ratio is expected to have worsened to one to one.

Once reform measures have become completely effective by 2012, the average social security pension will stabilize at a lower level, relative to earnings. The "income gap" opening up between this percentage and the income required to maintain the prior standard of living can only be closed by private retirement accounts and occupational benefits. The actual extent of the income gap depends not only on the social security level but also on the net income of active employees, which is determined by the percentage of gross income payable as taxes and social security contributions. This was 16 percent in 1960, 23 percent in 1970, 29 percent in 1980, and has risen to around 33 percent at present. The resulting de-

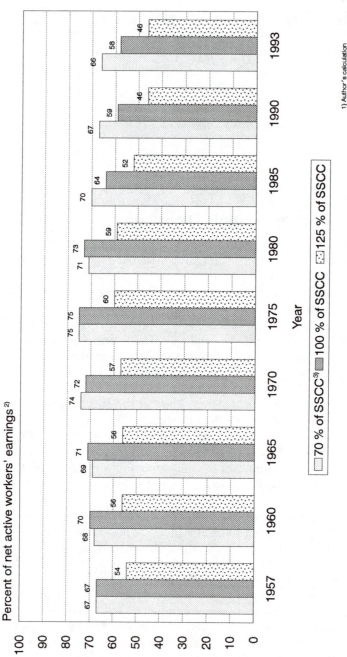

Figure 1. Net replacement level of social security, West Germany.[1]

velopment of the net replacement level of social security over the years is illustrated in Figure 1. The actual income gap for 1994 is shown in Figure 2. In this context it should be pointed out that for a large part of the population the possibility of making private provisions is quite limited since this has to be done from taxed income. In general, individuals cannot establish individual retirement accounts and receive a tax deduction.

Due to the reduction of the social security level in the long term, as well as to the restricted possibilities for private provisions, the subject of occupational pensions has become an important issue of social policy. To provide an overview of the general economic background to any benefit issues, the development of wages, the cost of living, social security, and productivity since 1957 have been depicted in Figure 3.

The Historical Development of German Occupational Pensions

The Early Stages

The first German company-sponsored pension plans were established in the middle of the nineteenth century by chemical companies and those in heavy industry. These were characterized by their patriarchal approach and the employee's personal dependence on the employer. Their purpose was to protect old people who could no longer rely on the social network of a large family, since the latter as a "workplace and household entity" disintegrated during the course of industrialization. Employers, therefore, were predominantly driven by "care" motives for their former employees. At the time when statutory disability insurance was introduced for workers (1891) and subsequently extended to salaried employees (1911) company pension plans were already becoming widespread. Their spread was further helped by the inflation of 1923, which completely destroyed any private retirement accounts employees might have made (devalued savings versus provisions out of current company earnings). Along with the change in the employer-workforce relationship that took place between the two world wars the provision of company-sponsored pensions became based more and more on objective reasons rather than on personal motives. The moral concept of responsibility for staff welfare was replaced by the principle that a pension was a fringe benefit provided by employers.

After World War II: Setting the Course for the Dominance of Internal Financing

High inflation in 1948, in the aftermath of the second world war, set the course for today's dominance of internal financing for occupational

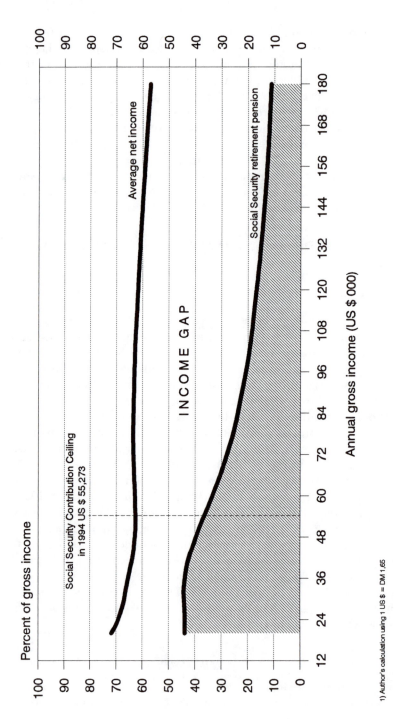

Figure 2. Illustration of the income gap, West Germany, 1994[1] (percentage of gross income).

1) Author's calculation using 1 US $ = DM 1.65

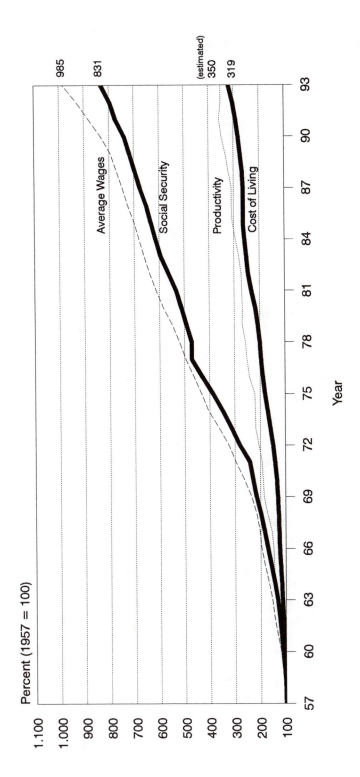

Percent (1957 = 100)

1.100
1.000
900
800
700
600
500
400
300
200
100

57   60   63   66   69   72   75   78   81   84   87   90   93

Year

Average Wages

Social Security

Productivity

Cost of Living

985
831

(estimated)
350
319

1) Author's calculation

Figure 3. Development of average wages, productivity, social security, and cost of living, West Germany.[1]

TABLE 1   Spread of Company-Sponsored Pensions in the Industrial Sector
in Germany (Western Laender)

Industry	Companies with an Occupational Pension Plan (% of companies belonging to the respective group)			Employees Entitled to Company-Sponsored Pensions (% of employees belonging to the respective group)		
	1981[1]	1987[2]	1993[3]	1981[1]	1987[2]	1993[3]
Number of Employees						
20–49	50	39	45	27	23	18
50–199	75	75	73	47	46	40
200–999	92	91	91	70	68	62
1000+	97	99	97	85	91	85
Industry Total	67	61	64	70	72	66
Basic and producer goods	77	72	71	76	83	78
Capital goods	70	62	66	75	78	69
Consumer goods	59	54	57	53	50	46
Food processing	68	64	65	62	59	57

Sources: [1]Ifo survey June/July 1981; [2]Ifo survey November/December 1987; [3]Ifo survey
June/July 1993.

pensions, to be examined shortly in more detail. According to the (currency) Transition Act June 1948 (*Umstellungsgesetz*) all pensions directly paid by companies had to be continued to be paid completely, whereas all other kinds of occupational retirement benefits were converted at a ratio of 10:1 from "Reichsmark" into "Deutschmark." Encouragement of the internal financing method, which until then was scarcely to be found, was due to economic and fiscal considerations.

Like all other economic sectors, the banking and financial sector was devastated, so reconstruction of the economy based on loan capital was impossible. In addition, the tax law of the allied forces (Allied Control Commission Act. No. 12 of February 1946) imposed marginal tax rates of up to 90 percent on company profits. Disclosing a liability for future pension obligations in the balance sheet meant that income taxes could be deferred and the means to finance reconstruction were made available.

For employees the extension of occupational pension systems meant an improvement in their retirement provisions. In 1948 the level of social security was around 25 percent of net earnings and was intended to provide the necessary means of existence. With the Social Security Reform Act of 1957 this objective was altered in favor of the maintenance of the prior standard of living. Today an employee with a salary of US$ 2,425 per month can expect to receive a pension of 47.5 percent after 45 insur-

TABLE 2   Spread of Company-Sponsored Pensions in the Trade Sector
in Germany (Western Laender)

Trade	Companies with an Occupational Pension Plan (% of companies belonging to the respective group)			Employees Entitled to Company-Sponsored Pension (% of employees belonging to the respective group)		
	1981[1]	1987[2]	1993[3]	1981[1]	1987[2]	1993[3]
Number of Employees						
3–5	21	23	28	12	9	12
6–9	28	38	36	12	19	11
10–19	40	32	42	12	11	12
20–49	50	47	55	15	15	16
50–199	67	71	61	27	28	23
200–499	81	85	70	30	44	27
500+	85	87	85	62	54	61
Trade Total	30	32	34	28	28	28
Wholesale trade	37	31	38	30	29	27
Retail trade	27	33	33	28	27	28

Sources: [1]Ifo survey June/July 1981; [2]Ifo survey November/December 1987; [3]Ifo survey June/July 1993.

ance years. However, it should not be forgotten that in former days all company pension entitlements were lost once the employee decided to move to another employer.

The extent to which company pension plans are now to be found in companies in industry and trade is illustrated in Tables 1 and 2.

Legal Foundations of Occupational Pensions

Only in very exceptional cases are German occupational pension plans mandated to provide company benefits, as is the case in countries like France, Finland, Sweden, and Switzerland. Occupational pensions in Germany are governed by tax law and labor law, as well as insurance control law and trade and company law. However, when company-sponsored benefits are granted by the employer on a voluntary basis, a pension obligation exists only if an actual liability has been established. Under the German legal system even an oral promise is binding, although a written statement is required if book reserves are to be disclosed in the tax balance sheet.

On a collective basis, a pension entitlement can be established either through an agreement with the works council or through a collective agreement. However, the benefit levels of such codetermined pension plans generally do not differ significantly from plans established without employee codetermination. Accordingly, the character of company pension systems is a voluntary and additional one following the principle of subsidiary.

Generally, the legal foundations of a company pension scheme can be of an individual or a collective nature. As regards the possible forms of individual contracts, special attention is required by the so-called "standard contractual regulation" and the "overall pension promise." The former represents a number of identical individual pension promises, whereas the latter describes a pension promise by established individual contract, yet given to the entire workforce or to a certain group of employees, either by publishing the pension plan on the notice board or by an oral or written announcement. Both are individual contractual pension promises to each individual employee, but they still contain a collective element, since all employees or groups of employees receive identical pension promises.

Further legal foundations for the creation of pension entitlements on an individual basis are the principle of equal treatment as well as the interpretation of "standard practice." According to the principle of equal treatment, equal facts have to be treated in the same way if there is no substantial reason for differentiation. With regard to occupational pension benefits this principle means that employees may not be excluded from pension promises if comparable employees are given pension promises.

The principle of "standard practice" applies if no formal written or unwritten pension promises or plans exist, but nevertheless the employer regularly provides benefits according to a certain scheme. This practice establishes a pension entitlement for active employees.

Important Aspects of Labor Law

Once an occupational pension scheme has been introduced by the employer, it is subject not only to the Law on the Constitution of Business Undertakings, the code of civil law, and extensive case law but also to the minimum standards set by the Improvement of Occupational Pensions Act (*Gesetz zur Verbesserung der betrieblichen Altersversorgung* [BetrAVG]) of December 1974, with a volume of 32 sections not including the tax provisions. This act was drafted for employee protection, improving their status in several areas.[2]

Vesting

This provision was intended to facilitate the mobility of employees, desirable in times when the economy is prospering, by recognizing that an employee's pension entitlement depends on the employee's having worked for a company until retirement. Irrespective of who initiated the termination of employment, an employee will keep his or her pension entitlement under section 1 BetrAVG if he or she has attained age 35 and the pension promise has been in existence for 10 years or if the employee has been with the company for at least 12 years and the pension promise has been in existence for at least three years. The amount of the vested entitlement will then be determined on a pro rata temporis basis. First, the entitlement has to be calculated on the basis of what the employee would have had if he or she had stayed with the company until normal retirement age. Then this theoretical entitlement is reduced by the ratio of actual service years to total possible service years.

Restrictions on Offsetting and Reductions

It is not permitted to reduce benefits in course of payment after the occurrence of the pensionable incident by taking into account the indexation of other benefits. Furthermore, it is also forbidden to take into account other benefits that have been financed entirely by the employee. This does not apply to social security benefits as long as they have been financed equally by the employer and the employee or to other benefits that the employer has financed by at least 50 percent.

Early Retirement

Under the BetrAVG the employee can claim the company pension before attaining normal retirement age (usually age 65) if the employee draws a full retirement pension from social security. However, the law does not mention the amount of this early retirement benefit, leaving it to the contracting parties to determine. In practice, an actuarial reduction rate is often applied for each month before the normal retirement date the pension is received. In the majority of cases this reduction rate has been set roughly actuarially neutral at 0.5 percent. Its purpose is to compensate for the longer payment period resulting from the earlier retirement date.

Insolvency Protection

Under the BetrAVG, provisions are made in the event the company should not be able to meet the claims arising from its pension scheme. All pension plans except those through pension funds and direct insurance with irrevocable rights are subject to the mandatory insolvency insurance established by the Act. Because of the fundamental importance of insolvency insurance for this chapter, this subject will be examined in more detail later.

Adjustment of Pensions in the Course of Payment

Regulation was introduced by the BetrAVG to protect pensions against inflation in the course of payment. It does not apply to deferred pension entitlements before payment and lump sum payments. Every three years the employer is obliged to review whether an adjustment is required. Specific factors to be considered include the needs of the beneficiary and the economic situation of the employer. As established by a decision of the Federal Labor Court, the needs of beneficiaries are described as compensation for the inflation rate according to a specific consumer price index. Only if the net incomes of the active employees have been growing slower than the rate of inflation during the past three years may the employer provide a benefit increase at this lower rate. The adjustment may be entirely or partially avoided if the economic situation of the company does not allow a full adjustment. This would be the case if the burden of adjusting all pensions under review would have to be met out of company assets.

Until recently it was generally accepted that at any review date adjustments only had to be made for the three-year period immediately prior and that a decision whether to adjust fully, partially, or not at all would be final without any consequences for later review dates. However, on April 28, 1992 the Federal Labor Court decided that any adjustments avoided since the beginning of pension payment will have to be made up for at a later date, once the economic situation of the company permits. Any former adjustments exceeding the cost of living requirement may be taken into account. Further, the development of the net incomes of the active employees of the company is used as a standard of comparison.

Germany is the only country within the European Community that has imposed an obligation to adjust pensions derived from voluntary occupational retirement benefit plans. In other countries, mandatory indexation of pensions exists but only as regards obligatory company pension systems. So, the difference concerns whether the company pension system is obligatory or not. Whereas in other European countries the adjustment is indirectly obligatory (because the company pension system as such is mandatory), in Germany the adjustment is obligatory but the company pension system is not mandatory.

Types of Financing Arrangements

Occupational pensions in Germany can be financed either directly by the company through accrued book reserves (internal financing) or through a legally independent institution (external financing), in which case actual contributions have to be paid. Consequently a differentiation is made between direct and indirect pension promises.

The employer may choose among four different financing methods: direct pension promise, support fund, direct insurance, and pension fund. The benefits granted usually include retirement, disability, and survivors' benefits and are paid as either a pension or a lump sum, although lump sum benefits are of little importance in Germany. A summary of their characteristics is given in Table 3.

Direct Pension Promise

Direct pension promises are the prevailing financing arrangements in Germany. The employer has a direct liability to pay the benefits to the employee or his or her survivors. Hence, the benefits are paid by the company, directly out of the company assets. In the balance sheet the book reserves represent a long-term unfunded pension liability that reduces the taxable company profit. During the time of accrual the deferred tax liability can be used for investments without borrowing from the financial markets. The company achieves a positive financing effect through the accrual of book reserves. Employee contributions, however, are not permitted.

Support Fund

A support fund is a legally independent institution with separate assets, set up by one or several companies. Its legal form is usually a "registered society" (*eingetragener Verein*, e.V.) or a "limited liability company" (*Gesellschaft mit beschränkter Haftung* [GmbH]). A special characteristic is that the employee or the employee's survivors have no legal entitlement to the benefits, since the fiscal treatment generally does not allow a sufficient accrual of funds during active employment, with the exception of current premiums for a reinsurance. Full financing through allocations by the company is possible after the occurrence of a pensionable incident. If the support fund does not have sufficient assets to cover benefit claims, the employer is liable for pension payments. Employee contributions to the support fund are not permitted. A support fund may provide ad hoc benefits.

Pension Fund

A pension fund is a legally independent institution set up by one or several companies. Its legal form is usually a "mutual insurance association"

TABLE 3 Summary of Financing Methods, Germany

Characteristics	Direct Pension Promise	Support Fund	Pension Fund	Direct Insurance
legal characteristics / carrier of benefit promise	company itself	legally independent entity (e.V. GmbH, seldom: trust foundation)	legally independent entity (VVaG)	insurance company
State insurance control	no	no	yes	yes
formal legal entitlement	required for accrual of book reserves in tax balance sheet; otherwise depending on plan	no	yes	yes
Insolvency protection through PSVaG for legally vested entitlements and current benefits	yes	yes	no	no, if irrevocable right; yes, if revocable right or if pledged, assigned or used as collateral
prefinancing of benefits	yes, through accrual of book reserves	no, only accrual for reserves; funds allocated after pension-able incident	yes	yes

employee contributions / investment of assets				
employee contributions	not possible	not possible	possible	possible
investment of assets	liberal, no obligation to invest	liberal, as long as business objective of support fund does not change; loan to sponsoring company possible and customary	only according to regulations of the Insurance Control Act; loan to sponsoring company only possible with approval of supervisory authority	loan of insurer to sponsoring company possible by raising a loan on the insurance policy
reinsurance	possible	possible	no	n/a
contributions taxable as income	allocations to book reserve not taxable as income	allocations by the company not taxable as income	taxation with flat rate through company possible, otherwise expenses for provisions within allowed limits	
taxation of pension payments	taxable as income, however tax-exempt amount of 40% (max. DM 6,000 p.a.) under section 19 (2) EStG		only interest part under section 22 EStG	
taxation of lump sum benefits	taxable as income with tax-exempt amount; possible to divide income by three and multiply the income tax on this amount by three [section 34 (3) EStG]		not taxable if duration of insurance was more than 12 years and contributions were acceptable as additional expenses for tax purposes	not taxable

(*Versicherungsverein auf Gegenseitigkeit*). Therefore, it is subject to state insurance control by the Federal Supervisory Office for Insurance Companies (*Bundesaufsichtsamt für das Versicherungswesen,* VaG). Employees or their survivors must have a legal entitlement to the benefits. The pension fund is financed by employer contributions, with employee contributions being possible and customary. This is the prevalent financing method among large companies and certain industry sectors (group pension funds).

Direct Insurance

In direct insurance, a life insurance is effected by the employer, who is the policy holder on the life of the employee. The employee or his survivors have to be fully or partially entitled to the insurance benefit. It is the insurance company who pays the benefits, and the insurance is financed by employer contributions, with employee contributions being possible.

Of the total funds of US$ 244 billion accumulated for all pension purposes in 1991, the individual financing methods accounted for the following percentages:

Book reserves	58 percent
Pension fund	22 percent
Direct insurance	11 percent
Support fund	9 percent

Total expenses for the provision of company-sponsored benefits in Germany, including all financing methods, amounted to US$ 18.45 billion in 1991. In the same year all benefits paid out totaled US$ 10.75 billion (ABA 1993).

Financing Principles

Financing of Direct Pension Promises

To finance a direct pension promise a book reserve has to be accrued and disclosed in the tax and trade balance sheet according to the following provisions.

The company has an obligation to disclose a liability in the trade balance sheet for pension promises effective after December 31, 1986, according to section 247 of the Commercial Code (*Handelsgesetzbuch,* HGB).

If pension promises were given before January 1, 1987 the company continues to have an option whether to disclose the book reserve fully, partially, or not at all under paragraph 28 of the Introductory Act to the Commercial Code (*Einführungsgesetz zum Handelsgesetzbuch*, EGHGB). Nevertheless, stock companies are obliged under paragraph 28 EGHGB to report in the appendix to the balance sheet any book reserves not disclosed in the balance sheet itself.

Under section 6a of the Income Tax Act (*Einkommensteuergesetz*, EStG) a tax-effective book reserve can be accrued for pension liabilities. However, the wording of section 6a EStG provides that the obligation to disclose a liability in the trade balance sheet is decisive for a disclosure in the tax balance sheet. The amount of the book reserve disclosed in the tax balance sheet may not exceed the book reserve determined under commercial law. Any possible deficits in the tax balance sheet may not generally be made up for at a later date. For pension promises effective before December 31, 1986 the option whether to disclose a liability for tax purposes follows the provisions under commercial law.

The main characteristics of book reserves are that they are borrowed capital and that they represent a liability of which the purpose but not the amount (kind and due date) is known. Valuation for tax purposes takes account of actuarial assumptions, such as mortality tables, invalidity tables, and a discount rate of 6 percent (in 1994). In 1955 the minimum discount rate had been set at 3.5 percent. With the Tax Reform Act of 1960 this minimum discount rate was increased to 5.5 percent. A further increase to 6 percent was brought about by the budget law of 1981 (*Haushaltsstrukturgesetz*, German Federal Law Gazette I, 1981, p. 1523). An increase of the discount rate has the effect that the annual allocations to book reserves are reduced, thus leading to higher taxable company profits. With the enactment of the Act on the Improvement of Occupational Pensions (1974) the minimum discount rate became an obligatory discount rate. The reason was the need for a uniform approach to calculate settlements for vested pension entitlements as well as the contributions to insolvency insurance, which are determined on the basis of the book reserves calculated with the "entry age normal" method.

Under this method, each employee is assumed to have entered the plan when first employed or as soon as becoming eligible (age 30 at the earliest to account for fluctuations). The current service cost is a level annual amount sufficient to provide the required benefit in the actuarial valuation, when invested at the rate of interest required by the German tax authority. A higher discount rate would result in lower settlement payments and in lower contributions to insolvency insurance. As another consequence of the entry age normal method, defined contribution plans, which do not focus on a defined benefit but focus instead on a periodic pension contribution volume for cost control purposes are not very widespread, because a pension increase due to a new contribution is also effective for the past.

The mere accounting procedure of accruing book reserves as a long term liability for pension purposes in the balance sheet reduces the taxable profit of the company and, thereby, its income tax burden. However, since the profit of the company increases once pension payments have started, due to the dissolution of the book reserve on an annual basis, the initial tax reduction only represents a long-term tax deferment. The financing effect of book reserve accrual results from the cash flow improvements and the interest payments saved on loan capital.[3]

Financing of Support Funds

The parent company transfers funds for benefit payments to the support fund under the provisions of section 4d EStG. Current benefits may be financed in full, whereas for future benefit entitlements only an overall allocation to a reserve is allowed. Financing as such is quite liberal. The company has no obligation to allocate funds to the support fund. Should the support fund not have sufficient funds for benefit payments, they can be directly paid by the company.

If the company has not transferred sufficient funds to the support fund, this liability does not have to be disclosed in the balance sheet. However, it is obligatory to show this liability in the appendix to the balance sheet (section 28, EGHGB). Allocations are limited in two ways: by the maximum annual allocation and the maximum permitted assets of the support fund. Both restrictions depend on the kind of benefits provided by the support fund—life annuities, annuities, or both.

Like book reserves, allocations to a support fund have a financial effect for the parent company. The allocations reduce its taxable profit and, thereby, the income or corporate tax burden. In addition, it is possible in Germany for the support fund to provide the parent company with a loan out of its funds. This procedure enables the company to substitute equity by loan capital without having to approach external financial markets.[4]

Financing of Pension Funds

A pension fund is a life insurance company in the form of a mutual insurance company and with a non-profit character. Pension funds are financed through contributions during the active employment of the beneficiary and employee contributions are not only possible but standard practice. Contributions have to be so calculated that the pension fund can accumulate the necessary funds for cover during the active employment period. The prescribed discount rate is 3.5 percent. Further, the contributions have to be so calculated that they cover the promised benefits as well as any administration costs, but they may also not exceed this level. On the other hand, the future pension payment must correspond to the contribution payments (principle of equivalence in insurance). This last point applies equally to the financing of direct insurance.

Taxation of German Occupational Pension Funds

To describe the taxation of the four possible financing methods, one has to distinguish between the employer and the employee as well as between the taxation of contributions and final benefits. Generally, taxation is governed by the "principle of income inflow." Accordingly, all different parts of total lifetime income may only be taxed once.

Depending on the financing method, either the pension-financing period is regarded as the effective date of individual taxable inflow (pension fund and direct insurance) or the period of benefit payment (direct pension promise and support fund). This differentiation is due to the historic development of the financing methods; in other words, it has traditional instead of rational reasons.

Taxation of Direct Pension Promises

As has already been explained above, with regard to the employer company the accrual and disclosure of book reserves in the balance sheet reduces the taxable profit and thereby the income tax burden (income or corporate tax and tax on trading profits). However, due to the profit-increasing effect of the dissolution of book reserves at the time of benefit payment, this reduction of the income tax burden merely represents a long-term tax deferment.

With regard to the employer the pension promise as such and the allocations to the book reserves do not represent taxable income. Once the benefits are being paid they are like wages, subject to income tax with several tax-exempt allowances that can be claimed. These tax-exempt amounts are the reason why the benefits are usually below the tax assessable limit. If the benefit is payable as a lump sum, it is fully subject to income tax at the time of inflow. However, it is possible to distribute the inflow over three years for tax purposes according to the Income Tax Act.

Taxation of Support Funds

For the parent company allocations to a support fund represent tax-deductible business expenses within the limits set by the Income Tax Act. The support funds themselves are exempt from corporation tax as well as from trade and wealth tax if the funds meet several conditions: if the support fund has its own legal status; if beneficiaries have no legal entitlement to benefits; if the fund is a social institution using its funds according to its statutes; if beneficiaries must be able to advise on the administration of the assets; and if there are no employee contributions. If the actual assets of the support fund at the end of the financial year are more than 1.25 times higher than the maximum allowed assets, the excess is subject to corporate, trade, and wealth tax.

With regard to the employee, the pensions from a support fund are subject to income tax once they are actually received, analogous to the benefits from a direct pension promise. The statements regarding lump sum payments apply as well.

Taxation of Pension Funds

The contributions of the parent company to a pension fund are tax-deductible without restrictions as business expenses as long as they are in accordance with the statutes of the pension plan or are required to cover deficits.

The pension funds themselves are tax-exempt if the same conditions mentioned for support funds are fulfilled; nevertheless, it must be noted that the maximum permitted assets are higher than for support funds since the restrictions concerning allocations for active employees do not apply. If the pension fund is overfunded, the surplus is subject to wealth and trade taxes. In other words, the contributions are treated like income of the pension fund. The tax liability can be revoked retroactively by using the excess assets for certain specified purposes, for example, for plan improvements.

For the employees, contributions are taxable, with the possibility of applying a flat tax rate. This system is analogous to the direct insurance approach described in more detail below. Of the benefits paid, only their interest portion is taxable.

Taxation of Direct Insurance Plans

With regard to the employer, the premiums for a direct insurance plan are tax-deductible as business expenses. Premiums are only non-deductible if the insurance was not installed for business reasons because of the contractual relationship between employer and employee. The employer is not required to disclose the insurance claim as an asset in the balance sheet, if the person on whose life the insurance has been taken out or his or her survivors are fully or partially entitled to the insurance benefit at the end of the financial year. Raising a loan on the insurance policy is possible without any adverse tax effects.

For the employees the contributions to direct insurance are regarded as taxable income (because of the benefit entitlement an inflow is assumed). The actual pension payments are only taxable on their interest portion. The amount of the assumed interest portion depends on the age of the beneficiary at the beginning of pension payment and has been determined by law. A possible lump sum benefit remains tax-free as long as the duration of the insurance exceeds 12 years and the contributions have been accepted as additional expenses for tax purposes.

By agreement with the employer, contributions can be taxed with a flat tax rate. However, this is restricted to a ceiling of US$ 1,820 per year per employee. To allow for the benefit requirements of older employees this ceiling can be raised to US$ 2,545 for an individual case, if the average of all contributions for all employees covered by a direct insurance contract or a pension fund does not exceed US$ 1,820. To calculate this average any premiums or contributions of more than US$ 2,545 may not be taken into account. The application of the flat rate tax is permissible only if the insurance benefit is not due before the attainment of age 60.[5]

Control and Insurance of Pension Risks

General Principles

As described above, the majority of pension assets in Germany (around 70 percent) are held within the company. Within limits this also applies for use of support funds as a financing method, which can be regarded as external funding only with some reservations, since the support fund does not give a legal entitlement to the benefits and the sponsoring company is still ultimately liable for any pension payments. This becomes particularly obvious if the support fund chooses to grant the company a loan out of the allocated assets. Under these circumstances the pension assets are again directly connected with the economic development of the parent company. Consequently before 1974 it was possible to lose all or part of the pension entitlement if the company became insolvent.

The Act on the Improvement of Occupational Pensions introduced an insolvency protection of pension entitlements in 1974 for all benefits from direct pension promises, support funds, and direct insurance contracts with a revocable claim (sections 7–15 BetrAVG).

Should the employer have pledged, assigned, or used the insurance policy as collateral, even direct insurances with an irrevocable entitlement are subject to insolvency insurance. In the event the insurance benefit is reduced because the employer did not pay all the premiums required, this part is still not covered by insolvency protection, according to a decision of the Federal Labor Court in 1992. Employees can decide to pay the premiums temporarily themselves or even to continue the policy with their own contributions. In any case, the contributions are regarded as part of the employee's salary in order to define his or her claim for compensation in case of bankruptcy and will be partially reimbursed by the labor bureau.

Benefits from pension funds are not subject to insolvency protection, since the beneficiary is the policy holder. Further, pension funds, which in Germany are always established as mutual insurance companies, are subject to the supervision of the Federal Supervisory Office for Insurance Companies. The fate of the pension entitlements, therefore, does not depend on the sponsoring company.

The Pensions-Sicherungs-Verein as the Carrier of Insolvency Insurance

According to section 14 BetrAVG, insolvency insurance is provided by the Pensions-Sicherungs-Verein (PSVaG), a mutual insurance corporation. It has the powers of an institution of public administration. This means, for example, that the contribution assessments of the PSVaG are acts of administration and that a fine may be imposed on employers who do not meet their legal duties concerning insolvency protection. These measures are intended to provide a high level of security for company pension benefits. The PSVaG does not pay the guaranteed occupational pensions itself; it uses a consortium of 74 life insurance companies (in 1992), which share the annuity business purchased from between 14.5 percent for the largest member of the consortium and 0.1 percent for the smallest. Through this solution the risks can be spread efficiently.

Under section 7 BetrAVG, the obligation of the PSVaG in the case of bankruptcy and in cases equal to bankruptcy are defined. These are the following:

(a) rejection of petition in bankruptcy because of no assets;
(b) institution of composition proceedings to avoid bankruptcy proceedings;
(c) settlement out of court after suspension of payments, only by formal consent of the PSVaG;
(d) suspension of operations within the purview of the Act on the Improvement of Occupational Pensions, if there was no petition in bankruptcy or if the petition would be rejected because of no assets;

(e) serious economic difficulties similar to bankruptcy, only in cases where a labor court or the PSVaG have agreed that entitlements may be restricted or suspended.

It is of no importance who is to blame for the bankruptcy. Even if the insolvency case is the consequence of criminal actions, the PSVaG is still obliged to provide coverage. Further, the employees have a claim even if their employer did not actually pay the PSVaG contributions legally due. The purpose of this principle is to avoid the situation where the security of employees' pension entitlements depends on whether the employer has been respecting the law. In spite of this principle, employers normally do pay the PSVaG contributions legally due, because fines can be imposed on those not paying punctually.

Benefits protected under insolvency insurance include pensions in course of payment (but the PSVaG does not accept an earlier retirement age than age 60) and pension entitlements that are already legally vested at the time of bankruptcy. As far as pensions in course of payment are concerned, the PSVaG has to cover the benefits from the moment of bankruptcy on. Coverage for vested entitlements is due once the pensionable incident has occurred. The PSVaG covers existing benefit entitlements by paying the single premium necessary to purchase annuity contracts from the consortium of life insurance companies.

Scope of Claims

In case of insolvency the PSVaG pays the beneficiaries a pension equal to the benefit the employer would have had to pay according to the original pension plan. However, the PSVaG will not adjust pensions according to section 16 BetrAVG; instead, it has to apply any indexation clauses that have been contractually fixed in the pension plan.

In the event that claims on the PSVaG represent an abuse under section 7, paragraph 5 BetrAVG, it has no obligation to provide coverage. A case of such abuse would be when improvements in the pension plan made within the year preceding insolvency exceeded improvements granted in the previous year. It should also be noted that the PSVaG is not obliged to pay a monthly pension of more than three times the Social Security Contribution Ceiling (three times US$ 4,606 in 1994).

Financing of the PSVaG

According to section 10 BetrAVG, employers are obliged under public law to provide the necessary means to finance the insolvency insurance on a pay-as-you-go basis. Contributions are related to the size of current

TABLE 4   Development of the Pensions-Sicherungs-Verein (PSVaG),
January 1, 1975–December 31, 1992

Financial Year	Members (through Dec. 31)	Final Contribution Rate (%)	Amount of Contributions (US$ millions)	Insurance Cases (no.)	Amount of Claim (US$ millions)	Beneficiaries Receiving Pension Payments (no.)	Beneficiaries with Vested Entitlements (no.)
1975	31,045	1.5	67.0	249	45.3	5,060	7,290
1976	31,685	1.9	96.7	267	99.2	8,614	8,795
1977	32,102	1.9	103.6	246	77.7	4,745	5,808
1978	32,778	0.7	43.2	187	47.0	4,765	6,785
1979	32,518	1.1	72.1	154	77.3	5,346	8,116
1980	32,547	1.4	101.8	161	103.5	6,879	6,985
1981	33,895	2.0	163.0	246	167.8	11,780	13,228
1982	33,977	6.9	607.5	363	739.6	39,564	55,498
1983	33,746	3.7	333.8	322	313.3	10,689	14,992
1984	33,968	2.6	259.1	369	237.3	8,036	15,601
1985	34,622	1.4	160.8	366	230.0	7,461	9,746
1986	34,848	1.1	138.0	332	226.4	8,135	13,448
1987	35,725	1.8	289.6	307	355.0	15,891	19,873
1988	35,813	0.9	222.4	200	188.3	4,460	7,606
1989	36,051	0.6	86.3	173	170.0	4,943	7,872
1990	36,712	0.3	46.1	156	201.7	5,774	6,837
1991	37,282	0.9	137.5	155	238.9	6,170	6,561
1992	37,758	0.8	136.9	185	257.0	9,914	11,216
Total			3,064.5	4,438	3,775.3	168,226	226,257

Source: PSVaG (1993, p. 147).

benefits and pension entitlements. A uniform contribution rate applies for all companies, not taking account of any individual risks and thus only insuring the abstract insolvency risk. The companies have to advise the PSVaG about their individual assessment bases for contribution. The contributions rate is then determined as the following fraction:

$$\frac{\text{total capital required}}{\text{total of assessment bases of all companies}}$$

For example, the annual contribution rate was 0.19 percent in 1976 and 0.078 percent in 1992. The highest rate charged so far was 0.69 percent in 1982, as a result of the composition proceedings concerning a major company in the electronics industry.

In 1992, 37,800 employers were contributing members of the PSVaG, which covered 7.2 million pension entitlements, of which 2.9 million were benefits in course of payment and 4.3 million were vested rights. Since 1974 the PSVaG has had to cover obligations for 168,000 pensioners and 226,000 employees with vested entitlements (PSVaG 1993). More detailed figures regarding the development of the PSVaG since 1975 are provided in Table 4.

State Guarantees

Should the PSVaG become unable to keep up its activities or should the Federal Supervisory Office for Insurance Companies withdraw permission for its business activities — both highly unlikely events — the assets of the PSVaG together with all its liabilities would be transferred by statutory order to the Deutsche Ausgleichsbank (Federal Bank for Compensation Payments).

General Principles to Ensure Investment Security in Connection with Direct Insurance

Pension funds, like mutual insurance companies and life insurance companies, are subject to the state supervision of the Federal Supervisory Office for Insurance Companies under the Insurance Control Act. In this context, the fund's business plans have to be approved and the investment of funds is subject to the following principles:

(a) Security of investment takes priority over yield;
(b) Profitability: appropriate returns must be ensured;
(c) Liquidity: the portfolio should be made up in such a way that there is access to any necessary current assets at any time;
(d) Diversity: no investment may dominate the portfolio; and
(e) Securing of cover funds, e.g., by investing the means in real estate.

Every three years the insurance company has to submit for review by the Federal Supervisory Office for Insurance Companies a balance sheet specifically set up according to insurance principles.

Current Issues Regarding the Security and Future of Occupational Pensions in Germany

The Situation of Occupational Pensions at Present

The present position of occupational benefits in Germany is marked by continuing recession in the German economy. High additional wage costs are too much for German companies in the current situation. Since no legal obligation exists to provide company-sponsored pensions and the introduction of a company pension plan is therefore purely voluntary, companies are increasingly inclined to economize in the occupational benefits area. This is manifest, for example, in the growing number of pension plans that are closed to new entrants; that is, new employees engaged after a fixed date no longer receive a pension promise. Furthermore companies are becoming reluctant to introduce new pension plans. According to a survey of the Ifo Institut für Wirtschaftsforschung (Institute for Economic Research) carried out on behalf of the Federal Ministry of Labor in November 1993, the number of employees in the industrial sector with a company pension promise has fallen from 70 percent in 1990 to 66 percent in 1993. This illustrates that the downward trend of occupational pension provision observed since the end of the 1980s, particularly in the industrial sector, is continuing.

This phenomenon does not alarm the pension market. In view of the continuing deep recession and the voluntary nature of occupational pensions, the extent to which a reduction of occupational pensions has been witnessed is surprisingly low. The extent of company-sponsored pensions in the trade sector has only decreased from 29 percent of employees in 1990 — the highest level so far — to 28 percent in 1993. In all, occupational pensions have maintained their position as the leading company benefit.

This leading role befits occupational pensions in Germany especially because of their function as a supplement to social security, as illustrated by the fact that the majority of company retirement benefits is provided as pension — as in the social security system — and not as lump sum payment.

As in other European countries, social security in Germany faces problems as increasing life expectancy and falling birth rates lead to an aging society and thus to a reduced contribution volume. The pay-as-you-go system of financing social security is hardly able to cope with these changes, a fact that has already necessitated reductions of benefits and will do so again in the future. Consequently, the importance of occupational pensions as the second source of retirement income in Germany is growing. This is reinforced by the fact that German reunification has created an immense need of the state for capital, a substantial part of which is recovered through high rates of taxes that render private retirement accounts almost impossible.

The government is well aware of this situation and tries to avoid putting pressure on the provision of occupational pensions by state measures. For example, in spring 1993 the government considered increasing the legally fixed discount rate for book reserves from 6 percent to 7 percent. This increase would have reduced the annual allocations to book reserves, leading to higher tax revenues for the state, but since it would also have substantially increased the burden for companies with their company pension plans, the whole initiative was rejected in order to avoid worsening the circumstances under which occupational pensions are provided.

For German employees it is not only the issue of occupational benefit provision as such that becomes more important because of the unfavorable developments in the social security system. What comes more and more into focus is the security of pension assets and their independence from the fate of the company, since the existence of many companies is endangered by the continuing recession.

Insured Pensions Promises

The majority of occupational pensions in Germany are financed internally through book reserve accrual; thus, no assets are accrued externally or available if the company becomes insolvent. In spite of this situation a high degree of security of pension entitlements and pensions in course of payment exists.

The distinctive and sophisticated system of insolvency protection provided by the Pensions-Sicherungs-Verein effectively protects current pensions and vested entitlements against the insolvency of the sponsoring company. This German system has proved to be a success even in several precarious cases. Not even the extensive composition proceedings concerning a major company in the electronics industry in 1982 with claims against the PSVaG of around US$ 576 million nor two other spectacular insolvency cases of major steel companies in 1993 with claims of US$ 242 million each could make the system of insolvency protection totter.

Moreover, the system will be further improved as part of the reform of the entire insolvency law that is currently under discussion in Parliament. Here, this reform will review the wording of the provisions of the BetrAVG concerning insolvency protection and enhance the position of the PSVaG as a creditor of the bankrupt's estate.

Entitlements Not Covered by Insolvency Insurance

Pension entitlements that are not yet legally vested are also protected by a special system developed by the decisions of the labor courts. Contractual pension promises once they are given can only be revoked or reduced by the employer under very restricted circumstances. Basically, such measures are only permitted in the case of serious economic difficulties that bring the company close to bankruptcy. In the case of the (partial) revocation of existing pension promises because of such serious economic difficulties, the employer has to bring in the PSVaG before the act of revocation, so that it can cover current pensions and vested entitlements. In case of pension promises established by an agreement with the works council, the possibilities of reducing the benefits are also very limited. Such changes will be scrutinized as to their adequacy and have to be in reasonable proportion to the reasons that caused them.

The Adjustment of Pensions in the Course of Payment

In Germany the current discussion regarding the security of company-sponsored benefits also focuses on the provisions of section 16 BetrAVG, which are intended to protect pension benefits against inflation. Following the decision of the Federal Labor Court in 1992, which held that any adjustments avoided on grounds of the economic situation of the company will have to be made up for at a later date, companies now face substantial financial burdens resulting from their pension plans. Additional problems are due to the fact that the expenses for adjustments can generally not be allocated to the period actually causing them (i.e., the period of active employment of the beneficiary), and thus be pre-financed, since the decision about an adjustment and its extent is always taken after the employee has left the company. This phenomenon of non-periodic pre-financing is even more relevant in the case of retroactive adjustments, as the company still has the accumulated adjustments before it.

As a result, discussion is underway to reduce the risk resulting from retroactive adjustments, so that the circumstances under which company benefits are provided do not deteriorate. In this context, an amendment to section 16 BetrAVG has been proposed that would stipulate that an adjustment of half the increase of the consumer price index would be sufficient and that any lower adjustments for economic reasons would not have to be made up for at a later date.

Occupational Pensions in the New Federal States

In the new federal states, occupational pension plans for the normal workforce are very rare because of the economic situation of companies. The introduction of a company pension plan is only reasonable once the company starts making profits.

Regional fiscal measures may be needed to facilitate the introduction of occupational pensions in the new federal states after the reconstruction of the economy there. Such a measure could include a reduced statutory discount rate for book reserve accrual that would provide tax advantages for the companies. Nevertheless, these proposals remain in the discussion stage at present.

The Success of Book Reserves

In view of the tax advantages granted to companies with pension plans, it has repeatedly been argued that Germany as a stock exchange location is heavily disadvantaged due to the book reserve system. However, the German system of book reserve financing has proven its worth. On the one hand, it would not be possible to separate capital accumulated for pension purposes from the company since it is mainly invested in internal fixed assets. On the other hand, it is not regarded as a disadvantage at all that due to the lack of separated assets there are no large pension funds that could dominate and influence the capital market and indirectly through this currency policy. Nor is the argument that book reserve financing is nothing more than an indirect subsidy to companies convincing. Here it is easily overlooked that the book reserve system fits smoothly with the German tax system and indeed has been created by it. Thus, according to the German tax system a separation of pension assets from the company would be immediately subject to tax, which is not the case in other countries.

The German system of book reserve financing has proved to be such a success that Germany's European neighbor countries have shown an interest in adopting the system.

European Integration: Tendencies and Outlook

The Progress of European Integration and Possible Effects on Insolvency Insurance

The trend seems to indicate that occupational pension systems will be increasingly influenced by European regulations and measures. However, national systems of insolvency protection always depend on the character and rules of their own national labor and tax laws. The definition of what are appropriate instruments for insolvency protection is particularly influenced by the way benefits are financed. If "internal financing" through book reserves is used, as in Germany, the safety of these funds will depend solely on the economic fate of the company.

In the course of European integration, unnecessary restrictions in the area of occupational pensions will likely be eliminated by the process of liberalization and deregulation. To achieve this goal, the European Commission presented a draft proposal in October 1991, the so-called "Pension Funds Directive," but this has not yet been passed by the European Council of Ministers because of the different approaches of the European member states.

The objective of this directive is to ease cross-border services relating to the investment and administration of pension fund assets. This would enable the institutions covered by the Pension Funds Directive — in Germany, the pension funds and support funds — that a company and its subsidiaries have in different countries of the European Community to pursue the joint investment and administration of all pension fund assets, within an overall investment strategy.

The effects of this draft proposal could possibly have an indirect influence on insolvency insurance policy in Germany. Benefits from direct insurance with an irrevocable entitlement of the employee, which are not pledged or used as collateral by the employer, as well as benefits from pension funds, are to date not subject to insolvency insurance in Germany. In each case the pension claim is independent of the economic fate of the company, and life insurance companies as well as pension funds are bound by the strict investment regulations of the Insurance Control Act. The result is a high degree of safety for pension entitlements. Under the draft Pension Funds Directive, these strict investment regulations would be considerably relaxed and thereafter the systematic supervision of investment decisions would be completely dropped (Article 4 of the draft Pension Fund Directive).

For life insurance companies, the strict requirements of the German Insurance Control Act are significantly relaxed by the 1992 Third Life Insurance Directive, which is headed toward national law. It provides that actuarial assumptions be no longer rigidly fixed. Further, it will abolish the approval procedure for rates and conditions, to be replaced by the principle of "single license," according to which only the single admission of the local (national) insurance supervision authority is necessary for a life insurance company to be able to offer the full range of its approved products throughout the European Community without having to set up an establishment in other member states. This might lead to an expansion of insolvency insurance obligations to irrevocable benefits from direct insurance that are not pledged or used as collateral and from pension funds, since pension entitlements based upon the liberal investment possibilities enjoyed by insurance companies and pension funds may no longer be considered sufficiently secure. In the long term, this could result in an increase in the contribution volume for the PSVaG.

Considerations regarding cross-border membership in occupational pension plans and the free movement of labor could also result in changes to the German insolvency insurance system. The existing vesting provisions are regarded by the Commission as a particular obstacle to the free movement of labor. However, reduced vesting periods would lead to an expansion of insolvency insurance, since in Germany under the provisions of the Act on the Improvement of Occupational Pensions only pensions in course of payment and vested rights are covered in cases of insolvency, leaving a considerable number of pension entitlements, that is, those that have not yet fulfilled the vesting period of 10 years, without the protection of the insolvency insurance carrier.

In all probability the expansion of insolvency insurance would result in an increase in the assessment bases. In this connection an essential feature of German insolvency insurance is the link to the tax law stipulation that book reserves can only be accrued from the age of 30. In the event that this age qualification were to be reduced to the European standard, some increase of premiums for insolvency insurance might take place, since pension entitlements could be acquired to a greater extent and, for reasons of employee protection, would probably have to be covered by the insolvency insurance. But such an increase would probably not be too far-reaching. Hence, no further and negative effects on the occupational pensions market are to be feared.

Equal Treatment: Decisions of the European Court of Justice

In the so-called 1990 Barber Judgment, the European Court of Justice ruled that different retirement ages for men and women in occupational pension systems violate Article 119 of the Treaty of Rome and are therefore inadmissible. Irrespective of when the statutory pension is paid, the employer may not differentiate between men and women as regards retirement age or the amount of the benefit. If the employer differentiates, a man can claim to be treated like a woman. Regarding the retroactive effect of this decision the European Court of Justice has supported the view that legal relationships already concluded will not be affected.

Belgian Advocate General van Gerven rendered his decision on four pension cases (using the Barber Judgment) in early 1993. In all four cases his opinion was that the Barber Judgment should have no retroactive effect. Further, the adjustment of retirement ages could be achieved by reducing the retirement age of the disadvantaged sex to the retirement age of the advantaged sex. However, deviating procedures should be allowed. The Advocate General spoke in favor of unisex rates for insurance purposes, but also not with retroactive effect. However, later in 1993 the European Court of Justice ruled in *Neath v. Hugh Steeper Ltd.* that the use of sex-based actuarial factors in funded defined benefit schemes is not contrary to Article 119 of the Treaty of Rome.

The decision on the *Ten Oever* case was given on October 6, 1993. In its judgment the European Court of Justice gave an affirmative answer to the question of whether occupational survivors' pensions represent remuneration in the sense of Article 119 of the Treaty of Rome and that this finding has no retroactive effect on periods before May 17, 1990.

The *Moroni* case was decided by the European Court of Justice on December 14, 1993. The male plaintiff, who was the beneficiary of a German occupational pension plan, claimed that under Article 119 of the Treaty of Rome he was entitled to a company pension from age 60 on, as female employees in the same situation would be. The European Court of Justice held that the definition of different retirement ages for men and women in additional pension plans remains contrary to Article 119 even if this difference is in accordance with the national social security system. Further, the Court decided that in this case the European Community directive 86/378 of July 24, 1986 "On the principle of equal treatment in occupational social security systems" does not conflict with the direct and immediate assertion of Article 119 of the Treaty of Rome before national courts.

Under Article 8 of this directive the member states must initiate steps to ensure that all provisions of occupational pension plans that violate the principle of equal treatment were amended before January 1, 1993. Thus, the European Court of Justice argued that Article 119 of the Treaty of Rome is directly applicable to any kind of discrimination that can be established according to the criteria of Article 119, and that directive 86/378 cannot restrict the consequences of Article 119.

In addition, the Court repeated its decision that equal treatment regarding occupational benefits can only be claimed for benefits resulting from employment periods after May 17, 1990 (Barber Judgment).

In respect of equal treatment, German vesting periods could probably become an issue again. The requirement of attainment of age 35 together with the 10-year service period could be regarded as indirect discrimination against women, since women quit or interrupt their employment careers much more frequently for family reasons.

Cross-Border Employment

In the meantime the European Commission has approached separately the issue of employee cross-border membership in occupational pension plans, a subject excluded from the draft Pension Fund Directive because acceptance did not seem possible at the time. Therefore in October 1992 the Commission presented a "working paper on cross-border membership of occupational pension plans for migrant workers." At present this working paper focuses only on the group of migrant workers. They are defined as employees who are employed by the same employer or group of employers in another country and who wish to remain in the occupational pension system of their home country.[6] It should be noted that all these considerations only concern a relatively small group of employees within the European Community, since according to the paper the number of migrant workers is not more than 260,000.

Conclusion

The provision of retirement income in Germany is based on three pillars: social security, private retirement accounts, and company-sponsored pensions. The expected worsening of the ratio of active employees to pensioners in the social security area will lead in the long term to a stabilization of benefits on a lower level. Hence, in view of the very limited possibilities for tax-efficient private provisions, the provision of company-sponsored benefits will become an even more important issue of social policy — as it is in a European context. Unlike the practice in other European countries, occupational pensions are provided in Germany on a voluntary basis. They are regarded, therefore, as an additional source of income.

Internal unfunded financing through book reserves is the dominating financing method, mainly for historical reasons, and has proved to be a success despite criticism. Apart from the chosen financing method, labor and tax law issues are of crucial importance. Also of considerable significance is the protection of benefits in the event of insolvency, since internal financing depends on the economic health of the company. The process of European integration also has an influence on national law, for example, regarding equal treatment of men and women, cross-border employment, and insurance control. Financially, the reunification of Germany imported serious economical problems. Because the introduction of a company pension plan is only reasonable once the company makes profits, pension plans for regular workers are very rare.

Notes

[1]Throughout this chapter all Deutschmark sums are converted into U.S. dollar figures at US\$ 1.00 = 1.65 DM.

[2]For further information see Ahrend and Jumpertz (1995) and Ahren, Foerster, and Roessler (1993).

[3]There are nevertheless some companies — in particular, subsidiaries of U.S. multinationals — that prefer to hold assets that correspond to the book reserve accrual. These are usually companies that have no need to fund their business other than through equity and earnings; in the case of U.S. multinationals, there can be tax and other financial reasons for having a "funded" pension plan. Traditionally, the asset most commonly used to back pension liabilities has been an insurance contract, which will provide the necessary cash to the company to pay the pension when it falls due. However, portfolios of stocks and bonds may also be used. Such portfolios can be especially attractive for U.S. multinationals,

which are more used to such investments for pension plans. Normally, the asset would not be tied legally to the book reserve or pension promise; thus the company remains free to disinvest the asset at any time. From a United States tax and legal perspective, such a pension plan would not be regarded as truly funded. Under section 404A of the Internal Revenue Code, this can have a negative impact on the U.S. parent of a German subsidiary. A solution to this problem would be to create a legal framework around the asset such that it is protected for the sole purpose of paying employees' pensions. This is done by pledging the assets to a fiduciary, an arrangement that comes as close as possible to the English Law concept of a trust. It should be noted, however, that for German accounting and tax purposes the assets would remain the commercial property of the company. The German tax deduction is obtained exclusively through the book reserve accrual, as before.

[4]A support fund also has the option to obtain the financial means for future benefit payments through the conclusion of reinsurances. If this involves annual premiums (not a single premium) the parent company can fully reimburse the support fund for these premiums under section 4d EStG, even if the premium exceeds the maximum possible annual allocations. In such a case the normal allocations have to be reduced by the ratio of the reinsured benefits to all benefits. A reinsured support fund as a form of "outside funding" combines the possibility of pre-financing benefits completely, without the tax problems arising with direct insurance or pension funds, with the easy "handling" of a support fund since no regulations concerning investment, control of the management, or accounting have to be observed.

[5]Interest received is generally regarded as taxable income. Under section 20 EStG interest from savings accounts is taxable as income from capital. After allowing for expenses, interest of up to US$ 3,635 for single persons and US$ 7,270 for married persons is tax-free each year. Any interest received above these ceilings is fully subject to income tax.

[6]Although the introduction of general regulations for cross-border membership in occupational retirement systems for employees working abroad is regarded as hardly realizable because of the different backgrounds in taxation, the paper concludes that a special regulation should be considered concerning a "mutual recognition for supervision and taxation purposes." This would mean that contributions from the country of employment would be tax-deductible on the same basis applicable for equivalent retirement systems in the country of employment.

References

ABA. Arbeitsgemeinschaft für betriebliche Altersversorgung. *Betriebliche Altersversorgung* 7/93 (1993): 239.

Ahrend, Peter, Wolfgang Foerster, and Norbert Roessler. *Steuerrecht der betrieblichen Altersversorgung mit ar beitsrechthiches Grundlegung*, 3, Auflage, Koln, 1993.

Ahrend, Peter and Bettina Jumpertz. "German Pension Law." *European Pension Law.* London: 1995.

Ifo Institut für Wirtschaftsforschung. *Ifo-Erhebung Juni/Juli.* Ifo survey, 1981.

———. *Ifo-Erhebung November/Dezember.* Ifo survey, 1987.

———. *Ifo-Erhebung Juni/Juli.* Ifo survey, 1993.

Pensions-Sicherungs-Verein Versicherungsverein auf Gegenseitigkeit (PSVaG). *Bericht über das Geschäftsjahr,* 1993. (annual report 1992)

Comments by Lucy apRoberts

My discussion of Peter Ahrend's chapter seeks to raise a few essential points of comparison for the pension systems of Germany, France, and the United States. The first two sections pinpoint the most "foreign" aspects of the German and the French systems from a U.S. point of view, namely book reserve financing in Germany and "complementary retirement plans" in France. The last section comments briefly on the U.S. retirement system from a German or a French perspective.

One obstacle to understanding a foreign social welfare system is the fact that what is politically or culturally acceptable in one country may be considered unacceptable in another. A negative value judgment on an aspect of a foreign system can impede understanding how it functions. German book reserve financing may be considered a case in point. In the United States (or in Britain), only financing through a pension fund is considered acceptable for company pension plans. Book reserve financing is frowned upon and is considered as inappropriate as any type of pay-as-you-go financing. It is, however, widely accepted in Germany, as Ahrend points out.

Another obstacle to comprehension is the fact that foreign systems can be based on concepts that do not exist in one's own country. When one first approaches a foreign system, it is natural to project concepts and categories that apply to one's own system onto the unfamiliar one. American retirement plans covering private sector employees are generally classified into two categories: social security and employer-based (or what the British call "occupational") or, alternatively, public and private. In France, much of the retirement income of private sector employees is provided through what the French call *régimes de retraite complémentaires* or *complementary retirement plans*. These plans are not part of the social security system and yet they are not exactly employer-based, at least not in the sense in which Americans usually employ the term. They do not fit into the U.S. classification system.

German Book Reserves

Peter Ahrend has written an excellent description of company-sponsored pension plans in Germany. Not only does he discuss legal and economic aspects of the system; he also touches on the history that has shaped it. He points out that accrual of book reserves is the most widespread financing method for company plans in Germany, accounting for almost 60 percent of total pension plan reserves.

In this method, the sponsoring company accrues book reserves corresponding to the present value of pension promises as liabilities on its balance sheet. As benefits become due, the company pays them out from its assets and the book reserves are drawn down. The term "funding" is generally used to refer to financing through a fund that is separate from the sponsoring employer's books and that invested largely outside the sponsoring company. By this definition, book reserve financing is not a form of funding. But does this mean that many German company plans operate on a pay-as-you-go basis? It depends on how the term is defined. If by "pay-as-you-go" one means a system where benefits are financed as they come due, without anticipation of future expense, then the German system is somewhat different.

The main difficulty of financing a defined benefit plan that covers a restricted group of employees, such as those of a single company, resides in fluctuations in the ratio of pensions being paid out relative to other labor costs. This problem is particularly acute during the long period of steady increase in pension expense that follows the creation of a plan, a period that spans a number of decades. The rise in pension expense is due to the increase over time in the number of retired employees who have qualified for pensions and to the fact that each new cohort of retirees has generally built up more pension rights than previous ones.[1]

If a new plan is financed on a pay-as-you-go basis, the cost in each period will be equal to the pensions actually paid out, and this expense will rise steadily relative to other costs, notably labor costs, until the plan matures. Companies operating in a competitive environment cannot normally afford to meet such a mounting cost; they need to level out pension costs over time, so that they become more or less constant relative to other expenses. The German book reserve system allows companies to do this: like a U.S. company with a funded plan, a German company makes actuarial forecasts of pension expense and accrues liabilities of a size adequate to finance this future expense. This technique allows the company to smooth out costs over time.

The book reserve system could be interpreted as a form of funding with an extreme asset allocation (Altman 1992; Frijns and Petersen

1988); it is as though the plan held only bonds issued by the sponsoring company. In a funded plan, the adequacy of financing depends on returns obtained on external markets; in the case of a plan financed through book reserves, the adequacy of financing depends on returns obtained by the company on its own capital. As Peter Ahrend does in his chapter, one could refer to book reserve financing and funding as two forms of "pre-financing" of pensions, to distinguish them from pay-as-you-go.

One objection to book reserve financing is that employee pension rights are not protected in the event of bankruptcy. In theory, funding insures against this problem: in the event of bankruptcy, the pension fund is used to pay out what is due to former employees. In a book reserve system, only whatever assets remain to the company can be used to cover pension obligations. The Germans have dealt with this problem through an obligatory national insolvency insurance system. This system is similar in many ways to the U.S. insolvency insurance system, and in fact the two were set up in the same year, 1974.

The fact that both countries have insolvency insurance might give pause to those who object that book reserve financing is riskier than funding: in reality, the security of pension rights in funded plans can be endangered by bankruptcy. The assets of a pension fund can fall short of what is required to cover pensions due, either because the sponsoring company has failed to set aside sufficient reserves or because of poor returns or actual losses on investments. When applied to defined benefit plans, the term "funded" is in fact quite vague. It refers to the existence of a fund, but it does not define the relationship between the value of the fund and plan commitments. It might be interesting to compare benefits paid out to retirees by the two national insolvency insurance systems as compared to total benefits paid out by insured plans in the two countries since 1974. Such a study could be a way of measuring which of the two financing methods has proven the most secure up until now.

In the book reserve system, a pension plan generates resources for the sponsoring company. It may be claimed that this system is too risky for employees, who are putting all their eggs in one basket. However, if a plan contributes to the prosperity of the employer, a prosperity that in turn ensures the future not only of pensions but also of wages and employment, it may not be such a bad basket for them to put their eggs in. Peter Ahrend points out that this pattern often applies in Germany even when financing methods other than book reserves are used: "support funds" may make loans to the sponsoring company; "pension funds" may invest in the company within certain limits; "direct insurance" may be used as collateral on loans to the company. Employees covered by a defined benefit pension plan could be considered to have made a kind of loan. In a book reserve system, they lend to their own employer; in the U.S. (or British) funded system, they lend to capital markets.

The commitments the employer makes to employees in a German plan financed through book reserves and in a U.S. defined benefit plan financed through a pension fund are more similar than appears at first glance. In setting up a defined benefit plan, an employer in either country makes a promise to employees concerning benefits, but not concerning financing. In Germany, the plan is often financed through company assets. In the United States, there must be a pension fund, but the plan is in fact backed up by the assets of the company. Should the pension fund fall short of the needs of the plan, the employer has a commitment to make up the difference.

Why do German and U.S. companies use different financing methods? The answer lies largely in fiscal policy: German companies can write off book reserve accruals for pension plans from their taxes and U.S. companies cannot. However, this answer only begs the question, because then one must ask why the tax systems differ. The explanation lies partly in historical factors. Peter Ahrend explains that the book reserve system became common following the Second World War. Tax rates imposed by the allied forces on company profits were high and companies had great difficulty obtaining capital: the banking sector was devastated, financial markets were inoperative, and firms could not obtain capital abroad. With encouragement from the state through tax exemptions, book reserves proved an efficient method of self-financing for many companies; they were able to raise capital internally without having to resort to issuing stock or borrowing. In 1986, pension reserves represented some 16 percent of total balance sheet liabilities of the 184 largest German corporations (Reynaud 1992). Generally, pension plan reserves constitute a large proportion of the balance sheet liabilities of many German corporations.

Cultural as well as historical factors may help to account for differences between the German and the U.S. system. German corporations seem to have a general dislike for financing through issuing securities. In addition, in the United States, it may be that employees — and unions — have little faith that employers will make good on pension promises. Financing through a fund invested outside the sponsoring company protects employees to some extent from the employer going back on the pension promise. The U.S. system originated at a time when funding was encouraged by tax law, but not obligatory. When unions exerted sufficient influence, as did the United Auto Workers, for example, they sometimes insisted on employers building up adequate reserves. Differences in pension plan financing may also be linked to differences in the industrial relations systems of the two countries. Through works councils and the system of codetermination, German employees generally have more of a say in how companies are run than U.S. employees do. Perhaps the fact that German employees often contribute to company finances through their pension plans gives them — and their employers — some sense that they have a right to a say in company policy.

Finally, it is important to remember that the German social security retirement system is far more generous, especially at higher salary levels, than the U.S. (or the British) system. It is explicitly designed to maintain employees' standard of living during retirement and replacement rates are generally quite high. Hence, for most employees covered by company plans, the company pension is only icing on the cake; the cake is their social security pension.

French Complementary Plans

The French retirement system is similar to Germany's in that nation-wide, pay-as-you-go plans provide most employees with pensions that are quite generous in relation to their salaries. It guarantees most employees with full careers a replacement rate of 70 percent or more of net salary, that is, salary after deduction of payroll taxes (Reynaud 1994). What is intriguing about the French system is that employers and labor unions have set up "complementary plans" that are similar to social security in some respects and yet are private institutions. Company plans are rare and provide very little retirement income. The complementary plans are not part of social security, nor are they employer-based, at least in the U.S. sense.

As in the case of the German book reserve system, some historical background is necessary to understand French complementary retirement plans. The French social security retirement system, which was set up at the end of World War II, levies contributions and pays out benefits that are more or less proportional to earnings under a ceiling that is a little above the average wage.[2] In 1947, the national employers' organization and the labor union confederations signed a collective bargaining agreement creating a national complementary plan: this plan pays out supplementary benefits to private-sector *cadres,* that is, high-level white-collar employees. This plan, called AGIRC (Association Générale des Institutions de Retraites des Cadres), collects contributions from employers and employees on salary above the social security ceiling and pays out benefits that are proportional to that salary bracket.

Many cadres had previously been covered by company or sectorial pension plans that had broken down during the War. The new plan paid out pensions on the basis of past service to retiring cadres as soon as it was created (Friot 1994). This measure was designed to compensate them at least partially for the disappearance of their former plans. It was possible because the financing was basically pay-as-you-go.

Originally, AGIRC covered only employees of companies that were members of the national employers' organization, but in 1950 the state made affiliation obligatory for all cadres through a legal process that is quite common in France under which a collective bargaining agreement may be made mandatory for employers who have not actually signed.

Little by little, complementary plans covering other employees were set up in the 1950s and '60s, some by individual companies and some through industry-wide collective bargaining (Lynes 1985). These plans levy contributions from employers and employees from the first franc of salary and pay out benefits proportional to salary. In 1961, they formed a federation called ARRCO (Association des Régimes de Retraites Complémentaires). By 1972, collective bargaining agreements had made affiliation mandatory for non-cadres in most sectors, and many cadres had also become affiliated. In 1972, legislation required that practically all private-sector non-cadre employees be affiliated to an ARRCO plan. By 1976, affiliation had become obligatory for all cadres, who pay in contributions and receive benefits on the basis of their salaries under the social security ceiling. Over time, the different plans in ARRCO have gradually uniformized their contribution rates and benefits and pooled their resources, so that today the federation functions practically like one large national pension plan covering all employees.

Together, ARRCO and AGIRC pay out around one-third of total private-sector retirees' pensions, the rest coming from social security. To draw a parallel with the U.S. private pension system, the French complementary retirement system is something like two nation-wide multi-employer plans: one for all employees and one restricted to the upper echelons. Like U.S. multi-employer plans, the complementary plans were created through collective bargaining and they are jointly run by labor union and employer representatives.

The complementary plans have some reserves, but their financing is basically pay-as-you-go. Technically, the plans could have built up much larger reserves, but employers and unions decided in favor of pay-as-you-go financing for a number of reasons. Because financing is quite centralized, there was some fear that large reserves would become the object of controversy over how the funds were invested and who was to control them. In addition, unions tended to be wary of funding, feeling that it would lead them to participate too closely in the capitalist system. Both employers and unions wanted to keep contribution rates down. Employers in particular felt it would be better to keep money in companies by keeping contributions down rather than building up reserves.

Pay-as-you-go financing enabled complementary plans to pay out benefits on the basis of past service from their creation. From its inception, AGIRC paid out pensions on the basis of past service to retiring cadres. When companies joined ARRCO, newly retiring employees received benefits on the basis of their whole careers with the company, even before their affiliation. This policy offered a certain advantage for financing: it did not take the plans very long to mature, and contribution rates, while high at first, have stayed relatively level; expenses rose over a shorter period of time than would have been the case if the system had not paid out benefits for past service.

There are probably a number of cultural attitudes that can help to explain the French complementary plan system. France generally has a highly centralized political system and its welfare system — even its private component — has become centralized as well. The French also have — or have had — a certain mistrust of financial markets, especially following the period between the two world wars, when inflation wiped out financial assets. It may also be that French employees are loathe to trust their employers to make good on pension promises, so that a national system is perhaps better suited to their expectations. Finally, employers in many industries may have wanted to avoid competition on the basis of labor costs; a national system helps to make them uniform.

The French complementary plans are private institutions, but they are national in scope. In fact, they have come to resemble a sort of second tier of the social security system. The security of their benefits depends on much the same factors as social security pensions. What is extraordinary is the way in which they were set up. Many employers, as well as labor unions, pushed for their creation and expansion. In most other countries, employers have opposed expansion of national retirement coverage and have fought to maintain their own, company-based pension plans.

In recent years, there has been much discussion about encouraging the creation of voluntary company pension plans in France. Some such plans do exist, but tax exemptions are not very generous. There is debate over whether financing should be only through funding or if tax exempt book reserves should also be authorized, as in Germany. Some current legislative proposals offer both options.

The United States as Compared to France and Germany

Compared to the U.S. retirement system, the French and German retirement systems are quite similar in that, in both countries, the vast bulk of old age pensions come from national, pay-as-you-go systems. Company plans are rare in France. They are more widespread in Germany, but provide only about 10 percent of private sector employees' retirement pensions (Reynaud 1992). In the United States, social security pensions are much smaller and employer-based plans pay out much more on average to retired employees who qualify to receive them.

The other characteristic that distinguishes the United States is the way in which social security pensions are calculated: the U.S. system is explicitly skewed in favor of low wage earners. In other words, it is somewhere between an earnings-related and a flat rate system. The German and French systems are not particularly redistributive on the basis of salary level: contributions and benefits are to a large extent proportional to salary; the two systems are basically earnings-related. They both evolved from less generous, more flat rate systems. The 1945 French system only paid out pensions equivalent to part of income under a ceiling; gradually, employers and unions fashioned a second tier of complementary plans that makes the present-day system comes close to providing a uniform total replacement rate (except for the very highly paid). Peter Ahrend refers in his paper to a major change in the German system in the 1950s. Previously, the social security system was designed to provide subsistence income for retired workers. When reform legislation was passed in 1957, the system's objective became to maintain beneficiaries' standard of living in retirement.

Americans often tend to assume that social security systems elsewhere are like their own, that is, that they pay out relatively small pensions, especially to highly paid wage earners. Germany and France, like many other countries in continental Europe, have a different tradition. Their retirement systems provide universal coverage that allows most retirees to come close to maintaining the standard of living they enjoyed during their careers.

Notes

[1] If a plan grants full retroactive rights at the outset, that is, rights for service completed before the plan was set up, the pensions of the first cohorts of retirees will be as large as those of later ones in proportion to their salaries. In this case, the period of maturation of the plan, that is, the time it takes for pension expense to level off (assuming stable salaries and a stable population of covered workers), will be shorter.

[2] In October 1993, the social security ceiling was 12,610 F per month, while the average monthly gross wage (before deduction of payroll taxes) in the private sector was 11,079 F.

References

Altman, Nancy. "Government Regulation: Enhancing the Equity, Adequacy, and Security of Private Pensions." *Private Pensions and Public Policy.* Social Policy Studies 9. Paris: OECD, 1992: 77–95.

Frijns, Jean and Carel Petersen. "Financing, Administration and Portfolio Management: How Secure Is the Pension Promise?" *Private Pensions and Public Policy.* Social Policy Studies 9. Paris: OECD, 1992: 97–113.

Friot, Bernard. "The Origins of French Complementary Retirement Pensions: The Founding of AGIRC." Paris: IRES International Conference on Supplementary Pensions, January 26, 27, 28, 1994.

Lynes, Tony. *Paying for Pensions: The French Experience.* London: London School of Economics, 1985.

Reynaud, Emmanuel. "Allemagne." In Lucy apRoberts and Emmanuel Reynaud, eds., *Les systèmes de retraite à l'étranger: États-Unis, Allemagne, Royaume-Uni.* Paris: IRES, 1992.

————. *Les retraites en France: le rôle des régimes complémentaires.* Paris: Documentation Française, 1994.

Comments by Marc M. Twinney

Most national private pension systems appear to be similar from country to country. The points in the German system that are different from the United States system are more numerous and important than with other countries. This makes it intriguing to study and compare the German system with the U.S. system.

Once a system is established, it is difficult to imagine whether any other choices might have been possible. When a pension system first comes into being, many choices may be open. Early choices are especially crucial, because they determine the basic structure. Whether a pension system will continue to change depends on the degree to which this structure reconciles what makes all the parties feel secure with what they consider equitable.

In the United States, a primary thrust for future change in defined benefit plans seems to revolve around the degree that underfunded plans can be accepted in the system of guarantees. The more common the features of the pension world become, the more likely that underfunded pensions will be unacceptable inside or outside the United States. This thrust could drive change in German pensions as well.

A second thrust for change worldwide will be to achieve cost effectiveness in the system. Low cost is a primary characteristic of quality in a system that, after all, only stores capital to be used at a later age. Low cost can be used to add more coverage, improve benefits, or reinvest in the economy to support other worthwhile goals that do not require funding, or permit funding that qualifies for tax deduction under U.S. rules. More about such rules later.

My discussion will focus on the few points of similarity between the United States system and the German system in order to understand better the points of difference. These points of difference are the ones most likely to be subject to change in the future, as the European community and North America become more closely integrated economically.

The Importance of Funding

Firms in the United States would prefer to fund their pension plan obligations externally for many reasons. These reasons have strengthened in recent years.

The traditional reason offered to explain why external funding is desirable is that it provides security that pension funds will be available to pay the benefits long term. This is, of course, the most important reason for participants, their representatives, the benefit guarantee system, and the public at large.

Other reasons for the firm to fund externally are to relieve future management of the burden of heavy cash outflows at some future time, to reduce the size of unfunded liabilities disclosed under U.S. accounting standards, and to improve the after-tax profit effect of accrued accounting for pensions. It is worth mentioning that the desire to reduce unfunded liabilities is not solely to make corporate financial statements look better, but also to achieve better credit ratings and lower the firm's cost of borrowing. Similarly, once the return on a diversified pension portfolio approaches or surpasses the firm's cost of capital, the profit effect turns positive. Note that funding the pension plan is a money-losing proposition at the margin if the investments are restricted to fixed income securities, because their performance is inferior both to equity returns and to the cost of capital long term. In some firms, the expected returns on investments in new product are cited as the breakeven for funding. Unfortunately, these returns are difficult to project. Further, the hurdle rates are often set at a high level to allow for variation in projections and to avoid projects whose returns could bring the firm's total return to a level below the cost of capital. As such, these rates are arbitrary and not the correct point to judge returns for pension funding.

Given the reasons for U.S. firms to fund externally, it is not surprising that their German subsidiaries are overrepresented among the funded alternatives and underrepresented in the unfunded book reserve alternatives. This means that German-based firms and, probably, non-U.S. multinationals, will tend to be overrepresented in the unfunded book reserve category.

In the September 2, 1993 *Wall Street Journal* article "Hopeful Assumptions Let Firms Minimize Pension Contributions" by Susan Pulliam, U.S. and non-U.S. underfunded pension obligations were added together for major U.S. multinationals. This was the first time this had occurred in the business press. Initial reaction of the listed firms was defensive, explaining that the results included overseas plans that were not required to be funded, but the article started new thinking inside and outside companies about the potential of funding the obligations worldwide.

German Practice

Many German firms have used an internal fund in the firm to support the book reserve or to diversify the investments of the direct insurance/pension fund arrangements. These "Spezialfonds" were begun in 1968. They have many points in common with the investment forms of a United States mutual fund and even some in common with United States pension trusts and ERISA. Some of the German investment law requirements include the following. (1) Only securities listed on stock exchanges may be used; this excludes notes and any unlisted securities and real estate. (2) Cash cannot exceed 50 percent of the assets. (3) All securities and cash must be held by a depository bank. (4) No more than 5 percent of the assets may be invested in a single issue. (5) No more than 5 percent of a single issue may be purchased. (6) Fund assets must be segregated from those of the management company and not be liable for any claims against the latter. (7) Shares in the fund must be redeemable at any time at net asset value. (8) The funds are regulated by the Federal Banking Authority.

The special funds also enjoy certain limited tax advantages. Transactions are not subject to sales tax, dividends and interest may be received free of withholding tax, the deferral of taxation applies to income from foreign as well as domestic sources, and capital gains are not taxed. These tax advantages do not equal that of the U.S. qualified plan nor of the invested insurance reserves, but they do apply to a higher-yielding, diversified portfolio of equities.

For German firms, these internal funds combined with the book reserve tax deduction begin to approach the cost effectiveness of the United States system. The German system is more complex because the tax deduction depends upon the tax calculation, "Teilwert," not on the amount of funds set aside. Because the firm is the beneficial owner of the special fund, it would be accessible to the firm's creditors.

For U.S. firms, the special funds in Germany fall short of what is needed for a funded plan. They are not treated as a funded plan under United States taxation in the consolidated return, and equally disadvantageous, they are not considered as a plan asset under U.S. accounting standards.

In an effort to counter these shortcomings, a new development sponsored by United States multinationals has been to add security provisions based on the U.S. pension law to the special funds in Germany. These contractual provisions emulate the requirements of ERISA and U.S. pension trusts. This development could become very important to United States firms if it solves the twin taxation and accounting problems that are specific to U.S.-based firms, but not to German-based firms. The reporting effect is taking on greater importance, as mentioned above, in the news media and credit ratings.

One of the issues in taxation is whether the provisions can be made tight enough to perfect the arrangement under U.S. requirements for exclusive benefit without setting off the taxation of the individual participants under local law in Germany as the funds are contributed.

There are a number of differences between the book reserve calculations for tax deductions and the U.S. calculations performed for U.S. accounting and tax purposes. There are also differences between the tax calculations allowed in the United States return for non-U.S. reserve plans. These issues include whether all benefits or only vested benefit accruals are included, the interest rate assumption, the projection of final average salary, the provision for subsidized early retirement, the extent to which mandated post-retirement benefit increases are projected, amortization periods for benefit amendments, changes in measurement methods and assumptions, and experience gains and losses.

Some of these differences mean that the German tax deduction method falls short of the need for a United States valuation for U.S. deductions or for the U.S. accounting standards.

Difficulties of Funding in Germany

A recent tax development in the United States is developing into a substantial problem for U.S. firms operating outside the United States. The problem came to a head in 1993 when the Internal Revenue Service proposed a regulation that combined the ERISA requirements and regulations with the 1986 and 1987 tax changes for pensions with a section of the code that applies to non-U.S. plan deductions and fund income exemptions. This section of the code (404a) was created to apply U.S. rules to deductions of contributions to funded plans and the deduction of book reserve accruals in unfunded plans such as in Germany.

In respect to a qualified funded plan, a U.S. company may reduce earnings by the amount of pension contributions to a trust or an equivalent of a trust, provided the level of local contribution is determined by actuarial valuation using reasonable methodology and provided that United States limitations on deductions, including the full funding limit, are not exceeded. This makes the United States tax limitations extraterritorial, for if the deductions are last in the local or the U.S. return, the contributions are effectively taxed.

The proposal limits the deduction in the United States return, not the amount that can be contributed locally. Thus U.S. practice for tax-deductible funding (not accounting) would prevail. This means that the benefits recognized, assumptions, methods, and amortization all must comply with United States tax law. Apparently the limitations on dollar benefits and contributions on the dollar amount of compensation are believed not to apply. But, the full funding limits and the 25 percent of payroll limitation must be reckoned with. This poses a problem for years in which major changes were made in German plans, such as in coverage, vesting, or benefit increases, and were funded or accrued in one to five years locally.

The 1993 regulation proposes to apply United States tax rules to the exemption of pension fund income as well as to deductions for contributions. The regulation would make the foreign pension fund a passive investment unless the plan is treated as a "qualified" funded plan. This is a much more serious problem than the mere lowering of deductions for funding in the U.S. tax calculations. It attacks the very concept of overseas pension funds for a U.S. firm.

The proposal would make the pension fund non-qualified under certain circumstances, subjecting the income of the fund to U.S. taxation. Failure to meet all the requirements imposed means that the investment income, including past accumulations, would become taxable in the United States.

To meet the requirement in the code, the local "trust" arrangement must comply with all the rules on prohibited transactions, including restrictions on real estate, loans, and investments in the firm sponsoring the plan. The reversion of assets, even if surplus from a non-terminated plan, would fail these tests. It is the legal ability to make an unsecured loan or to take a surplus reversion that creates these disqualifying conditions even if a plan is never in surplus or never takes a loan.

One way to avoid this U.S. taxation is to reduce funding overseas. This is impractical for many firms. Another way would be to attempt to revise the foreign pension fund to meet U.S. requirements. This may be possible to do in many common law countries where trusts exists, but is nigh impossible in civil law countries. It is especially difficult in Germany with the funded pension arrangements as they are described here today.

The effect of the 1993 proposal is to cast a pall over the local funding of pension plans of non-U.S. subsidiaries by U.S. parent firms. This is contrary to an economic policy that would allow or even encourage foreign subsidiaries of U.S. firms to be as competitive an employer as other local and foreign national employers in providing benefits and their financial security. It also restricts firms in non-U.S. markets and the hiring of significant numbers of people at the local site.

The U.S. tax authorities see little justification, given the code, to avoid the effect of their position related to funded plans. The U.S. regulators rationalize this outcome as preserving competitiveness between doing business in the United States and doing business outside the United States, even though that is probably not their effect, given local law and practice.

Pension Fund Investments

Long-term rates of return are key to being efficient in operating a pension fund. In the United States the historical long-term rates, nominal and real, on the three major investment classes are quite familiar. The dominant long-term asset class is common stocks or equities, with fixed income securities and money market instruments clearly behind. The differential in real yield can be as much as three to five percentage points.

Whether this differential is as pervasive in foreign markets or will be as available in the future is unclear. The exchanges and investment bankers in London and Frankfurt provide evidence and arguments that the advantage in favor of common stocks is not much different than in the United States. The size of the Frankfurt market is substantial, reaching 442 billion in U.S. dollars at year-end 1993. The developments reported by Dr. Ahrend concerning the insurance industry's deregulating the investments behind annuities, and the development of the security arrangement with special funds, could hold out the prospect of progress and future efficiency for pension funding in Germany.

Concluding Questions

We have discussed the German conditions and practice of German firms and contrasted them with the German conditions and practice of U.S. multinationals. It would be interesting to examine U.S. practice and conditions for the German multinational. Because a few of the German-owned U.S. subsidiaries have substantial underfunded United States plans, one cannot help but wonder if the book reserve view of funding is not affecting German funding decisions outside Germany.

Finally, one cannot resist asking the larger question about the future of the guarantee system in Germany. The cost trend of the guarantee system is favorable. Over 50 percent of the private benefit values (in 1991), however, appear to be in book reserves, based on the statistics in Ahrend's paper. In the United States, the frequently quoted US$ 53 billion of underfunding (in 1993) is 5 percent of the private pension obligations and assets. In the United States there is a clamor to mandate a solution for this 5 percent problem. One wonders whether similar questions are being raised in Germany about the future of the guarantee system and the book reserve system at their level of funding.

Chapter 4
Private Pension Plans in Japan

Noriyasu Watanabe

For over two thousand years, Japan has had a very different civilization from that in the West. It should thus not be surprising that Japan has developed a retirement income system that differs from those in Western countries. Western pension scholars who understand the Japanese pension system in terms of Western concepts of retirement plans miss important aspects of the Japanese pension system.

Overview of the Japanese Retirement System

The Japanese system for providing retirement income has three pillars: social security, private pension plans, and individual savings plans. The social security plans are the most important source of retirement income. The original system of social security was established in 1941, but at that time many workers were not included. A major change in the Japanese retirement income system occurred in 1961, when the National Pension plan was established to cover all Japanese citizens. A further major change occurred in 1985, when the present two-tier structure of social security was established. The first tier is a flat benefit related to years worked but not earnings. The second tier is related to both years worked and earnings. The most recent addition to retirement income plans occurred in 1991, when the National Pension Funds Plan was introduced as a supplementary pension for self-employed workers.

The two-tier structure of social security is composed of the National Pension plan and five plans covering different groups of workers, including plans for national and local government workers.

The National Pension plan covers every Japanese citizen aged 20 and over. The earliest age at which workers can receive full benefits is 65. The National Pension provides three types of benefits: (1) an old age pension,

(2) a disability pension, and (3) a survivors pension. The National Pension plan covers 68.4 million people and provides average benefits of 35,000 yen a month (about US$ 330, or about US$ 4,000 a year) to beneficiaries age 65 and older. The monthly contribution is the same for all workers, and was 10,500 yen (about US$ 100) for fiscal year 1993. (Fiscal years end on March 31 of the following calendar year.) There were 19 beneficiaries per 100 covered workers in that year.

Because contributions have been larger than benefit payments, each year the reserves for the National Pension increase. The National Pension had 4.4 trillion yen (about US$ 35 billion) in accumulated reserves in 1992.[1]

There are five mandatory earnings-related social security and public employee plans. The Employees' Pension Insurance covers most workers in the private sector and thus corresponds most in terms of coverage to the United States' social security system. Government employees and small groups of private sector employees are covered by the Mutual Aid Associations for National Public Servants, the Mutual Aid Association for Local Public Servants, the Private School Personnel Mutual Aid Association, and the Agriculture, Forestry and Fisheries Employee Mutual Aid Association.

These five earnings-related plans cover 37.8 million active participants with 7.2 million beneficiaries. They have 117.7 trillion yen (US$ 930 billion) in accumulated reserves as of 1994. As for the National Pension, it has an average of 19 beneficiaries per 100 workers, but with large differences in this ratio, ranging from eight per 100 for the Private School Personnel Mutual Aid Association, to 169 per 100 for the Japan Railways Mutual Aid Association.

Employees' Pension Insurance has 31.9 million insured participants and 5.0 million beneficiaries. It has 15.6 beneficiaries per 100 covered workers. It pays average monthly benefits of 151,000 yen (about US$ 1,400, or about US$ 17,000 a year). This amount combined with the National Pension is higher than that received by social security beneficiaries in most other countries. The contribution for both men and women in 1994 was 14.5 percent of wages. The contribution is not charged on the twice-yearly bonuses that most career workers receive, and thus the effective contribution rate on total earnings is somewhat lower than the stated rate.

Social security accumulated reserves have increased 22-fold in the National Pension plan and 51-fold in the Employees' Pension Insurance plan between 1965 and 1991. The assets of these plans are required by law to be managed on a sound and profitable basis. In order to manage the investment of social security and public pension fund money, the money is deposited with the Trust Fund Bureau of the Ministry of Finance, but does not become part of the national government budget. The Trust Fund Bureau uses the social security and public pension fund reserves to finance a complex network of government investment and lending operations.

Future Funding of the Social Security System

The generosity of Japanese social security systems improved greatly during the rapid economic growth of the past several decades. Social security expenditures in Japan in 1989 were 13.9 percent of national income, compared to 15.8 percent in the United States and 28.4 percent in West Germany.

The ratio to national income of all taxes, including contributions for social security, was 38.5 percent for Japan, 36.5 percent for the United States, and 52.5 percent for West Germany. Population aging will increase the burden of tax and social security expenditures. That burden is projected to exceed 50 percent early in the next century. The Japanese government, however, has indicated it intends to keep the ratio of taxes and social security contributions to national income to less than 50 percent. In order to cope with the cost increases for pension benefits associated with a growing number of beneficiaries and a longer period of receipt of benefits (due to increasing life expectancy), the government will need to raise the social security tax rate.

The government estimated in 1989 that, if the present benefits provided at age 60 remain unchanged, a contribution rate of about 35 percent would be required in 2025 to maintain the social security trust funds. If the pension age were to be raised gradually from 60 to 65, with a reduced benefit available to those ages 60 to 64, the required contribution rate would fall to 28 to 29 percent.

Population aging may affect the overall government budget. The Organization for Economic Cooperation and Development (OECD) has estimated that the Japanese government deficit will be worse relative to the Japanese economy than the United States government deficit in 1995. Further, it estimates that if social security funds are excluded from the calculation, the Japanese government deficit was worse than the United States deficit in 1993. In 1993, the Japanese deficit was 4.5 percent of gross domestic product (GDP), compared with the United States deficit of 4.4 percent (Organisation for Economic Development, 1993). To calculate the government deficit correctly, social security funds, which are composed mainly of funds for social security, should be excluded. The worsening Japanese government deficit reflects the worsening economic situation and the heavy burden of a rapidly aging society.

To adjust to an aging population, changes in social security will be needed. The Pension Council advises the Ministry of Health and Welfare. It is composed of academics, employee representatives (usually union officials), and employer representatives (usually officials of major employers' organizations). Although not required by law, the Japanese government always asks the opinion of the Pension Council when considering major changes in pension laws. In October 1993, the Pension Council (1993) made two recommendations: (1) that the age for receiving a full pension benefit from Employees' Pension Insurance be raised from 60 to 65, with reduced benefits available at age 60, and (2) that benefit amounts be indexed to changes in real disposable income, rather than to prices. The initial benefit at retirement under the indexation proposal would be based on a portion of the worker's real disposable earnings immediately before retirement. Indexing after retirement would be tied to the increase in real disposable income rather than the increase in prices. The two main reasons for the recommendations are that the Japanese economy has moved from a period of rapid growth to a period of slower growth, and that the rapid aging of the Japanese population will increase the tax burden rapidly over the next century.

The Japanese government intends to amend social security laws according to these recommendations. These changes in social security programs will cause private pension plans to become increasingly important.

Private Pension Plans

In Japan private pension plans have traditionally been defined benefit plans. Defined contribution plans have not been considered to be pension plans but rather are thought of as individual savings plans.

Lump sum benefit plans are an important part of the defined benefit private pension system. These plans predate the Japanese social security system. They have decreased in importance over the past 20 years but still are important. They are the predecessor of the current pension plans in many companies.

A Short History of Retirement Income Systems in Japan

Contrary to many Westerners' views of Japanese history, Japan had a well-developed economy before the 1868 Meiji revolution.[2] The first lump sum retirement benefit plans may have been introduced in the late seventeenth century. Initially, they were severance pay plans, but gradually they came to be a retirement income security system. The oldest document concerning a lump sum retirement benefit plan is the will in 1722 of a Mr. Sozin, President of Mitsui Company, which shows that the Mitsui Company had a retirement income system for its managers and white collar workers (but not blue collar workers) with the managers and white collar workers contributing (Kurozami 1966).

In 1876, a government shipbuilding factory established a lump sum retirement benefit plan. In 1883, the Japanese government established a public pension plan covering military personnel and upper level government officials.

In 1885, the Ohzi Papermaking Company established a lump sum retirement benefit plan for its workers. This plan is historically important because it is the first modern plan that covered blue collar workers. The minimum service requirement for eligibility for a lump sum retirement benefit was 10 years. In 1897, the Mitsui Company established a lump sum retirement benefit plan with minimum vesting of three years. In 1914, the Mitsui Company amended its plan and introduced the first life annuity pension benefits plan in Japan.

Between 1900 and 1910, lump sum retirement benefit plans became popular for managers and white collar workers, but they did not become widespread for blue collar workers until the 1920s and 1930s.

Traditionally in Japan, labor mobility was high, even in the nineteenth century. But starting about 1910, industries began establishing the Tei-nen-seido system, which is the current system of lifetime employment followed by mandatory retirement. Contrary to popular understanding of Japanese labor customs, the lifetime employment system in Japan has had a relatively short history.

In 1936, the Lump Sum Retirement Benefit Plans law was enacted. It was the first law regulating retirement income security for workers. In 1941 the Workers Pension Insurance law was enacted, and it was amended by the Employees' Pension Insurance law in 1944, which created the first social security pension plan. After World War II, the new Japanese constitution guaranteed the rights of workers to organize, bargain, and act collectively. Unionization spread rapidly. By 1947, the unionization rate had increased to 45 percent, compared with 8 percent in 1931.

Immediately after World War II, one of the main goals of the labor movement was to establish better lump sum retirement benefit plans. These were viewed as a right of employees guaranteed by the new constitution. A government survey in 1951 showed that 96 percent of companies with more than 500 employees had those plans, as did 90 percent of companies with 100 to 499 employees, and 78 percent of companies with 30 to 99 employees. A survey in 1955 showed that over 70 percent of companies had the current system of lifetime employment with mandatory retirement, and by 1959 all companies with more than 1,000 employees had such a plan.

Conditions Prior to the Introduction of Private Pension Plans

As Japanese industries destroyed during World War II regained their strength, employers wanted to encourage long tenure by their workers. Employers increasingly introduced the system of lifetime employment, followed by mandatory retirement with a lump sum benefit at a relatively early age. The lump sum retirement benefit plans, however, required companies to pay large sums when each employee reached the mandatory retirement age, usually 55.

The lump sum benefit plans were financed by the book reserve financing method. The 1952 amendment of tax laws established the current system of book reserve financing. In the lump sum benefit plans, the benefit an employee receives at mandatory retirement or mandatory job separation is much larger than the benefit he or she receives if he or she leaves the job voluntarily. In the book reserve financing method, employers can only take a tax deduction based on the amount of benefits the employee would receive if he or she leaves voluntarily. Employers can take a tax deduction at the point of mandatory retirement for the difference between the benefit for voluntary retirement and the benefit for mandatory retirement.

Because lump sum benefits are not advance-funded, financing lump sum benefits for retiring employees was a big burden for employers. They sought a funded system for providing retirement benefits. In 1962, by amendment of the Corporation Tax law and the Income Tax law, Tax Qualified Pension (TQP) plans were introduced. In 1966, a further major legal change occurred when Employees' Pension Fund (EPF) plans were introduced.

In some firms, Tax Qualified Pension plans or Employees' Pension Fund plans replaced lump sum benefit plans, but in many other firms the lump sum retirement plans have continued along with those plans. Even if the plan is not a lump sum benefit plan, when employers and employees negotiate benefits from private pension plans, they usually compare benefits in terms of their lump sum value.

There are four types of defined benefit plans in Japan today: (1) Lump Sum Retirement Benefit plans funded by book reserve; (2) Tax Qualified Pension plans; (3) Employees' Pension Fund plans; and (4) non-tax qualified defined benefit plans. Though of considerably less importance, there are also three types of defined contribution plans: (1) Middle to Small Enterprise Private Pension Mutual Aid plans; (2) Zaikei-tyotiku plans; and (3) National Pension Fund plans for employees not covered by Employees' Pension Insurance plans. We consider each in turn.

Lump Sum Retirement Benefit (Book Reserve) Plans

The lump sum retirement benefit plans receive preferential tax treatment under corporate tax law, which allows employers tax deductions for an amount equal to 40 percent of the accrual of voluntary retirement lump sum benefits. The amounts of the lump sum benefit at voluntary and mandatory retirement are determined by contract with the labor union in unionized firms.

No accurate statistics on the total number of book reserve plans are available, but the most useful information is from the Tax Administration of the Finance Department of the Japanese government. These data contain about 65,000 companies, or 2.7 percent of all companies in Japan. They contain all companies with capital value of 1.0 billion yen or more, and 40 percent of companies of between 0.1 and 1.0 billion yen. According to these data, 5 percent of companies have book reserve plans, and the total value of the plans equals 18 percent of the value of the companies.

The percentage of companies using book reserve plans increased from 7.1 percent in 1971 to 8.0 percent in 1974, and then decreased to 5.4 percent in 1992. The main reason for the decrease is that firms have established Employees' Pension Fund and Tax Qualified Pension plans instead. Book reserve plans are much more common in large firms than in small ones. In 1992, 74 percent of companies with capital value of one billion yen or more had those plans. In comparison, only 1.5 percent of companies having a value of less than 5 million yen had book reserve plans. Large firms have thus used not only Employees' Pension Fund plans and Tax Qualified Pension plans but also book reserve plans.

Tax Qualified Pension Plans

Employers with 15 or more full-time workers can contract with financial institutions to establish Tax Qualified Pension plans.[3] The main requirements are that (1) the plan must be established for the sole purpose of paying retirement pension benefits, with employees having the option of receiving lump sum benefits; (2) the plan must be funded through a trust bank or life insurance company; (3) contributions must be calculated on a predetermined basis, such as a fixed percentage of salary or a fixed amount (at least every five years, the plan must recalculate the fixed percentage or fixed amount to adjust for overfunding or underfunding); (4) the plan must follow prescribed actuarial assumptions, with actuarial reviews conducted at least every five years; (5) although reserves may be transferred to another Tax Qualified Pension plan or Employees' Pension Fund plan, they cannot revert to the employer; (6) if the plan is terminated, the reserves must become the property of the participants; (7) the plan may not discriminate against any group of employees in terms of eligibility and benefit provisions (it must cover all full-time employees but may exclude part-time employees); and (8) the owners and directors of the company generally must be excluded from the plan.

In 1993, there were 10.4 million employees in 92,000 Tax Qualified Pension plans. Benefits were paid from life annuities in 21 percent of plans, but were paid for 10 years in 46 percent of plans, and 15 years in 30 percent.

Employees' Pension Fund Plans

The Employees' Pension Fund plans are contracted-out plans. The term "contract out" means that a qualifying company, with the permission of the Health and Welfare Ministry, can establish the pension fund as a legal entity different from the plan sponsor and can pay a reduced social security tax rate. In exchange, the plan must provide a pension benefit that is at least 30 percent more generous than the social security benefits being replaced. Changes in pension laws in recent years have reduced the participant size requirements for employers to establish Employees' Pension Fund plans (Watanabe, Turner, and Rajnes 1994).

There are four types of Employees' Pension Fund plans: single company fund plans, established with a single company as plan sponsor, and requiring at least 500 full-time participants; allied company fund plans, established with the sponsorship of affiliated companies within a company group, and requiring at least 800 full-time participants; multi-employer plans, established with a national or regional trade association as plan sponsor, and requiring at least 3,000 full-time participants; and regional plans, established with employers in different industries within the same prefecture as plan sponsor, and requiring at least 3,000 full-time participants.[4]

In 1993 there were 11.7 million employees participating in Employees' Pension Funds in 1,735 plans.

Because the government relaxed the laws for establishing Employees' Pension Fund plans, the coverage of these plans has been growing. The Japanese government has the goal that these plans cover half the workers covered by the Employees' Pension Insurance, up from a third in the early 1990s. Employees' Pension Fund plans have increased in popularity in recent years and cover more employees than do Tax Qualified Pension plans. The reasons for their popularity are that they receive more favorable tax treatment than do Tax Qualified Pension plans, that they pay annuities rather than lump sum benefits, and that they are portable. The

Pension Fund Association, an association of the Employees' Pension Fund plans, provides a portability system for job changers. The Tax Qualified Pension plans cannot belong to this system.

In 1992 there were 11.7 million participants in Employees' Pension Fund plans and 10.4 million in Tax Qualified Pension plans, for a total of 22.1 million participants. The figure of 22.1 million participants gives a coverage rate of 54 percent of the labor force. However, excluding the double counting of participants in both Employees' Pension Fund and Tax Qualified Pension plans, the coverage rate would be about 50 percent (Watanabe 1993a).

Defined Contribution Plans

Compared to defined benefit plans, defined contribution plans have a short history. In 1959 Middle to Small Enterprise Private Pension Mutual Aid plans were established. Employers with fewer than 300 employees can contract with the Middle to Small Enterprise Private Pension Mutual Aid Association for establishing a pension plan. Employers pay all the contributions, but the government pays the costs of the Association.

In 1972 Zaikei-tyotiku plans were established as individual savings plans. Employees, whose participation is voluntary, can contribute to them and receive a tax deduction. Employers can also contribute for employees.[5]

In 1991 the National Pension Fund plans were established for the self-employed as a defined contribution plan. These plans give employees not covered by Employees' Pension Fund and Tax Qualified Pension plans the opportunity to benefit from a defined contribution plan, but they do not receive employer contributions.

Problems to Be Solved in Private Pension Schemes

Because social security plan financing is made more difficult by population aging, private pension plans have grown increasingly important in the Japanese retirement income system. There are many problems to be solved, however, concerning private pension plans. The Pension Council (1993) recently recommended that several problems be addressed, including the need to cover more employees in medium and small companies, the need to pay benefits to retired workers age 60 to 65, the need to prevent adverse selection in terms of the Employees' Pension Fund plans that contract out of the Employees' Pension Insurance, and the need to abolish unreasonable pension fund investment regulations. Other problems that also need to be addressed are the need to encourage greater self-reliance by employees and beneficiaries, the need to establish a pension accounting system, and the need to establish legal pension fiduciary requirements.

Labor Market Problems

The labor force participation rate of males aged 65 and older in Japan in 1991 was 38.0 percent, compared to 15.5 percent in the United States. The rate in Japan is relatively high because of the strong work ethic. Also, in Japan there are more opportunities for older workers in family businesses in agriculture, retail sales, and restaurants than in other countries. Differing from the United States, many volunteer activities in Japan provide some pay, and older volunteers are included as labor force participants. However, the comparative study of the percentage of wage income in the income of older families, indicates that Japan (18 percent) and the United States (17 percent) are similar in this regard, perhaps indicating that the pay older Japanese workers receive is very low (Watanabe 1993a).

Characteristics of Private Pension Systems in Japan

Lump sum retirement benefit amounts differ by employer size and by the education, career, and sex of workers. The average lump sum retirement benefit for a male university graduate with 35 years of service in a company with more than 3,000 employees is 27.0 million yen (about US$ 250,000). For a similar male who was a high school graduate, the average lump sum benefit is 21.4 million yen (US$ 200,000), and for a high school graduate in a company with 100 to 299 employees the average amount is 15.7 million yen (US$ 150,000). Females on average only receive about 85 percent of what males receive because they tend to have lower wages and shorter service.

Trends in the Lifetime Employment System

An important aspect of the lifetime employment system is mandatory retirement. The percentage of employers with compulsory retirement age at 60 increased from 68 percent in 1988 to 82 percent in 1992. Employers with a compulsory retirement age of 61 or over increased only from 1.3 percent in 1988 to 2.4 percent in 1992. The government has tried to persuade employers to postpone the compulsory retirement age to 65, but employers have strongly resisted because of the high wage cost of older workers who have received seniority-based wage increases. Japan does not have an Age Discrimination Act that would prevent employers from forcing workers to retire because of their age.

Distribution of Private Pension Plans

On average, 89 percent of employers with more than 30 employees have private pension plans. Even for employers with 30 to 99 employees, 86 percent had pension plans. For employers that have pension plans, 49 percent have only book reserve plans, 11 percent have a Tax Qualified Pension and/or Employees' Pension Fund plan, and 39 percent have a book reserve plan and a Tax Qualified Pension and/or Employees' Pension Fund plan. The percentage of employers with a book reserve plan decreased from 67 percent in 1975 to 49 percent in 1989. Tax Qualified Pension and/or Employees' Pension Fund plans have been preferred by employers with 1,000 or more employees. Excluding book reserve plans, among employers that have private pension plans 16 percent have an Employees' Pension Fund plan, 70 percent have a Tax Qualified Pension plan, and 8 percent have an Employees' Pension Fund and Tax Qualified Pension plan. Among employers that established an Employees' Pension Fund or Tax Qualified Pension plan, 77 percent reduced the amounts of their book reserve plans.

The Japanese government designed Tax Qualified Pension plans to be simple to establish and as good plans for small and medium-sized companies. It designed Employees' Pension Fund plans to be suitable for medium and large companies. But many large companies, including Nippon Steel, the largest steel company in the world, have established Tax Qualified Pension plans.

The Employees' Pension Fund plans are contracted out from the Employees' Pension Insurance social security program. With Employees' Pension Fund plans, a fully funded private sector pension plan replaces a public plan that has low funding. These plans also receive a rebate from the Employees' Pension Insurance for each worker in the plan. There is currently a single rebate amount not depending on the average age of the employees in the plan, but depending only on the earnings of the employees. Because it is cheaper to provide benefits for younger workers, firms with young workforces are more likely to contract out than are firms with older workers. The Japanese government is considering a rebate schedule that would vary with the average age of a firm's workforce.

The government has made it easier over time to establish single company Employees' Pension Fund plans. For example, at first those plans required a minimum of 1,000 employees. That minimum requirement is now 500 employees. Further, employees of small firms can without much difficulty establish an Employees' Pension Fund plan through a multi-employer fund or through a regional fund.

The main reason that the two types of plans—Employees' Pension

Fund and Tax Qualified Pension — coexist is that the Finance Department regulates Tax Qualified Pension plans while the Health and Welfare Department regulates Employees' Pension Fund plans. Each department wants to maintain its power by maintaining the type of plan it regulates.

Taxation of Pension Plans

As in other countries, in Japan private pension plans receive favorable tax treatment. Before the 1962 amendments, tax laws had only provisions for the book reserve financing of lump sum retirement benefits. Japan had no tax law provisions for annuity benefits. Regarding annuity benefits, neither employer nor employee contributions for funding pension benefits were tax-deductible; pension fund earnings were taxable; pension benefits were taxable to the beneficiary when received; and pension benefit amounts were tax-deductible to the employer only when paid to the beneficiary.

Since 1962, private pension plans (other than non-tax-qualified plans) have enjoyed favorable tax treatment compared to other forms of savings. For other savings, the investment earnings are taxable at a rate of 20 percent (a 15 percent income tax and a 5 percent regional tax). For people aged 65 and older, however, the investment earnings on savings is not taxable. Employer contributions to employee savings are deemed to be wage income to the employee and are immediately taxable.

Tax Treatment of Employer Contributions to Pension Plans

For both Employees' Pension Fund plans and Tax Qualified Pension plans, employers may deduct 100 percent of contributions for involuntary retirement annuity benefits if the amount of the contribution is determined on a reasonable actuarial basis. Contributions for past service liability are also tax deductible. For book reserve plans, the employer may deduct 40 percent of the amount equivalent to the accrual of lump sum voluntary benefit amounts.

It is easier for employers to accumulate the money necessary to pay annuity benefits through an Employees' Pension Fund plan or a Tax Qualified Pension plan than it is to accumulate money to pay annuity benefits or lump sum benefits through a book reserve plan. The present tax laws are not favorable to book reserve plans. However, many large companies have book reserve plans because they can use the money that would have been put into a pension plan as working capital.

Employee contributions to an Employees' Pension Fund plan receive a tax deduction because they are like social insurance contributions. For a Tax Qualified Pension plan, employees may receive a tax deduction up to a maximum of 100,000 yen a year (about US$ 950) for contributions. There are no employee contributions to book reserve plans since they are not funded.

A special corporate tax of one percent and a regional tax of 0.75 percent are levied on the proportion of Employees' Pension Fund plan assets that exceed a stipulated limit. The limit is set at 2.7 times the required funding to substitute the Employees' Pension Fund pension for Employees' Pension Insurance. For a Tax Qualified Pension plan, pension assets held by a life insurance company and/or in a trust bank are not subject to the regular personal income tax or corporate income tax. They are subject to the special corporate tax of 1.0 percent and regional tax of 0.75 percent, which is levied on pension assets after excluding employee contributions. The special corporate tax was originally set at 1.2 percent in 1962, but was reduced to 1.0 percent in 1968.

Book reserve plans are generally invested in the working capital of the company, and the earnings on the working capital are subject to the corporate tax, which is roughly 50 percent (including a regional tax).

The special corporate tax payments have grown as private pension plans have developed. The amounts in 1991 were 950 million yen (US$ 7 million) for Employees' Pension Fund plans (paid by 30 plans) and 12.7 billion yen (US$ 94 million) for Tax Qualified Pension plans. Many groups, including the Japan Employers' Association, have proposed that the taxation of pension assets be abolished.

In April 1993, the Japanese government amended pension law to establish Special Tax Qualified Pension plans, which enjoy favorable tax treatment in comparison to other Tax Qualified Pension plans. These plans do not pay the 1.75 percent special corporate tax. Two main requirements for a Special Tax Qualified Pension plan are that the firm must employ fewer than 500 employees (so that the firm does not qualify to establish a single firm Employees' Pension Fund plan) and the pension benefits provided by the plan must be life annuities. The government established this type of plan to encourage more small employers to establish pension plans and to encourage the offering of lifetime annuities.

Taxation of Annuity Benefits

Annuity benefits paid by an Employees' Pension Fund plan are subject to the same tax as on social security benefits. The tax is applied after certain deductions are made. For a married annuitant under age 65, the maximum annuity on which no tax would be paid is 1.71 million yen (about

US$ 16,000). For the annuitant who is aged 65 or older with a spouse who is aged 70 or older, the maximum annuity on which no tax would be levied is 3.05 million yen (about US$ 29,000).

In a Tax Qualified Pension plan, annuity benefits after excluding the amount equal to employee contributions are subject to the same tax as on an Employees' Pension Fund plan. Book reserve plans do not pay annuity benefits; so that tax question does not arise for them.

Taxation of Lump Sum Benefits

An Employees' Pension Fund plan must pay a life annuity for those benefits that are contracted out from the Employees' Pension Insurance social security program. However, in Tax Qualified Pension plans, 93 percent of all plans have a lump sum benefits option, and more employees take that option than take annuity benefits. The popularity of lump sum benefits arises in part because the tax law provides more favorable tax treatment of lump sum benefits than of annuities. The taxable amount is calculated as follows:

$$\text{Taxable amount} = \frac{\text{lump sum benefit} - \text{deduction amount}}{2}.$$

Some analysts feel that this preferential tax treatment of lump sum benefits is undesirable because annuity benefits would be better for employees. Often employees have little knowledge as to how to invest their lump sum benefits.

Financing

Private pensions in Japan are funded mainly by employer contributions. In 1988, cash wages were on average 84 percent of employers' total labor costs and other aspects of compensation accounted for the remaining 16 percent.[6] Cash wages are divided into the regular monthly salary, which is 75 percent on average, and the twice a year bonus, the remaining 25 percent.

Private pensions are on average 4.2 percent of employers' total labor costs. This 4.2 percent is divided into the costs for book reserve plans (2.6 percent), the costs for Employees' Pension Fund plans and Tax Qualified Pension plans (1.6 percent), and the costs for Smaller Enterprise Retirement Allowance Mutual Aid plans and other plans (0.1 percent).

Private pension plan costs are a larger share of labor costs in large companies than in small companies. For companies with 5,000 or more employees, pension plan costs average 6.2 percent of total labor costs, and book reserve costs average 4.2 percent. For companies with 30 to 99 employees, private pension costs average 2.1 percent and book reserve costs average 1.1 percent.

For Smaller Enterprise Retirement Allowance Mutual Aid plans, companies with 100 to 299 employees pay 0.3 percent of their total labor costs for those plans.

As a share of total private retirement income costs, book reserve costs have decreased from 72 percent in 1975 to 61 percent in 1988. Costs for Employees' Pension Fund plans and Tax Qualified Pension plans have increased from 27 percent in 1975 to 37 percent in 1988.

Employees' Contributions

In 1989, for firms with 1,000 or more employees, employee contributions were made in 10 percent of Tax Qualified Pension plans and 16 percent of non-tax-qualified plans. In 35 percent of Employees' Pension Fund plans, employees contributed above the minimum required for contracting out. Employees may voluntarily contribute in order to increase their benefits. Employees' contributions are commonly 25 percent to 35 percent of the total (employer and employee contribution).

The average share employee contributions were of total contributions was 31 percent in Tax Qualified Pension plans, 33 percent in Employees' Pension Fund plans, and 25 percent in non-tax-qualified plans. Between 1981 and 1989, there was little change in the percentage of Employees' Pension Fund plans with employee contributions, but the percentage of plans with employee contributions decreased in Tax Qualified Pension and non-tax-qualified plans.

In Tax Qualified Pension plans for employers of all sizes (including small employers), 5.4 percent had employee contributions in 1981 and 4.8 percent had employee contributions in 1989. Employee contributions were more common in large plans. In 1989, they occurred in 10 percent of plans with 1,000 or more employees, and in 5 percent of plans with 30 to 99 employees. The average employee contribution was 27 percent of total contributions, with the figure being 31 percent in plans with 1,000 or more employees and 23 percent in plans with 30 to 99 employees.

Assets in Private Pension Plans

Over the past 30 years, assets in private pension plans have grown rapidly. The assets in private pension plans have increased from 6.7 trillion yen (US\$ 22 billion) in 1975 to 59.9 trillion yen (US\$ 475 billion) in 1992, an increase valued in yen of 890 percent.

Private pension assets have also grown in importance relative to total financial assets in Japan. At the end of fiscal year 1992 total assets in financial institutions equaled 1,488 trillion yen (US$ 14.1 trillion), and the assets in life insurance companies were 152 trillion yen (US$ 1.4 trillion). The percentage of total financial assets accounted for by private pension plans has increased to 4.0 percent of all financial assets and to 39.5 percent of the financial assets of the life insurance industry.

The book value of book reserve plans has increased from 4.2 trillion yen (US$ 14 billion) in 1975 to 12.7 trillion yen (US$ 100 billion) in 1992, an increase valued in yen of 300 percent. Assets in Tax Qualified Pension plans have increased from 1.0 trillion yen (US$ 3 billion) in 1975 to 15.0 trillion yen (US$ 119 billion) in 1992, an increase valued in yen of 1,500 percent. Assets in Employees' Pension Fund plans have increased from 1.5 trillion yen in 1975 (US$ 5 billion) to 32.2 trillion yen (US$ 255 billion in 1992), an increase of 2,150 percent. The value of book reserves has decreased as a percentage of total pension assets from 63 percent in 1975 to 21 percent in 1992, while the assets in Tax Qualified Pension and Employees' Pension Fund plans have increased from 37 percent to 79 percent.

Financial Institutions

The major financial institutions that manage pension plans and invest pension assets are life insurance companies and trust banks. In 1982, Employees' Pension Fund plans were managed 24 percent by life insurance companies and 76 percent by trust banking companies. In 1993, the shares were 36 percent for life insurance companies, 62 percent for trust banks, and 2 percent for investment adviser companies.

In 1982, Tax Qualified Pension plans were managed 47 percent by life insurance companies and 53 percent by trust banking companies. In 1993, the shares were 56 percent for life insurance companies, 43 percent for trust banking companies, and one percent for investment adviser companies.

As financial markets have been deregulated, banking and security companies have entered the business of managing private pension funds by establishing investment advisor trust banking companies. This has increased competition among financial institutions that manage pension funds.

Accounting Rules for Pension Plans

Perhaps the most important problem in the management of Japanese public and private pension plans is to establish an economically meaningful accounting systems (Watanabe 1992). In Japan, good accounting rules for pension systems have not yet been established. Contrary to United States accounting practice, pension assets are measured based on their historical or book value rather than their market value. This type of accounting makes it impossible to measure the financial situation of pension plans accurately in periods when security prices and currency exchange rates are changing. It also makes calculating meaningful rates of return difficult.

The Japanese stock market dropped dramatically from its peak of about 40,000 yen on the Nikkei Dow Jones at the end of 1989 to about 20,000 yen at the end of January 1994. This decline has had a large negative effect on not only financial institutions but also pension assets. News reports have indicated that pension assets with trust banks have suffered losses of more than 10 percent.

Statutory Guidelines for Pension Asset Management

For Employees' Pension Fund plans, each plan and each trust bank must comply with the following restrictions on the asset mix of the portfolio:

Assets with guaranteed principal	>50 percent
Equities	<30 percent
Foreign currency denominated assets	<30 percent
Real estate	<20 percent

These percentages are based on the book value of the assets. These percentages limit the ability of plans to achieve higher returns through investment in equities. Recently the Pension Fund Association, the association of Employees' Pension Fund plans, proposed to the government that these rules be abolished in order to allow pension funds to take on greater risk and receive greater expected return.

Control of Financial Risks

As just discussed, perhaps the most important change that needs to be made in Japan concerning the control of financial risks in the pension system is to move to a market value accounting system. With the current historical value accounting system it is not possible adequately to assess the financial risks facing plans.

Contrary to the regulation of United States private pension plans, Japanese plans are not required to be managed independently of the sponsoring company. This is a source of financial risk to pension plans (Watanabe 1993b). One main reason why independence has not been established is that fiduciary laws are not well developed in Japan. In addition, a Tax Qualified Pension plan is not a separate legal entity, but is only a contract between the employer and the company labor union, and enjoys little legal protection. Finally, an Employees' Pension Fund plan is a separate legal entity from the employer, but it has little legal protection.

There are also social reasons why pension plans in Japan have received little legal protection. One is that employers have not understood the importance of pension plans and have treated them as another account of company money. In addition, labor unions have not understood the importance of pension plans. They have focused on reforming social security plans but have devoted little attention to private plans. Finally, the government has rigidly regulated Employees' Pension Fund plans. Many high level government employees from the Health and Welfare Department have taken positions as managing directors of Employees' Pension Fund plans after retiring from the government. These employees know the legal regulations concerning Employees' Pension Fund plans, but have little knowledge about managing investments.

Thus, the financial institutions that manage pension money have been chosen mainly by employers. Employers expect the financial institutions that manage their pension assets to provide favorable treatment for the other financial activities of the firm, but have been less interested in securing the best performance for their pension fund investments.

For Tax Qualified Pension plans there are no special regulations. They are regulated only by general civil laws. The Employees' Pension Insurance law section 125-2 regulates the responsibility of the Employees' Pension Fund plans director. However, the regulation is weak.

One aspect of pension risk is the risks associated with job change. As for pension benefits for job changers, the Pension Fund Association runs a unique pension clearinghouse. The Pension Fund Association was established by the Health and Welfare Department in 1967 as a separate legal entity. The Employees' Pension Insurance Law regulates the management and administration of pension benefits for withdrawing Employees' Pension Fund plan members. There is no pension clearinghouse, however, for Tax Qualified Pension plans.

Pension Insurance

The median monthly pension benefit in Tax Qualified Pension plans has grown from 62,000 yen in 1989 (US$ 449 a month or US$ 5,400 a year) to 71,000 yen in 1992 (US$ 563 a month or US$ 6,800 a year). The percentage of monthly benefits exceeding 100,000 yen has grown from 19 percent in 1989 to 28 percent in 1992. In 1991, the average annual benefit from an Employees' Pension Fund plans was 481,000 yen (US$ 3,600). For single company plans, the average was 911,000 yen (US$ 6,700). For allied company plans, it was 516,000 yen (US\$ 3,800). For multi-employer plans, it was 285,000 yen (US\$ 2,100).

As private pension plans have developed, guaranteeing pension benefits for employees has become one of the most important problems (Watanabe 1989). Following the rapid increase in asset prices of the bubble economy of the late 1980s, the number of bankrupt companies has grown.

The financial situation of trust banking companies, which manage pension funds, has grown weaker, as has that of the life insurance industry. Since 1966, when Employees' Pension Fund plans were established, the life insurance industry has guaranteed the investment rate of return of 5.5 percent for Employees' Pension Fund plans. By government regulation, the guaranteed rate is the same for all companies. Starting on April 1, 1994, the industry has dropped the rate to 4.5 percent. But there is growing criticism of the fixed rate and growing support for deregulation, so that the guaranteed rate would not be set by law but rather all companies could decide on their own rates.

The Ministry of Finance has indicated it intends to establish a Guarantee Fund for protecting insurance consumers starting in 1995. This would be the first time such a fund has existed in Japan.

Lump Sum Retirement Plan (Book Reserve Plan)

After the recession following the oil shock of 1973, company bankruptcies increased. Many employees lost their jobs, and firms could not pay their unpaid wages and lump sum retirement benefits. The regulations of bankruptcy law, labor law, and commercial law were insufficient to protect workers.

To solve this problem, in 1976 a law guaranteeing wages was enacted. Through it the government guarantees 80 percent of unpaid wages. For the lump sum retirement benefit the law requires the employer to guarantee the amount through a contract with a financial institution.

Because of insufficient regulations, most employers do not guarantee their book reserve plans. The percentage of employers who guarantee their book reserve plan through a financial institution has increased from 12 percent in 1981 to 24 percent in 1989. For employers with 1,000 or more employees, only 16 percent guarantee their book reserve plan through a financial institution. The percentage is higher for smaller employers — 24 percent the employers with 30 to 99 employees.

Tax Qualified Pension Plan

By corporate tax law, when an employer goes bankrupt, the present value of a Tax Qualified Pension plan would be paid to the employee. However,

Tax Qualified Pension plans do not have a pension insurance system. This is perhaps the most serious problem to be solved concerning Tax Qualified Pension plans.

Employees' Pension Fund Plan

The Pension Guarantee Program established in 1989 only insures Employees' Pension Fund plans. The guarantee program is managed by the Pension Fund Association. Employees' Pension Fund plans are required to participate in the insurance program. Under this program an Employees' Pension Fund plan can be terminated with insufficient assets only if the sponsoring company declares bankruptcy, the business of the sponsoring company or the industry deteriorates, or other unavoidable circumstances occur under which continuation of a fund is deemed to be extremely difficult.

The level of contributions to the pension benefit insurance program are computed for different sizes of plans on the basis of the statistical likelihood by size group of plan termination with an unfunded liability. The required contributions are roughly proportional to the number of participants in the pension plan, with the contribution per participant decreasing gradually as the number of participants increases. The amount of the required contribution is recalculated every year based on the average number of participants in the plan in the previous year. Total contributions were 766 million yen in 1992.

As of 1994, only one plan had terminated since establishment of the benefit insurance program (Table 1). Because the terminated fund had sufficient assets for financing 1.3 times the substitutional component of the Employees' Pension Fund plan, no claim was made on the insolvency insurance program.

After three years of the Payment Guarantee Program, the first actuarial valuation of funding levels was carried out on March 31, 1992. As a result of the actuarial valuation of liabilities in comparison to the book value of assets, the required contribution per member of all funds was calculated to be unchanged from its previous level.

Conclusion

Japanese private pension plans have grown rapidly but serious problems need to be addressed. These include establishing better accounting rules using market valuation of assets, establishing better fiduciary responsibility rules, and abolishing the rigid regulation of pension investments with fixed maximum and minimum percentage asset allocations. With

TABLE 1 Number of Terminated Employees' Pension Fund Plans, 1975–1992

Fiscal Year	Number of Funds (FY End)	Terminated Funds	Number of Cases Guaranteed under Insurance Program
1975	929	2	—
1980	991	4	—
1985	1,091	2	—
1989	1,358	0	0
1990	1,474	1	0
1991	1,593	0	0
1992	1,735	0	0

Source: Pension Fund Association, "Pension Insurance System in Japan," p. 21.
Note: Four funds would have made a claim on the insurance program out of 16 funds terminated before 1989, if the Payment Guarantee Program had existed.

population aging placing financial pressure on public social security plans, private pension plans will be asked to play a larger role in providing retirement income in the future.

Notes

[1]Monetary figures for different types of retirement plans are quoted as of March 31 of the year.

[2]Following the Meiji revolution, Japan reestablished trading and cultural ties with the West. During the preceding Tokugawa era, Japan had been largely closed to the West.

[3]The terminology may be confusing for U.S. readers because both Tax Qualified Pension plans and Employees' Pension Fund plans receive preferential tax treatment.

[4]A prefecture is a governmental unit corresponding to a county.

[5]There are three types of these plans: (1) Ippan-zaikei — a general savings plan; (2) Zyuutaku-zaikei — saving for buying a house; (3) Zaikei-nenkin — a defined contribution annuity plan. The available data do not separate out the asset amounts in the different types of plans.

[6]In contrast to U.S. statistics on labor costs, paid holidays are not included in the statistics about labor cost in Japan.

References

Kurozumi, Akira. "Teninen-Seido, Lump Sum Retirement Benefit Plans and Private Pension Schemes." Tokyo: Yuhikaku Publishing Co., 1966.

Organization for Economic Cooperation and Development. *OECD Economic Outlook* 54 (December 1993): 14–15.

Pension Council. "Proposal for Amending Public Pension Laws." Tokyo: Health and Welfare Department of the Japanese Government, 1993.

Watanabe, Noriyasu. "Comparative Study of Labor Force Participation Rates in Advanced Countries." *Aging and Work* 11 (1993): 90–105.

——. "Comparative Study of Private Pension Schemes in Advanced Countries." *Aging and Work* 9 (1991): 110–146.

——. "Fundamental Problems in Pension Fund Investments." *Tokyo Economist Magazine,* Special Issue (November 1993): 98–102.

——. "The Most Important Problem in Pension Fund Investment." *Japan Pension Academy Magazine* 12 (1992): 45–56.

——. "PBGC System in ERISA: A Comparison with the FDIC System." *Pension Academy Magazine* 9 (1989): 64–130.

Watanabe, Noriyasu, John Turner, and David Rajnes. " 'Pay or Play' Pensions in Japan." *Contingencies* (November/December 1994): 63–65.

Comments by Robert L. Clark

Noriyasu Watanabe has done an excellent job of providing a brief, up-to-date review of private pensions in Japan. His analysis provides a nice review of the basic characteristics of the Japanese employer pension system. He notes that Japanese pensions are virtually all defined benefit plans and that the development of the pension system has occurred since 1960. There are two primary types of pensions in Japan: Tax Qualified Pension plans (TQP), first established in 1962, and Employees' Pension Fund plans (EPF), established in 1966. The TQP plans are similar to United States-style pensions and are used primarily by small employers. EPF plans are based more on the British concept of pensions and require firms to contract out of the national social security system. EPF plans pay a benefit that replaces the earnings-related component of social security. The total pension benefit must be at least 30 percent greater than the social security benefit that has been replaced.

The Tax Qualified Pension plans are overseen by the Ministry of Finance. Firms with as few as 15 workers can establish a TQP. Employees' Pension Fund plans are overseen by the Ministry of Health and Welfare. EPF plans are primarily adopted by large firms. A single employer must have at least 500 workers to establish an EPF. Watanabe relates many important details concerning the administration of both types of plans and provides considerable coverage and financial data. He also notes how the pension system was developed in conjunction with the traditional lump sum severance system. In addition, Watanabe includes a brief assessment of the Japanese social security system.

I have relatively few comments concerning what is actually said in the chapter. In my remarks I will place this review of Japanese pensions into a broader context of political, economic, and demographic changes that are now unfolding. My comments examine problems facing private pensions, identify several puzzles concerning pensions and labor market activity, and finally, venture some predictions for the further development of employer pensions. I will do better on identifying the problems and puzzles than in making accurate predictions. The main objective of my comments is to provide a broader context in which to examine the continued development of Japanese pensions. International comparisons are an excellent method of extending our knowledge base and considering a more diverse set of policies prior to adopting them.

Analysis of Trends

One criticism of the Watanabe chapter is that it does not link changes in the population age structure, labor market institutions, and social policies to likely changes in employer pensions. Several key developments must be examined if we are to understand the future of Japanese pensions.

First, major demographic shifts are occurring in Japan. The Japanese population is the most rapidly aging developed country in the world. If maintained, current fertility and mortality rates will lead to a declining population in the first half of the next century. How will these changes alter employer pensions?

Second, significant changes are occurring in the social security system. Major changes include efforts to raise the age of eligibility for retirement benefits and projections of rapidly increasing tax rates to support the system. How will these changes alter employer pensions?

Third, the industrial relations system is continuing to evolve in response to demographic and political pressures. Mandatory retirement ages are being increased, the importance of seniority-based pay systems is declining, and new employment policies for older workers are being introduced. How will these changes affect employer pensions?

Population Aging in Japan

The population of Japan is aging extremely rapidly. In 1950, only 5 percent of the population was 65 and older. By 1990, this proportion had increased to 13 percent. Watanabe reports that current projections indicate that over one-fourth of the Japanese population will be 65 and older by 2025. This rapid aging of the population will require substantial modifications of the social security programs and the system of industrial relations.

Current projections indicate that the payroll tax rate necessary to support currently promised benefits will increase from 14.5 percent to 35 percent within 35 years. The pressure of the increasing cost of social security programs has led the government to introduce legislation to raise the age of eligibility for full benefits in the Employees' Pension Insurance system from 60 to 65. This change would reduce the required tax increase by approximately five percentage points.

In addition, the projected cost increases have influenced social policies toward work and retirement. The government is encouraging later retirement by subsidizing employment programs for the elderly and pressing firms to increase their mandatory retirement ages to 65. How will firms respond to these changes? Will firms modify their pensions in response to later social security retirement ages and higher payroll taxes?

The industrial relations system is also adjusting to the aging of the population. There is a decline in the use of seniority-based pay increases and a greater reliance on merit pay systems. Turnover rates appear to be increasing, and the prevalence of lifetime employment is declining. Even as they have raised the ages for mandatory retirement, firms have attempted to encourage earlier retirement from career jobs. The Japanese pension system was built around lifetime employment with a single firm coupled with an early age of mandatory retirement. How will employer pensions adjust to these changes in compensation?

Japanese Social Security and Employer Pensions

United States business leaders, politicians, and scholars often are amazed at the extent of the Japanese retirement system. Many believe that Japanese workers have little or no retirement income. They believe that this explains why older Japanese continue to work. They believe that it explains some of the cost advantages of Japanese firms. And finally, many believe that this is one of the reasons why Japanese save so much.

Watanabe clearly demonstrates that this perception is wrong. Coverage by the social security systems is almost universal and coverage rates by employer-based retirement plans exceed those in the United States. Almost 90 percent of the Japanese labor force is covered by an employer pension or a lump sum severance plan. In recent years there has been a trend toward greater use of pensions and less reliance on traditional lump sum payments. Currently about half of all workers are participating in an employer pension plan — a pension coverage rate similar to that in the United States.

The social security system provides replacement ratios to retired workers comparable to those provided by the social security system in the United States. The average monthly benefit paid from this system in 1991 was 150,000 yen, or approximately US$ 1,500 at 1994 exchange rates. Watanabe reports that the median monthly benefit paid by Tax Qualified Pension plans was 71,000 yen in 1992, or around US$ 700. In contrast, the 1991 median monthly benefit from Employees' Pension Fund plans was 481,000 yen, or approximately US$ 4,800.

Why are so many foreign observers ignorant of the Japanese system? Perhaps this misunderstanding of the Japanese retirement system is due to the relatively recent development of social security and employer pensions. The Employees' Pension Insurance system (the social security system that covers most private employees) was established in 1941, while the National Pension system (the social security system that covers self-employed, spouses, and family workers) was only established in 1961. As noted above, employer pension plans date only to the 1960s.

Watanabe shows that social security payments provide a significant base of retirement income for all Japanese workers and that employer pensions add a significant supplement to retirement income for many workers. Despite this system of retirement income, labor force participation rates in Japan are the highest in the developed world. Over one-third of Japanese men 65 and older remain in the labor force compared to 16 percent of older men in the United States and only 3 to 5 percent in western Europe. These data are the basis for a puzzle concerning individual behavior in Japan. Why are the labor force participation rates for older Japanese so high compared to other developed countries if their retirement income is comparable?

Evolving Industrial Relations System

In response to the aging of the population, the Japanese system of employee compensation and lifetime employment is changing. The use of seniority-based pay is declining, especially for older workers. An increasing number of firms have introduced merit pay systems to replace or supplement the traditional seniority pay systems. As a result, the age earnings profiles for career employees is becoming flatter.

Mandatory retirement is an integral component of the Japanese system of industrial relations. Approximately 90 percent of all firms have mandatory retirement policies. Twenty-five years ago, 55 was the most prevalent age for compulsory retirement. Over time, the age set by most firms has increased, with 60 now being the modal mandatory retirement age. Virtually no firms have ages higher than 60. The government is actively encouraging firms to increase the age of mandatory retirement to 65. If firms comply, how will employer pensions adjust?

Even as mandatory retirement ages have increased, firms have been known to encourage early retirement. Some workers are transferred to client firms or subsidiaries while others are given dead-end jobs as encouragement to retire. Will pensions be modified to further encourage the trend toward earlier retirement from career jobs in Japan?

It is puzzling how a country where most firms impose mandatory retirement at relatively young ages has such a high labor force participation rate among older persons. Such high work rates are due, in part, to several institutional factors. First, many firms reemploy workers after they have been mandatorily retired. The "retired" workers are typically employed in lower status jobs at lower wages. Such activities are permitted in Japan since there are no age discrimination laws. Workers are also outplaced to client firms and subsidiaries. Thus, the "retiree" finds new employment while these smaller firms gain access to quality older workers.

The continued aging of the population will require further changes in the industrial relations system in Japan. Compensation policy will also be changed. A key factor influencing retirement patterns and the economic well-being of the elderly is how firms will modify their pension plans in response to these events.

Conclusions and Predictions

The future of employer pensions in Japan depends on how plan sponsors adjust their retirement plans to the changes described above. Some trends are clear, while others are still uncertain.

Japan will lead the developed countries in facing the super aging of the population. In the next 20 years, Japan will confront a rapid increase in its elderly population. As a result, the costs of social security programs will skyrocket. Payroll taxes will sharply increase. The age of eligibility for unreduced social security benefits will be increased to 65 if not higher in the first quarter of the twenty-first century.

Firms will continue to develop new human resource policies to cope with an aging labor force. The entire system of lifetime employment along with its compensation policies will be reconsidered. A fundamental conflict between the government and private employers will continue to increase in intensity. The government will accelerate its efforts to promote the employment of older workers and to get firms to raise the age of mandatory retirement to at least 65. Employers will increase their efforts to accommodate an aging workforce and to encourage early retirement. How will these conflicting desires be resolved in the future? What will be the effect of policy changes on employer pensions?

Answers to the questions posed throughout these remarks will determine the future of employer pensions in Japan. Changes in the population age structure will occur. In response to the aging of the population, social policies will be revised. Within this framework, employer pensions will surely be amended to conform to the new national norms.

II
Pensions in Emerging Economies

Chapter 5
Mandatory Saving Schemes: Are They an Answer to the Old Age Security Problem?

Estelle James and Dimitri Vittas

As the world's population ages, old age security systems are being reevaluated. This chapter is part of and draws heavily from a broader study (World Bank 1994) that analyzes alternative methods of providing old age security, with an emphasis on developing countries. One important model is the mandatory retirement saving scheme. These schemes are motivated by the belief that some people will not save on a voluntary basis when they are young because they are shortsighted or lack reliable savings instruments. From the perspective of old age they may wish they had saved more (time inconsistent preferences) or may become a charge upon the rest of society (moral hazard). Mandatory saving schemes avert these problems by forcing people to shift consumption from their earlier to their later years and by providing financial institutions for this purpose.

Their basic mode of operation is as follows. Workers' contributions are deposited in personal accounts, and benefits depend on these contributions plus the investment income they earn. These schemes are thus fully funded defined contribution plans not sponsored or differentiated by employer. In their purest form, mandatory retirement saving schemes imply no redistribution; the capital accumulation before retirement equals the present value of expected post-retirement income.

Full funding implies capital accumulation, and a key question is how these funds are managed and invested. In most mandatory saving schemes currently operating, the government determines the use of the funds and sets the rate of return. Examples of such "national provident funds" are found in Singapore, Malaysia, and several African countries. These centrally managed plans can involve capital and labor market distortions and capricious redistributions similar to those in many public defined benefit plans, because required contribution rates may be high and returns low and uneven. As an alternative, mandatory saving schemes may be privately and competitively managed, in which case they are likely to have fewer distortion effects, fewer incentives for evasion, and less political manipulation. At this point Chile is the only country that has fully implemented a decentralized mandatory saving scheme, but several other Latin American countries are in the process of introducing one.

Like funded occupational plans, mandatory saving schemes can foster long-term saving and capital market development. But unlike defined benefit occupational schemes, they are fully funded by nature rather than by regulation. Their coverage can be broad. They do not imply portability problems or inhibit labor mobility. They permit workers to diversify risk. And unlike defined contribution occupational schemes, they allow workers, who bear the investments risk, to choose the investment manager.

Mandatory saving nevertheless creates a new set of problems. Most notably, privately managed schemes fail to insure workers against poor investment performance of the funds, a problem especially great where many workers have had little financial experience or information. In addition, they do not assist workers with low lifetime incomes or provide adequate pensions in the start-up years of the plan. For these reasons, a decentralized mandatory saving scheme requires a regulatory structure that protects workers against ill-informed investment choices. And it must be supplemented by a redistributive public plan that alleviates poverty. Three central dilemmas are posed:

(1) If mandatory schemes are imposed because of myopia among workers, how can we count on these same workers to make wise investments decisions?

(2) If governments have mismanaged their centrally administered pension plans, how can we count on them to regulate private funds effectively?

(3) If government regulates and guarantees, won't it eventually end up either controlling or bailing out these funds?

This chapter begins with a brief history of mandatory saving schemes, followed by a summary of their major design features. Theoretical and empirical evidence about their effects on the broader economy includes discussion of labor market, capital market, government fiscal stability, and the income distribution effects. In some cases we contrast these effects with those of the more common pay-as-you-go publicly managed systems. The regulatory structure that may be needed to implement such a scheme is also presented, drawing heavily on the Chilean experience.[1] Our conclusion, which summarizes the major findings, suggests that privately managed mandatory saving schemes deserve careful consideration as an important part of the old age security system in countries with the human capital, financial markets, and regulatory capacity to run them effectively or the potential to develop these institutions and capacities quickly.

Brief History

The first nationally mandated provident fund was established in Malaysia in 1951; the largest such fund is Singapore's Central Provident Fund (CPF), created in 1955. India and Indonesia established provident funds in the early 1950s, but with limited coverage. Several African countries set up national provident funds in the 1960s, and several Caribbean and Pacific island countries in the 1970s and 1980s. Currently some twenty countries, mostly former British colonies in Africa, Asia, and the Pacific and Caribbean islands, have such schemes. These countries, and others that adopted this model later, had no public pay-as-you-go pillar at the time they established their national provident funds.

Chile is the only country that has fully replaced an existing public pay-as-you-go pension scheme with a government-mandated retirement saving scheme. Chile is also the only country whose mandatory saving program is privately managed, initiated in 1981. It is known as the AFP system, named after the private companies called Administradoras de Fondos de Pensiones that are authorized to run it. The public pension system was replaced because of widespread evasion, unsustainably high contribution rates, and an inequitable benefit structure. One of the main arguments used by the Chilean authorities to promote the AFP system was the failure of the public system to maintain the real value of pensions in inflationary periods. For similar reasons other Latin American countries, including Peru, Mexico, and Argentina, are now in the process of partially replacing their financially strained public pension schemes with a system of the Chilean type. It is curious—although not surprising in view of their age structures and historical experiences—that this transition to a mandatory saving scheme is occurring in older Latin American countries at the same time that several younger African countries are contemplating a transition in the opposite direction.

How Do Mandatory Retirement Saving Schemes Work?

Designing a mandatory saving scheme requires that policy makers answer many crucial questions:

- What should its coverage, wage replacement, and contribution rates be, and should they be uniform for all workers?
- At what age should workers be allowed to withdraw funds and should payouts take the form of annuities or lump sum withdrawals?
- Should management be centralized or decentralized, and if it is decentralized, how much choice should workers have?
- What regulations are needed to ensure that funds are prudently managed, and what guarantees should the state provide?
- What is the best way to minimize costs and maximize returns?
- How can a mandatory retirement saving scheme be integrated with the redistributive objectives of the old age system as a whole?

This section explores these issues briefly. The following sections examine the management and regulatory issues in greater detail.

The Contribution and Target Replacement Rates

In a mandatory saving scheme, the worker's pension is financed by the saving account that accumulates before retirement and its size depends on the contribution rate, the growth rate of earnings, the interest rate, and the number of working and retirement years. If a higher wage replacement rate is desired, a higher contribution rate is required. The required contribution rate rises the longer the retirement period is relative to the working period (the passivity ratio) and the smaller the rate of return is relative to the growth rate of real earnings (Table 1).

The required contribution rate is higher in plans that make poor investments, incur high administrative costs, index pensions to prices or wages, or permit accumulated balances to be used for other purposes such as housing, education, or health care — as is common in national provident funds. Traditionally, pension specialists have assumed that real rates of return are about two percentage points higher than the growth rate of real earnings. But data in World Bank (1994) show that in many countries over long periods the differential has been greater, giving an advantage to mandatory saving plans.

A well-run mandatory saving scheme — with a real rate of return two to three percentage points higher than the growth rate of real earnings, a passivity ratio of about one-half, and price or wage indexation — requires a contribution rate of 10 to 15 percent to cover a replacement rate of 40 percent of gross final year salary, survivors' and disability benefits, and moderate plan expenses (Table 1). A contribution rate much lower than 10 percent will, to a large extent, replace voluntary saving and be used up in transaction costs, rather than increase retirement income. If people retire early or withdraw from the labor force for part of their adult years,

TABLE 1 Contribution Rate Needed to Pay Pension = 40% of Final Salary under Mandatory Saving Scheme[1]

	Non-Indexed Pension				Pension Indexed to Prices			
Passivity Rate	1/2		1/3		1/2		1/3	
Real Wage Growth	0	2	0	3	0	2	0	3
Real Interest Rate								
0%	13	18	9	14	20	29	13	20
2%	7	11	5	8	11	16	7	11
5%	3	5	2	3	5	7	3	5
Real Pension Rate at Death[2]	15	15	19	19	40	40	40	40
Relative Pension Rate at Death[3]	15	10	19	14	40	27	40	30

Source: Schwarz (1992); Vittas (1992a).
Notes: [1]Plan expenses and disability and survivors' benefits are not included. These would raise the required contribution rate three to five percentage points in a well run plan. A 5 percent inflation rate is assumed. The one half passivity rate stems from an assumption of forty working years and twenty years of retirement. The one third passivity rate implies 45 working years and 15 years of retirement.
[2]Real pension in year of death as proportion of final year's salary.
[3]Pension relative to average wage at the economy in year of death.

or if the real rate of return is lower than the growth rate of earnings, or if objectives are pursued besides saving for retirement, a contribution rate higher than 15 percent will be required. Differences in the basic parameters of the plan, especially the use of funds for purposes other than retirement, may explain why the contribution rate is as high as 22 percent in Malaysia and Sri Lanka and 35 percent in Singapore, but only 13 percent in Chile (Table 2).

Should young workers be exempted or permitted to pay lower contribution rates, to offset their lower productivity? What about for older workers who have passed normal retirement age and peak productivity? If these workers receive special treatment, higher contribution would then be required in the middle years, which are generally the high point of life cycle earnings. Singapore requires a lower contribution rate for low income workers and recently introduced a lower rate for workers over the age of 55. This schedule helps smooth consumption over the worker's lifetime, a major purpose of the scheme.

Investment and Inflation Risk

In mandatory saving schemes workers assume the investment and inflation risks for their own retirement funds. Investment risk arises from variations in investment performance and is closely related to pension fund solvency risk. Investment risk is particularly high at the time of

TABLE 2   Payroll Tax Rates for Mandatory Saving Schemes, 1991
(percentage of wages) [1]

| Country | Percentage of Wages | | | Combined as a Percentage of Wage Plus Employer Tax |
	Employee	Employer	Combined	
Africa				
The Gambia	5.0	10.0	15.0	13.6
Ghana[2]	5.0	12.5	17.5	15.6
Kenya	5.0	5.0	10.0	9.5
Nigeria	6.0	6.0	12.0	11.3
Swaziland	5.0	5.0	10.0	9.5
Tanzania	10.0	10.0	20.0	18.2
Uganda	5.0	10.0	15.0	13.6
Zambia	5.0	5.0	10.0	9.5
Asia				
Fiji	7.0	7.0	14.0	13.1
India	10.0	10.0	20.0	18.2
Indonesia	1.0	2.0	3.0	2.9
Kiribati	5.0	5.0	10.0	9.5
Malaysia	9.0	11.0	20.0[3]	18.0
Nepal	10.0	10.0	20.0	18.2
Singapore	25.0[4]	10.0	35.0	32.0
Solomon Islands	5.0	7.5	12.5	11.6
Sri Lanka	8.0	12.0	20.0	17.9
Western Samoa	5.0	5.0	10.0	9.5
Latin America (1994)[5]				
Argentina	11.0	0.0	11.0	11.0
Chile	13.0	0.0	13.0	13.0
Colombia	2.9	8.6	11.5[6]	10.6
Peru	13.3	0.0	13.3	13.3

Source: Social Security Administration (1993); Columbia (1993); World Bank (1994).
Notes: [1]African and Asian schemes are publicly managed provident funds; Latin American
schemes are privately managed.
[2]The provident fund is being converted to a social insurance scheme.
[3]This was raised to 22 percent in 1993.
[4]The contribution varies from seven to 30 percent of gross wages for workers.
[5]For Argentina and Colombia a new plan started in 1994, for Peru in 1993.
[6]This will rise gradually to 14.5 percent in 1996.

retirement, when many workers use their accumulated assets to purchase
a lifetime annuity; the level of interest rates and the state of the financial
market on the date the annuity is purchased are critical. As we will see
below, it is important that schemes include some method of spreading
this risk across time.

As for inflation risk, an important question is whether pensioners should be required to purchase indexed annuities and, if so, whether they should be indexed to wages or prices. Indexed annuities cost more than non-indexed annuities, whether in higher contribution rates or in lower initial benefit payments (Table 1), but they maintain the pension's real value. In a mandatory saving scheme individual workers pay the cost of their own indexation, whereas in a pay-as-you-go scheme, current workers bear this risk to protect current retirees. Whether private companies will be willing or able to guarantee indexed pensions is another matter.

Publicly managed pay-as-you-go defined benefit plans are supposed to protect retirees by transferring these risks to the more adaptable younger generation. In reality, however, retirees are never entirely protected. "Defined" benefits are never completely defined over the long run. They are rarely fully indexed against inflation in developing countries; even OECD countries have skipped cost of living increases in recent years. Thus participants in both types of plans face variants of these risks, and the variants are only partially correlated. For example, mandatory saving plans can invest in equities and real property (whose nominal values generally rise with inflation), in foreign assets (thereby avoiding country-specific shocks), and in indexed instruments (thereby passing inflation risk on those who are willing to bear it). Pay-as-you-go plans do not have these options. Consequently, it is not clear which type of the plan will provide the best inflation insurance and a mixture of the two may reduce risk through diversification.

Centralized or Decentralized Management

In capital-scarce middle income countries, an efficient system of forced long-term saving can lead to high rates of return and economic growth — if the savings are channeled to productive uses and away from precautionary or speculative investments in real estate, precious metals, and land. Risks, costs, and rate of return are strongly influenced by whether the fund is centralized or decentralized. In their ideal state, centralized provident funds that are run by the national government invest productively and benefit from economies of scale that minimize operating costs. Singapore and Malaysia are examples of national provident funds that have low costs and earn stable, though modest, returns. However, more typically, managers of centralized provident funds, which are compulsory monopolies, may have little incentive to operate efficiently or to earn reasonable returns — and may be subject to political pressures to invest unproductively (see Table 3 and Figure 1).

Decentralized competitive plans, by contrast, face market pressures to operate efficiently and maximize returns and are at least partially insu-

TABLE 3   Operating Costs and Investment Returns

Cost or Returns	Chile 1990	Malaysia 1989	Singapore 1990	Zambia 1988–89
Operating Costs as Percentage of:				
Annual Contributions	15.40	1.99	0.53	51.73
Average Total Assets	2.30	0.18	0.10	6.80
Covered Annual Wages	1.54	0.40	0.21	5.17
Affiliates Times Per Capita Income	2.31	0.54	0.16	4.48
Real Investment Returns on				
Individual Accounts Net of Fees	9.2	4.6	3.0	−23.4
Period for Investment Returns	1981 to 90	1980 to 90	1980 to 90	1980 to 88

Source: World Bank (1994); Asher (1992a and b); Vittas (1992b). Calculations of investment returns by
    World Bank staff.

lated from political pressures to misallocate capital. Workers choose the
fund in which they want to place their savings, presumably based on its
record of returns and risk. But these plans require a complex regulatory
structure to ensure the financial soundness and integrity of funds managers and to prevent workers from making big mistakes. Regulating decentralized mandatory saving schemes requires considerable human
capital and institutional capacity, including the ability to enact clear rules
and penalize malfeasance in predictable ways. Some elements of modern
financial markets are also needed, though these are likely to develop in
response to the scheme. For countries that satisfy these criteria, privately
managed mandatory saving plans deserve careful consideration.

Impact on the Broader Economy

Proponents of the mandatory saving pillar argue that these plans have
beneficial effects on the broader economy, while critics argue that the
effects are minimal or even negative. Among the important effects to
consider are the impacts on long-term saving, capital allocation, labor
markets, income distribution, poverty reduction, and the government's
fiscal position.

Implications for Capital Markets

The mandatory saving pillar can be an important instrument for acceler-
ating capital market development, increasing long-term saving, boosting
investment in productive capital formation, and monitoring corporate
performance. If the current rates of long-term saving and capital accumulation are below optimal levels—as many analysts believe—such
changes have the potential to enhance economic growth.

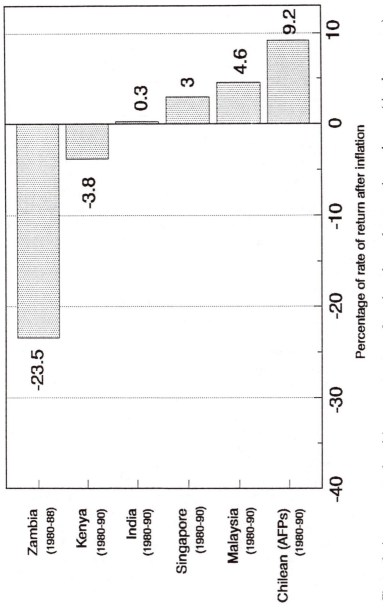

Figure 1. Average annual real investment returns for selected mandatory savings schemes (simple averages). All funds publicly managed except Chilean AFPs. For provident funds, rates are credited to members. Source: World Bank (1994).

Impact on National Saving

One of the most hotly debated issues in pension economics is the effect of pay-as-you-go versus funded schemes on household and national saving. Some analysts argue that pension schemes have no effect on total national saving, that consumers substitute taxes or saving under the scheme for other forms of saving. Other analysts maintain that pay-as-you-go schemes reduce national saving while funded pension schemes displace some personal saving but not on a one for one basis, so total national saving increases.[2]

The crowding out of voluntary saving may be only partial because people are shortsighted and will not save as much on their own for old age. Some of their voluntary saving may be for bequests or for precautionary motives, which are not easily satisfied by mandatory retirement saving schemes. Limits on consumer borrowing may prevent people from dissaving against future pension benefits. Workers may opt for earlier retirement than the system allows; so they may have to continue saving outside the mandatory system. And people may have little faith in the new system, and hence treat their contributions as a tax and continue to save privately for their old age.

The influence of each of these factors is likely to vary by country. Crowding out would be expected to be more substantial in countries where the voluntary saving rate is high, as in most East Asian countries, and smaller in countries where it is low, as in eastern Europe, where private saving was unknown under socialism, or in Latin America, where saving has been discouraged by inflation. Crowding out would be less for poor and young workers, who save little on their own. Also, as the system matures, covered workers begin to retire and dissave their accumulated assets; so the increase in natural saving comes to a halt, albeit at a higher level of capital stock than before.

Overall, then, it seems likely that a mandatory saving scheme will increase saving relative to the situation with no mandatory scheme, but the effect may not be large. However, the positive effect on saving is likely to be much greater relative to a mandatory pay-as-you-go scheme. A pay-as-you-go scheme gives a windfall consumption gain to the first few cohorts of covered workers, and may thereby reduce national saving (other factors remaining unchanged), while a funded scheme does not. The very factors that offset this negative effect of pay-as-you-go plans — myopia, capital market imperfections, increased saving for early retirement, precautionary motives for saving, and lack of faith in the pension system — tend to increase the positive effect of mandatory saving on saving. In Chile private saving went up sharply in the decade after the mandatory saving scheme was introduced, but because many other factors were changing at the same time it is difficult to pin down how much of the higher saving, if any, was due to the mandatory saving scheme.

In sum, the arguments seem strong for expecting a mandatory retirement saving scheme to have a more positive effect on capital growth than a pay-as-you-go scheme — but the size of the effect is difficult to predict.

Impact on Long-Term Savings

Perhaps more important is the shift in the composition of savings in favor of long-term financial assets controlled by large financial institutions. How quickly long-term resources are accumulated depends on the age of the system, its coverage, and the levels of contributions. In Singapore the resources of the Central Provident Fund rose from 28 percent of GDP in 1976 to 76 percent (despite large withdrawals for housing). In Malaysia the balances of the Employees Provident Fund increased from 18 percent of GDP in 1980 to 41 percent in 1987. In Chile resources in the AFP systems totaled 35 percent of GDP by 1991, often ten years of operation (Table 4).

Thus the mandatory saving pillar can generate substantial long-term financial savings in a relatively short time. Consider the case in which labor income represents 50 percent of national income. A compulsory scheme covering 50 percent of the labor force and imposing a 10 percent contribution rate would annually accumulate funds equal to 2.5 percent of national income. If the rate of return on fund balances equals the rate of growth of GNP (and because pension payouts would be minimal in the early years of operation), such a scheme would accumulate resources equal to 12.5 percent of GNP over five years and 25 percent over ten years. After the first ten years the growing volume of benefits payments would slow the pace of accumulation, although expanded coverage and a rising share of labor income would accelerate the rate of accumulation.

In the very long run — in a closed economy, and even in an open economy if funded plans become commonplace — the marginal productivity of capital and the real rate of return may tumble as long-term savings accumulate. At some point the productivity of capital may fall so far that further high saving is no longer efficient. Since the problem in many countries and from a worldwide point of view now appears to be a scarcity rather than an overabundance of capital, this effect is far off in the future. It can be further forestalled by international diversification, investment in human capital that is complementary to physical capital shifts of labor from the informal to the formal sector, and capital-intensive technological change.

TABLE 4   Assets of Selected National Provident Funds (percentage of GDP) [1]

Country	1983	Most Recent	Year Available
Singapore	53.8	75.6	1991
Malaysia	24.4	40.8	1991
Solomon Island	15.4	—	—
Zambia	9.1	5.8	1989
Sri Lanka	8.1	15.2	1990
Swaziland	6.0	5.4	1987
Nepal	3.8	—	—
India	1.9	4.5	1990
Indonesia[1]	1.0	1.4	1990
Ghana[2]	—	0.6	1986
Fiji	—	43.9	1987
Nigeria	—	0.7	1988
Barbados	—	16.0	1986
Kenya	—	11.5	1989

Source: World Bank (1994).
Notes: [1]Refers to main provident fund in each country.
[2]Refers to both public employees' and national provident funds.
[3]Provident funds are being replaced by social insurance systems.

Impact on Capital Allocation

Establishing a mandatory savings scheme presents an opportunity to stimulate capital markets and expand the supply of productive capital. Nevertheless, the allocation and productivity of this capital depends on whether the funds are publicly or privately managed. Most centrally managed provident funds have been invested in government bonds or in failing public enterprises at low nominal interest rates that become negative during inflationary periods. This is also true of centrally managed reserves of defined benefit plans (World Bank 1994). If government has exclusive access to the funds, spends them wastefully, and pays workers an arbitrary interest rate, the potential advantages of mandatory saving schemes are lost. In fact, such schemes become very much like pay-as-you-go schemes in their capital and labor market effects.

Because of the fungibility of money once it becomes part of the government budget, the real productivity of these provident funds is not known. The funds may increase government consumption or investment beyond what they would have been otherwise — or they may substitute for explicit taxes while holding government spending unchanged. Each has a different impact on national output and its composition and distribution. It is known, however, that the real returns credited to worker accounts was around zero in India and highly negative in Zambia and other African countries (Figure 1). So, for the worker, these systems have failed. And for the broader economy, their allocations have not been subject to any competitive market test or even public scrutiny.

Even in Singapore, more than 90 percent of fund assets have been invested in non-tradable government securities with an average rate of return of 3 percent in the 1980s (Asher 1992b), similar to that on 12-month time deposits and less than what long-term contractual savings could have earned in the market. The Singapore government claims that it has used these funds productively, both domestically and for investments in foreign assets, but these returns have not gone to the provident fund. The relatively low interest rate paid to the fund could thus be viewed as a hidden tax on workers to finance general government expenditures and reserves.

Most countries with national provident funds allow employees to use part of their balances for housing and other specified purposes, and Singapore now allows limited investments in approved private sector securities. Members are obliged to redeposit the funds with the provident fund if they sell the houses or other investments (Asher 1992a). This use of funds has a positive effect on home ownership and the housing market but reduces the impact of national provident funds as a source of productive capital investment and retirement income. It is not clear that mandatory saving for housing is justified on efficiency grounds.

By contrast, in a decentrally managed competitive system such as that in Chile, workers pick their management company from a small number of authorized AFPs and can transfer their accounts from one company to another. This gives decision-making authority to workers, who are clearly interested in maximizing returns and minimizing risk, and avoids the problem of earning below market returns and encouraging excess government spending. But workers may not have the information needed to make wise choices. Their investments may be too risky in some cases and too conservative in others; so they may eventually become charges on the rest of the society. To counter this problem, the Chilean government has imposed strict regulations to protect the safety and profitability of investments (see below).

Given the decentralized management and the block on personal withdrawals, the Chilean pension system has become a dominant player in the capital market — a force facilitating privatization and growth. Initially the AFPs invested predominantly in government bonds, but gradually they shifted to corporate securities — especially equities, as the Chilean stock market boomed and investment rules were liberalized (Vittas and Iglesias 1992). Now the government must compete for access to funds and pay the competitive market price. The AFP system also invested heavily in the privatization of public utilities in the mid-1980s, accounting for 10 to 35 percent of the equity capital of the privatized utilities — and even more of the domestically held equity capital. By 1991, 38 percent of AFP funds were in state securities, 24 percent in corporate equities, and about 13 percent each in corporate bonds and bank deposits. AFPs hold more than one-third of all public bonds, two-thirds of all private sector bonds, and 10 percent of all corporate equities in the country (Superintendencia de AFPs, Banco Central Chile).

Perhaps more important, the pension system has stimulated the development of other institutions and practices that have deepened Chilean financial markets over the past decade. These include modern bank supervision, new securities and corporation laws, increased disclosure requirements for public companies, risk classification agencies for bonds, a long-term corporate bond market and a second stock market, new types of mortgage bonds, and improved regulation of insurance companies.

The rate of return to workers in the Chilean system has been much higher than in countries with centrally managed mandatory saving pillars. During the first ten years, the gross annual real return averaged 13 percent, and the average net yield to workers, after fees, was about 9.2 percent, albeit with large variations among different funds and individuals (Acuna and Iglesias 1992). Such high gross returns cannot be expected in the long run, but the high start-up costs of the first two years also will not continue; they have already been reduced from 14.7 percent of assets in 1982 to 1.6 percent in 1992. Overall, this experience is consistent with the observation that decentralized funded plans have earned far higher returns than centralized plans — perhaps reflecting their competitive nature and the market tests for their allocations.

Pension Fund Concentration and Corporate Governance

Mandatory pension funds, if invested in the private sector, could eventually come to dominate the ownership of financial assets that represent claims on the economy's real assets — land, housing, stock, commercial property, and industrial equipment. This ownership structure has implications for corporate governance, since pension funds would become major stockholders and could exercise voting rights and power over corporate management.

The concentration of ownership means that mandatory pension funds could not simply buy and sell shares without disrupting the market, as smaller investors can do. It also makes it worthwhile for them to incur the costs of gathering and processing information, which they can use to monitor the management performance of corporations, thereby estimating corporate efficiency. On the other side of the coin, that may give a small number of pension funds an influential voice in interlocking directorates, an anti-competitive force in strategic corporate decisions. Centralized provident funds are even more concentrated. If these funds were to invest in corporate equities, public officials could gain control of corporate affairs, a back door to nationalization.

In Chile, the three largest companies account for more than 60 percent of total funds and a big chunk of total corporate equity. So far, the AFPs have not attempted to monitor or control corporations, and publicly managed provident funds have not invested in private corporations. But funded plans in other countries are doing so. In the United States, funded occupational plans have begun to monitor the governance of the corporations in which they have an ownership stake. Because this channel allows pension funds to have a far-reaching influence on the economy, it becomes particularly important for them to be concentrated — but not too concentrated — and to have incentives that encourage the right performance from corporations.

Implications for Labor Markets

Mandatory saving plans, unlike public or occupational plans (particularly defined benefit plans), have relatively little impact on the labor market. Since workers eventually recoup their contributions, with interest, they are less likely to see savings as taxes, to be evaded. And since they "own" their accounts, they can carry them along from one job to another with no penalty for mobility. In this sense, the important story is that there is relatively little labor market story, compared with the other types of plans.

Even so, some distortions remain. First, when contribution rates are much higher than households' desired saving rates (presumably the reason for a mandatory scheme), incentives are created to evade by shifting to the informal market, understating covered wages, and substituting in-kind benefits for wages. When interest rates are below market, as is often the case for provident funds, this effect is exacerbated. If workers cannot evade they may be induced, by their higher accumulated savings and compulsory savings rate, to retire early. Thus, mandatory saving plans may reduce the supply of labor, especially experienced labor, in the formal sector. In addition, wage rigidities may prevent employers from shifting their share of the payroll tax to workers — and may decrease employment instead. Singapore seems to have experienced this effect in 1984, when it raised the contribution rate to 50 percent of wages, shared equally by employers and employees. The employers' rate was cut in half the following year because of the belief that this had affected employment adversely. Both these factors imply a tax element that distorts the labor market and limits the efficient contribution rate.

Fiscal Implications

A mandatory saving plan also has few fiscal implications than a pay-as-you-go public plan since workers receive only the value of their contributions plus investment earnings. Political pressure to increase public spending on pension benefits is absent. In fact, governments have borrowed from provident funds at below market interest rates, cutting future pension benefits and current public borrowing costs. But these low rates could increase public deficits if they induce the government to spend more on other goods and services. The danger is that the spending, financed by a hidden tax on workers, may not be productive. (This is similar to the problem posed by large reserves in a partly funded public plan.) Decentralized schemes that charge market rates avoid this problem. But if the government guarantees their benefits, this constitutes another state obligation that could become surprisingly large if strategic manipulation and moral hazard are not controlled.

Another important fiscal effect stems from the tax treatment of pension savings. Tax incentives are not essential for mandatory schemes, but they improve compliance and are therefore common. The tax loss may force the government to reduce spending or to raise other taxes, which could have a high efficiency cost (Valdés-Prieto and Cifuentes 1993).

Contributions to most mandatory saving schemes are deductible for income tax, as is the current investment income from the funds. Workers in Chile are allowed to contribute additional amounts on a voluntary tax-exempt basis. In most schemes, withdrawals are subject to tax, like any other income. The benefits of tax deferral are greater for higher income workers, because their initial tax savings are higher and they are likely to be in a lower tax bracket after retirement. To avoid this perverse redistribution, limits may be placed on the tax-advantaged benefits or a tax credit may be offered rather than making contributions tax-deductible, as has been proposed for occupational plans.

Malaysia and Singapore exempt the contributions and the withdrawals — as well as the interest earned in between — from taxation. The total tax benefits of Singapore's national provident fund (and the government tax revenue forgone) were estimated at slightly more than one percent of GDP for 1987, roughly the tax expenditures for the United States occupational pension system (Turner and Beller 1989). The Singapore fund thus provides a valuable tax shelter for contributors, especially high income workers who would be subject to higher marginal tax rates on other investment income (Queisser 1991). The higher tax benefits received by upper income groups may be one reason they go along with the high contribution rates and low interest rates.

Redistributive Effects and Poverty

Because of the direct link between contributions and benefits, mandatory saving plans, in principle, do not involve redistribution either across or within generations. Non-transparent and perverse redistributions can still occur, however, particularly in centrally managed pension funds, so the system needs to be designed to avoid this possibility.

If the government borrows from provident funds at below market rates, in lieu of increased taxes to finance general public expenditures, this has a redistributional effect since the incidence of the payroll tax is not the same as that of general revenue taxes and is generally more regressive. Or, if the government uses the funds to finance public expenditures that it would not otherwise have undertaken, income is redistributed from fund contributors to the beneficiaries of the additional government spending. Such transfers are difficult to trace (doing so requires knowing what would have happened had the funds not been available) — which is precisely why the transfers are likely to benefit privileged groups, who are in a position to influence government transactions.

Allowing contributors to withdraw funds before retirement also benefits middle and upper income groups. Singapore's national provident fund permits early withdrawals for education, home ownership, and alternative investments as long as contributors maintain a minimum balance in the plan, a condition few low income workers can meet. In some countries plan members are permitted to borrow against their savings at below market rates for specified purchases — an option that again is used mainly by high income groups. A more competitive system for investing pension funds, yielding a higher rate of return, would reduce this problem of perverse redistribution.

Perverse redistribution may also result if retiring workers are compelled to purchase annuities that pool people with long and short life expectancies. Public policies that prohibit distinctions among different demographic and socioeconomic groups in setting the terms of annuities and life insurance contracts have this effect. For example, if regulations require that retiring mine workers and white collar employees pay the same price for annuities, the result would be regressive. This effect could be offset by reducing annuity prices for lower socioeconomic groups, by topping up their accounts directly, or by paying large benefits to their survivors. Similarly, regulations that pool men and women redistribute expected lifetime income from the former to the latter, who live longer.

Most mandatory saving schemes avoid this problem by paying lump sums instead of annuities on retirement. But this means they do not provide longevity insurance and do not protect the very old against poverty. Chile gives workers a choice between purchasing an annuity or taking phased withdrawals that are scheduled to last an expected lifetime and that avoid the redistribution problem. Chile also requires all employees to purchase term life and disability insurance, in which mine workers get a net benefit if they are in the same pool with white collar workers.

Another problem with mandatory retirement saving schemes is their failure to protect low wage workers with interrupted careers, such as women, who may never accumulate enough in their pension accounts to support themselves in old age. Along similar lines, the pensions may fall below subsistence standards because of inflation or low investment returns. For that reason, mandatory saving can leave considerable old age poverty.

Some of these possible sources of poverty can be handled without public transfers. In Chile, the purchase of private disability insurance and term life insurance is compulsory. Most provident funds do not provide or require such insurance, leaving survivors and disabled workers largely unprotected and poor. Regulations could require joint contributions and joint ownership of retirement savings accounts between spouses, protecting women whose labor force participation has been interrupted. Beyond that, governments can deal with the problems of long-term poverty alleviation and extreme investment risk by guaranteeing a minimum pension based on years of employment — or by redistributive social assistance programs; this might be considered an accompanying role of the public plan. Chile provides such assistance and guarantees, financing them from general tax revenues.

Regulatory Issues in Decentralized Schemes

Decentralized competitive systems are more likely than centralized provident funds to maximize investment returns and contribute to capital market development. But decentralized plans raise a host of public policy issues related to the fiduciary standards of pension companies, the safety of their investments, the range of products offered and of information disclosed, the size of fees and commissions, the kind of advertising and other marketing expenses incurred, the guarantees provided by government, and the regulatory apparatus needed to monitor all these elements. Extensive regulation is needed because workers often lack the expertise needed to invest wisely. Private pension companies, if left unchecked, might mislead their members or might take too many risks in order to maximize yield and attract new accounts, or might be too conservative to keep up with inflation. Given the long-term nature of pension investments, once the damage becomes evident it may be too late for the worker to recover financially through new saving. Trying to remedy this flaw through government guarantees may create moral hazard problems, if the guarantees exacerbate a tendency toward risky investments. Regulations are designed to protect both individual workers and society from perverse competition in the face of information deficiencies. This protection is particularly important in a mandatory program.

Can governments be counted on to regulate decentralized systems well, having already shown that they cannot control centralized pension funds very well? And, at what point does a strict regulatory structure wipe out competition and become government control? The experience of Chile is used to explore what kinds of regulations are workable and may — or may not — be advisable.

Ensuring the Solvency of Funds and the Integrity of Managers

Which funds qualify as custodians of mandatory saving accounts? To ensure competent and responsible administration of pension funds and to protect their solvency, criteria must be established on entry and minimum capital margin and fund managers must be vetted by the supervisory authorities. The shortage of local expertise in many developing countries can be overcome by using foreign fund management companies in joint ventures with local firms. Developing countries that are reluctant to use joint ventures may have a hard time assembling the expertise needed to run pension funds well, especially in the early years.

Chile limits participation in the mandatory scheme to the Administradoras de Fondos de Pensiones, or AFPs, specialized pension fund management companies. The AFPs are regulated and supervised by the Superintendency of AFPs, which has authority over charter approval. The AFPs are set up as joint-stock companies. Any group of shareholders, including large corporations, trade associations, labor unions, and other financial institutions (but not banks), can establish an AFP. Until recently, the three largest AFPs, serving about two-thirds of the market, were joint ventures.

The pension fund is an independent entity, segregated both legally and financially from the AFP and its other activities. The assets of the pension fund belong exclusively to individual members, are not attachable, and are not affected by any financial losses suffered by the AFP. AFPs are required to maintain investment reserves equal to one percent of the total assets of the pension fund they manage. Reserves must be invested in the same assets as the pension fund under AFP management to ensure that AFPs apply the same professionalism in investing the resources of the pension fund as they do for the AFP's own resources. Pension funds are valued daily at market prices (much like mutual funds) or, for assets for which there are no daily market values, according to a valuation model developed by the Superintendency of AFPs.

In Chile, workers choose their own AFP and are permitted to switch their accumulated balances to another AFP if they are dissatisfied, creating competition among AFPs. To simplify matters, regulations impose a strict limit of one account per worker and one fund per management company. These regulations are very restrictive — and controversial. Allowing workers to have accounts with more than one company would let them hedge their bets and reduce their dependence on the performance of a single company. Similarly, allowing management companies to operate a wider range of funds would allow them to tailor products to different tastes and age groups. For instance, equity funds might appeal to younger workers, mixed stock/bond funds to middle-aged workers, and money market funds to older workers. The unit account-unit fund rule reduces variety and choice, two of the potential advantages of competition.

These two restrictions are aimed at preserving the simplicity and transparency of the system, characteristics that are considered important for a compulsory scheme involving large numbers of financially unsophisticated people. Allowing companies to manage a wider range of investment funds would complicate compliance monitoring. For example, it would become more difficult to prevent withdrawals or a concentration of workers' portfolios in risky assets. As the system matures, and workers gain financial experience, regulations may become less restrictive. But in the meantime, the cost of simplified regulations is the loss of choice and risk diversification.

Keeping Investment Risk Within Reasonable Bounds

Financial regulation aims to ensure fairness for all participants, including protection from fraudulent or imprudent behavior by the managers of financial institutions — a task that assumes particular importance in mandatory retirement saving schemes because of their compulsory nature and long-term contracts. One way to provide such protection is through regular disclosure of information. AFPs in Chile are required to provide statements to contributors three times a year, disclosing the last four monthly contributions paid by employers, the financial performance of the pension fund, and the accumulated balance and rate of return on individual accounts.

Participants are further protected through investment rules. Chile started out with rigid investment regulations, and gradually eased them as funds and experience increased. The limits on equity investments, for example, have been steadily increased, and investments in overseas securities, which were not allowed initially, have been authorized.

Investment rules are guided by two operating principles: safety and profitability. Safety implies that pension funds are invested in approved assets and properly diversified, while profitability implies that fund management companies are free to seek the highest returns subject to these rules. Thus only upper limits are imposed on investments, to control the exposure of pension funds to particular risks. There are no floors requiring purchase of government bonds or other "socially useful investments." Currently, the upper limits are 50 percent on government bonds, 30 percent on corporate equities, 10 percent on foreign securities, and similar limits on bank deposits, mortgage loans, and other assets (Vittas and Iglesias 1992). Ceilings also apply to permissible investments in the securities of individual companies. Ceilings are higher for "Chapter 12" companies, which accept severe restrictions on their management independence. So far only recently privatized utilities have opted to qualify for Chapter 12, which has allowed pension funds to play an important role in their privatization.

The dispersion in returns across AFPs is reduced through the regulation of maximum and minimum returns. If a fund's real investment return over a rolling 12-month period is 50 percent or two percentage points higher (whichever yields the higher rate of return) than the average for all pension funds, the AFP has to place the difference in a profitability reserve, which becomes an asset of the pension fund, not the AFP. Similarly, if the real investment return for a pension fund is less than half the average of all pension funds or two percentage points lower (whichever yields the lower rate of return), the AFP is required to make up the difference by transferring funds from the profitability reserve and, if this is inadequate, from its own investment reserves. If an AFP is unable to make up the shortfall, it is declared bankrupt, its pension fund assets are transferred to other AFPs, and the government makes up any remaining difference. So far, the dispersion in returns among AFPs has been so low that no profitability reserves have been established; three AFPs have been dissolved or merged because of failure to maintain the one percent investment reserve.

Maximum and minimum limits on pension fund returns are designed to protect workers against excessive fluctuations in returns and to avoid wide dispersion across AFPs. But they may also induce herd behavior, since firms are penalized for being different, not for being wrong. In addition, using a 12-month average in calculating returns unduly emphasizes short-term performance, an undesirable attribute for long-term contracts that may span 60 years or more. An AFP that persistently performs at the lower end of the permitted range would produce substantially lower than average returns over a period of many years. An alternative approach would apply narrower limits (say 25 percent rather than 50 percent) on performance over longer periods of time, say three to five years. Another alternative would specify the maximum and minimum returns in terms of the top and bottom 10 percent of funds, or those that are more than two standard deviations away from the average. The better informed workers are, the less need there will be for such regulations, as workers shift savings away from consistently poor performers.

To protect against inflation, pension fund managers could be required to invest a portion of their portfolios in assets that provide an effective hedge against inflation, such as equities, real estate, foreign assets, or indexed bonds. Though Chile does not require indexation by AFPs, this position is widespread in Chilean financial markets — a response to demand in an environment in which inflation has historically been a problem. More than 95 percent of AFP assets are invested in equities, indexed bonds, or real assets, including indexed bonds issued by banks or private firm. This counters the common assertion that the private sector cannot offer indexed securities or insure against inflation. Hedging against inflation would be much more difficult, however, in countries with less developed financial markets, poorly indexed financial instruments, and a high and volatile inflation rate.

Allowing Investments in Overseas Assets

There are strong advantages to international diversification of pension funds, particularly for countries with small or concentrated domestic economies. Lower risk and sometimes higher returns are possible over the long term through international investment, which reduces the exposure of investors to country-specific risks such as inflation and gives them an opportunity to move their capital to countries that offer the highest return. Open capital markets may also impose fiscal discipline which is badly needed in some countries. But they also raise fears of institutionalized capital flight, loss of control by mandatory authorities, and depriving local markets of the benefits of the increased availability of long-term funds.

Perhaps because of these fears, few countries with national provident funds invest abroad, a major reason for negative returns in countries with high inflation. Singapore is an exception. Using assets borrowed from the provident fund, among others, two public agencies have invested abroad, the Monetary Authority of Singapore in short- and medium-term securities, and the Government of Singapore Investment Corporation in longer-term foreign equities and other assets. The authorities claim the returns on these foreign investments have been high, but the claims cannot be corroborated since no published data are available and the accounts of the two agencies are not audited. At any rate the returns go to the government, not to the provident funds, which receive low interest rates from the government. Pressures are mounting in Fiji and in Malaysia to allow their national provident funds to invest in foreign securities, since the funds are now large and government borrowing needs have subsided.

Chile did not allow the AFPs to invest in foreign securities until 1991, and then only on a gradual schedule, beginning at one percent of funds and rising to 10 percent (perhaps higher) by 1995. Authorizing investment in foreign securities represents a recognition of the maturity of the system, the large size of the pension funds, the saturation of domestic markets, and the growing need for diversification of country risk. It is also a response to the large capital inflow that Chile has been experiencing in recent years. Conversely, liberalization of capital outflows may encourage inflows by convincing foreign investors that they will be able to get their money out.

Chile's approach may be too cautious. In particular, saturation of the domestic market would come sooner in smaller countries, suggesting a need to relax investment rules at a much earlier stage and to a much larger extent. The new scheme in Argentina permits investments of up to 10 percent in foreign securities from the start.

Regulating Fees and Commissions

In principle, competition among plan administrators should make regulation of fees and commissions unnecessary. In practice, agency and information problems often lead to distortions in the structure of fees and commissions, as Chile's experience suggests. Since mandatory saving schemes are, by definition, compulsory, and economies of scale in the pension industry may result in concentration, investment companies may end up charging more than they would in a purely voluntary competitive scheme.

Chile regulates the types of fees that AFPs can levy but not the level of fees or the structure of commissions paid to agents. Authorized fees include a fixed fee per contribution, a prorated fee on wages subject to pension contribution, fees for opening new accounts, fees per pension payment, and fees for voluntary savings accounts. No AFP has imposed the last two fees, and only one has levied a fee on new accounts. Fees may not be assessed for closing an account, to prevent AFPs from discouraging account transfers. AFPs were initially allowed to charge a management fee on the total value of funds under their management, but this fee has since been disallowed because of its depleting effect on the accounts of those who were out of work and no longer contributing.

The flat fee per contribution is probably the most controversial. This fee would seem to be regressive, but it may simply reflect the real costs of handling an account. This fee was high in the early years of the program, leading to lower net rates of return to lower income workers, but competition combined with negative publicity has led most AFPs to abolish or greatly diminish it. A prorated fee of about 1.5 percent of covered wage is currently the major fee, and net returns have been largely equalized across income groups (Acuna and Iglesias 1992).

Keeping a Lid on Operating Costs

Decentralized systems that allow workers to choose management companies and transfer accounts tend to incur higher operating costs than efficiently run centralized plans. Decentralized systems cannot achieve the same economies of scale, they incur high marketing and transactions (switching) costs, and they perform additional functions, such as investment research and processing (which may, however, result in higher rates of return). At the same time, decentralized plans have more incentive to operate efficiently than centralized plan that have a monopoly in a compulsory system. These factors help explain why, in 1990, operating costs were 1.5 percent of covered wages and 2.3 percent of total assets in Chile's decentralized system, compared with 0.2 percent and 0.1 percent in Singapore's and 0.4 percent and 0.2 percent in Malaysia's centralized systems, while the costs of Zambia's centralized system were 25 times higher than Singapore's and ate up half of all contributions (Table 3).

Competition may be very imperfect in financial markets that are serving a mass, relatively uneducated clientele. Where investors are unable to collect and analyze information about prospective rates of return, they are susceptible to intensive marketing campaigns, which create barriers to entry and increase costs. Promotional expenses are estimated to account for as much as 30 percent of operating costs for Chile's AFPs. Paying salespeople by commission leads to high turnover of accounts and high transaction costs, which are eventually passed on to consumers in the form of high fees. Advertising campaigns also tend to emphasize short-term performance.

Requiring companies to provide data on fees and commissions as well as investment performance over longer periods (three, five, and 10 years) would provide a more accurate picture of relative returns and might also help to keep operating costs down. Marketing costs and account turnover would decline if transfers, which workers might choose during an open enrollment period, were limited to one per year. Marketing costs might also fall if AFPs were allowed to pass along the savings to long-term affiliates in the form of a bonus on their rate of return or a reduction in their required fee. The entry of new AFPs in a competitive market may eventually lead to lower costs and fees. Economies of scale and learning by doing as the system grows will undoubtedly enhance efficiency. Indeed, costs fell dramatically through the 1980s, are now about 1.6 percent of total assets, and are lowest for the largest AFPs.[3]

Regulatory Annuities

Under Chile's mandatory retirement saving program, workers must purchase term life and disability insurance. Chile's scheme also provides for the voluntary purchase of annuities at the time of retirement. These insurance-related elements give rise to a host of potential problems in the annuities market.

In Chile, insurance agents receive large commissions up front, giving them an incentive to withhold information or to shade the truth in order to gain a customer. Since the purchase of an annuity is an irreversible act, a wrong decision by an ill-informed retiree may have disastrous consequences that cannot be readily corrected. Chile imposes no restrictions on these commissions or on the sale or range of acceptable annuity products, other than to require price indexation, but it is considering various measures to control commissions and inform workers about their options. One proposal is to limit annuity products to two or three standard options, such as partially indexed life annuities for the retiree combined with survivor benefits for a 10- or 20-year period, or joint annuities that cover the entire lifetime of the retiree plus a designated beneficiary. That would simplify comparison shopping for annuities offered by different companies. Broad disclosure on premiums and commissions would also be required. Other proposals call for independent professional advisers to assist retirees in evaluating annuity choices and for the establishment of an ombudsman to investigate complaints and arbitrate disputes. These proposals, which focus on increased information flows, should help the market work better. Some analysts believe that increased competition will eventually lead insurance companies to move toward direct sales of annuities, which would reduce the price by cutting out the commission.

Another problem concerns the worker's exposure to the risk of a sharp decline in the market at the time of retirement, when the annuity is purchased. This risk could be reduced by requiring workers to purchase small annuity contracts periodically once they reach a predetermined age, such as 50. By reducing the lumpiness of the purchase this method would diversify the interest rate risk, but would, at the same time, increase workers' exposure to the risk of insurance company insolvency, making regulation of fiduciary standards all the more important. The timing problem could be mitigated more effectively by developing variable annuities, whose value would rise and fall with the market rather than being fixed at the retirement date. This would reduce the worker's to market conditions at retirement time, but would continue the investment risk throughout retirement. Such variable annuities are used in South Africa and the United States. Caps on annual movements in value of variable annuities might make this risk more acceptable to retirees. Similar variable instruments, with caps on annual movements, have been developed in the mortgage markets.

Monitoring Compliance by Investment Companies

Close monitoring of investment company behavior is essential to ensure compliance. Supervision in Chile's AFP system includes daily reports on investment transactions and monthly reports on each company's financial position and performance. Compliance with investment limits is monitored continuously. On-site inspections are undertaken periodically to ensure the accuracy of submitted returns. Though the arrangement works well in Chile, countries with weaker regulatory capacity might have difficult time in effectively monitoring decentralized firms.

Chile's system is supervised and controlled by the Superintendency of AFPs, an autonomous agency linked to the Ministry of Labor and Social Security. The Superintendent is appointed by the President, and the agency enjoys considerable independence and authority. The Superintendency has the right to authorize and revoke the license of AFPs, to issue detailed regulations for the smooth functioning of the system, and to promote changes in the law. The agency, which employs more than 100 lawyers, financial auditors, examiners, and others, supervises the investment of AFPs, the operation of profitability reserves, the crediting of member contributions, and the payment of pensions.

An ever present danger in regulatory systems is that the regulated will "capture" the regulators and prevent them from operating effectively. Although this does not seem to have happened in Chile, countries with a weaker regulatory capacity might have a more difficult time monitoring decentralized firms. Countries should assess their institutional and human capital capacities for regulating effectively before understanding a decentralized mandatory saving plan.

Guaranteeing Pensions and Pension Returns

Various types of government guarantees are designed to ensure at least some pension coverage for everyone. In countries with mandatory saving plans social assistance is often provided to people who are not covered by the scheme and a minimum return or minimum pension may be guaranteed to those who are covered. These guarantees have a redistributive function and are usually financed out of general revenues.

Singapore provides modest benefits (12 percent of the average wage) to poor old people, widows, and orphans through a social assistance program financed from general revenue. It specifies the rate of return that is paid to the provident fund. But it does not provide a guaranteed minimum pension.

Chile's system includes four types of state guarantees. First, the government pays a low social assistance benefit of about 12 percent of the average wage to old people not covered by the mandatory saving plan. Second, for workers who have contributed to the mandatory saving plan for at least 20 years, the state guarantees a minimum pension of about 22 to 25 percent of the average wage. Third, a minimum profitability rate is guaranteed for each pension fund relative to the average for the country. Any shortfall in rate of return is covered first through the profitability reserve and then through the investment reserves of the AFP. If these are inadequate, the AFP is forced into liquidation, and the state makes up the shortfall. Finally, the government guarantees annuity payments for old age pensions and disability and survivorship benefits in case of insurance company failure. The guarantee covers 100 percent of the minimum pension and 75 percent of the difference between the minimum pension and the value of the benefit involved up to a specified limit. These guarantees are financed out of general revenues.

What are the likely costs of such guarantees? As long as the rate of return remains at least two percentage points above the growth rate of wages, most people who work full-time during their active years (about 40 years) will receive a pension far above the minimum without any public transfers (Table 1). But a problem arises if low income workers contribute just long enough to qualify for the subsidized minimum pension (20 years) and then escape to the informal sector to avoid making further payments. As many as 30 to 40 percent of covered workers in Chile may fall below the minimum if strategic evasion is common or if fund performance falls drastically. But even then the government has to make up only the shortfall between the minimum pension and the benefit payable by the pension fund.

Simulations indicate that these guarantees will cost less than one percent of GDP, easily absorbed in a country such as Chile that has only a small budget deficit (Gillion and Bonilla 1992; Diamond and Valdés-Prieto 1994; Wagner 1991). But the cost of a minimum pension ought to be carefully calculated in advance to ensure that the state is not taking on a large unfunded liability that it will be unable to meet. If the cost is expected to be high, the minimum guarantee should be lowered or the required contribution rate raised, unless the government wishes to use general revenue finance as a redistributive instrument.

A contrasting problem is that a minimum pension of 22 to 25 percent of the average wage, as in Singapore and Chile, is well below the poverty line in most countries and the social assistance of 12 percent is below subsistence. One way to attack both the evasion and the poverty problems is to guarantee a higher minimum pension to workers who have contributed for more years. For example, the guarantee could be set equal to 12 percent of the average economy-wide wage (the universal floor for everyone over age 65) plus 5 percent for every year of contributing and employment, up to a specified maximum. A worker with 20 years of service would then be guaranteed 22 percent of the average wage and one with 45 years' service would be guaranteed 35 percent, which might be the maximum guarantee. Given the 10 percent contribution rate and the link to years of employment, this scheme would not cost the government much more than the current one in Chile, and might even cost less.

Conclusion

Mandatory personal saving schemes require workers to accumulate a pool of long-term savings for consumption in old age. Since the schemes are not tied to place of employment, they are more portable and diversify risk more than occupational plans. They are also likely to be more concentrated and therefore benefit more from economies of scale than occupational plans. Since they make benefits directly contingent on contributions, they are less likely than public plans to induce evasion and shifts of labor to the informal sector. Political pressures for poor design features — such as early retirement, non-sustainable pension levels, and hidden redistribution to influential groups — are avoided because each person's contribution determines the benefits that person ultimately gets. If evasion or early retirement does take place, the costs are borne by the individual worker, not by others in the plan.

Mandatory saving schemes have the potential to stimulate capital accumulation and the development of modern financial instruments and institutions. But if governments are given exclusive or favored access to the funds, many of these potential advantages are lost. When the pension funds are publicly managed, they are invariably required to be invested in government debt as a source of general revenue in return for low nominal rates of interest that become negative during inflationary periods. Often the government has used the funds for consumption rather than productive investments, canceling out the positive effect of these plans on long-term saving.

In principle, centralized national provident funds could become competitive by turning them over to one or more private managers on the basis of competitive bidding and with the authority to invest in private sector securities. This procedure, which has been considered in Malaysia, would enable the fund to minimize marketing costs, reap economies of scale, and possibly earn a higher rate of return. But the potential for corruption and cronyism in the bidding process would outweigh this advantage in many countries. Another option would retain centralized control but passively index the fund to the domestic and international stock markets, a procedure that is followed in the voluntary occupational plan for federal government employees in the United States. But many developing countries lack the necessary securities market for indexation. In any event, most governments have demonstrated that they do not want to relinquish privileged access to national provident funds.

Empirical experience indicates that decentralized mandatory saving schemes are likely to achieve higher returns and allocate capital more efficiently than centralized schemes. Political interference over investments is always a possibility, but decentralization makes this explicit and sets up a constituency against it — private pension funds and their worker affiliates. The danger is that workers' choice of investment might be ill informed, eventually leaving many people without adequate pensions. Regulation must walk a fine line between adequately protecting workers and giving funds enough latitude that competition and investment choice are not stamped out. To minimize risk:

- Only prudent companies, including joint ventures with experienced foreign firms, should be allowed to manage pension funds.
- Information disclosure should be emphasized.
- Investments should be diversified and subject to ceilings, not floors.
- There should be no requirement to invest funds in public securities.
- The range of funds, marketing expenses, and annuity products could be limited in the early years of the system and then gradually expanded.
- Investment in overseas securities should be encouraged in order to reduce exposure to country-specific risk.

Decentralized mandatory saving schemes will function best in middle or high income countries with a population well enough informed to make intelligent investment decisions, with financial markets that offer (or could be prompted to offer) a variety of debt and equity instruments, and with effective regulatory institutions or the capacity to develop the institutions quickly. Because financial market development and a regulatory apparatus are necessary for continued economic growth of all countries, funded pension plans are more viable as countries develop and can also speed up the development process.

Mandatory saving plans can provide an adequate pension for middle and high income workers, but they fail to protect workers with low wages as they grow old or to insure against sharp dips in investment performance. To alleviate long-term poverty and to help diversify risks, these plans must be accompanied by a minimum pension guarantee or other publicly financed redistributive benefits, thereby ensuring old age security for all.

This chapter draws on and extends chapter 6 of World Bank (1994). The work is a product of the staff of the World Bank and the judgments made do not necessarily reflect the views of its Board of Directors or the government they represent.

Notes

[1]Major sources on Chile are Acuna and Iglesias (1992); Diamond and Valdés-Prieto (1994); Gillion and Bonilla (1992); Valdés-Prieto (1993); Vittas and Iglesias (1992); Wagner (1991). For a discussion of broader issues concerning defined contribution plans see Bodie and Merton (1988); Valdés-Prieto (1994); Vittas (1992a and b); Vittas and Skully (1991). Additional background is available in World Bank (1994); see especially chapter 6.

[2]Most of this literature focuses on public pay-as-you-go schemes and occupational pension plans. For surveys of this literature see Atkinson (1987) and World Bank (1994).

[3]For a further discussion of pension costs see Valdés-Prieto (1993); Mitchell, Sunden, Hsin, and Reid (1994); and James and Palacios (1994).

References

Acuna, R. and Augusto Iglesias. *Chile: Experience con un regimen de capitalizacion 1981–1991.* Regional Project on Financial Policies. Santiago: Economic Conference for Latin America and the Caribbean-United Nations Development Program (ECLAC-UNDP), 1992.

Asher, Mukul. "Income Security for Old Age: The Case of Malaysia." National University of Singapore Department of Economics and Statistics mimeo, 1992. (1992a)

——. "The Singapore Central Provident Fund." National University of Singapore Department of Economics and Statistics mimeo, 1992. (1992b)

ASTEK (Indonesian Provident Fund). *ASTEK Annual Report.* Jakarta, Indonesia. 1992.

Atkinson, Anthony. "Income Maintenance and Social Insurance." In Alan J. Auerbach and Martin Feldstein, eds., *Handbook of Public Economics,* Vol. 2. Amsterdam: North Holland, 1987: 779–908.

Bodie, Zvi, A. Marcus, and R. Merton. *Defined Benefit Versus Defined Contribution Pension Plans: What Are the Real Trade-Offs?* Chicago: University of Chicago Press, 1988.

Colombia, Government of. *Ley de la Reforma de Pensiones.* Bogotá: December 1993.

Diamond, Peter and Salvador Valdés-Prieto. "Social Security Reform." In Barry Bosworth, Rudiger Dornbusch, and Raul Laban, eds. *The Chilean Economy Policy Lessons and Challenges.* Washington, DC: Brookings Institution, 1994.

Dixon, John. *National Provident Funds: The Enfant Terrible of Social Security.* London: International Fellowship for Social and Economic Development, 1989.

Gillion, Colin and Alejandro Bonilla. "Analysis of a National Private Pension Scheme: The Case of Chile." *International Labor Review* 131, 2 (1992): 171–95.

India Employees' Provident Fund. *Annual Report* 37, 1989–90. New Delhi: Employees' Provident Fund Organization, 1991.

International Social Security Association. "Conjugating Public and Private: The Case of Pensions." Geneva: International Labor Office, mimeo, 1987.

James, Estelle and Robert Palacios. "Comparing Administrative Costs of Pension Scheme." Washington, DC: World Bank Policy Research Department mimeo, 1994.

Johnson, Paul and Jane Falkingham. "Is There a Future for the Beveridge Pension Scheme?" London: London School of Economics, mimeo, 1992.

Kenyan National Provident Fund. Nairobi: mimeo, 1989.

Mitchell, Olivia, Annika Sundén, Ping Lung Hsin, and G. Reid. "An International Appraisal of Social Security Administration Costs." Washington, DC: World Bank, 1994.

Queisser, Monika. "Social Security Systems in South East Asia: Indonesia, the Philippines and Singapore." *International Social Security Review* 44, 1–2 (1991): 121–35.

Schwarz, Anita. "Basic Parameters of Mandatory Retirement Savings Schemes." Washington, DC: World Bank, mimeo, 1992.

Schwarz, Anita and Dimitri Vittas. "Policy Issues in Pension Guarantees." Washington, DC: World Bank, mimeo, 1992.

Turner, John and Daniel Beller. *Trends in Pensions* (annual). Washington, DC: US Department of Labor, 1989.

U.S. Social Security Administration. *Social Security Programs Throughout the World — 1991.* Washington, DC: U.S. GPO, 1993.

Valdés-Prieto, Salvador and Rudrigo Cifuentes. "Credit Constraints and Pensions." Santiago: Catholic University of Chile, working paper, 1993.

Valdés-Prieto, Salvador. "Administrative Costs in the Chilean Pension System: Evidence from an International Comparison." Washington, DC: World Bank Policy Research Department, 1993.

———. "Distributive Concerns When Substituting for a Pay-as-You-Go Scheme with a Fully Funded Pension System." *Revista de Analisis Economico* 9, 1 (1994): 77–103.

Vittas, Dimitri. "The Simple(r) Algebra of Pension Plans." Washington, DC: World Bank Policy Research Department WPS 1154. (1992a)

———. "Contractual Savings and Emerging Securities Markets." Washington, DC: World Bank Policy Research Department WPS 858. (1992b)

Vittas, Dimitri and Augusto Iglesias. "The Rationale and Performance of Personal Pension Plans in Chile." Washington, DC: World Bank Policy Research Department WPS 867, 1992.

Vittas, Dimitri and Michael Skully. "Overview of Contractual Savings Institutions." Washington, DC: World Bank Policy Research Department WPS 605, 1991.

Wagner, Gert. "La seguridad social y el programa de pension minima garantizada." *Estudios de Economia* 18, 1 (1991): 35–89.

World Bank. "Averting the Old Age Crisis: Policies to Protect the Old and Promote Growth." Washington, DC: World Bank and Oxford University Press, 1994.

Zambian National Provident Fund. *Annual Report.* Zambia.

Comments by Alan J. Auerbach

This is a difficult study to discuss because its arguments are both compelling and non-controversial. In large part, this is because the chapter never really confronts the question its title poses, namely, are mandatory saving schemes the answer to the old age security problem? What the chapter does do admirably well is to describe how these forced saving schemes work, in theory and practice, what the economic and political pitfalls are in different approaches, and how these pitfalls can be overcome. Thus, we are given a manual for how to implement a mandatory saving scheme, but remain uncertain whether we should do so, alone or in conjunction with other pension reforms. I do not mean this as a criticism of the study, but rather of the title. It is not clear exactly what the "old age security problem" is. Indeed, it is probably several things, not all of which can be addressed using mandatory saving schemes.

The chapter does answer a number of important questions about mandatory saving schemes. Among these are the following.

How can such schemes be justified?

The primary purpose of such schemes is to give workers a retirement income that is closely tied to the contributions they make while working. Unlike a defined benefit plan, in which the benefits tend to be loosely tied to any implicit or explicit worker contributions, a forced saving scheme is relatively transparent from the worker's perspective. This has the economic advantage of reducing the labor supply distortion that might be associated with systems, like the United States social security system, in which contributions and benefits are only very loosely related. It has the reinforcing political advantage of establishing property rights of workers to the accumulating assets.

How should assets of such schemes be invested?

To preserve the sense of ownership that workers have to their mandatory saving accounts, Estelle James and Dimitri Vittas stress the importance of not allowing the government favorable access to the funds. That is, there should be no forced holdings of government bonds at below market interest rates. This objective will be furthered by having private sector portfolio management.

However, there is a serious question of how much choice individual workers should have over their investment options. Even in a country like the United States, with a very developed financial system, there may be a need to provide such regulation to limit the fleecing of unsophisticated worker-savers. In a developing country, with developing financial markets, the problem is likely to be greater.

To me, though, there is an obvious solution, which James and Vittas view with ambivalence: invest most of the money abroad. In addition to the usual argument in favor of doing so — that this provides optimal portfolio diversification — there is the strong advantage of not having to worry about the shenanigans of local portfolio managers or the stability of the domestic economy. The chapter suggests at one point that such overseas investment should occur only gradually, once domestic investment opportunities have been used up. Otherwise, one of the potential advantages of forced saving, the access to more investment capital, would be lost. But this seems inconsistent with the idea of letting investors earn their best returns. Forcing them to invest domestically is only slightly less invidious than forcing them to invest in government bonds with below market returns.

How should retirement income be structured?

When workers do near retirement, there is a question of how they should receive their accumulated funds. A simple answer is to give them a lump sum and leave the decision up to them. As James and Vittas point out, though, this goes against one of the reasons for having the forced saving in the first place, that workers need protection against their own myopia. The lump sum may be spent quickly, leaving the elderly without the assets needed to finance consumption. The authors favor forcing retirees to buy an annuity with some or all of the funds. To prevent adverse selection, they advocate forcing this to be done upon retirement. But they worry about the fact that this exposes retirees to "investment risk" in the sense that, on the day their assets are converted into an annuity, the market may be "abnormally low." I am not sure what abnormal means in this context, nor do I see the obvious benefit to the "smoothing" of annuity purchases over a period of several years. But I do agree with their alternative solution, which is to allow the use of variable as well as fixed annuities. James and Vittas suggest that one problem of private annuity provision is overall longevity risk, because this cannot be pooled and may cause annuity providers to become insolvent. I do not see why this is a problem, as long as the rate paid on the annuity is allowed to vary with group mortality experience.

Can mandatory saving schemes help the current elderly?

The chapter argues that a mandatory saving scheme is, by its nature, a funded scheme. Thus, it cannot be used to bail out current retirees. Although I agree in substance, there is nothing preventing the government from issuing marketable debt as it establishes the scheme, and giving this debt to the current elderly to mimic the assets they would have accumulated had the system been in force while they were working. (See, e.g., Auerbach, Gokhale, and Kotlikoff, 1992.) Why one would wish to do so is another matter.

Can mandatory saving schemes be used for redistribution within a cohort?

James and Vittas argue that a forced saving scheme "can provide an adequate pension for middle and high income workers, but fails to protect workers with low wages as they grow old." They argue that an old age pension plan needs low income supplements to make it work. This is, of course, the philosophy behind the United States social security system, but it makes no sense to me. If an individual has low wages his or her entire life, and is forced to save the same fraction of these wages as a higher income individual, in what sense is the resulting asset accumulation inadequate? It is inadequate to provide the low wage individual the high wage individual's standard of living, but it may be perfectly adequate to maintain the low wage individual at his or her own lifetime living standard. The issue, in other words, is not old age poverty, but all poverty. Why should there be a separate program for the poor elderly? But, then, why should other countries be more rational about this issue than we have been?

In short, then, forced saving schemes can be used to insure against worker myopia or the equivalent problem of individuals purposely not saving for their old age because they believe that society will take care of them if they do not. The schemes should not be viewed as a source of cheap capital or as a means for redistributing income. However, there is significant benefit to attacking different problems with different programs. This will protect mandatory saving schemes from political pressure. It may also lead policymakers to reevaluate the logic of their different goals.

References

Auerbach, Alan J., Jagadeesh Gokhale, and Laurence J. Kotlikoff. "Social Security and Medicare Policy from the Perspective of Generational Accounting." In James M. Poterba, ed., *Tax Policy and the Economy*, 6. Cambridge, MA: MIT Press, 1992: 129–45.

Comments by Donald S. Grubbs, Jr.

This stimulating chapter provides information and ideas on mandatory savings schemes in developing countries. I also find it interesting to consider how the concepts might apply to the United States and other industrialized countries, and in turn how the experience of industrialized countries applies to developing countries (see also Watson, Salazar, and Stroinski, 1993).

Mandatory savings schemes serve the dual purposes of providing capital formation and meeting retirement income needs. James and Vittas recognize that the mandatory savings schemes leave gaps in meeting retirement income needs, and accordingly they state that such programs must be supplemented by a public program that ensures a basic income floor. They do not report the extent to which most countries that have established a mandatory savings scheme have such a public basic income floor. In the United States the social security system provides a basic income floor, and public policy encourages voluntary programs established by employers to supplement the basic income floor, but somewhat fewer than 50 percent of all private sector employees are participants in a plan of their current employer. To solve this problem in 1970 I began advocating that a mandatory supplemental program be established in the United States; in 1981 the President's Commission on Pension Policy endorsed a variation of my proposal (PCPP 1981).

Lifetime Inflation-Adjusted Incomes

A primary reason for having a mandatory system is that individuals need the retirement income that it can provide. If such a system is to succeed, it must assure that the income will continue throughout the lifetime of the retiree (and the retiree's spouse where appropriate). The income needs to be one that does not increase in purchasing power during the retirement years. To the extent that retirement benefits do not continue throughout the retiree's lifetime and keep pace with inflation, a program fails in meeting human needs.

James and Vittas discuss the difficult problem facing defined contribution plans in providing such a flow of income to meet retirement needs. Many of the programs described are clearly failures in this regard. The failure of countries to adopt programs that can meet retirement income needs may be the result of faulty analysis or shortsightedness, but it should not be surprising. Many U.S. employers and individuals are following the same shortsighted approach.

Most employees are not able to convert a lump sum distribution into a lifetime income that keeps pace with inflation. Chile's alternative of providing an income for the number of years in the retiree's life expectancy may leave about half of retirees destitute in their later years.

It was encouraging to read that the marketplace in some countries has responded by making available inflation-adjusted life annuities, financed through inflation-indexed bonds. Mandatory defined contribution systems would better accomplish their objectives if they were required to make all distributions in the form of indexed life annuities, funded either with private insurers or a federal portability system. (For a discussion of how such a system might work see Grubbs 1983.)

The authors describe the "perverse redistribution" that results from pooling people with long and short life expectancies. Of course every issuance of annuities is based upon such pooling. A system may pool males and females, educated and uneducated individuals, smokers and non-smokers, overweight and average weight individuals, people of different races, healthy individuals and those with health problems, and so on. These various groups have differing life expectancies, and an argument can be made that the amount of annuity provided to each category should differ accordingly. While not recognizing all such differences in experience can arguably be termed "redistribution," it is not necessarily perverse. Women, for example, have as much need for monthly income as men. Making determinations of which distinctions in life expectancy to recognize and which not to recognize, and making determinations of who is in which group and how much annuities should vary for each group, can waste dollars in administration that would be better spent providing benefits, and can create as many inequities as it relieves.

Governmental or Private Operation of the Programs

The programs described by the authors are defined contribution plans that fall into two categories: "provident funds" administered by the government and privately managed programs. The privately managed programs are invested primarily in corporate stocks and bonds, while the provident funds are invested in governmental obligations that have been less effective in contributing to long-term saving and capital market development and that have generally provided lower rates of return. The authors indicate that investment in governmental securities is a disadvantage of provident funds. Apparently none of the developing countries have tried having a governmentally administered program invested in private sector investments and the authors do not discuss this possible alternative. In the United States we have two examples of governmental investment of pension funds in private sector investments, the trust funds of terminated pension funds being administered by the Pension Benefit Guaranty Corporation and the Thrift Savings Plan for federal employees.

The authors report that Malaysia and Singapore have allowed the provident funds and equivalent private plans to operate side by side, but that in practice most private plans have been absorbed into the provident funds. It would be helpful to know why most employers have elected to use the provident funds, and to consider designing a program that would encourage both programs to operate simultaneously. This has a parallel to the United Kingdom and Japan, which allow employers to contract out of the public program if they provide equivalent benefits. If contracting out is permitted, it would be logical also to allow contracting out by employers with defined benefit plans that provide equivalent benefits.

Contribution Rates, Benefit Levels and Rates of Return

James and Vittas's first table shows that a program that indexes pensions to inflation, that has a passivity rate (ratio of payout years to accumulation years) of one-third and a zero real rate of return requires contributions of 13 percent of pay to provide pensions of 40 percent of the final rate of pay, but would require contributions of 20 percent if the passivity rate were one-half. The United States social security system is fairly comparable, since workers who work 45 years and retire at age 65 have a passivity rate of about $1/2.5$ and receive benefits that have a median of approximately 43 percent of pay (decreasing to about 37 percent for future retirees). Costs of the OASI (Old Age and Survivor Insurance) program are currently 10.2 percent of pay but are projected to increase to 16.1 percent in 75 years. Thus the benefits and costs of the OASI program are roughly comparable to the benefits and contributions shown for the mandatory savings scheme with a zero real rate of return. However, their Table 1 shows that, if the real rate of return can be increased to 2 percent, required contributions are cut approximately in half. Thus maximizing the rate of return within acceptable levels of risk is extremely important for the funded system.

Investment in Government Securities

James and Vittas state that, by investing in government securities, the provident funds receive lower returns and "can involve capital and labor market distortions and capricious redistributions similar to those in many public defined benefit plans." Lower returns are a natural concomitant of low risk securities, but investing in government bonds does not necessarily affect capital and labor markets significantly differently than investing in corporate bonds. While any significant economic program distorts capital and labor markets from what they would otherwise be, such distortions can have both positive and negative effects. In the United States, for example, the social security system has tended be a stabilizing factor in the economy, helping slightly to reduce the erratic swings in capital and labor markets. The redistributions of such programs are usually not capricious, but are intentional and carefully planned.

The trust funds of the United States social security system are invested in United States government securities, but this has little effect upon the total outstanding governmental securities. The total outstanding governmental securities must be sufficient to finance the excess of governmental expense over governmental income. If the social security system's trust funds were to switch from purchasing United States government bond to purchasing corporate bonds, the Treasury would merely have to sell more bonds in the public marketplace. The greater demand for corporate bonds and lower demand for governmental bonds would tend to decrease interest rates for corporate bonds and increase interest rates for government bonds. Greater investment returns of the social security system's trusts would reduce the cost of the social security system, but higher interest rates on government bonds would increase the general revenue expense. Thus by purchasing government bonds instead of private sector securities, social security systems and provident funds tend to subsidize general revenues.

However, the authors were not discussing this minor subsidy through interest rates, but rather the tendency of some governments actually to spend more because the provident funds provide the facility to finance government debt. The authors apparently believe that this facility has reduced a discipline that would otherwise restrain governmental spending in some countries, and I assume that there is a basis for this assertion. On the other hand, if government spending is required for development and other needs and if the government has limited ability to finance its debt, this facility may enable the government to make needed expenditures that it would not otherwise be able to make. In addition, financing part of the government's debt through the provident funds will help hold down the interest rate not only on the debt held by the provident fund but on all the government's debt. Any government must balance the advantages and disadvantages of these approaches.

Other Investment Considerations

For privately managed investments, the authors point to the advantage of investing in foreign assets to provide diversification. This also introduces an exchange rate risk, particularly if there is a possibility that the currency of the investing country will generally become stronger in the future. This is not a reason to exclude foreign investments, but it is a consideration in deciding how extensive they should be.

The chapter describes the problems of decentralized private investment, which include malfeasance and the regulatory burden of attempting to control it, the additional expense resulting from individuals' switching back and forth between competing funds, and the charges for commissions and other selling costs. All such problems can be avoided by utilizing a single governmentally administered fund invested in private sector investments, the approach taken in the United States by the trust funds of terminated pension funds being administered by the Pension Benefit Guaranty Corporation and the Thrift Savings Plan for federal employees.

The Thrift Savings Plan invests in equities using the index fund method. This method not only reduces investment expenses but in most periods produces higher rates of return than most actively managed pension funds. It also removes the government from political considerations in making investment decisions. Some developing countries may lack a suitable index for this approach.

Because of the fungibility of assets, whether an additional dollar of retirement savings is invested in government bonds or private sector investments may have little effect on the allocation of capital. If the new dollar is invested in government bonds, that amount of bonds will not be purchased by other investors, who will then have one more dollar available for private sector investments. This will not be the case, however, if the purchase of government bonds causes the government to make more total expenditures and to issue more bonds.

The authors raise the specter of backdoor socialism if a governmental program controls private sector investments, and particularly if it exercises control through voting rights. This is usually not a problem with debt instruments. The problem can be avoided for equities if the government avoids voting its stock.

The authors list potential problems if employees are not permitted to make investment choices. In my opinion most employees would be better served by having diversified investments made either by professional portfolio managers of a single fund or by the index method, resulting in better gross investment results and lower sales and administrative expenses.

Conclusion

Mandatory savings schemes can provide little retirement income for those who are close to retirement at the time the program is established. Therefore a universal defined benefit system is essential to meeting retirement income needs, at least until the mandatory savings scheme has been in effect for many years. Even then, the mandatory savings scheme will be ineffective in meeting retirement income needs to the extent it does not have the following characteristics:

- universal coverage;
- mandatory application of the account balances to provide a lifetime income for the retiree, and for the retiree's spouse if applicable;
- cost of living adjustments after the pension commences.

Even if a mandatory savings scheme is not fully effective because it does not completely meet these criteria, it may still be a very valuable supplement to the basic defined benefit program of a social insurance system. For the United States such an addition would help millions of workers achieve adequate retirement incomes and would substantially increase capital formation.

References

Grubbs, Donald S. Jr. "Proposal for Mandatory Pensions." *Actuary* 4, 3 (1970).
———. "Vesting and a Federal Portable Pension System." *Journal of Pension Planning and Compliance* 9, 5 (1983).
Watson, Charles, Camilo Salazar, and Krzysztof Stroinski. "Privatization of Social Security Programs." *Record* 19, 1B(1993): 721–40. Schaumburg, IL: Society of Actuaries.
President's Commission on Pension Policy (PCPP). *Coming of Age: Toward a National Retirement Income Policy*. Washington, DC: President's Commission, 1981.

Chapter 6
Private Pension Systems in Transition Economies

John A. Turner and David M. Rajnes

In many countries around the world, a debate is occurring over the structure of retirement income systems. Following the downfall of communism, countries in central and eastern Europe are considering private pensions to complement their state-run social security systems. In these countries and elsewhere, the state social security retirement income systems face severe financial problems caused by benefits that are overly generous and entitlement rules that allow eligibility at too young an age. In response to the heavy burden on government, private pension systems are seen as reducing the government spending needed to support an increasingly elderly society.

Establishing private pension systems in countries where they have not existed has proven to be difficult. Major institutional changes needed to establish private pension systems may be dependent on other financial institutions' being developed first.

This chapter provides analysis and a new perspective on issues surrounding the development of private pension systems. Recognizing that there are major differences between countries, the chapter considers within a general framework the initial steps toward establishing private pension systems. The development of a private pension system also needs to consider the particular situation of individual countries. This chapter draws its examples from central and eastern Europe, but much of the analysis is applicable for other countries.

Private pension systems, once established, tend to evolve as an experienced group of professionals develops to manage them, and as changing economic and demographic conditions warrant. Features of a new private pension system that are appropriate at the beginning stages may need to be changed later as conditions change.

In considering the development of private pension systems, two primary questions arise. First, what are the necessary preconditions before a private pension system can established? Alternatively, what is the necessary sequence in which legal, economic, and institutional developments need to occur? Second, what form should new private pension systems take?

Because of the close connection between social security and pension systems, social security retirement income reform must be addressed at the same time as private pension reform. Such reform may involve raising the minimum retirement age, eliminating special categories of beneficiaries, reducing real benefit levels, changing the benefit formula to tie benefits more closely to earnings, or alternatively moving to a flat benefit where all beneficiaries receive the same amount.[1] The complex issues of social security reform are not considered here.

Preconditions for Establishing Private Pension Systems

The private pension systems of North America, western Europe, and Japan are supported by complex legal, financial, and service provider systems. These support systems involve sophisticated institutional arrangements and highly trained specialists. These support systems appear to be prerequisites for the pension systems they support.

Factors necessary for establishing private pensions can be identified by studying the historical development of private pensions in other countries. Historical experience concerning the pension systems in other countries provides insights on ways to deal with problems arising due to the limitations of existing economic and institutional conditions.

Economic Preconditions

Capital Markets

The countries of central and eastern Europe, like many countries without private pension systems, do not have well-developed capital markets. At best, they have fledgling stock markets with few securities traded, and few regulatory safeguards found in Western countries' capital markets. Because of government subsidies of businesses and the financial instability in the economies, it is difficult for capital markets to determine accurate, stable values for financial assets and for firms.

For small countries with a limited industrial base, optimally diversified pension portfolios would have a relatively small percentage invested domestically. This pattern of pension investment is seen in another small country, the Republic of Ireland, which in the mid-1990s had a population of 3.5 million and which had pension plans with larger amounts invested in foreign equities than in domestic equities. However, the countries of central and eastern Europe do not have sufficient foreign currency to invest in foreign securities. Investment of pension funds abroad under new private pension laws in Hungary (1993) and the Czech Republic (1994) is exceedingly difficult. It is virtually impossible under the Hungarian foreign exchange regulations, while very difficult in practice under current Czech exchange restrictions (Batty, Stumpa, and Kovari 1994).

Alternative portfolio diversification options that limit domestic exposure could include investment in multinational subsidiaries, international joint venture firms, and export-oriented enterprises. The lack of domestic financial instruments and assets in which to invest and the inability to invest in foreign markets create problems for the development of funded pension systems.

The historical experience of Chile, Japan, and Germany, however, suggests that having a developed financial market is not necessarily a precondition for developing a private pension system. Chile in 1981 established a fully funded mandatory defined contribution system to replace its public defined benefit social security system. At that time, Chile had few financial assets in which its pensions plans could invest and it did not permit international investments. During the early years, private pension funds were invested almost entirely in government bonds, and subsequent demand for financial securities by Chilean pension funds encouraged development of a successful stock market.[2]

In both Japan and Germany after World War II, the banking sector and financial markets were destroyed. Nonetheless, private pensions were developed using the book reserve method of financing (Ahrend, Chapter 3, this volume, and Watanabe, Chapter 4, this volume). With this method, funds that might have been invested outside the firm are instead retained within the firm. A liability for the promised future pension benefits is then reported on the financial accounts of the firm.

Investing the pension fund entirely in the sponsoring firm entails high risk, especially in an uncertain economic environment. In Germany, this liability must be insured. Without insurance, workers may bear considerable risk because of the uncertainty surrounding the financial future of many enterprises.

Pension funds in countries developing new pension systems could invest in government bonds, as in Chile, or finance their pensions through book reserve financing, as in Japan and Germany. They could also invest in former state enterprises now being privatized. In Chile in the mid-1980s, stock in state enterprises was offered for sale on the Santiago Stock Exchange. Initially, only the large pension funds were permitted to buy it.

Chilean economists felt that only the large pension funds had sufficient financial expertise to evaluate the stocks and determine a realistic price.

Privatization — the transfer of state property to private ownership — presents unique opportunities for the development of private pensions. Significant progress has been made almost everywhere in central and eastern Europe in privatizing small firms, although privatizing larger enterprises has proceeded more slowly (Slay 1993).

Besides directly purchasing stock, pension funds could invest in newly privatized enterprises through mutual funds or investment funds. Such investment funds would be able to assist people in investing privatization vouchers that they had received (either distributed freely or purchased). Instead of themselves selecting a firm or firms in which to invest, people could exchange their vouchers against the shares of these specialized financial institutions, which would invest the public's vouchers for them. Such a system provides investment diversification, as funds would invest in dozens of companies. In effect, the government creates shares in enterprises that it wishes to privatize, selling or giving those shares to individuals or mutual funds. In this way, pension funds could also buy or be granted mutual fund shares.

Privatization through the distribution of free vouchers has occurred in the former Czechoslovakia, and continued in the Czech Republic and Slovakia. In the Czech Republic and Slovakia, the shares of privatized firms are held by large Investment Privatization Funds. Individuals own shares in these funds through their vouchers (International Monetary Fund 1994). Such funds have been proposed in Poland. One of the most extensive programs so far is in Russia, where the government has encouraged capitalism by giving away most state property, issuing 144 million vouchers free to citizens.

Pension funds can play an important role in privatizing an economy, as they did in Chile, because of their financial expertise and because their funds create a demand for a financial market (James and Vittas, Chapter 5, this volume). Thus, rather than arguing that capital markets must precede the development of private pension funds, this approach suggests that pension funds will create a demand for capital markets. Conversely, the prevalence of book reserve financing by German pension funds, which can be used in the absence of well-developed capital markets, may explain the relatively small stock market in that country.

Inflation

In many central and eastern European countries, inflation during the early years of the economic transition was high and variable. In some countries, this problem has declined considerably. For example, Poland's annual inflation rate was 251 percent in 1989, 586 percent in 1990, 70 percent in 1991, 43 percent in 1992, 35 percent in 1993, and estimated to be 27 percent in 1994 (International Monetary Fund 1994). High and unpredictable inflation rates create uncertainty for both firms and savers. This environment penalizes savers when interest rates do not reflect an inflation premium (as in those administratively set).

If inflation is not to destroy a funded pension system, such a system must invest in assets that preserve their value in an inflationary market. Generally, equities preserve their value in an inflationary environment, provided the tax system does not cause the relative tax burden on equities to increase with inflation.

Alternatively, as was done in Chile, the government could offer inflation-indexed bonds. That was facilitated by the Chilean government's inflation-indexing the tax system and other aspects of the economy. Although inflation-indexed bonds have desirable features, few governments offer them. Further, in the United Kingdom where they have been offered, few pension plans have used them, presumably because the liabilities for active workers are generally effectively indexed by wages rather than prices.

Interest Rates

As well as determining the value of assets, capital markets determine the present value of liabilities for benefit payments due in the future. In countries where interest rates are not determined by the market but are administratively set, problems can arise. The combination of administered interest rates and decontrolled prices with widely fluctuating inflation rates can lead to wide fluctuations in real interest rates (Korczyk 1993). During 1990, for example, the real interest rate on low risk lending in Poland ranged from +75 percent during the low inflation early part of the year to about −300 percent during the high—inflation latter part of the year (OECD 1992). In such a situation, it is difficult to determine stable economic values for assets and liabilities because market-based valuations vary considerably.

Real Income

Real income in the central and eastern European countries declined during the early part of the transition phase from communism to a market economy. During a period of declining real income, workers are unlikely to save for future consumption. Rather, in an attempt to maintain their former level of consumption, they will dissave. Thus, a period of declining real income is not a good time to start a mandatory funded pension system, but a voluntary system could be launched.

Institutional Preconditions

As well as economic preconditions for the development of private pensions, several institutional preconditions may need to be established.

Social Security

In many central and eastern European countries, social security reform is urgently needed because of the high costs of the existing systems. The seriousness of that problem suggests to some analysts that social security reform should be the top priority in the retirement income area; thereafter, private pension reform would be considered. However, reductions in real social security benefits and postponement of age of eligibility will be more easily achieved if a private pension alternative is available to workers (Fox 1994).

The Legal System

Many of the countries of central and eastern Europe do not have legal systems that clearly protect individual property rights and that establish legal rights in bankruptcy. It has been argued that laws governing prudence, self-dealing, and other aspects of fiduciary behavior, and concerning settlement of property disputes and bankruptcies are necessary prerequisites to developing of a funded private pension system (Korczyk 1993). These protections need to be established to reduce financial risks, and until they are, uncertainty about prospective changes in the legal system add to the uncertainties facing individuals and firms.

Regulation

Because of the money that accumulates in pension plans, these funds may be the target of theft and fraud. To prevent financial malfeasance from jeopardizing the retirement income of many people and shaking public confidence in a newly established private pension system, financial safeguards must be established at an early stage.

Pension fund regulators in Western countries rely on other regulators, such as those governing investment markets and financial institutions. In most central and eastern European countries, the regulation of banks, stocks and bonds, and insurance markets is in its early stages.

The Chilean experience, however, demonstrates that pension reform can be started without having a sound regulatory structure in place (Diamond and Valdés-Prieto 1994). Modern bank regulation was not fully operational in that nation until 1982, a year after the pension reform had been implemented. Reforms to the securities and corporation laws were passed in 1981. Later during the 1980s and 1990s, financial reform occurred several times, in part in response to the growth of pension funds.

Trained Personnel

The sophisticated private pension systems found in the United States, Japan, and other developed countries depend on the services of actuaries, accountants and auditors, financial management experts, attorneys, and computer specialists. Decentralized fund management requires more trained personnel than centralized fund management. While decentralized fund management may be more efficient than centralized management in developed countries (Davis, Chapter 8, this volume), that only applies in economies with an ample supply of trained personnel. Countries developing a new pension system can economize on skilled personnel by initially limiting the number of alternatives for fund management. Foreign expertise can also substitute for the lack of domestic expertise while domestic expertise is being developed. The Hungarian-American Enterprise Fund provides an example, where Western experts initially were used to evaluate the projects the fund invested in.

Policy Options

In considering policy options, any proposal for a private pension system should:

- Reduce the fiscal burden on the government,
- Protect the security of retirement benefits,
- Maintain regulatory simplicity, and
- Be politically acceptable.

Any proposal that is not politically sustainable is ultimately self-defeating. While this chapter does not directly analyze the political acceptability of proposals, all the proposals it considers are policies that have been implemented in other countries, and thus have met the test of political acceptability at least in the context of one country.

This section draws on the experience of a number of countries in considering specific proposals for dealing with problems that arise in developing private pension systems. It concludes with a timetable suggesting an ordering of policy developments.

Financing the Transition

The transition from a retirement income system with only a pay-as-you-go social security system to a system where social security has a reduced role and there is a funded private pension system is generally difficult because of the paying twice problem. The "paying twice" problem is the situation facing the transitional working generation that must set aside savings to fund its own future benefits, while at the same time paying for the existing social security system, which is financed on a pay-as-you-go basis.

The double payment burden of the transition can be eased. First, if the new system is phased in gradually, the burden is spread over a longer time period and thus over more tax-paying cohorts.

Second, an abrupt transition from a pay-as-you-go social security system to a funded private pension system could be financed, as was done in Chile, by the issuance of government bonds. Workers having past service credits in the old social security system were issued these bonds to compensate them for their past service credits. The bonds are interest-bearing but no payments can be made until the worker reaches retirement. The bonds are financed out of general revenues. By postponing the payments, the Chilean government has been able to spread out the cash payments required to finance the transition to its funded pension system (Diamond and Valdés-Prieto 1994).

Third, in Chile the transition was also financed by a surplus in the government's general revenues. The Chilean government, in anticipation of costs of transition from a pay-as-you-go to a funded retirement income system, purposively accumulated a government surplus in its general revenues. For most countries, this is not a feasible option. An alternative to that approach is to build up a surplus in the social security trust funds. While these approaches are available to some countries, neither are available to the countries of central and eastern Europe because of the financial strains on their government budgets and social security funds.

Fourth, revenues from government-owned assets or proceeds from their sale can be used to finance the government's past-service pension obligations (Jenkins 1992). Argentina in 1994 helped finance the transition to a partially privatized system by the sale of government-owned enterprises.

Normally the establishment of funded pension plans that provide meaningful benefits takes decades because of the large sums that must be accumulated to pay benefits over a worker's retirement years. The assets of socialized enterprises, however, can be used to make up for the lack of initial assets in the pension funds (Holzmann 1993; Hanke 1991).

Fifth, in addition to government policies to ease the transition, supporting changes may occur in the private sector. To the extent that generations are connected by intergenerational transfers, the shift in assets between generations that occurs during the transition to a partially privatized system can be offset by private intergenerational transfers. The transition generation can adjust by making fewer private intergenerational transfers, and other generations can increase their transfers to the transition generation. To the extent that generations are linked by private intergenerational transfers, such adjustments may naturally occur.

Financial Incentives

In a market economy, the primary force driving economic development is financial incentive. In all countries with well-developed private pension systems, a major factor in the development of those systems has been tax incentives.

Personal income tax systems are envisaged in all countries of central and eastern Europe. They have already been implemented in Hungary (1988) and Poland (1992), and by the Czech Republic (1993) and Slovakia (1993). Tax incentives for pensions are generally provided through the tax exemption of contributions and investment returns of the pension funds. The taxation of pension plans generally takes the form of taxation of benefits (Dilnot, Chapter 6, this volume). The 1993 Hungarian private pension law takes this form. In an interesting variation to this approach, the Czech Republic provides matching funds to encourage pension growth.

Postponing taxation of pensions until benefits are received reduces the short-run cash flow for the government. In the transition economies, which are facing governmental cash flow problems, deferral of tax payments may pose a problem for the governments.

Alternatively stated, the deferral until retirement of taxes on pensions implies a loan by the public sector to the private sector, thereby enlarging the fiscal deficit. The loan is equivalent to the taxes that would have otherwise been paid but that are, in effect, given back to the worker in exchange for their repayment at retirement. At the same time, private individuals need to save more in order to meet their future income tax payments on their pension benefits while maintaining their after-tax pension benefits. Therefore, if private sector workers anticipate future tax payments, private pension saving and other saving should in effect compensate for part of the public dissaving (Holzmann 1993). However, the populations in central and eastern Europe, because of the expectation of rising incomes, wish to consume more now than their current income permits but are prevented from doing so because of the difficulty of borrowing against expected future income. In light of this liquidity constraint, it seems unlikely that the private sector will compensate for potential public dissaving. Thus, the phasing in of private pensions supported by tax incentives may initially decrease rather than increase national savings. In the early phases of the transition, the introduction of tax incentives for pensions may be too expensive for government budgets. However, the effect of not introducing tax incentives is that the private pension system will be an unimportant source of retirement income.

Social Security

The generosity of social security benefits limits the development of private pension plans. This occurs particularly if benefits are generous for individuals at higher income levels (Davis, Chapter 8, this volume). Therefore, a first step toward developing private pensions is to limit social security benefits at higher income levels. This could be done by not providing cost of living adjustments in retirement for social security benefits above a certain level, as was done in Hungary. It could also be done, as in Ireland, by providing a flat social security benefit to all workers.

A Decentralized Competitive System for Pension Asset Management

In a decentrally managed competitive system for pension asset management, workers and firms pick their own management company from a number of management companies. They can transfer their accounts from one management company to another. Decentralized management systems are less vulnerable to pressure to invest pension funds for political reasons than are government-run centrally managed systems (James and Vittas, Chapter 5, this volume).

The governments of central and eastern Europe currently do not have personnel with the requisite training for regulating pension funds and financial markets. For this reason, the transition economy countries should probably have their newly established pension funds managed by large financial management firms controlling the assets of numerous individual pension fund accounts, as is done in Chile. With this structure for managing pension funds, regulatory authorities only have a few large entities to oversee.

This is the thinking of the Czech government, which is stressing a small number of large funds that can easily be supervised. That approach is quite different from the Hungarian approach, where there is a desire to establish a significant number of Voluntary Mutual Benefit Funds (VMBFs) for the employees of individual companies. But even in the Hungarian approach, employer-specific plans are not the sole method available. Funds can be established on a regional, occupational, or trade basis (Batty, Stumpa, and Kovari et al. 1994).

Chilean Pension Portfolio Regulations

Two approaches can be used to regulate private pension investments. The first approach, used by the United States and the United Kingdom, is the "prudent man rule." This approach places few specific restrictions on allowable investments. Instead, pension plan managers are required to diversify their asset holdings and in all other respects to invest plan assets consistently with what would be done by a prudent person acting in such circumstances. Failure to perform carries civil and possibly criminal penalties.

The second approach places specific maximum and possibly minimum restrictions on the percentage of a pension portfolio that may be invested in certain types of assets. This approach is used by Chile, Japan, and many other countries. The second approach gives plans less flexibility in deciding their investments. It is, however, a simpler approach for regulators to monitor and for that reason may be preferable.

Hungarian pension law follows this second approach. It lays down strict provisions as to the proportions that can be invested in four classes of assets rated by risk factor (Batty, Stumpa, and Kovari et al. 1994). Czech restrictions, by contrast, do not limit types of investments but focus on the permissible investments in a particular company or particular share issue.

British-Style Voluntary Personal Pension Plans

An early step toward developing pension institutions and capital markets is to allow voluntary tax-deductible personal pension plans. To limit the tax revenue lost, a restriction should be placed on tax-deductible contributions, such as 15 percent of earnings up to a fixed ceiling amount, with a flat minimum amount that exceeded 15 percent of earnings for low earners. These pensions are simple to administer and do not impede labor mobility.

An alternative would be to allow such pensions in conjunction with partial contracting out, as is done in the United Kingdom (Daykin, Chapter 2, this volume). For example, workers could reduce their social security tax payments by a small amount if they contributed to a personal pension. Administratively, this could be handled by the employee's requesting that at the end of the tax year that amount be transferred to his or her personal pension account.

A Voluntary or a Compulsory System

An option for developing a private pension system involves establishing a universal mandatory savings system as a second tier in the retirement income system. This savings plan would supplement or replace a traditional defined benefit social security system (Fox 1994). The savings plan would be similar to that found in Chile. France, Switzerland, Australia, and Sweden also have compulsory national private funded pension systems. At least 20 countries have compulsory provident funds, or forced savings funds (James and Vittas, Chapter 5, this volume). The two private systems currently operating in the central and east European region — Czech and Hungarian — are both voluntary. A voluntary system is politically appealing to some people because it provides freedom of choice.

A mandatory funded pension system or a mandatory provident fund system would accumulate a large amount of funds. That would strain the financial and regulatory systems of those countries. At the same time, the potential for dynamic interaction between rapidly accumulating pension funds and the financial sector should not be overlooked.

Contracting Out by Employers Meeting Japanese Criteria

Both Japan and the United Kingdom allow employers to contract out of the social security system. In these countries, employers and employees can reduce their social security tax payments, and in exchange, the employer provides a private pension plan that meets certain requirements. While all employers and all employees in the United Kingdom are permitted to contract out, in Japan only large employers or groups of employers may do so, provided that they meet profitability and other requirements. The Japanese approach to contracting out could be adopted. For example, employers of 5,000 or more employees would be eligible if they had growing or stable workforces for the previous three years and had earned a profit for the previous three years. These employers could then reduce their social security payroll tax payments. Such a system would only be available to economically stable firms, but it would allow a small reduction in the total size of the social security system.

German Vesting Rules

Defined benefit plans are generally not portable, meaning that workers who change jobs receive lower benefits than do workers who stay with one employer. Lack of portability may create a barrier to efficient labor market adjustment. During the economic transition, many workers need to change jobs as the economies restructure. During the transition period the accumulated value of pension benefits, and the associated barrier to mobility caused by their loss, would be small.

The development of employer-based defined benefit pensions creates longterm employer liabilities. These liabilities could make it more difficult to restructure enterprises during the transition (Fox 1994). In addition, enterprises will become bankrupt or cease to exist during the transition, which implies that pension promises may not be kept. This phenomenon can prompt calls for pension insurance with its attendant dangers (Pesando, Chapter 9, this volume).

If mandatory vesting were set at 10 years, for the first few years of participation pension plans would have little effect on labor mobility because the date of vesting would be sufficiently far off. In Germany, mandatory vesting occurs at 10 years of participation in a pension plan for workers age 35 and older and 12 years for younger workers. Adoption of this vesting rule would limit the disruption from impeded job mobility or due to firm bankruptcy during the transition phase.

British Funding Rules

In the United Kingdom, full funding is only required in contracted-out plans for the guaranteed minimum benefit. In a sense, book reserve funding may be used for benefit amounts above that level. The funding and capital market requirements of new pension plans could be eased initially by requiring only that funding cover a minimum level of benefits provided by defined benefit private pension plans. Workers would be informed of the funding level of their plan and would understand that, for unfunded benefits above the minimum level, they faced greater risks.

Defined Benefit and Defined Contribution Plans

Defined benefit and defined contribution plans have desirable features for different types of workers and firms. The choice between them need not be made by the government but can be left to individuals and firms. While defined benefit plans are more complex to administer and regulate, those problems are not insurmountable. Many of the complications of defined benefit plans are related to their providing annuities. A simplified form of defined benefit plan could be initially offered, for example one that only paid benefits for a fixed number of years.

Defined contribution plans, however, have qualities that commend their use (Holzmann 1991). They do not require a great number of financial professionals nor comprehensive government regulations. Sophisticated financial markets would also be unnecessary, since defined contribution plans could incorporate the distribution of privatized assets through vouchers. Important to the transformation process as well is the fact that defined contribution plans would not create impediments to enterprise restructuring because the defined contribution plans would be unrelated to firm liabilities. They would also not create an obstacle to labor mobility since they would be portable. Hungarian Voluntary Mutual Benefit Funds are expected to be predominantly defined contribution plans. The Czech law does not yet allow for defined benefit plans.

The Chilean Model

The success of pension reform in Chile, combined perhaps with cultural affinity, has caused that approach to appeal to other Latin American countries. That approach has also been recommended by some pension consultants for central and eastern Europe. In Chile, all new entrants to the labor force, except the self-employed, must establish an individual account pension plan to which they contribute a minimum of 10 percent of their earnings, up to a maximum level of earnings that is roughly five times the average salary of all covered workers. The self-employed can participate voluntarily. Participants in the old social security system have the option of continuing in that system or joining the new system.[3]

This mandatory funded defined contribution pension system replaces the traditional defined benefit social security system in Chile. An additional contribution pays for administrative expenses, disability insurance, and pre-retirement survivors benefits. Employees wishing to contribute more to their accounts may do so. The funds must be invested with investment management companies that have been established solely for the purpose of managing the individual account pension plans. These companies are regulated by the national government.

Most social security systems redistribute income toward low income workers. The Chilean pension system also has that feature in that it guarantees a minimum pension that is funded through general revenues. To the extent that the individual's account is insufficient to provide the minimum, the difference is made up from general revenues.

In traditional defined benefit pension systems, the financial market risk is borne primarily by the employer. In the Chilean pension system, the financial risk is borne primarily by the worker. However, if the pension fund earns a rate of return substantially below that earned on average by all funds, the management company must bear some of the risk. Larger employers are presumably better able to bear pension fund risk because they can pool the risks that many workers with different retirement dates would face individually.

The Chilean pension system provides less diversification than mixed pension systems that also contain defined benefit plans and social security pay-as-you-go plans. It also provides less freedom of choice than do other pension systems.

Pension Benefit Insurance

Most countries have not established pension benefit insurance programs. Most countries with such programs have experienced serious problems.[4] In addition, countries with pension benefit insurance programs have adopted regulations whose primary purpose is to protect the insurance programs. Some of these regulations have restricted the investment options of pension plans in ways that otherwise would not need to have been restricted (Davis, Chapter 8, this volume). There are alternative regulatory frameworks that can be established to protect pension benefits. For example, the funding level of pension plans can be regulated to maintain minimum funding levels. In addition, workers should be informed on a regular basis as to the funding level of their pension plan.

Begin Slowly and Have Realistic Expectations

Because the countries starting new pension systems are inexperienced in managing private pension systems, they may make mistakes in the early stages. For that reason, new pension systems should be developed initially on a modest scale. They should be simple to understand, to administer, and to regulate.

Private pension systems for central and eastern Europe have been criticized because they will cover only part of the labor force. This could increase income inequality. Voluntary private pension systems in practice nearly always cover less than half of the labor force (Daily and Turner 1992). Private pension systems are generally designed to provide retirement income to middle and upper income workers. This fact should be realized so that unrealistic expectations as to coverage levels are not raised.

An Approach Toward Implementation

Table 1 outlines a proposal for the steps to take in developing a private pension system. The essence of this proposal is training for government and private sector pension professionals and incentives to private sector individuals and firms for establishing pensions. The proposal divides the development of a private pension system into three phases.

TABLE 1   Timetable for Establishing an Employer-Provided Private
            Pension System

Phase I
- Limit inflation through macroeconomic policy, deregulate interest rates
- Train pension personnel — development of human capital
- Draft and discuss pension reform proposals and alternatives
- Establish a personal income tax system
- Gradually increase social security retirement age and eliminate special categories of social securities benefits

Phase II
- Establish voluntary individual pension accounts that receive preferential tax treatment
- Establish several pension management firms
- Grant tax exemption for pension contributions and investment earnings
- Reduce the real level of social security benefits for middle and upper income workers
- Establish the regulatory framework for pension management firms

Phase III
- Draft pension law with preferential tax treatment or subsidy for pensions

---

In the first phase, some preconditions are established. We assume that a transitional economic reform plan is being implemented. This would include macroeconomic policies to address inflationary pressures and to promote factor and product markets, new social safety net institutions, removal of foreign exchange restrictions, and institutional and legal measures to establish property rights and allow for the privatization of state assets. With this body of generally accepted policy prescriptions implemented, movement to study private pension alternatives, train pension personnel, and reform the social security system should quickly follow.

In the second phase, a simplified voluntary individual pension system is established. The monetary and financial sector reforms introduced during the first phase allow functioning banks and insurance companies to develop. Incentives built into the tax code for corporations and individuals are intended to stimulate economic agents to establish private pensions in an increasingly flexible labor market.

In the third phase, a framework for an employer-provided pension system is established. We have suggested features such a system might include.

Conclusion

Using the experience of other countries with private pension systems as a guide, as well as Hungary and the Czech Republic, small steps could be taken immediately in central and eastern Europe and elsewhere to start the development of private pension systems. Taking these steps will have a number of immediate benefits. First, they will make social security reform easier. Second, they will aid in privatization of state enterprises. Third, they will aid in the development of financial markets. Fourth, they will develop an understanding and appreciation of market institutions among the citizenry. Fifth, they will be a positive step toward greater financial security in retirement.

This chapter is the responsibility of the authors and does not represent the position of any institution with which they are associated. The work on this chapter was undertaken while Turner was a Senior Fulbright Scholar at the Institut de Recherches Economiques et Sociales in France.

Notes

[1]Tying benefits to earnings would make social security into a mandatory savings program with no redistributive aspect. Providing a flat benefit would change social security into a purely redistributive program with high earners contributing more but receiving the same amount as low earners.

[2]Diamond and Valdés-Prieto (1994) provide a good description of the Chilean pension system.

[3]The Chilean pension system is described in Hanke (1991), Myers (1992), and Santamaria (1992).

[4]See Pesando (Chapter 9, this volume), Weaver (Chapter 9, this volume), and Turner (1993) concerning the United States.

References

Ahrend, Peter. "Pension Financial Security in Germany." This volume.

Batty, Iain, Radomil Stumpa, and Istvan Kovari. "Pension Reform in Eastern Europe." *Benefits and Compensation International* (May 1994): 8–14.

Daily, Lorna and John A. Turner. "U.S. Pensions in World Perspective, 1970–89." In John A. Turner and Daniel Beller, eds., *Trends in Pensions 1992*. Washington, DC: U.S. GPO, 1992: 11–34.

Daykin, Christopher D. "Occupational Pension Provision in the United Kingdom." This volume.

Davis, E. Philip. "An International Comparison of the Financing of Occupational Pensions." This volume.

Diamond, Peter and Salvador Valdés-Prieto. "Social Security Reforms." In Barry Bosworth, Rudiger Dornbusch, and Raul Laban, eds., *The Chilean Economy: Policy Lessons and Challenges*. Washington, DC: Brookings Institution, 1994: 257–320.

Dilnot, Andrew. "The Taxation of Private Pensions." This volume.

Fox, Louise. "What To Do About Pensions in Transition Economies?" *Transition* 5 (February–March 1994): 3–6.

Hanke, Steve. "Private Social Security: The Key to Reform in Eastern Europe." *Contingencies* (July/August 1991): 18–21.

Holzmann, Robert. "The Provision of Complimentary Pensions: Objectives, Forms and Constraints." *International Social Security Review* 44 (January/February 1991): 75–93.

Holzmann, Robert. "Reforming Old-Age Pensions Systems in Central and Eastern European Countries in Transition." *Journal of Economics* Supplement 7 (1993): 191–218.

IBIS. "Multinationals Prefer Risk Benefits in Slow Entry Into Eastern Europe." *IBIS Review* (December 1992): 36–37.

International Monetary Fund. *World Economic Outlook.* Washington, DC: International Monetary Fund, 1994.

James, Estelle and Dimitri Vittas. "Mandatory Saving Schemes: Are They an Answer to the Old Age Security Problem?" This volume.

Jenkins, Glenn. "Privatization and Pension Reform in Transition Economies." *Public Finance* 47 (Supp.) (1992): 141–51.

Korczyk, Sophie. "Prospects for Private Pensions in Poland, the Former Czech and Slovak Federal Republic, and Bulgaria." Washington, DC: Report to the U.S. Department of Labor Pension and Welfare Benefits Administration, January 28, 1993.

Myers, Robert. "Chile's Social Security Reform, After Ten Years." *Benefits Quarterly* 8 (Third Quarter 1992): 41–55.

Organization for Economic Cooperation and Development (OECD). *Poland 1992.* Paris: OECD, 1992.

Pesando, James E. "The Government's Role in Insuring Pensions." This volume.

Santamaria, Marco. "Privatizing Social Security: The Chilean Case." *Columbia Journal of World Business* (Spring 1992): 38–51.

Slay, Ben. "Roundtable: Privatization in Eastern Europe." *RFE/RL Research Report* 2 (August 1993).

Turner, John A. "U.S. Pension Benefit Insurance." *Benefits Quarterly* 9 (January 1993): 77–85.

Watanabe, Noriyasu. "Private Pension Plans in Japan." This volume.

Weaver, Carolyn L. Comment on "The Government's Role in Insuring Pensions." This volume.

III
Instruments of Pension Policy

Chapter 7
The Taxation of Private Pensions

Andrew Dilnot

As governments throughout the developed world faced up to growing pressure on public finances in the 1980s and 1990s, one natural question has been whether more tax could be raised from the pension sector. Alongside the desire to raise more revenue, there have been some tax reformers who have called for a broader tax base and lower tax rates, while others have argued for special tax privileges in an attempt to boost saving. Contributions to private pensions represent a major part of private sector savings flows, and thus their taxation must fit sensibly with the taxation of other forms of saving. Where private pensions are based on funds, as is typically true within the Organization for Economic Cooperation and Development (OECD), the pension funds are of enormous importance as suppliers of capital to industry; any taxation must aim to avoid distorting the capital market. And, finally, private pensions are an important and growing source of retirement income. The taxation of pension benefits should aim to distort choices as little as possible for the retired, and in particular should not necessarily distort the decision as to the mix of benefits to be taken between lump sum and pension. All these are complex issues; the aim of this chapter is to attempt to highlight areas where discussion and debate are needed rather than to define answers.

We begin by examining the range of possible tax regimes in which private pensions might operate. Next we describe the tax systems for private pensions in a number of countries, and consider alternative aims for a tax system as it affects retirement saving. Possible routes to raising additional revenue from private pensions for those countries at present giving substantial relief are evaluated along with the debate over tax expenditures.

Taxing the Provision of Private Pensions

Three main transactions constitute most private pension plans, and it is these transactions that are the possible occasions for taxation:

- Contributions into the scheme, from employer or employee
- Income derived from the investment of contributions
- Payment of retirement benefits from the accumulated fund.

As we discuss in the following section, there are examples within the OECD of regimes that tax pensions at almost every conceivable combination of these points. However, certain possible combinations are more common than others, and certain combinations characterize alternative ideals for the tax system.

Table 1 illustrates four possible tax regimes, describing them in terms of whether tax is imposed at each of the three possible points. Thus the EET regime is exempt taxed. We assume for these examples that there is a single income tax rate of 25 percent, that the rate of return that can be earned on investment is 10 percent, and that we are considering a single contribution derived from earned income of 100, five years before retirement.

Regime A: Tax Free Contributions and Fund Income, Taxed Benefits (EET)

This regime allows deductibility of pension contributions from taxable income, allowing the whole 100 of earnings into the pension fund. No tax is charged on the investment income of the fund, but tax is charged in full on withdrawal. This type of tax treatment confers a post-tax rate of return on saving equal to the pre-tax rate of return. Faced with this regime an individual earning 100 can either choose to spend now, paying 25 of tax and consuming goods worth 75, or save now and consume goods worth 120.79 in five years. The figure 120.79 is simply $75 \times (1.1)^5$. It is easy to think of this regime as being a way of deferring pay until retirement, and simultaneously deferring the payment of tax on that pay until retirement.

Regime B: Taxed Contributions, Tax Free Fund Income and Benefits (TEE)

This regime does not allow deductibility of contributions, thus reducing the initial size of the fund from 100 to 75. As for Regime A, investment income is free of tax. Withdrawal of retirement benefits attracts no tax. As for Regime A, this type of tax treatment preserves the equality of pre- and

TABLE 1 Alternative Tax Regimes

Characteristic	A (EET)	B (TEE)	C (TTE)	D (ETT)
Earnings	100	100	100	100
Taxes Paid	—	25	25	—
Pension Fund	100	75	75	100
Net Income Over Five Years	61.05	45.79	32.67	43.56
Fund at Retirement	161.05	120.79	107.67	143.56
Tax on Withdrawal	40.26	—	—	35.89
Benefit Withdrawn	120.79	—	120.79	107.67

Source: Author's simulation.

post-tax rates of return. In the case of Regime B it is easy to see the non-taxation of investment income that ensures this.

Regime C: Taxed Contributions, Taxed Fund Income, Tax-Free Benefits (TTE)

This regime is basically that applied to interest-bearing short-term saving in most OECD countries. There is no tax deductibility of contributions, investment income is taxed in full, and there is no tax on withdrawal of benefits, since there is no untaxed investment income. Unlike Regimes A and B, this tax treatment brings the post-tax rate of return below the pre-tax rate of return. Here, the post-tax rate of return is 7.5 percent [$107.67 = 75 \times (1.075)^5$].

Regime D: Tax Free Contributions, Taxed Fund Income, Taxed Benefits (ETT)

This regime produces the same outcome as C, and therefore the same post-tax rate of return. Taxation of benefits and exemption of contributions is substituted for taxation of contributions and exemption of benefits.

Other combinations of taxing and relieving at each of the three points are possible, and indeed exist. There are no regimes within the OECD less favorable than C, but many more favorable than A or B.

If taxing pensions were as simple as implied by the above examples, much of the complexity of both legislation and of the pensions industry itself would be unnecessary. We discuss below some of the problems associated with attempting to increase revenue in this area that are related to the complexity of pension regimes in practice. We have, for example, assumed that contributions can be identified. Non-contributory employer-funded schemes make this quite difficult. We have assumed that funds exist, although there are many examples of unfunded schemes and, in some countries, of effectively pay-as-you-go schemes. We have also ignored the problems of identifying investment income, in particular where the income is in the form of unrealized capital gains, and of allocating investment income to individuals in a fund held on behalf of individuals with varying marginal tax rates.

Finally, and perhaps most important, we have ignored inflation. For Regimes A and B, which do not tax investment income, inflation causes no problem; for Regimes C and D, where investment income is taxed, difficulties arise. If investment income is taxed ignoring inflation, the post-tax real return will fall still further below the pre-tax real return. Imagine that in our earlier examples 7.5 percent of the 10 percent interest rate simply reflects inflation. To maintain the real value of savings a 7.5 percent post-tax rate of return is required. The outcome of Regimes C and D was 107.67, which is precisely $75 \times (1.075)^5$. So Regimes C and D, if they ignore inflation, would in this case remove the whole of the real return. If the balance between inflation and real returns were to shift further towards inflation, Regimes C and D would confer a negative post-tax rate of return. Regimes A and B retain their characteristic of real pre- and post-tax real rates of return whatever the mix of inflation and real return in the nominal return. In the case of 7.5 percent inflation the real return in Regimes A and B is 2.32 percent per year, equal to the pre-tax real return $(1.075 \times 1.0232 = 1.10)$. Regimes of type A and B correspond to an expenditure tax-type treatment, while Regimes C and D correspond to a comprehensive income tax type treatment.[1] These brief descriptions of possible tax regimes should provide some benchmarks against which to assess the actual regimes summarized in the next section, and to provide a basis for our discussion of the criteria for a "good" tax system for private pensions.

Taxing Pensions

Our discussion thus far has outlined a range of possible regimes for taxing private pensions. In this section we describe briefly some actual regimes, and attempt to relate them to the hypothetical regimes just presented. Table 2 is inevitably a simplification.

Almost all the countries shown impose upper limits on the level of contribution and/or benefits that can be paid, although typically these limits affect only a small proportion of the workforce. Many countries treat lump sum payments out of pension funds more generally for tax purposes than they do regular payments: Australia, Ireland, Japan, and the United Kingdom fall into this category. Some other countries such as Canada and France take quite the opposite route, disallowing lump sum payments out of tax-privileged pension regimes, while the remainder

TABLE 2   Taxation of Private Pensions

Country	Contributions	Fund Income	Benefits	Regime
Australia	Employer deduct Employee partially deduct	tax at 15%	partially taxed	?
Canada	Deduct	exempt	taxable	EET
France	Deduct	n/a	taxable	EET?
Germany	Employer deduct Employee taxed	exempt	taxable	EET?
Ireland	Deduct	exempt	taxable	EET
Japan	Employer deduct Employee rare	low tax rate	taxable	?
New Zealand	Taxable	taxable	exempt	TTE
Denmark	Deduct	taxed on real returns	taxed	ETT?
Greece	Deduct	exempt	taxed	EET?
Netherlands	Deduct	exempt	taxed	EET
Portugal	Employer deduct Employee limited deductibility	exempt	taxed	EET?
Sweden	Deduct	tax at 10 to 15%	taxed	ETT?
United Kingdom	Deduct	exempt	taxable	EET
United States	Employer deduct Employee taxable	exempt	taxable	EET

Source: Author's compilation.

subject lump sums to tax in broadly the same way as regular payments. It is clear from Table 2 that the bulk of countries still operate systems most like the EET regime referred to above, which itself corresponds quite closely to the expenditure tax, and can also be thought of as a system of deferred pay. These apparently quite generous schemes have typically operated over quite lengthy periods.

It is worth noting that two countries that have recently reformed their taxation of pensions, Australia and New Zealand, have both moved toward less generous systems, at least partly with the aim of raising extra revenue but also with the aim of improving the efficiency and equity of the tax system as a whole. New Zealand has taken perhaps the boldest steps, making all contributions taxable, taxing all fund income (with no allowance for inflation), and then leaving all pensions untaxed. As argued at the time in New Zealand, this puts pension saving on the same basis as saving in an ordinary interest-bearing account.

The reforms in Australia moved in a similar direction, but have produced a substantially more complex system. Employer contributions continue to be deductible. Employee contributions are partially deductible up to certain limits contingent on employer support being below a given level, and all concessions are phased out beyond roughly average earnings. These limits discourage employers from increasing their contributions beyond the level at which employees lose their rights to deductibility and create a number of other distortions. Contributions that have been deductible are subject to a 15 percent withholding tax. Investment income of the fund is taxed at 15 percent, as are capital gains, but capital gains are taxed after adjustment for inflation, thus making capital gains far more attractive than income from the point of view of the funds. Lump sum benefits are taxed at 15 percent beyond a threshold, and pension benefits are taxed at the individual's marginal rate less 15 percent.

Two other regimes deserve special mention since they do not fit into the framework outlined above — those of France and Germany. Occupational pensions are provided in France through a pay-as-you-go system known as "repartition." Employers make contributions to a collective pension plan; these earn a certain number of points for the employee on whose behalf they are made. At retirement the worker concerned will have a points score to his or her credit that determines the pension to be received. The value of a pension point is reviewed annually and moves in line with earnings. The cost of a pension point is set by the annual outflow from the fund. Thus there is no funding of future liabilities, and hence no pension fund assets or liabilities of great significance. Contributions made by employers on this basis are deductible against corporation tax paid by employers, and employee contributions can be deducted from taxable income. Pensions are taxable as ordinary income, although subject to some special concessions.

The normal method of private pension finance in Germany is through the use of "book reserve" accounting. There is no special fund; prospective pension liabilities are charged each year against the company's profit and loss account and balance sheet. Charges computed in accordance with bases agreed on by the tax authorities can be deducted in assessing corporation tax liabilities. Scheme members rank with other creditors in the event of insolvency of the parent company; hence legislation requires that vested benefits and pensions in payment should be insured. Premiums for such insurance are in turn tax-deductible. There is no charge to employees until pensions are paid. Pensions are then taxed as other income, subject to a lower rate of tax on small incomes. If a German employer does establish a segregated fund, the employee will be liable for tax on contributions made on his or her behalf. Such funds are correspondingly rare.

Although the French and German institutional arrangements are rather different from those in most countries, they fit into the group of countries including Canada, Ireland, the United Kingdom, and the

United States for which the only significant source of tax revenue from pensions is the taxation of pensions in payment. The United States does deny relief to employee contributions to defined benefit plans, but the consequence is that there are few employee contributions.

Despite their long histories, and widely varying institutions, the taxation arrangements for private pensions in the OECD have much in common. Yet there are many calls for reform, and some countries have already implemented quite dramatic change. In the following section we consider the possible objectives for a pensions tax regime, and the feasibility of achieving them.

Objectives for the Tax System

Many considerations seem to lie behind attempts to review the tax treatment of savings in general, and private pensions in particular. One is the concern for fiscal neutrality, the desire to achieve a tax structure that as far as possible avoids discrimination between different kinds of activity and that leaves choices unaffected by tax considerations. A second is a desire to raise revenue by eliminating subsidies to particular activities that take the form of favorable tax treatment rather than explicit items of public expenditure. A third is concern about the aggregate level of saving. And in developing and transitional economies, questions are often raised about the most appropriate form of savings taxation.

There is no feasible tax regime that both raises revenue and is fiscally neutral in all aspects. Taxes inevitably distort economic behavior; so the best we can do is remove unnecessary deviations from neutrality and choose those that are least damaging in their overall economic effect. Two kinds of incentive are particularly important in considering the tax treatment of pension funds. One is the incentive to save rather than consume. The second is the choice of the form in which to save. We consider each kind of incentive in turn. There are two ways of interpreting fiscal neutrality in relation to the decision to save. We might seek to be neutral between consumption and savings, or we might seek to be neutral between present and future consumption. Neutrality between consumption and savings is achieved by a comprehensive income tax on real income of all types. Whatever the source of revenue, whether it be from work or from savings, and whether it is consumed or saved, it is taxed in the same way and at the same rate. This approach appears to be gathering support, as evidenced by the reforms in Australia and New Zealand, and by debates throughout the OECD. However, it is worth noting that there are peculiarities associated with this approach. With a comprehensive income tax (TTE in our earlier discussion), savings are treated as if they are simply another commodity, akin to consumption.

But people do not, in the main, save for saving's own sake; savings are not a commodity in themselves, but a means to future consumption. In relation to retirement savings, this perspective is particularly obviously the appropriate one. The relevant concept of neutrality is not between consumption and savings but between consumption now and consumption in the future.

It is this neutrality in the impact of the tax system on the decision between current and future consumption that is achieved by tax systems of the EET type most common in the OECD. Such systems offer the alternative of paying now or deferring tax by means of contributing to private pension plans and paying tax when the benefits are derived. Thus both present and future consumption are taxed on the same basis. And, as noted above, the EET regime maintains equality of pre- and post-tax returns, another reflection of the lack of distortion imposed on the decision as to whether to consume now or in the future.

The comprehensive income tax, or TTE approach, by contrast, reduces future consumption because less is saved as compared to that would exist in a no tax world; in an inflationary world with nominal investment income taxed, it could actually impose a penalty on deferred consumption. Thus, if fiscal neutrality between current and future consumption is desired, the appropriate tax system is an expenditure-type system along the lines of those commonly used in OECD countries.

The second concept of fiscal neutrality that is of interest to us concerns the way in which different kinds of savings are taxed. Here, neutrality demands that all forms of saving be taxed in the same way. If not, more generously treated forms of saving will tend to attract greater flows of saving, regardless of their underlying economic efficiency. In general, different forms of saving are taxed very differently in countries across the OECD.

Although it is hard to make generalizations in this area, two forms of saving stand out as being conceded relatively favorable tax treatment in many countries: owner-occupied housing and private pensions. Governments in the 1980s made many statements to the effect that fiscal neutrality between forms of saving was an important goal, but few made much progress toward it. There were two main reasons. First, although most statements were in favor of a comprehensive income tax-type treatment, nowhere was any serious attempt made to adjust investment income as well as capital gains for inflation. Second, very few governments had the courage to remove the "privileges" associated with owner-occupied housing or private pension plans. Part of the reason for lack of action in this second field was the widespread belief that there are strong arguments for providing special incentives for private pension provision. It is to a discussion of these which we now turn.

Two types of argument are often advanced to defend the special tax advantages of private pensions: one that pension saving is more important than other saving; the second that saving in general should benefit from tax incentives.

Households save for a variety of reasons. They save in order to redistribute income over their lifetime to use it when they are old, sick, or unemployed, or when young children reduce the family's income and increase its outgoings. They save in order to accumulate assets from which they may derive benefits (housing services from owner-occupied housing) or that they might use to establish or develop a business. They may also save in order to leave money to their children.

It is not immediately easy to see why retirement savings should be singled out in this list. They are all worthy motives, which is no doubt why, at one time or another, in one place or another, all have been singled out for fiscal privilege, although frequently in an uncoordinated manner. Several possible arguments exist.

First, individuals may fail to perceive accurately their likely needs in old age, and this failure of perception/information is more serious here than in other areas. It would be plausible to argue that this could be so simply because at the beginning of the period when saving for retirement might make sense, old age can seem very distant. This is a basically paternalistic argument that asserts that governments know better than their people what is good for them and should distort choices using the tax system in an attempt to correct the deficiencies of individual preferences.

A second argument for singling out retirement savings is that they can be particularly significant in reducing other forms of state expenditure. If individuals fail to save for their old age, the state will have to provide incomes for them during that period. Certainly in most countries at least a part of the social security system that supports the elderly pays benefits that are related to income. If governments can encourage more people to save for their retirement, and also those who already are saving to save more, expenditure on means-tested benefits to the retired would fall. The importance of this argument will obviously vary from country to country.

A third argument might be that private pension plans are superior to other financial intermediaries. This could relate either to their investment performance or to the broader social and economic implications of their investment policies. Although this is a possible argument, it is not one that has been put forward much, and it is difficult to give it much weight, not least because in many instances private pension funds are organized by financial intermediaries engaged in a wide range of business other than the provision of pensions.

There is no suggestion that private pensions are anything other than a

TABLE 3   Household Savings Rates as Percentage of Disposable
Household Income

Country	1988	1993
United States	4.5	4.6
United Kingdom	5.7	11.5
Australia	6.5	4.2
Japan	14.3	14.6
Germany	12.8	12.1

Source: Dilnot and Johnson (1993).

desirable thing, and there are some arguments for particularly favorable tax treatment for them. The strength of these arguments depends on the extent to which pension saving would fall in the absence of any special privilege. The recent experience in New Zealand is the best evidence available on this. Thus far there are insufficient data to draw firm conclusions, although there does seem to have been some move away from employer-provided pension. If it is the case that pension saving falls if tax treatment is made less generous, the important issue for policymakers is determining the most appropriate form in which to provide some incentive for pension saving.

The remaining argument for tax incentives for pensions relates to the overall level of saving. Across much of the OECD there is concern that savings rates are too low. The United States, United Kingdom, and Australia would be obvious examples, while in countries like Japan and Germany such a problem seems not to exist. Table 3 illustrates the diversity of personal savings rates. One of the longest-running debates in applied economics has been the extent to which new tax incentives for saving in a particular form will increase the overall level of saving. It is clear from the experience of Registered Retirement Savings Plans in Canada, Individual Retirement Accounts in the United States, and Personal Pensions in the United Kingdom, for example (Carroll and Summers 1987, Venti and Wise 1986; National Audit Office 1991, respectively), and the popularity of private pension saving in general, that new or existing generous tax regimes for certain types of saving can be enormously "successful," if we measure success only in terms of amounts of money flowing into the favored regime.

Such a measure of success is of little interest. Of course, tax incentives for saving in a certain form will attract funds. We need to know what impact this has on funds held in, and flowing into, other forms of saving, and the impact of the new scheme on government tax revenue, since if we are concerned about any measure of saving it is national saving, which includes public sector saving, not simply personal sector saving.

It would be quite possible for a new savings incentive to appear to be successful while in fact reducing both personal sector saving and public sector saving, and thus diminishing national saving (Munnell 1982). If we started from a world in which individuals had a relatively fixed demand for an income level in retirement, but in which savings were harshly treated by the tax system, the introduction of tax incentives would allow a reduction in current savings without any reduction in the level of retirement income, thus reducing the level of personal sector saving. At the same time, since the tax incentive would reduce tax revenue, public sector saving would fall.

There has been a great deal of empirical work using microeconomic data to attempt to provide conclusive evidence on the likely effect of tax incentives. This is an extremely difficult area, since the data requirements are very severe: complete answers would require detailed information on all assets, incomes, preferences, and expectations for a large sample of individuals over a long period. To the extent that there is a consensus, it seems to be that tax incentives can increase personal saving, and that after taking account of the reduction in tax revenue there may be a small increase in national saving (Bovenberg 1989; Feenberg and Skinner 1989; Feldstein 1992; Poterba, Venti, and Wise 1993; Venti and Wise 1987, for some representative views). Some, however (e.g., Gravelle 1991), cast doubt that even a small increase in national saving occurs. These results are still debated, and would tend to vary enormously from country to country as a function of the nature of the tax system and the determinants of saving. Certainly differences in tax systems can go only a little way toward explaining cross-country variation in saving.

All too often, it is simply assumed that more saving is a good thing, and that the tax system imposed on pensions is an effective and appropriate way of achieving a change in the level of national saving. Even if we accept that there is some argument for higher saving, it is not obvious that tinkering with the tax system is a good way of raising national saving. But it does seem reasonable to assert that we would not want a tax system that imposed a post-tax rate of return on deferred consumption lower than the pre-tax return. If our concern is not to depress saving, then we must expect to impose a tax treatment for saving in general and for pensions in particular that does not tax the return to saving. Starting from a tax system that does tax the return to some or all forms of saving, moving to one that taxes the return to fewer or no form of saving might increase national savings. But the taxation of savings in most developed countries is enormously variable (OECD 1984) with some forms of saving having a post-tax rate of return higher than the pre-tax rate and some far lower than the pre-tax rate. Consequently, confident prediction in this area is very difficult.

One problem with the common EET/expenditure tax treatment is the cash flow implication for government. While for a mature scheme and economy the deferral of tax payment until retirement is not too great a problem, in a young or developing economy such a scheme might cause problems. Given this, a TEE-type scheme may be preferable in such circumstances, providing an earlier payment of tax where governments may genuinely be constrained. Such a scheme also has the advantage that government revenue is not vulnerable to emigration prior to retirement. Schemes of this kind have been attracting more attention in recent years (Munnell 1992).

Increased Revenue from Pensions?

As tax reform gathered momentum in the second half of the 1980s, a common theme of "broadening the base and lowering the rate" could be discerned in much of the debate about what to do, and much of the description of what was done, although perhaps not so clearly in what was done. This objective seemed to imply changes in the taxation of pensions with a view to raising more revenue, which could be used to cut tax rates. As we have already noted, some countries have already moved in this direction, and many others seem to be considering the option.

Starting from a tax treatment of the EET type, there are three areas in which changes could be made in an attempt to raise more revenue: the taxation of contributions, the taxation of pension funds themselves, and the taxation of benefits paid out. We examine each in turn.

The Taxation of Contributions

One seemingly obvious way of raising revenue from taxing pensions is to give no relief, or only limited relief, to employees for contributions to pension plans. Such relief could be abolished where it exists, or restricted to a low rate of tax, or be subjected to a maximum. Yet it would be pointless to make such a change without simultaneously reviewing the tax treatment of employer contributions. Indeed, it seems inevitable that all forms of contributions to pension funds be given identical tax treatment. If not, employees, employers, and pension funds will so arrange their affairs as to make all contributions in the most tax-efficient manner. The losers in such a position will be the ill advised, or those unable to take advantage of the most lightly taxed route. As we noted earlier, the general non-exemption of employee contributions in the United States means that very few employee contributions are made, not that large amounts of tax are raised.

If employees' contributions are to be subject to tax, it seems that employers' contributions must also be. There are few practical problems in subjecting employees' contributions to tax; tax due would simply be calculated on income inclusive of contributions rather than exclusive of them. Difficulties do arise in the case of employers' contributions, however. In principle, contributions made by employers on behalf of their employees would be treated as a benefit to the employee, and taxed as income of the employee. This causes no problem where employers' contributions are clearly defined and linked to particular individuals, but difficulties arise in the much more common procedure where an employer makes general contributions to a fund related to aggregate payroll. Here the task of allocating the employer's contributions to employees is challenging. One possibility is simply to require employers to attribute general contributions to individual employees, but this would not be easy to implement.

An alternative would be to levy tax on employees who are members of defined benefit schemes on the value of their pension rights, rather than on contributions. Contributions to defined benefit schemes would remain tax-deductible, but the benefit in kind in the form of increased pension rights would be taxable. This route requires an answer to the question of what the value of the rights is; valuing such rights may be at least as difficult as allocating general contributions. Valuation is especially hard where the final pension is a function of years of employment and final salary. It is also worth noting that rights within pension plans are frequently defined quite narrowly, with pensions paid frequently far exceeding rights. If tax authorities imposed a tax on the annual increase in the value of an individual's pension rights, it is easy to imagine that such rights would very soon be all but replaced by discretionary payments. The alternative of trying to tax as income the expected value of discretionary payments many years in the future is not a task that would appeal to many revenue authorities.

The problems outlined above are not insuperable; the difficulties of taxing general unallocated contributions, for example, can be dealt with, as in New Zealand, by imposing a flat rate tax. This solution is reasonably fair if most taxpayers face the same marginal income tax rate, and somewhat inequitable in countries with multiple-rate income taxes. And although calculating the value of accrued pension rights is hard, we must remember that such calculations are already made, for example, to determine transfer values. If a country is determined to tax pension contributions, it can certainly be done.

If there is no tax relief for pension contributions, then it is inappropriate to tax the whole of any pensions in payment as income, since part would already have been taxed. The easiest solution to this, adopted by New Zealand, is to tax the income of pension funds as well, making any further taxation of pensions in payment unnecessary. But if the income of funds is not to be taxed, full exemption from tax of pensions in payment produces a TEE regime equivalent in impact to the EET regime, although with the timing of tax payments advanced. If the aim is to move to a system that raises more revenue, without taxing contributions twice, rules to distinguish between the underlying contributions and the return on them would be needed, so that only the previously untaxed elements would be taxed. These rules would probably be quite complex, and inevitably cause some distortions. The Australian system, which imposes partial tax on contributions, fund income, and benefits illustrates some of the problems.

The Taxation of Fund Income

Taxing fund income is an alternative (or additional) route to raising revenue from pensions schemes. There is no obvious lack of logic in a system that taxes both contributions and fund income, as is done in New Zealand, although pensions in payment should then be relieved of tax. If not, pension funds would suffer a substantial fiscal disadvantage relative to other means of saving, and could be expected to decline rapidly in popularity and importance.

If the problems with taxing contributions outlined above are thought to rule out such a regime, the alternative of taxing fund assets or income while leaving contributions untaxed and benefits taxed is also open. This is the type of system that operates in Japan, although with a very low rate of tax. There is an apparent element of double taxation in a procedure that taxes the income of funds as it is received or their assets and imposes tax again when benefits are paid out. But it is the same element of double taxation that is intrinsic to the taxation of income in general, where both the capital and the returns on capital are taxed.

If fund income is to be taxed, a decision as to the rate at which it is to be charged is needed. The most obvious candidate is the marginal tax rate of the majority of members of the scheme, provided that this majority is a large one. If there is a wide divergence of tax rates among scheme members, then any single tax rate will inevitably be unfair, but the problems of attempting to allocate fund income to specific individuals and then tax it at their marginal tax rate seem likely to be too great to consider such a route seriously.

Perhaps the greatest problem in this area is designing a system that deals properly with inflation, since a system that taxes full nominal income will be very vulnerable to inflation. In New Zealand and Australia no adjustment is made to fund income to account for inflation, producing a position where at high inflation rates the post-tax rate of return can become negative. This clearly makes little sense, but the difficulties of adjusting income for inflation would be very great. The area that is most frequently chosen for the attempt to adjust for inflation is capital gains; many OECD countries now have capital gains taxes that adjust for inflation.

The combination of taxing full nominal fund income and taxing real capital gains in the fund, as in Australia, provides a strong bias to the fund in favor of assets producing capital gain rather than regular income, and this bias is a function of the rate of inflation, being stronger the higher the rate of inflation becomes. This sort of distortion will tend to affect the portfolio behavior of funds, and is clearly undesirable.

One further problem in this area relates to the way in which such a tax could be introduced if it did not already exist. One possible transition mechanism would be to close all existing schemes to new contributions, and allow these schemes to continue to accumulate tax free income and pay out taxable pensions. New contributions would go into new funds with taxable incomes. Such a transition would be challenging for pension funds, actuaries and tax authorities, but ought to be possible. An alternative route would simply be to subject fund income to a relatively low rate to begin with, reflecting the large share in the fund of "old" contributions, perhaps increasing the rate steadily over time.

The Taxation of Pension Benefits

As already noted, the main form of taxation levied on the activities of private pensions in the OECD is of benefits in payment. While it is true that if contributions and/or fund income are taxed, it is not necessarily appropriate that all benefits be taxed; where relief exists for contributions, there is a strong case for taxing benefits.

The most significant area for debate over the taxation of benefits is the appropriate treatment of lump sum payments. In several countries (Australia, Ireland, Japan, and the United Kingdom, for example), lump sum payments are taxed more leniently than pensions. Given our belief that all forms of contribution to private pensions should be taxed in the same way, we might expect to believe that all forms of withdrawal should be taxed in the same way.

Two arguments in support of preferential tax treatment for lump sums are frequently advanced. The first is that such provisions are an accepted part of the regimes where they exist, and therefore should not be changed. This is a weak argument; although it is vital to avoid too great a disruption to established expectations, and thus avoid too dramatic a change for those approaching retirement, we cannot accept the status quo simply because that is what it is.

The second argument relates to personal capital accumulation and general capital formation and suggests that the availability of tax-free lump sums may encourage this. It is certainly the case that private capital accumulation may stimulate enterprise and risk taking in the economy. But a relief whose receipt is conditional on reaching retirement age seems somewhat inappropriate if this is the aim. There are arguments for supporting retirement savings, but these do not imply encouraging lump sum provisions — rather the reverse. There may be arguments for encouraging the accumulation of capital sums by individuals, but not especially individuals past retirement age — rather the reverse.

There seem to be no very strong reasons for treating the lump sum more favorably than pension payments for tax purposes. If lump sums are taxed, the question of whether they should be taxed in the year of receipt becomes relevant. Once more, the question is unimportant in a single-rate income tax, but significant with a graduated tax system. Under a graduated system, any lump sum might attract a marginal rate of tax well in excess of the recipient's expected average marginal tax rate during retirement. One possibility would be an averaging provision, but it could also be argued that the disincentive to lump sums caused by graduation was appropriate, and should be allowed to stay.

Most countries could raise more revenue from private pensions than they do at present. However, serious problems are associated with taxing of both contributions and fund income: it is not an accident that neither are taxed in most regimes. The one area where increased taxation seems appropriate in many countries is lump sum benefits, but even here, entrenched expectations may make raising more revenue quickly difficult.

Tax Expenditures

The last two decades have seen growing interest in the concept of tax expenditures (Surrey 1973; OECD 1984). Many countries now publish lists of tax expenditures, or lists that are widely thought of or described as being of tax expenditures, and a growing number produce such figures for the tax treatment of private pensions. These figures are widely used in the debate over tax reform, but merit rather more critical analysis than is often given them.

According to Willis and Hardwick (1978), a "tax expenditure is an exemption or relief which is not part of the essential structure of the tax in question but has been introduced into the tax code for some extraneous reason — e.g. in order to ease the burden for a particular class of taxpayers, or to provide an incentive to apply income in a particular way, or perhaps to simplify administration. The term is used to cover, not merely specific exemption but also gaps in the charge as a result of which receipts . . . are not subject to tax."

The most obvious problem with the concept of tax expenditures, as is made clear above, is the complete subjectivity on which they are based in the case of items such as private pensions, because of the difficulty in deciding on the "essential structure" of the tax system. If we believe that the essential structure of the tax system is or should be an expenditure tax, we will argue that tax expenditures on private pensions are in general relatively small, being mainly the common relief for lump sum payments and, in cases such as Australia and New Zealand, negative. If, on the other hand, we are advocates of the comprehensive income tax, we will believe that tax expenditures on private pensions are in general very substantial. In the United Kingdom, for example, taking an expenditure tax as the base implies a tax expenditure of less than 0.1 percent of GDP, while using an income tax unadjusted for inflation as the base implies a tax expenditure around 0.7 percent of GDP (Dilnot and Johnson, 1993). These arguments, very appropriately, point us back toward the realization that the crucial debate is over the aims and structure of the whole tax system as it affects saving.

Even if we can come to some agreement over the "essential structure" of the tax system, the task of calculating the tax expenditures associated with private pensions is a very difficult one. It makes very little sense, as is too often done, to assume that we can change the tax system without changing behavior as a result. At a very simple level, if we move from a system where contributions are free of tax to one where they are taxed, either gross contributions must rise or the size of the fund and subsequent benefits will fall.[2] Either way, there will be some loss of tax to offset the tax gained from taxing contributions. If gross contributions rise, company taxes will fall if the contributions are from employers, and taxes on consumption will fall if the contributions are from employees. If the size of the fund and subsequent benefits decline, both income and consumption taxes paid by benefit recipients will fall, social security benefits paid to the retired will rise, and to the extent that fund income was taxed, that source of revenue will also decline.

More important than this, and even more difficult to quantify, is the extent to which a less favorable treatment for private pensions would lead individuals to switch their saving to other forms. If we imagine a tax regime in which private pensions are the most tax privileged form of saving, but in which other forms of saving are only marginally less privileged, it is easy to see that a major increase in the tax burden on private pensions would probably lead to dramatic switching of savings flows to the previously marginally less privileged form of saving, resulting in very little additional revenue to the government.

Any sensible measure of the tax expenditure associated with a given tax regime for private pensions requires a clear view of the overall objectives of the tax system, of the likely impact of any change in the tax system on employee and employer contributions, the size of pension funds, the composition and level of their income, the level of benefits, the likely extent of switching to different savings vehicles or to consumption, and the tax revenue and public expenditure consequences of all of these.

This long list of difficulties is not meant to suggest that the concept of tax expenditure is without interest or value. It is important that those who argue for concessions through the tax system should provide estimates of the cost of such concessions that can be compared to alternative means of support. But in the field of private pensions, producing an informative estimate of tax expenditures is likely to be possible only when we have achieved a clear idea of the aims and effects of the tax system. Measures of tax expenditure that ignore the arguments set out above may well do more harm than good.

Conclusion

Finding an appropriate tax system for private pensions is not easy, and cannot be done without considering the rest of a country's tax system, especially as it affects saving. Much of the interest in this area has been a result of the belief that substantial extra revenue could be raised here. It may be possible to raise some additional revenue without major dislocation, but significant increases in taxation may not be desirable from all points of view, will inevitably be difficult, will lead to much behavioral change, and should not be seen as an easy answer to anything. It is no accident that the basic form of pensions tax regime that is most common is the EET type, for which there is a strong economic case.

Notes

[1] On comprehensive income taxation, see Carter Commission (1966). On expenditure taxes see Kaldor (1955), Andrews (1974), and US Treasury (1977), and Pechman (1980).

[2] The United Kingdom authorities, for example, note that their estimates of the costs of tax allowances and reliefs "make no allowance for the fact that changes in tax reliefs may cause people to change their behavior. For example, removing the tax privileges of one form of saving may lead people to switch to another tax privileged form of saving" (HMSO 1992).

References

Andrews, William D. "A Consumption-Type or Cash Flow Personal Income Tax." *Harvard Law Review* 87 (1974).

Bovenberg, Alans. "Tax Policy and National Saving in the United States: A Survey." *National Tax Journal* 42, 2 (1989): 123–38.

Carroll, Chris and Lawrence Summers. "Why Have Private Savings Rates in the United States and Canada Diverged?" *Journal of Monetary Economics* 20 (September 1987): 249–80.

Carter Commission. "Report of the Royal Commission on Taxation." Ottawa: Queen's Printer, 1966.

Dilnot, Andrew and Paul Johnson. *Taxation of Private Pensions.* London: Institute for Fiscal Studies, 1993.

Feenberg, Daniel and Jonathan Skinner. "Sources of IRA Saving." Cambridge, MA: NBER Working Paper 2845, 1989.

Feldstein, Martin. "The Effects of Tax-Based Saving Incentive on Government Revenue and National Saving." Cambridge, MA: NBER Working Paper 4021, 1992.

Gravelle, Jane. "Do IRAs Increase Savings?" *Journal of Economic Perspectives* 5, 2 (1991): 133–48.

HMSO. Inland Revenue Statistics. London: HMSO, 1992.

Kaldor, Nicholas. *An Expenditure Tax.* London: Allen and Unwin, 1955.

Munnell, Alicia. *The Economics of Private Pensions.* Washington, DC: Brookings Institution, 1982.

———. "Current Taxation of Qualified Plans: Has the Time Come?" *FRB-New England-Economic Review,* 1992 (2) (1992): 12–25.

OECD. *Tax Expenditures: A Review of the Issues and Country Practice.* Paris: OECD, 1984.

Pechman, Joseph, ed. *What Should Be Taxed: Income or Expenditure?* Washington, DC: Brookings Institution, 1980.

Poterba, James, Steven Venti, and David Wise. "Do 401(K) Contributions Crowd Out Other Personal Saving?" Cambridge, MA: NBER Working Paper 4391, 1993.

Surrey, Stanley S. *Pathways to Tax Reform.* Cambridge, MA: Harvard University Press, 1973.

U.S. Treasury. *Blueprints for Basic Tax Reform.* Washington, DC: U.S. GPO, 1977.

———. *Tax Reform for Fairness, Simplicity and Economic Growth.* Washington, DC: U.S. GPO, 1984.

Venti, Steven and David Wise. "Tax-Deferred Accounts, Constrained Choice and Estimation on Individual Saving." *Review of Economic Studies* 53 (1986): 579–601.

———. "IRAs and Saving." In M. Feldstein, ed., *The Effects of Taxation on Capital Accumulation.* Chicago: University of Chicago Press, 1987.

Willis, J. and P. Hardwick. *Tax Expenditures in the United Kingdom.* London: Heinemann, 1978.

Comments by Angela E. Chang

The chapter by Andrew Dilnot reviews the tax treatment of pensions in a number of developed countries and lays out several issues that deserve further discussion and research.[1] In reviewing the favorable tax treatment of pensions in 14 countries, the chapter focuses on common "themes" observed in the various countries. For example, the form in which pensions receive favorable tax treatment is similar across the countries. Favorable tax treatment is granted to one or more of the following transactions that occur as related to pensions:

- tax-deductible contributions to the pension plans, by employers and/or employees;
- tax-exempt earnings from investment of the pension funds; and
- tax-exempt payment of retirement benefits from the pension funds.

Another common theme concerns the motivation for granting favorable tax treatment to pensions. Dilnot discusses several possible motivating factors that may have led policymakers in these countries to grant the specific favorable tax treatment that we observe, such as a desire to raise the aggregate level of savings and to reduce the financial burden on social security programs.

Lastly, in several countries, the value of favorable tax treatment of pensions is becoming the subject of increasing policy debate in light of the desire for fiscal restraint in these countries. The debate is about whether the benefits from encouraging pensions outweigh the cost of the foregone tax revenue. In particular, if the favorable tax treatment of pensions is curtailed, would that cause national saving to fall? This is a question about the sensitivity of pension decisions to taxes.

There is substantial literature about the tax sensitivity of individuals' contributions to pensions, so I will briefly discuss what we have learned from the literature. Research in this area has concentrated on individuals' contributions to individual retirement-saving vehicles, such as IRAs and 401(k)s.

Several studies on IRAs (Feenberg and Skinner 1989, Venti and Wise 1990) and 401(k)s (Poterba, Venti, and Wise 1993) indicate that saving in these instruments does not "crowd out" other forms of saving, suggesting that an increase in IRA or 401(k) saving raises personal saving. There is also evidence that the increase in personal saving associated with IRAs outweighs the foregone tax revenue (Feldstein 1992). This suggests that curtailing the favorable tax treatment of these vehicles may diminish national saving.

In contrast to the substantial literature on the impact of taxes on individuals' contribution to pension plans, there has been little research about the following issues:

- tax sensitivity of pension contributions by firms;
- tax sensitivity of the investment of pension funds; and
- the effects of the taxes imposed on the payment of pension benefits, particularly the tax treatment of lump sum distributions.

Let me expand on the discussion of areas for future research beyond the issues mentioned in Chapter 7. An interesting explanation has emerged from the literature about the tax sensitivity of individuals' saving decisions — that individuals may not always make saving decisions based on rational utility maximization. For example, one explanation for the high participation rates in 401(k)s is that the payroll deductions of 401(k) contributions serve as a self-control mechanism. Several economists (e.g., Thaler 1990) are exploring the importance of self-control factors, rules of thumb, mental accounting, and other behavioral models of saving decision.

Another thought-provoking observation concerns the 10 percent tax penalty on pre-retirement lump sum distributions that are not rolled over into IRAs or other tax-deferred instruments. Congress imposed this tax penalty in 1986, anticipating to raise little tax revenue from it. For 1987–89, Congress expected to raise about US$ 500 million in tax revenue from the tax penalty. The actual tax receipt from the tax penalty during the period was over US$ 1.8 billion.

One explanation for the low impact of the tax penalty on rollovers is liquidity constraints. Many more individuals may be liquidity-constrained than expected, such that they spent their lump sum distributions even though they paid the 10 percent tax penalty (Chang 1993).

Thus, while more data in terms of quality and quantity would further our knowledge about the tax sensitivity of individuals' saving decisions as regards pensions, refining the economic framework to take account of the possibility of individuals' using self-control mechanisms and rules of thumb to make saving decisions and the possibility of liquidity constraints may also produce important insights. Finally, until we have an adequate economic framework and sufficiently accurate data, it would be premature to answer one way or the other that curtailing the favorable tax treatment of pensions will raise national saving.

The views expressed are solely those of the author and do not necessarily reflect the official position of the Federal Reserve Bank of New York, the Board of Governors, or the Federal Reserve System.

References

Chang, Angela E. "Tax Policy, Lump Sum Pension Distributions, and Household Saving." Unpublished PhD dissertation, Massachusetts Institute of Technology, 1993.

Dilnot, Andrew. "The Taxation of Private Pensions." This volume.

Feenberg, Daniel and Jonathan Skinner. "Sources of IRA Savings." In Lawrence Summers, ed., *Tax Policy and the Economy 1989*. Cambridge, MA: MIT Press, 1989: 25–46.

Feldstein, Martin. "The Effects of Tax-Based Saving Incentives on Government Revenue and National Saving." Cambridge, MA: NBER Working Paper 4021, 1992.

Poterba, James M., Steven Venti, and David Wise. "Do 401(k) Contributions Crowd Out Other Personal Saving?" Cambridge, MA: NBER Working Paper 4391, 1993.

Thaler, Richard. "Anomalies: Savings, Fungibility, and Mental Accounts." *Journal of Economic Perspectives* 4, 1 (1990): 193–206.

Venti, Steven and David Wise. "Have IRAs Increased U.S. Savings: Evidence from Consumer Expenditure Surveys." *Quarterly Journal of Economics* 105 (1990): 661–98.

Comments by Sylvester J. Schieber

Andrew Dilnot's chapter presents a concise analytical framework for assessing the implications of alternative tax treatments of pension savings. This framework is used to show how the alternative timing of taxation of contributions to plans, income accruing to plan assets, and benefit payments under pension plans results in a variety of tax and benefit outcomes. He employs the framework to show how several of the major economies represented in the OECD tax pension accruals. He assesses the overall objectives for a taxing system and some of the dilemmas that these systems pose relative to pension design and sponsorship. He discusses the governmental revenue issues that are pushing some, if not all, of the countries he covers in his analysis to reevaluate their tax treatment of pension plans. He informs us that another of the United States' great cultural creations, tax expenditures, has spread like Mickey Mouse and the Golden Arches around the world. Finally, he leaves us with the conclusion that increases in the taxation of pensions relative to the traditional treatment accorded them in most countries "may not be desirable from all points of view, will inevitably be difficult, will lead to much behavioral change, and should not be seen as an easy answer to anything."

I like Dilnot's chapter, though having said this, I believe it has two shortcomings. The first shortcoming is that I believe the chapter fails to probe deeply the countervailing policy tensions that persist between the motivations for pension and retirement policy, on one hand, and, on the other hand, analysts who argue that the comprehensive income tax is the appropriate base by which to assess pension policy. The second shortcoming is that Dilnot's presentation is incomplete, not in its broad and analytical framework, but in the detailing of pension outcomes that result from alternative taxing policies. Before I turn to these two points specifically, I feel compelled to address an issue that Dilnot raises in his analysis of the objectives for tax systems.

Clarifying the Analytical Framework

In assessing the goals of a taxing system, Dilnot looks at their treatment of consumption and savings and the desirability minimizing distorting behavior. He states that "neutrality between consumption and savings is achieved by a comprehensive income tax on real income of all types." While this statement is true, its misapplication in the development of the concept of tax expenditures accorded pensions in many countries and in the development of pension policy in others must be understood. The problem is that the actual application of the concept that Dilnot so simply states generally ignores that the "neutrality between consumption and savings is achieved by a comprehensive income tax on *real* income," while when operationalized, the analytical models and estimates are generally derived using nominal rather than real incomes.

In order to understand this point, consider a simple case where there are no taxes applied against income. In this case, a consumer can enjoy a level of consumption (C) equal to his or her entire income (Y) in the time period in which it is earned (P),

$$(1) \quad C_P = Y_P.$$

Alternatively, the consumer can invest his or her income and earn interest at a rate (i), and enjoy future income as follows:

$$(2) \quad C_F = Y_P (1 + i).$$

The consumer can trade off current versus future consumption at the rate

$$(3) \quad \frac{C_P}{C_F} = \frac{Y_P}{Y_P(1 + i)} = \frac{1}{1 + i}.$$

Under this model, the consumer is paid an interest premium for deferring consumption. The way our income tax system works, an individual is faced with a slightly different scenario than that laid out in equations (1)–(3). Under the current federal tax system, if an individual consumes current income, taxes have to be paid on that income first. That is,

$$(4) \quad C_P = (1 - t) Y_P,$$

where t is the income tax rate. Under the IRC provisions favoring retirement plans, workers are faced with the opportunity of saving out of current income before taxes, but they have to pay taxes on the amount distributed at retirement. In this case, future consumption can be specified as

$$(5) \quad C_F = (1 - t) \, [Y_P (1 + i)].$$

If a comprehensive income tax is introduced into this world, the special treatment of retirement plan contributions would no longer be allowed. Future consumption in this regime is

$$(6) \quad C_F = (1 - t) \, Y_P [1 + i (1 - t)].$$

Under this regime the consumer would trade off current versus future consumption at the rate

$$(7) \quad \frac{C_P}{C_F} = \frac{1}{1 + i(1 - t)}.$$

The application of the "comprehensive" income tax to qualified retirement plans would equalize the tax treatment of pension savings with the tax treatment of a regular savings account under our tax laws. Comparing equations (5) and (6) shows that the existence of tax-free earnings for retirement savings enhances the efficiency of the tax-qualified plan. The difference between the two is that in the former the effective tax rate on the interest accruals in the account is zero, but in the latter it would be the statutory rate.

The problem is that the current measurements of tax expenditures accorded pensions in the United States are based on the concept of the comprehensive income tax applied to the nominal income accruing to pension assets. This approach overlooks the fact that some portion of the returns on assets over time does not reflect real economic return for deferring consumption, but rather makes up for the decreased purchasing power of money resulting from price inflation. That is, the interest rate i in equation (6) above is composed of two elements:

$$(8) \quad i = \frac{dP}{P} + r$$

where P is the price level in the current period and dP is the change in prices from the current period to the future period, and r is the real rate of return on assets in excess of inflation. In other words:

$$(9) \quad \frac{C_F}{C_P} = \frac{1}{1 + (dP \, / \, P)(1 - t) + r(1 - t)}$$

TABLE 1   Relative Value of Money in a Normal Savings Account Paying a Rate
of Return Equivalent to a 5 Percent Inflation Rate and Subject
to 25 Percent Tax Rates

Year	Nominal Value of Constant Purchasing Power	Nominal Value of Savings	Gross Interest	Net Interest	Purchasing Power of Savings (% of original earnings)	Effective Tax Rate on Original Earnings
0	1,000.00	750.00	37.5	28.1	75.0	25.0
1	1,050.00	778.13	38.9	29.2	74.1	25.9
2	1,102.50	807.30	40.4	30.3	73.2	26.8
3	1,157.63	837.58	41.9	31.4	72.4	27.6
4	1,215.51	868.99	43.4	32.6	71.5	28.5
5	1,276.28	901.57	45.1	33.8	70.6	29.4
6	1,340.10	935.38	46.8	35.1	69.8	30.2
7	1,407.10	970.46	48.5	36.4	69.0	31.0
8	1,477.46	1,006.85	50.3	37.8	68.1	31.9
9	1,551.33	1,044.61	52.2	39.2	67.3	32.7
10	1,628.89	1,083.78	54.2	40.6	66.5	33.5
20	2,653.30	1,566.11	78.3	58.7	59.0	41.0
30	4,321.94	2,263.10	113.2	84.9	52.4	47.6

Source: Wyatt Company simulations.

In order for deferred consumption to be at least of equal value to present consumption, the rate of return on deferred consumption has to equal at least the rate of inflation. Since the return defined by the factor dP/P is merely maintaining the purchasing power of income across periods, taxing that factor subjects income to an added tax if it is not consumed immediately. It is this conception of a "comprehensive tax" where the return on assets that covers inflation is taxable that is the theoretical basis for measuring tax preferences for retirement and savings plans. Under this model, if there is any inflation at all in the economy, income deferred for retirement purposes outside a tax-qualified plan is subjected to a higher tax than if it is used for immediate consumption purposes.

Using a hypothetical situation where the marginal statutory tax rate is 25 percent and the annual rate of return on assets just equals the inflation rate, Table 1 shows that deferring consumption under this type of regime results in a gradual deterioration of the purchasing power of money saved relative to the purchasing power of the income originally earned. If the earnings are put toward consumption in the year earned, the taxpayer can consume 75 percent of the value of earnings. If consumption is deferred just one year, the purchasing power of the account is only 74.1 percent of the value of the initial earnings. This loss in pur-

TABLE 2   Effective Tax Rates on Current versus Future Consumption When
Consumption Is Deferred through a Regular Savings Account at 5
and 10 Percent Interest and Inflation Rates

	Statutory Tax Rate	
Consumption Time Frame	25 Percent	33 Percent
5 Percent Interest and Inflation Rates		
Immediate	25.0	33.0
After 10 years	33.5	42.8
After 20 years	41.0	51.2
After 30 years	47.6	58.3
10 Percent Interest and Inflation Rates		
Immediate	25.0	33.0
After 10 years	40.4	50.6
After 20 years	52.6	63.6
After 30 years	62.4	73.1

Source: Wyatt Company.

chasing power results because the inflationary return on the asset is
taxed. No added income accrues to the account holder under the assumptions, just added tax because of the decision to defer consumption.
If the savings are held in this environment for 10 years, the effective tax
on the original earnings rises to 33.5 percent. After 20 years it is 41.0
percent, and after 30 years it is up to 47.6 percent.

Further analysis of this phenomenon shows that the effective tax rate
on earnings not immediately consumed varies in relation to a number of
factors as shown in Table 2. The results in the table show that the effective
tax rate varies with the underlying statutory tax rate, the duration of time
that consumption is deferred, and the economy's underlying inflation
rate. Under these assumptions, 50 percent goes to keep up with the
eroding purchasing power of money, and 25 percent of the gross interest
goes to pay taxes. The effective yield on the deferred consumption in this
case implies a 50 percent tax on the real return, double the statutory tax
rate assumed in the development of this example. In other words, the
concept of the comprehensive income tax behind the measurement of
tax expenditures related to tax-qualified retirement plans in the United
States would penalize people who deferred consumption during their
working career.

Conflicts Between Pension and Tax Policies

While the measurement of the tax expenditures related to employer-
sponsored retirement plans raises several methodological issues, there is

an even more fundamental problem with the estimates in that the theoretical concept is inconsistent with other stated public policies. Most governments of developed economies around the world would be reluctant to espouse publicly a national retirement policy that would advocate that retirees should lead reduced standards of living in retirement. Matching retirement living standards with pre-retirement standards does not imply that pre-retirement income levels have to be maintained. Retirees no longer have the direct expenses related to an active working life. If workers help to finance the national retirement scheme through the payment of payroll taxes, they will no longer be burdened by payroll taxes after quitting work, and other tax obligations may be reduced as well. If workers help to finance their own retirement security through steady savings in either tax-favored or unfavored plans, they will no longer be required to make such provision in retirement. But after taking into account all the differentials in expenses related to working relative to retirement, typical government policy is to encourage, if not provide, that generally acceptable living standards be attainable in retirement.

Indeed, one of the stated goals of public policy of the United States federal government, as specified in the Older Americans Act of 1965, is that the older citizens of this nation enjoy "an adequate income in retirement in accordance with the American standard of living."[1] One of the problems with the Older Americans Act is that it is not specific about the levels of income that would satisfy "the American standard of living." There are other conventional measures of adequacy that we might consider in this context, however. At the lower end of the income spectrum there are absolute measures of adequacy that are implied by the federal government's official poverty line. At income levels above these minimalist measures, adequacy of retirement income is often measured against the ability to maintain pre-retirement living standards.

An analysis of the measures usually used to assess the adequacy of benefits provided through retirement programs shows that most countries' social security benefits by themselves are inadequate to finance consumption levels commensurate with generally acceptable standards of living across a broad range of the income spectrum. This means that, in order to attain adequate retirement income to sustain acceptable standards of living, individuals must accumulate other financial resources during their working careers by deferring consumption until their retirement. This public policy goal is inconsistent with the concept of the comprehensive income tax and its application to the tax deferrals on retirement plan accumulations in the United States and elsewhere around the world. If attaining government retirement policy goals implies that individual workers have to save some of their lifetime wages to help meet their own retirement needs, why would government impose a "tax penalty" on them for doing so?

At times, past U.S. federal budget documents submitted to Congress have been unequivocal in their support of the issues being raised here regarding the measures of tax expenditures related to retirement savings. For example, the 1993 Budget observed that decisions on whether specific provisions of the tax law are preferential exceptions to the baseline provisions "is a matter of judgment."[2] The fiscal 1993 budgetary document specifically addressed the issue of taxing the inflationary return on savings. It states: "A comprehensive income tax would adjust the cost basis of capital assets and debt for changes in the price level during the time the assets or debt are held. Thus, under a comprehensive income tax baseline the failure to take account of inflation in measuring . . . interest income would be regarded as a negative tax expenditure (i.e., a tax penalty)."[3]

If including the inflation component of interest earnings on retirement assets results in a "negative tax expenditure," it should exactly offset the positive inflation component of returns on pension assets that is built into the annual estimates of these tax expenditures included in the annual federal budgets. In other words, the tax expenditures related to tax-qualified retirement plans included in the annual federal budget estimates are not only inconsistent with other federal policy, but are exaggerated by the amount of inflationary return on assets in all the respective plans. If the inflationary return on pension assets is not included in the calculations, the overall magnitude of the tax preferences accorded employer-sponsored retirement plans declines significantly.

The Comprehensive Income Tax at Work

Until 1987 New Zealand followed the normal practice of providing tax deductions for employer and employee contributions to pension plans. In addition, exemptions from tax on investment income were provided to the plans. Benefits paid by the plans were taxed on a concessional basis. The changes introduced in 1987 eliminated the tax deductibility of employee contributions, subjected employer contributions to a withholding tax, and subjected investment income to a tax. The goal of these changes was to remove all tax incentives for retirement savings and achieve tax neutrality between all forms of personal savings.

By implementing tax neutrality in this fashion the government actually subjected any earnings deferred for retirement purposes to much higher tax rates than if the earnings were used for immediate consumption purposes as shown earlier. While the new tax structure was neutral between savings within an approved retirement scheme versus some other forms of savings, it was not neutral between income earned and consumed in this period versus income earned in this period but saved for later consumption. Under this model, the only way to equalize the statutory tax rate on earnings that are saved relative to those that are not is by reducing the inflation rate in the economy to zero.

In addition to its tax treatment of private pensions, the government of New Zealand has had another structural problem in regard to its support of retirement programs. This particular problem has to do with its public social security program. This program has paid relatively high benefits, equal to 45 percent of average salaries in the economy for a single individual living alone. For a retired couple the benefit is approximately 65 percent of the average wage level. These benefit levels suggest that New Zealand's national retirement program is providing benefits at a level that would come close to sustaining the pre-retirement living standards for a significant portion of the workers reaching age 60. The problem that New Zealand has faced is that it cannot afford benefits at this level of generosity.

Under the 1991 New Zealand government's budget proposals regarding the move from the guaranteed retirement income (GRI) scheme to a revised national superannuation scheme, an income test would begin to tax away the national retirement benefit at incomes above US$ 4,160 for couples at a rate of a 50-cent reduction in the government benefit for each additional dollar of employer-provided benefit through a life insurance annuity or from a registered superannuation scheme. If that 50 percent tax rate were to be applied to the nominal value of accumulated saving in the examples we were discussing earlier, it would basically reduce the net real return on savings to zero or negative rates if the asset were held for any significant period of time. Under this model it is possible to conceive of easily plausible scenarios where workers would be better off burying their retirement savings in a jar in their back yard than investing them in an approved retirement scheme. From a macroeconomic policy perspective, encouraging people to bury their retirement savings in jars should be discouraged.

As of 1994, the budget proposal outlined by the government during 1991 has not been implemented because of the concerns voiced about it. The revised phase-out arrangement, which applied from April 1992, provides for a reduction in national superannuation by 25 percent of each dollar earned in excess of US$ 4,160 for single people and US$ 6,240 for couples. Only 50 percent of benefits paid by registered superannuation schemes and annuities paid by life offices are included in the phase-out calculation because the balance is, in effect, deemed to be a repayment of the earnings originally contributed to the plan.

A further complicating and distorting element of the New Zealand tax law is that housing continues to receive preferable tax treatment. If the goal is tax neutrality, then the preferential treatment of housing is inappropriate. While tax neutrality may be the stated goal for the current tax treatment of some forms of wealth accumulation, the inconsistency with which it is being applied undoubtedly will distort behavior.

Notes

[1] Public Law 89-73, USC.
[2] *Budget . . . Fiscal Year, 1993,* Part Two, p. 23.
[3] Ibid.

Chapter 8
An International Comparison of the Financing of Occupational Pensions

E. Philip Davis

This chapter analyzes the diverse scope of private pension funding, pension investments, and the risks and returns obtained in the capital markets in 12 major industrial countries — the United States, the United Kingdom, Germany, Japan, Canada, France, Italy, the Netherlands, Denmark, Sweden, Australia, and Switzerland.[1] The marked differences in national experience raise a number of economic issues, which I seek to address. For example, it aims to consider the role of private funding in retirement financing relative to social security, the role of government regulation of pension funds' financing; and appropriate contribution rates to private pensions. There are clear links between these issues: for example, regulations may influence appropriate contribution rates (via asset returns), and they may also influence the scope of funding itself. This chapter seeks to illustrate the varying choices made in this field by the countries concerned, their benefits and costs, and their consequences for the scope and efficiency of the privately funded sector. In this discussion I first consider the arguments for and against private pension funding per se, before outlining the differences in the scope of funding between the major countries and their determinants. I then assess the differing regulation of pension fund financing and the performance of funds in capital markets; together these enable an assessment to be made of appropriate contribution rates.

Before commencing, I offer four key definitions. In a funded pension plan, pension commitments are covered in advance by accumulation of real or financial assets. In pay-as-you-go plans, by contrast, contributions of employers and current employees are relied on to pay pensions directly. Social security systems are pay-as-you-go in most countries, while private pension plans tend to be funded. In a defined benefit pension plan the pension formula is defined in advance by the sponsor, independently of the contributions and asset returns. In contrast, in defined contribution pension plans only contributions are fixed, and benefits therefore depend solely on the returns on the assets of the fund. The key difference between defined benefit and defined contribution plans is that with defined benefit plans there can be risk sharing between worker and company as well as between younger and older members.[2] These risk-sharing features are absent with defined contribution plans.

Why Fund Pensions?

The costs and benefits of funded occupational pensions can be shown in the context of the economic issues raised by the overall choice between funding and pay-as-you-go. Under the simplifying "steady state" assumptions of a constant population and population distribution, with pension contributions proportionate to salary, and benefits proportionate to contributions,[3] the transfers received by pensioners under pay-as-you-go relative to their contributions earlier in their working lives depend on the growth of average earnings (which determines the growth in total contributions by the workforce). Meanwhile the corresponding growth of receipts under funding depends on the rate of return on the assets accumulated during the working life. In other words, the "rate of return" to pay-as-you-go is indicated by earnings growth, and that of funding by the return on physical and financial assets (Aaron 1966).[4] The actual pension received per annum under pay-as-you-go also depends on the ratio of contributing workers to pensioners (the dependency ratio), while that received in the case of funding varies with the number of years of retirement relative to working age (the passivity ratio).[5] Allowing for population growth, the steady state rate of return to pay-as-you-go increases to the growth rate of average earnings plus population growth (i.e., total earnings).

The reasoning above implies, ceteris paribus, that funding can offer higher total benefits to retirees for the same outlay if asset returns exceed the growth rate of average earnings (or, with constant factor shares, that of productivity and real GDP). Historical experience and economic theory suggest this will generally be the case.[6] Data in Table 1 indeed suggest that, in most of the countries studied, asset returns over 1970–90 did exceed growth in average earnings; hence underlying economic conditions favored funding even in a steady state, particularly if international diversification of investment is permitted where domestic returns are relatively low. Risk may be a partially offsetting factor favoring pay-as-you-go relative to funding, if asset returns are more volatile than growth in the wage bill and the dependency ratio. Risk is particularly important to

TABLE 1 Indicators of the Comparative Advantage of Pay-as-You-Go versus Funding (percentage)

Country	Average Population Growth (1970–90)	Growth Rate of Real Average Earnings	Real Return to Pay-as-You-Go in Steady State[1]	Real Return on Balanced Portfolio[2]	Real Return from Pension Funds[3]	Real Return on Equity[4]	Ratio of Population over 65/15 to 65 in 1980 and 2050
United Kingdom	0.1	2.6	2.7	3.7	5.8	8.1	23.1/30.4
United States	1.0	0.2	1.2	2.8	2.2	4.7	18.7/31.8
Canada	1.1	1.7	2.8	2.2	1.6	4.5	16.8/36.4
Japan	0.85	4.2	5.05	5.3	4.0	10.9	16.6/37.6
Germany	−0.5	4.0	3.5	6.2	5.1	9.5	22.5/42.3
Netherlands	0.6	2.4	3.0	4.2	4.0	7.9	18.5/38.1
Sweden	0.15	1.5	1.65	3.7	0.2	8.4	27.4/35.8
Denmark	0.2	2.8	3.0	4.6	3.6	7.0	22.7/39.8
Switzerland	0.2	1.9	2.1	2.0	1.5	6.2	25.0/46.0
Australia	1.45	0.7	2.15	2.8	1.6	8.1	16.6/32.0
France	0.5	4.0	4.5	4.9	n/a	9.4	21.0/37.8
Italy	0.35	3.3	3.65	2.0	n/a	4.0	20.3/37.8
Chile	1.65	6.6	8.25	n/a	n/a	n/a	n/a
Singapore	1.3	3.6	4.9	n/a	n/a	n/a	n/a

Source: Davis (1994a).
Notes: [1] Sum of population growth and earnings growth.
[2] 40 percent domestic equities, 40 percent domestic bonds, 10 percent foreign equities, 10 percent foreign bonds.
[3] Average 1967–90 (see Table 6).
[4] Average 1967–90 (see Table 6).

defined contribution funds as there is no back-up from the sponsor and pensions must typically be taken in a lump sum (to buy an annuity) at the precise point of retirement.

In practice, the calculations in Table 1 are excessively favorable to pay-as-you-go since the key assumption of the steady state — a fixed population distribution — will not be fulfilled in the coming decades. Slower population growth and aging of the population will put increasing strain on pay-as-you-go systems. In terms of the analysis above, the dependency ratio is set to rise sharply relative to the passivity ratio, driving down the rate of return to pay-as-you-go relative to funding, other things being equal.[7] In line with this, the OECD (1993) calculates that, under pay-as-you-go, contribution ratios in the G-7 countries would have to rise to a peak of 4.4 to 11.9 percent of GDP to eliminate net liabilities of social security, whereas for funding it would have to rise 1.1 to 5.3 percent, and the overall cost would be lower to the extent that the return on financial assets exceeds the growth of average earnings.[8] Such problems are leading governments to seek to reduce social security promises, thus also showing the "political risks" to which social security is vulnerable when labor market conditions are unfavorable. However, if there were to be crises in the capital market equivalent to this "crisis in the labor market," funded plans could equally be disadvantaged.[9]

There are also differences in the implications of the alternative approaches for economic efficiency. If pay-as-you-go social security contributions are seen as taxes, they will distort the labor supply decision, which is particularly likely if the rates of contribution are high and there is a great deal of redistribution; this does not occur with funding to such an extent. Again, pay-as-you-go may discourage saving and hence capital formation, notably for the first generation of recipients. This in turn makes labor relatively abundant in relation to capital, reducing the wage and raising the interest rate, thus reducing the welfare of future generations (Kotlikoff 1992). In the context of an aging population, if contribution rates under pay-as-you-go are not adjusted sufficiently to allow for benefits, fiscal deficits will be engendered, which may lead to crowding out of private investment. Even if deficits do not occur, pay-as-you-go with an aging population implies net unfunded government liabilities, which could again have crowding-out effects on investment. Meanwhile, funding tends under certain plausible conditions to increase saving, thus lowering the interest rate and raising the capital stock and hence future output for both workers and pensioners. Indeed, as noted by Estelle James and Dimitri Vittas in Chapter 5, the conditions under which funding will have a positive effect on saving, namely myopia, credit rationing, and lack of credibility of the pension plan, are precisely those whose absence will lead pay-as-you-go to reduce saving. So a switch from pay-as-you-go to funding is unambiguously likely to raise saving. If higher saving engenders capital investment, which itself raises productivity (e.g., by introducing new working methods), the overall economic growth rate may be endogenously boosted (Romer 1986). Funding can also benefit the capital markets via the composition of saving (in long-term instruments such as equities and bonds), notably if asset allocation is decentralized, as is the case for private pension funds.

There are nevertheless some arguments against funding. Funded pension plans may be vulnerable to confiscatory taxation or diversion of investment to unprofitable projects or asset categories for political reasons. Funding may adversely influence the exchange rate and the current account if ex-ante domestic investment is less than the increase in saving. The increase in saving may over the very long term depress the domestic rate of return to capital; in other words the return on assets may be affected by the scope of funding, reducing its advantage relative to pay-as-you-go, although international investment in countries with a younger population can in principle offset this problem.[10]

A transition from pay-as-you-go to funding can be difficult because one generation has to "pay twice": once for existing pensioners via pay-as-you-go, and once for their own pensions via funding. Also, in a closed economy, and abstracting from the increase in saving that funding may induce, the problem of competition over domestic resources raised by the intergenerational transfers inherent in pay-as-you-go is not entirely removed by funding. Instead it is switched from pensioners seeking a share of labor income (via taxation) to claims over the returns on the capital stock (Vittas 1992).[11] But again international investment can mitigate this problem. Pay-as-you-go plans can offer immediate pensions without waiting for assets to build up, and hence are more favorable to the first generation after their introduction than funded plans. They can remove inflation risk to pensioners by being able to link future benefits to wages (assuming a steady-state in the economy with positive population and productivity growth). Pay-as-you-go may be superior in terms of insurance of risks to labor and capital income (factor share risk), since in its absence workers tend to be wholly dependent on labor income and pensioners on capital income.[12]

From a welfare point of view funding may be objectionable for intergenerational equity where some redistribution may be justified, for example, if the growth rate is rapid and the young are much more productive and therefore have higher incomes than the elderly (Pestieau 1992). This is because, with funding, no transfers are possible between generations to compensate for a changing economic environment. With an actuarially fair funded plan, there can also be problems of equity within generations whereby well-paid workers and those who stay with one firm benefit disproportionately from the fiscal benefits offered, whereas groups with broken work histories may get an inadequate net income.[13] Only social security is able to redistribute to offset poverty within generations.

As regards methods of funding, a social security trust fund may face particular problems, which makes private funding relatively attractive (Thompson 1992). A large trust fund may induce higher government consumption or even fiscal deficits, thus defeating the object of the exercise, and its management could be subject to political interference (although it could be privatized or devolved). Investment in government bonds, which is typical of such funds in the United States, Japan, and Singapore, has ambiguous consequences. As pointed out by Bodie and Merton (1993), it is not clear that governments' willingness to repay bonds (or at least, not to devalue them by a bout of inflation) should be any more reliable than the promise to pay pensions, unless the funds are used for productive capital investment, with revenues hypothecated to pay pensions. Even if used to fund investment, finance may be diverted to unprofitable projects for political reasons. Also, lack of international investment, which is typical of such funds, leaves them dependent on the performance of the domestic economy. Investment performance of one such public trust fund, the ATP fund in Sweden, is examined below.

To summarize, these arguments suggest that funding is superior in terms of economic efficiency (e.g., less distortion of incentives to work and save), so a shift from pay-as-you-go to funding may raise work incentives and saving. Also the rate of return to funded plans tends to exceed that on pay-as-you-go plans. However, funding has some disadvantages in terms of equity that suggest that a wholesale switch to funding would be inappropriate. Diversification reasons (the differing risks to which funded and pay-as-you-go plans are exposed) are also a point in favor of retaining pay-as-you-go. The ability of social security to redistribute suggests a role for pay-as-you-go in providing basic needs, while funding caters for transfer of saving to old age. And international investment may be needed to mitigate some of the difficulties that funding may entail with an aging population. With these considerations as background, we go on to examine the actual determinants of private funding in 12 countries.

What Determines the Scale of Private Pension Funding?

The data in Table 2 show pension fund assets in the twelve countries studied, first on a narrow definition of funded non-insured company plans, and secondly on a broader definition including pension funds managed by life insurers and certain other funded plans. For each measure, a contrast is apparent between the role of pension funds in the

TABLE 2   Assets of Pension Funds End of 1991 (US$ billion)

Country	Narrow Definition[1]			Broad Definition[2]		
	Stock of Assets (end of 1991)	% of Personal Sector Assets	% of GDP	Stock of Assets (end of 1991)	% of Personal Sector Assets	% of GDP
United States	2,915	22	51	3,780	29	66
United Kingdom	643	27	60	786	33	73
Germany	59	3	3	80[3]	4	4
Japan	182	2	5	303[3]	3	8
Canada	187	17	32	205	19	35
Netherlands	145	26	46	242	43	76
Sweden	87	n/a	33	—	—	—
Denmark	22	n/a	16	82	n/a	60
Switzerland	173	n/a	70	—	—	—
Australia	62	19	22	110	34	39

Source: Davis (1994a).

Notes: [1] Includes only independent (private and public sector) funded pension schemes, except Sweden — public ATP scheme.

[2] For the United States, Australia, Canada and Denmark includes data for pension reserves of life insurers; for the United Kingdom and Japan includes estimates of life insurance companies' pension fund reserves; for Denmark includes funds managed by banks; for the Netherlands includes the Civil Service Pension Fund (ABP).

[3] In Germany and Japan there are large reserve funded (or "booked") pension plans with assets held directly on the sponsoring firm's balance sheet. The value of these in 1991 was US$ 150 billion in Germany and an estimated US$ 120 billion in Japan.

Anglo-Saxon countries (the United Kingdom, the United States, Australia, and Canada), the Netherlands, Denmark, and Switzerland, where they account for a sizable part of personal sector wealth and GDP, versus that role in other continental European countries such as Germany. Japan occupies an intermediate position, with sizable total assets but low ratios to personal wealth or GDP. Note the Swedish data are for the funded earnings-related social security system (ATP); private funded plans exist, but their assets are relatively small.

Taking the asset/GDP ratio as an imperfect proxy for the size of the funded sector, what types of influences could account for the differences in the importance of funded sectors in the provision of pensions? The most crucial point is that private funded plans cannot usefully be viewed in isolation; the principal alternative to a private pension fund is the state social security pension system. Not surprisingly, the growth of private plans can be related to the scale of social security pension provision, which imposes limits on private sector plans, particularly if there is generous provision for individuals at higher income levels. Second, where provision is voluntary, taxation and regulatory provisions make it more or less attractive for the firm to offer a pension fund. For example, exemption of funds from taxation, "prudent man" rules for asset management, and flexible funding rules will increase funds' attractiveness. However, in some countries these factors may be overridden, imposing compulsory pension plans on employers. Since accrued rights within occupational pension plans comprise assets of the employee, it is natural also to consider their motivations. For example, high marginal tax rates may increase the attraction to employees of tax deferral via pension funds. Employees will also be attracted by the quality of retirement income insurance that is on offer, which differs between defined benefit and defined contribution plans and varies with factors such as indexation of pensions to prices or wages (Bodie 1990). But note that regulations making funds attractive to employees, such as compulsory indexation and short vesting periods, may make them less attractive to employers.

Of course not all funds are company-based. Personal pensions, which are invariably defined contribution plans, have grown in importance in a number of countries in recent years, the main aims being to provide the tax incentives of pension plans to those not in company plans, to enable company plans to be supplemented, and/or to offer greater portability than is available from company plans. A further factor influencing the size of pension funds is the maturity of the plans, that is, whether they have a stable long-run ratio of contributing to benefiting members. Coverage is obviously also important (i.e., the proportion of employees covered by pension plans). However, this is a consequence of the economic features as discussed below, rather than a separate cause of growth in itself.

Accrual of pension rights in a defined contribution plan is synonymous with accumulation of assets, which will thus be larger the higher the contribution rate, coverage of the workforce, and rates of return. But a defined benefit plan is not necessarily synonymous with a fund; rather it is a way to collateralize the firm's benefit promise. In order for assets to be built up, it is essential for fiscal or regulatory provisions to encourage funding of defined benefits; otherwise defined benefit plans may be unfunded. Only if external funding is encouraged, as opposed to "booking" of pension liabilities on the balance sheet, will funds be available in the form of assets of the capital market intermediated via pension funds. And only then one can one also assert for defined benefit funds that the more generous the benefits offered and the wider the coverage, the more financial assets funds will require.

Table 3 offers a summary of the way these various features stand in the twelve countries studied. To summarize, the influence on the development of private plans of the scale of social security, compulsion, the tax regime, and maturity can be discerned in each country. Key regulatory features that may also influence funding, notably funding rules per se, are assessed in more detail in the next section.

TABLE 3   Determinants of the Size of Funded Sectors

Country	Social Security Replacement Rate 1992 (%)[1]	Form of Taxation[2]	Coverage of Funded Schemes (%)	Maturity of Funded Schemes
United States	65–40	EET – Contributions and asset returns tax free. Benefits taxed.	46 (voluntary)	Mature
United Kingdom	50–26[3]	EET – Contributions and asset returns tax free. Benefits taxed, except for tax free lump sum.	50 (company) 25 (personal); (voluntary)	Mature
Germany	70–59	TET – Employers' contributions taxed as wages; employees' contributions and asset returns tax free. Benefits taxed at low rate. (For booked benefits, employers contributions tax free, benefits taxed at normal rate.)	42 (voluntary)	Immature
Japan	54[4]	ETT – Contributions tax free. Tax on asset returns. Benefits taxed, except for tax free lump sum. (Partial tax exemption of contributions to booked benefits.)	50 (voluntary)	Immature
Canada	34[4]	EET – Contributions and asset returns tax free. Benefits taxed.	41 (voluntary)	Mature

Country	Ratio	Tax treatment	Coverage	Maturity
Netherlands	66–26	EET – Contributions and asset returns tax free. Benefits taxed.	83 (voluntary)	Mature
Sweden	69–49	ETT – Contributions to ATP tax free; contributions to ITP/STP subject to social security tax. Tax on asset returns of ITP/STP. Benefits taxed at low rate.	90 (ATP compulsory; ITP/STP voluntary)	Mature
Denmark	83–33	ETT – Contributions tax free. Tax on real asset returns. Benefits taxed, including 40% of lump sum payments.	50 (voluntary)	Mature
Switzerland	82–47	EET – Contributions and asset returns tax free. Benefits taxed.	90 (compulsory)	Mature (pre-BVG) Immature (post-BVG)
Australia	28–11	TTT – Contributions, asset returns and benefits taxed.	92 (compulsory)	Immature
France	67–45[5]	E(E)T – Contributions to ARRCO/AGIRC tax free; separate funded schemes forbidden; insured pension contributions tax free.	100 (compulsory)	Mature
Italy	77–73	EET – Contributions and asset returns tax free, benefits taxed.	5 (voluntary)	Immature

Source: Davis (1994a).

Notes: [1] Based on final salary of US\$ 20,000 and US\$ 50,000, for married man; source Wyatt (1993).
[2] The abbreviations refer to taxation of contributions, returns and benefits, hence EET means contributions and returns are exempt and benefits are taxed.
[3] Includes state earnings related pension scheme (SERPs). For those contracted out, the ratios are 35% and 14%.
[4] Ratio to average earnings in 1986.
[5] Includes ARRCO.

As regards social security, replacement ratios are shown to be relatively low in Australia, which is a country that relies heavily on private pensions even for low earners, but comparable for those on low incomes in other countries. In such cases, the shape of the relation of replacement ratio to final earnings is a crucial determinant of the scope of private funds; if social security provides high replacement ratios to high earners, there will be little incentive to develop private funded plans at all. In line with this suggestion, the replacement ratio declines rapidly with earnings in Denmark, the Netherlands, the United States, and the United Kingdom — countries with large funded sectors. Italy and Germany, by contrast, are notable for comparable replacement ratios to those retiring on earnings equivalent to US\$ 20,000 and US\$ 50,000. Their private funded sectors are much less important.

As regards taxation, the Netherlands, the United Kingdom, Switzerland, the United States, and Canada offer generous treatment (exemption of contributions and asset returns from tax, while pensions in payment are taxed, denoted EET in Table 3). "Booking" is discouraged in these countries by withholding tax privileges from reserve-funded plans (or outright bans, as in the United States and Canada). High general tax rates of up to 68 percent, as in Denmark, can encourage private funding even if their fiscal treatment is less generous (a tax is imposed on real asset returns to pension funds above a certain level). In Germany and Japan, tax incentives to "booking" of corporate pension liabilities and some tax disadvantages to pension funds have, at least until recently, accompanied smaller funded plans.

Compulsion is a feature of the Swedish public and the Swiss and Australian private national funded systems, all of which are designed in the light of demographic concerns to provide a sizable proportion of retirement benefits. Coverage is hence extremely high: only in the Netherlands do voluntary plans reach similar levels of coverage. Because the plans are compulsory, the tax regime is less important; in particular, the Australian fiscal treatment of taxation of contributions, returns, and benefits would be unlikely to encourage voluntary pension provision. The French supplementary plans are also compulsory, but pay-as-you-go financing is enforced.

Funded sectors differ in terms of maturity, which also influences the current and prospective asset/GDP ratio. In the United States, the United Kingdom, Canada, Sweden, and the Netherlands, defined benefit plans are largely mature and hence the asset/GDP ratio is near a peak, although personal and defined contribution funds could spur further growth in the United Kingdom, Canada, and the United States. In Denmark, Japan, and Germany, immaturity of company plans indicates further growth is likely. In Australia and Switzerland, the relatively recent introduction of mandatory pension funds means that a significant proportion of pension funds will again be immature.

A simple regression analysis was carried out to test the main influences on the "broad" pension asset/GDP ratio, using as independent variables the key factors identified above, namely the scope of social security, the tax regime, whether the scheme is mandatory, and maturity of the scheme. Of course, such a regression cannot prove causality. Subject to this caveat, the equation does indicate the importance of these factors in discriminating between countries with small and large private funded sectors. It suggests that every one percentage point increase in the difference between social security replacement ratios at US\$ 20,000 and US\$ 50,000 is associated with a 1.2 percent higher asset/GDP ratio; a deviation from favorable "expenditure tax" treatment of pensions is related to 21 percent lower funding; countries where there is compulsion have a 23 percent higher ratio, ceteris paribus, and those with mature systems a 27 percent higher asset/GDP ratio. All variables were significant at the 95 percent level.

Detailed study of national funded sectors (Davis 1994a) suggests that other important factors in the development of occupational pension funds are the ability of employees to opt out of earnings-related social security for an equivalent private pension (as in the United Kingdom and Japan), funding of civil service pensions (Netherlands), widening of coverage via encouragement of personal pensions (United Kingdom, Canada, United States, Switzerland), and encouragement of supplementary defined contribution plans (United States). On the other hand, development can be stopped by simply banning company-based externally funded plans, as in France (Syatt 1993), and funding of social security in Sweden ensures private funds remain small.

A striking feature of this analysis of the determinants of private funding is that it appears to be tenuously related to the underlying fundamentals that were outlined above. This is not surprising, as in most countries social security and private provision have evolved piecemeal, without coordination. Only in Australia (and Chile) does social security provide solely for basic needs. There is little correlation between the wage-interest differential and the size of funded sectors, nor, as yet, to the future aging of the population in the different countries. These should predispose countries such as France, Italy, Japan, and Germany to extend the scope of funding. Retirement system reform has nonetheless been marked in Japan, with a reduction in social security promises, partial funding of social security, and reduction of tax benefits to "booking" (Watanabe, Chapter 4, this volume), but elsewhere it has been slow.[14] Taxation costs and transition problems, as well as preference for the "social solidarity" of comprehensive pay-as-you-go, are among the reasons.

What Are the Principal Pension Regulations Affecting Financing?

A final factor that may influence the size of the funded sector is regulation, by requiring external funding of benefits per se and/or affecting the attractiveness of provision of funds to companies. This section assesses the main regulations affecting pension fund financing, namely regulations of funding and portfolio regulations, and considers their influence, together with other factors, on the portfolio distribution, the returns, and hence the cost of providing a given level of benefits. In terms of the framework set out in the first section, funding rules can be seen as ensuring that assets actually are accumulated to cover benefit promises under funding, while portfolio regulations seek to influence the nature of the return to funding. The basic regulations are summarized in Table 4.

Regulation of the funding of benefits is a key aspect of the regulatory framework for defined benefit pension funds. Note that, by definition, a defined contribution plan is always fully funded, as assets equal liabilities, whereas as noted with defined benefit plans there is a distinction between the pension plan (setting out contractual rights to the parties) and the fund (a pool of assets to provide collateral for the promised benefits). When the fund is worth less than the present value of promised benefits, there is underfunding; when the opposite is the case, there is overfunding. Calculation of appropriate funding levels requires a number of actuarial assumptions, in particular the assumed return on assets, projected future wage growth (for final salary plans), and projected future inflation (if there is indexing of pensions), as well as estimates of death rates and the expected evolution of the relative number of contributors and beneficiaries over time. Minimum funding limits set by regulation seek to protect security of benefits against default risk by the company, given that unfunded benefits are liabilities on the books of the firm and therefore risk is concentrated and pensioners (or pension insurers) may have no better claim in case of bankruptcy than any other creditor.[15] Funding offers a diversified and hence less risky alternative back-up for the benefit promise, as well as offering the possibility of unplanned benefit increases if the plan is in surplus. Extra protection against creditors of a bankrupt firm is afforded when the pension fund is independent of the firm and when self-investment is banned or severely restricted, as is the case in most countries except Germany and Japan. There are usually also upper limits on funding, to prevent abuse of tax privileges (overfunding). Bodie (1990) suggests that the three main reasons why firms fund, besides regulations per se, are because of the tax incentives, in order to provide financial slack (when there is a surplus) that can be used in case of

TABLE 4   Summary of Pension Asset Regulations

Country	Portfolio Regulations	Regulation of Funding[1]
United States	Prudent man concept; 10% self investment limit for defined benefit funds.	ABO must be funded. Maximum 50% overfund of the ABO. Higher insurance premiums if underfunded.
United Kingdom	Prudent man concept; five percent self investment limit, concentration limit for defined contribution plans.	Maximum 5% overfund of PBO or IBO. Funding only obligatory for contracted out part of social security.
Germany	Guidelines; maximum 20% equity, five percent property, four percent foreign, 10% self investment limit.	Funding obligatory up to PBO. Option of book-reserve funding.
Japan	Guidelines; maximum 30% equity, 20% property, 30% foreign, 10% in one country; minimum 50% in bonds.	Tax exempt up to ABO only. Option of book-reserve funding.
Canada	Prudent man, tax on foreign assets over 10%, seven percent limit on property.	Maximum 5% overfund of PBO. Funding obligatory.
Netherlands	Prudent man concept, five percent self investment limit.	Funding obligatory for IBO or PBO.
Sweden	Majority to be in listed bonds, debentures and retroverse loans to contributors.	IBO is funded. Contribution rate adjusted 5-yearly to balance fund.
Denmark	Property, shares and investment trust holdings limited to 40%, foreign assets to 20%; 60% to be in domestic debt. No self investment.	Irrelevant as defined contribution; benefits must be funded externally.
Switzerland	50% limit on domestic shares, 50% on property, 20% foreign currency assets.	Funding only obligatory for ABO; PBO usually funded. Four percent to be credited to accounts annually.
Australia	Prudent man rule.	Irrelevant as defined contribution; minimum contribution rate enforced.
France	Assets of supplementary funds to be invested 50% in government bonds and less than 33% in loans to sponsors.	Funded company schemes forbidden; book reserve funding subject to tax discrimination.
Italy	No pension law.	No pension law.

Source: Davis (1994a).
Note: [1]ABO refers to the accrued benefit obligation; PBO to the projected benefit obligation.

financial difficulty, and because pension benefit insurance may not cover the highest-paid employees.

Certain definitions are useful as background to a discussion of funding rules. The "windup" definition of liabilities, the "solvency" level at which the firm can meet all its current obligations absent any projections of salary, is known as the accumulated benefit obligation (ABO).[16] The assumption that rights will continue to accrue, and be indexed up to retirement, as is normal in a final salary plan, gives the projected benefit obligation (PBO).[17] The indexed benefit obligation (IBO) assumes indexation after retirement.[18] An important argument in favor of the PBO/IBO over the ABO is that it ensures advance provision for the burden of maturity of the plan, when there are many pensioners and fewer workers, by spreading costs over the life of the plan (Frijns and Petersen 1992). This may be better for the financial stability of the sponsor.[19]

In the United States the ABO must be funded; unfunded plans are forbidden in theory, though in practice some forms are less fully funded. Together with absence of obligatory indexation, this has an important influence on portfolio distributions, since underfunding (shortfall risk) can be avoided, and tax benefits to the firm maximized, by holding bonds, or at least by portfolio insurance strategies; unhedged equities are only suitable for overfunded plans. The United States Pension Benefit Guaranty Corporation (PBGC) guarantees (up to a limit) benefits of defined benefit funds in default, funded by contributions from all defined benefit plans; the funding requirement can be seen partly as a protection for PBGC. Higher PBGC insurance premiums are charged to underfunded plans.

The United States illustrates the interaction of funding rules with accounting standards and tax law in influencing funding. Under the United States accounting standard FASB 87, if pension assets fall below the ABO, the unfunded liability must be reported in the firm's balance sheet, and since they are senior debt, they act as a major problem for the firm in raising funds. However, a surplus cannot be included on the balance sheet, although it can be implicitly recouped by reducing in contributions, as discussed below. The accounting standard requires presentation of the PBO, as well as the ABO, thus ensuring at least partial focus on future liabilities. Again, overfunding in the United States has since 1987 been limited by tax law to 150 percent of the ABO. This implies that a rise in interest rates could prevent further funding, leaving the plan underfunded when interest rates fall. This would not have been the case for a PBO definition, taking projected rises in benefits into account, as long as the Fisher effect holds, that is, interest rates rise with expected inflation.

Other countries show similar interactions. In Germany, various laws or court decisions have enforced minimum standards of funding for pension funds (while leaving open the choice of a book reserve system) and what amounts to inflation indexing of pensions. These provisions were felt to be particularly burdensome, and have helped blunt the growth rate of externally funded private pension plans as opposed to "booked" benefits (Deutsche Bundesbank 1984). In both Germany and Switzerland, accounting conventions have an impact on funding decisions, as shortfalls (defined at the lower of cost and market value of assets) are included in the company accounts (Hepp 1992). It is suggested that this helps to account for conservative investment strategies, independently of portfolio regulations discussed below. Rules forcing employers in Switzerland to credit at least 4 percent to pension accounts annually may have a similar effect. In Japan, the traditional means of providing retirement benefits was via booked benefits, with a special reserve account on the balance sheet as benefits accrue. Externally funded plans must be funded only up to the ABO, and there is reportedly very little overfunding, partly because contributions that would raise funding levels above the ABO are taxed. In Canada plans must be funded as going concerns, including projections of salary rises (i.e., the PBO); unfunded plans are forbidden, and any unfunded liabilities must be paid off in 15 years.

In the United Kingdom, plans that contract out of earnings-related social security must fund sufficiently to provide an equivalent "guaranteed minimum pension" (GMP), but this is far below actual benefit promises. Funding above this level is not legally required — although trustees are bound by their duty of care to ensure funding is in place — nor is there a requirement to include deficits in company balance sheets. In practice a continuance basis such as the PBO or IBO tends to be used, on which overfunding is limited to 5 percent. A crucial difference from other countries is that adequacy of funding is judged by current and projected cash flows from assets and not current market values; this allows volatile assets such as equities to be heavily used. This is reflected in accounting standard SSAP24, which also bases fund valuation on such actuarial valuations and long-run smoothing. Historically, this has not conflicted with the need to cover obligations if the fund is wound up, since the PBO has tended to exceed the ABO. But compulsory indexation, currently being introduced, will increase the ABO and could put the system under threat (Riley 1993).[20] Meanwhile, although the government guarantees to pay the GMP if a plan fails, there has to date been no system to guarantee non-GMP pension benefits in the United Kingdom; partly for this reason regulations have historically been less strict than elsewhere, and managers could adopt a high return/high risk portfolio strategy. However, the Goode Committee on United Kingdom pension law — set up to report on regulatory shortcomings in the wake of the

Maxwell scandal, and which reported in 1993 — recommended a minimum funding rule based on the ABO, with only a three-month grace period to top up the fund, albeit with a 10 percent shortfall being permitted without the immediate need to top up. Insurance against fraud was also recommended. The government launched a bill in mid-1994 approving these proposals, although funding rules will be less strict for immature funds. This raises issues similar to those outlined above for the United States, and might alter quite significantly the asset mix of United Kingdom funds toward less volatile but also less profitable assets.

The importance of the choice of discount rate in funding calculations is shown by a 1993 United States Department of Labor estimate that a one percent fall in the bond yield would raise pension liabilities by 10 percent for the average fund.[21] Feldstein and Morck (1983) report that many underfunded plans in the United States tended to use a high rate to discount fund liabilities. One answer to these problems is to take a long-run view of asset returns, or possibly, where inflation is low and stable, a fixed benchmark discount rate. The latter is the case in the Netherlands, where funding of the PBO is compulsory and the government sets a maximum real interest rate assumption of 4 percent, as well as an assumption for wage growth. Since in practice Dutch funds have been able to earn over this level, surpluses estimated at 30 percent were present by 1990; a special tax levy is planned. In the United States, in the light of the tendencies noted above, the Securities and Exchange Commission (SEC) has insisted that interest rate assumptions follow actual bond yields closely. In Japan contributions are set assuming a 5 percent nominal rate of return on fund assets. In Canada a nominal return of 8.5 percent and 5.75 percent wage growth are standard assumptions. In the United Kingdom the government accepts the (varying) judgment of the actuaries, and generally also allows for an assumption of wage growth.

Finally, since most Danish and Australian funds (as well as a proportion of funds in Switzerland and the Anglo-American countries) are defined contribution plans, the issue of funding does not arise. However, the issue of limiting tax privilege does arise, and is dealt with (in Australia) via contribution limits and (in both countries) via taxation of returns.

Quantitative regulation of portfolio distributions is imposed in a number of countries, with the ostensible aim of protecting pension fund beneficiaries, or benefit insurers, although motives such as ensuring a steady demand for government bonds may also play a part. Limits are often imposed on holdings of assets with relatively volatile returns, such as equities and property, as well as foreign assets, even if their mean return is relatively high. There are also often limits on self-investment, to protect against the associated concentration of risk regarding insolvency of the sponsor.[22] Apart from the control of self-investment, which is clearly necessary to ensure that funds are not vulnerable to bankruptcy of the sponsor, the degree to which such regulations actually contribute to benefit security is open to doubt, since pension funds, unlike insurance companies, may face the risk of increasing liabilities as well as the risk of holding assets, and hence need to trade volatility with return. Moreover, appropriate diversification of assets can eliminate any idiosyncratic risk from holding an individual security or type of asset, thus minimizing the increase in risk. Again, if national cycles and markets are imperfectly correlated, international investment will reduce otherwise undiversifiable or "systematic" risk (see Davis 1994b and Table 9 below). Portfolio limits may be particularly inappropriate for defined benefit pensions, given the additional "buffer" of the company guarantee and risk sharing between older and young workers, and if benefits must be indexed. Clearly, in such cases, portfolio regulations may affect the attractiveness to companies of providing pension funds, if it constrains managers in their choice of risk and return, forcing them to hold low-yielding assets and possibly *increasing* their risks by limiting their possibilities for diversification.[23] It will also restrict the benefits to the capital markets from the development of pension funds; in particular, in the case of restrictions that explicitly or implicitly oblige pension funds to invest in government bonds, which must themselves be repaid from taxation, there may be no benefit to capital formation and the "funded" plans may at a macroeconomic level be virtually equivalent to pay-as-you-go.[24]

Japanese funds face ceilings on holdings of certain assets such as 30 percent for foreign assets and for equities, which Matsuhiro Tamura (1992) suggests (inappropriately) "imitate regulations devised for trust banking and life insurers." German pension funds, besides a 10 percent self investment limit, remain subject to the same panoply of regulation as life insurers (4 percent limit on foreign asset holdings, 20 percent limit on equities, 5 percent on property). It is arguable that these are particularly inappropriate for German pension funds given the indexed nature of their liabilities.[25] Note that by offering tax privileges to "booking," Germany and Japan effectively impose no limits on self-investment of book reserves (although the Germans do insist on insurance of such reserves). Swiss limits are similarly structured, but since the end of 1992 have been much less restrictive than the Germans': a 50 percent limit on shares, 50 percent for real estate, and 30 percent on foreign assets (Meier 1993). Scandinavian limits are in many ways even tighter than the Germans', in that minima are also specified. The Swedish ATP, as well as private funds, have historically been obliged to hold the majority of its assets in domestic listed bonds, debentures, and retroverse loans to contributors (although recent deregulations have permitted limited investment in property, equities, and foreign assets, of which some private plans have reportedly taken advantage). Historically, restrictions on equity investments were justified on the additional ground that for ATP they would involve backdoor nationalization and worker control. Danish funds have to hold 60 percent in domestic debt instruments, although since 1990 they have been allowed to hold 20 percent in foreign assets. Investment in the sponsor is forbidden. Mutual societies providing pensions in France (via group insurance policies) must follow insurance regulations that insist that they invest at least 34 percent in state bonds, and a maximum of 40 percent in property and 5 percent in shares of foreign insurers.

Such limits are not, however, imposed in all the countries studied. For example, pension funds in the United States are subject to a "prudent man rule" that requires managers to diversify portfolios; the primary limit to portfolio distributions is a 10 percent limit on self investment for defined benefit funds and some defined contribution funds.[26] United Kingdom pension funds are subject to trust law and implicitly follow the "prudent man" concept; as long as trust deeds are appropriately structured they are not constrained by regulation in their portfolio distribution except for limits on self-investment (5 percent) and concentration.[27] Australian funds' investment has been unrestricted since exchange controls were abolished in 1983 and public sector funds were deregulated in 1985, except for a 10 percent limit on exposure to the sponsor. Dutch private funds face no legal restrictions, except for a 5 percent limit on self-investment (Van Loo 1988). In contrast, the Dutch public service fund (ABP) faces strict limits, being able to invest only 10 percent abroad and 20 percent in shares or real estate. Some countries have switched to "prudent man" rules; Canadian funds were strictly regulated until 1987 (when the "prudent man" concept was introduced) and have until recently faced limits on the share of external assets.

To conclude, funding and portfolio regulations differ quite significantly, with some countries using only accrued benefit-based funding and others projected benefits. The division for portfolio regulations, between countries with "prudent man" rules and regulations, is even more stark. In the next sections we probe the consequences of such rules for portfolios.

How Are Pension Assets Invested?

The portfolio distribution and the corresponding return and risk on the assets held are the key determinant of the cost to the company of providing a pension in a defined benefit plan and the replacement ratio obtainable via a defined contribution fund (and hence in each case the yield that can be obtained by funding relative to that of pay-as-you-go). This section seeks to trace the various influences on portfolio distributions, in particular those of the portfolio and funding regulations outlined above.

How might funds be invested in the absence of portfolio regulation? As shown by Black (1980), for both defined benefit and defined contribution funds, there is an incentive to maximize the tax advantage of pension funds by investing in assets with the highest possible spread between pre-tax and post-tax returns. In 1980 in the United States this was bonds, but some analysts suggest that since 1986 the relative tax advantage of equities has declined sharply, making them candidates for pension fund investment on this basis (Chen and Reichenstein 1993).[28] Apart from this a defined contribution pension plan would seek to diversify, seeking to maximize return for a given risk, and shift to lower risk assets for older workers as they approach retirement.

More complex considerations arise for defined benefit funds. First, there is an incentive to overfund to maximize the tax benefits, as well as to provide a larger contingency fund, which as noted is usually counteracted by government-imposed limits on funding. Meanwhile, appropriate investment strategies will also depend on the nature of the obligation incurred. If it is the ABO and is purely nominal, with penalties for shortfalls, it will be appropriate in theory to match (or "immunize") the liabilities with bonds of the same duration to hedge the interest rate risk of these liabilities, or at least to hedge against the risk of shortfall when holding more volatile securities. With a projected benefit obligation target, an investment policy based on diversification may be most appropriate, in the belief that risk reduction depends on a maximum diversification of the pension fund relative to the firm's operating investments (Ambachtsheer 1988).[29] Moreover, if the projected liability includes an element of indexation, then fund managers and actuaries typically assume that it may be appropriate to include a proportion of equities and property in the portfolio as well as bonds (Christopher Daykin, this volume). This should minimize the risk of longer-term shortfall of assets relative to liabilities, implicitly diversifying between investment risk and liability risk (which are largely risks of inflation).[30]

An essential counterpart to such an approach is that regulators allow gradual amortization of shortfalls, or even focus in solvency calculations on income from assets rather than market values as in the United Kingdom. Allowing inflation indexation of pension to be discretionary, as is the case in most countries other than the United Kingdom and Germany, is another way to reduce the risk of shortfall; implicitly it is a form of risk sharing between firm and workers. Maturity will also affect optimal portfolios. For example Blake (1994) suggests that given the varying duration of liabilities it is rational for immature defined benefit funds having "real" liabilities to invest mainly in equities (long duration), for mature funds to invest in a mix of equities and bonds, and for funds that are winding up mainly in bonds (short duration).

It is important to note that many financial economists disagree with the implicit assumptions that may underlie a strategy of equity investment, namely that equity is a hedge against inflation, and that raising the share of equity reduces costs, as opposed to merely raising expected returns, and offering benefits of diversification (Bodie 1990). We do not seek to take sides in this debate in this chapter. Suffice to note here that Tepper (1992) suggests that the debate hinges on whether returns on equity are statistically independent from year to year. If they are, it is quite conceivable that a long series of bad returns could lead to significant real losses from equities even over a long time horizon relevant to pension funds. But proponents of the view that equities outperform bonds over long time horizons would maintain that there are reversals in trends in returns to ensure that owners of capital are compensated over the long term. They suggest that although underperformance of equities is quite common in the short term, long-term underperformance would entail economic collapse, which governments would seek to resist. Also of interest in this context is the suggestion that the premium in returns of equities over bonds is more than can be explained by relative risk (Mehra and Prescott 1985), which if correct implies that risk-neutral investors such as pension funds can gain from holding equities.

The actual patterns of portfolio distributions over the past two decades are shown in Table 5. Marked differences emerge: for example, in 1990 equity holdings varied from one percent in Sweden to 63 percent in the United Kingdom, and foreign assets from one percent in Denmark to 18 percent in the United Kingdom. As background, estimates of real total returns and their standard deviations for 1967 to 1990 are shown in Table 6. Davis (1994a) offers a detailed analysis of these patterns of portfolio distributions and their determinants. So here I offer an overview of certain key determinants, grouping by type of influence.

In line with the discussion above, liabilities are a major influence, for example affecting the share of bonds. In countries such as Canada, with a high share of bonds, only nominal returns have historically been promised after retirement, while in the United Kingdom, where bond holding is low, a degree of inflation protection both before and after retirement is expected. Similar indexation promises are made by the Swedish supplementary national plan, despite which the bond share is extremely high, suggesting an inefficient portfolio allocation.

Historically the higher taxation on bonds than on equities made the former an attractive investment to tax-exempt investors such as pension funds, but as noted recent analyses suggest that equities are now less advantaged in the United States, and hence should be more attractive,

TABLE 5   Pension Fund Portfolio Distributions (percentage)

Country		Equities	Bonds	Loans and Mortgages	Property	Liquidity and Deposits	Of Which Foreign Assets[1]
United	1970	49	32	0	10	4	2
Kingdom	1980	52	24	0	18	5	9
	1990	63	14	0	9	7	18
United	1970	45	45	6	0	1	0
States	1980	41	41	2	0	8	1
	1990	46	36	2	0	9	4
Germany	1970	4	19	50	12	3	0
	1980	9	24	52	9	2	0
	1990	18	25	45	6	2	1
Japan	1970	6	12	52	27	2	0
	1980	9	51	33	6	2	1
	1990	27	47	14	2	3	7
Canada	1970	27	53	11	1	5	0
	1980	26	50	12	2	9	4
	1990	33	47	4	3	11	6
Netherlands	1970	11	15	54	16	3	7
	1980	5	10	69	14	2	4
	1990	20	23	43	11	3	15
Sweden	1970	0	76	22	0	1	0
	1980	0	74	26	0	1	0
	1990	1	84	10	1	3	0
Switzerland	1970	3	25	48	16	7	0
	1980	9	28	37	18	6	0
	1990	16	29	22	17	12	3
Denmark	1970	0	72	7	0	3	0
	1980	3	63	7	0	2	0
	1990	7	67	7	0	1	1
Australia	1970	15	51	0	2	n/a	0
	1980	15	33	0	13	n/a	0
	1990	27	20	0	16	23	13

Source: National flow-of-funds data.
Note: [1]Foreign assets are included in the categories to the left.

and indeed bond shares in the United States have declined somewhat. Often portfolio regulations force funds to hold tax-disadvantaged assets, as in Denmark, where funds must hold 60 percent fixed interest assets, despite the real interest tax on such assets.

Asset returns, both absolute and relative to other assets, are a key influence on the structure of any portfolio. This is confirmed by econometric analysis of the portfolio distributions of pension funds, which shows they are strongly influenced by relative asset returns, particularly where there are few regulations governing portfolio distributions and low transactions costs, as in the United Kingdom and the United States (Davis

TABLE 6   Returns on Pension Fund Portfolios, 1967–90: Mean (and Standard Deviation) of Annual Real Total Returns (percentage, domestic currency)

	United States	United Kingdom	Germany	Japan	Canada	Netherlands	Sweden	Denmark
Estimated portfolio return[1]	2.2 (11.9)	5.8 (12.5)	5.1 (4.4)	4.0 (9.4)	1.6 (9.8)	4.0 (6.0)	0.2 (7.6)	3.6 (12.0)
Average earnings growth	0.2 (2.1)	2.6 (2.5)	4.0 (3.1)	4.2 (4.2)	1.7 (2.8)	2.4 (3.2)	1.5 (3.5)	2.8 (3.0)
Portfolio return less average earnings	2.0	3.2	1.1	-0.2	-0.1	1.6	-1.3	0.8
Inflation (CPI)	5.8 (3.0)	8.9 (5.3)	3.5 (2.1)	5.5 (5.3)	6.4 (3.0)	4.9 (3.1)	8.1 (2.7)	7.7 (3.0)
Returns on								
Loans	3.5 (2.9)	1.4 (5.0)	5.3 (1.9)	0.9 (4.3)	4.0 (3.7)	3.8 (3.6)	3.4 (3.1)	6.1 (3.0)
Mortgages	2.0 (13.4)	2.0 (5.2)	4.7 (1.4)	3.0 (4.9)	2.4 (12.3)	4.3 (2.6)	2.6 (3.0)	5.8 (3.0)
Equities	4.7 (14.4)	8.1 (20.3)	9.5 (20.3)	10.9 (19.4)	4.5 (16.5)	7.9 (28.2)	8.4 (23.3)	7.0 (27.0)
Bonds	-0.5 (14.3)	-0.5 (13.0)	2.7 (14.9)	0.2 (12.8)	0.0 (12.1)	1.0 (13.1)	-0.9 (8.5)	3.4 (16.0)
Short-term assets	2.0 (2.5)	1.7 (4.9)	3.1 (2.1)	-0.5 (4.6)	2.5 (3.3)	1.6 (4.0)	1.3 (3.5)	1.6 (1.0)
Property	3.4 (6.4)	6.7 (11.4)	4.5 (2.9)	7.2 (6.8)	4.6 (6.2)	4.6 (15.0)	n/a n/a	n/a n/a
Foreign bonds	1.6 (14.9)	-0.1 (15.0)	3.0 (11.2)	1.3 (14.6)	-1.7 (12.7)	-0.7 (11.2)	-0.2 (12.6)	-2.0 (11.0)
Foreign equities	9.9 (17.2)	7.0 (16.2)	10.4 (13.5)	7.8 (18.7)	5.8 (14.3)	6.6 (14.4)	7.1 (14.0)	5.5 (14.0)
Memo: portfolio return[2]	3.9 (7.6)	6.3 (10.7)	5.5 (3.0)	2.9 (5.7)	4.1 (5.0)	4.3 (5.5)	2.8 (2.9)	5.8 (3.0)

Source: Davis (1994a), using national flow of funds data (for portfolio distribution see Table 5) and BIS macroeconomic database (for asset returns).
Notes: [1] Using holding period returns on bonds (all countries) and on fixed-rate mortgages (United States and Canada).
[2] Using redemption yields on fixed rate instruments.

1988). Adjustment to a change in such returns is generally rapid. Assuming adequate information and appropriate incentives to fund managers, this should imply an efficient allocation of funds and correct valuation of securities. In my research, these results did not all hold where transactions costs are high and regulations are strict, as in Germany, Japan, and Canada. In these countries adjustment to a change in returns is somewhat slower and allocation of funds less efficient. The results also contrast with those for households and companies, where adjustment to changes in returns tends to be slow, due to higher transactions costs and poorer information. Examples in Table 6 of responses to relative returns include the high levels of liquidity held temporarily after stock market collapses in the United Kingdom in the mid-1970s, and in the longer term due to structural changes in yields arising from deregulation and expansion of short-term markets in the United States and Canada. Inter-country differences in bond holding may also relate to asset returns; partly owing to low and stable inflation, real returns on bonds and other fixed interest assets are relatively high in Germany, Denmark, and the Netherlands, thus motivating a high portfolio share. But in Sweden and Switzerland, bonds have a high portfolio share due to portfolio regulations despite poor returns.

Risk reduction is the main motivation for portfolio diversification, as well as being required by "prudent man" rules. For example, the fall in the United Kingdom bond share since 1980 partly reflects alternative means of diversification; after abolition of exchange controls United Kingdom funds sold bonds to buy foreign assets (although the contraction in the supply of public debt in the late 1980s also played a role). Portfolio regulations may operate contrary to this; Swedish and Danish funds have considerable exposure to housing markets via mortgage-related bonds and loans to housing credit institutions. Together with mortgages, these amounted to no less than 57 percent of Swedish funds' assets in 1990, while Danish funds had 63 percent of assets in mortgages or mortgage association bonds. These imply an enormous exposure to potential effects of recession and falling house prices. Meanwhile, as discussed below, the United Kingdom funds may have portfolios excessively concentrated on equities.

As noted, international diversification can offer to fund managers a better trade-off of risk to return by reducing the systematic risk of investing in domestic markets arising from the cycle or medium-term shifts in the profit share. In the longer term, international investment in countries with a relatively young population may be essential to prevent battles over resources between workers and pensioners in countries with an aging population (Davis 1994b). Table 6 shows that foreign asset holdings have grown sharply over the 1980s in the United Kingdom, Australia, and Japan. In all three countries, this pattern followed abolition of exchange controls, at a time particularly in the United Kingdom and Japan when the economies were generating current account surpluses and overseas investment returns looked attractive. In Japan, portfolio restrictions on overseas investment were also progressively eased over the 1980s. Meanwhile Dutch funds have long held a significant proportion of assets abroad, partly due to the large volume of pension fund assets compared with domestic security and real estate markets. Growth has been much less marked in the other countries; in Germany, Switzerland, Denmark, Sweden, and Canada this is partly due to portfolio restrictions.

Risk aversion of trustees or managers may limit portfolio distributions, and at times appears directly counterproductive. In the Netherlands equity holding remains low — 20 percent — despite absence of portfolio restrictions. Van Loo (1988) suggests that this may relate to risk aversion of pension fund trustees.[31] Partly reflecting portfolio regulations, although probably also due to conservatism of managers (since the limits do not currently bind) the equity share in countries such as Sweden and Denmark is exceptionally low, despite the Danish tax on real returns to debt instruments, which encourages substitution of equities for bonds. Risk aversion may also play a role in many countries in limiting international investment, whereas it actually reduces risk over a time horizon relevant for pension funds. Risk aversion appears particularly marked for defined contribution funds; this is partly rational, given the lack of risk sharing and because workers nearing retirement will be anxious for low risk assets to be held.[32] But this risk aversion may be excessive. Indeed, evidence from the United States suggests that when employees have control over investment, as is often the case for defined contribution funds, the vast majority goes into fixed interest bonds; when equities are held and their value declines, dissatisfaction is often expressed (Rappaport 1992). Even for defined benefit funds, pressures to hold low risk assets may be sizable with an aging membership and employee trustees. But such pressures also seem to occur when the fund is composed of younger workers.[33] Again, for personal pensions, there is anecdotal evidence in the United Kingdom that persons free to choose their asset backing often select highly cautious combinations of assets. In the United States only 25 percent of 401(k) plan assets are invested in equity, where individuals are free to choose their portfolio allocations (Frijns and Petersen 1992). Mitchell (1994) expresses concern that, because of conservative approaches to investment, future retirees may find their pensions inadequate.

Portfolio regulations have a clear and widespread influence on portfolios, a number of which have already been mentioned. Bonds constitute over two-thirds of pension fund assets in Sweden and Denmark, largely because of portfolio regulations and the nature of the domestic financial markets, which require that 60 percent of Danish assets be invested in domestic debt instruments, while the majority of Swedish assets be in listed bonds, debentures, and retroverse loans. The fact that a fifth of the Swedish quasi-public funds' assets are invested in government bonds casts some doubt on their efficacy as a means to protect against future risks to social security, given the bonds are to be repaid by the taxpayer in the same way as they would if they were to be used to finance future social security burdens via pay-as-you-go. Similar comments can be made about the Dutch civil servants' pension fund (ABP), which is subject to such severe portfolio restrictions that at the end of 1991 it held 48 percent of its assets in the form of public sector bonds and loans. The decline in public bond holding in Australia parallels the removal of portfolio requirements that formerly required the majority of assets to be held in government securities. As regards equities, it was noted above that in Germany funds are limited to a maximum of 20 percent by regulation and in Japan to 30 percent; hence at 18 percent and 27 percent respectively in 1990 the German and Japanese ceilings were almost binding. Unlike other sectors, which have decreased holdings of property in recent years, Swiss funds retain around a fifth of their assets in property; one of the few assets that were relatively under their pre-1993 portfolio restrictions. This focus may drive up the price of land, it does not contribute to capital formation, and funds may face decreasing returns on (domestic) property in the future, as the population declines.

Funding rules also have an effect. In the United States, where minimum funding regulations make it optimal to hold a large proportion of bonds to protect against shortfall risk, despite their weakness as an inflation hedge, bonds form around 40 percent of pension funds' portfolios. Bodie (1991) suggests that given such funding rules, it is a paradox that United States defined benefit funds invest in equities, since a drop in market values can cause underfunding which has to be reflected in the employer's profit and loss account. He suggests investment in equities occurs because management sees a plan as a trust for employees, and manages assets as if it were a defined contribution plan (i.e., for employee welfare), with a guaranteed floor given by the benefit formula. Swiss bonds offer low returns, but given the low target yield of 4 percent nominal, fund managers there historically saw little need to diversify into riskier assets.

As regards accounting standards, in Japan, assets are held at book value, and a fixed return on the fund (based on interest and capital gains) is targeted for every year. This gives perverse incentives to sell well-performing equities as general share prices fall and retain those showing price declines, as well as to hold more bonds than portfolio optimization would imply (Tamura 1992). In Germany and Switzerland, Hepp (1990,

1992) suggests, application of strict accounting principles, which are more appropriate to banks than to pension funds, restrains equity holdings by funded plans independently of the portfolio regulations in Switzerland, evidenced by the fact that funds' equity holdings are far below the ceilings permitted. These conventions, for example, insist on positive net worth of the fund at all times, carry equities on the balance sheet at the lower of book value and market value, and calculate returns net of unrealized capital gains. In contrast, the United Kingdom accounting standard permits long-run smoothing and focuses on dividends rather than market values, and hence enables funds to accept the volatility of equity returns. The concern of some commentators in the United Kingdom is rather whether equity holdings are *too high* given the risks; however, note that 18 percent of the 63 percent equity share in 1990 was actually in foreign equities, thus reducing risk somewhat. In 1992 the equity share was 80 percent, of which 58 percent were domestic and 22 percent foreign. No other country has anything comparable to this portfolio share of equities. And as noted, new legal proposals may lead funds to reduce their equity shares.

The structure of fund management in countries such as Japan has had counterproductive effects, according to some commentators. There the share of loans has fallen sharply, although these medium-term floating-rate yen loans to firms were consistently the most profitable investment in Japan in the 1970s. It can be argued that this highlights a general point, that protection of fund managers from external competition (as was the case in Japan until recently) may lead to a suboptimal investment strategy from the point of view of plan beneficiaries.

Finally there is administrative fiat. Much of the past growth of Japanese funds' bond holdings may reflect the high share of public bonds purchased under government pressure, a practice that has now been abandoned.

Fund Performance

It is evident from the discussion above that a wide variety of often extraneous influences impinge on pension fund portfolios, which may in turn restrict funds from portfolio optimization, reduce return, and raise risk relative to feasible alternative investment strategies. We suggest that a useful means of judging the cost of these regulations and market imperfections, as well as of devising appropriate contribution rates, is to assess pension fund performance relative both to that in other countries and to that of artificial portfolios. The patterns of portfolio distributions (Table 5) and risks and returns on assets can be used to derive estimates of the returns and risks on portfolios (Table 6), and hence the cost to the firm of providing a given level of pension benefits (for a defined benefit fund) or the return to the member (for a defined contribution fund).[34] The estimates suggest that over the period 1967 to 1990, pension funds in the United Kingdom obtained the highest real return, those in Sweden, Switzerland, Canada, and the United States the lowest.[35] The result of course partly reflects risk and the share of equity and property, the United Kingdom having the highest standard deviation of returns (together with Denmark), and by far the highest share of real assets. Meanwhile, Swedish, Swiss, U.S., and Canadian funds held high proportions of bonds, which performed poorly over this period. Note that U.S. funds are also high risk in real terms despite relatively conservative portfolios; this is mainly due to unanticipated inflation in the 1970s, but it may also relate to funding rules and tax incentives. Interestingly, portfolios in Germany and the Netherlands had a high real return and low volatility, despite their focus on bonds and loans. This relates to relatively high returns on fixed-rate instruments in those countries. However, as discussed below, Table 9 shows that real returns for German and Dutch funds could have been boosted significantly by an increased share of equities. Investment in international equities would ensure that the associated increase in risk was mitigated.

Several observations can be made regarding these results. The publicly sponsored Swedish fund does poorly. The low-return Swedish and Swiss (and latterly the Australian system) are also compulsory, thus in principle reducing competitive pressures. In the case of Australian and Danish funds, occupational defined contribution funds imply that those who select the managers (companies themselves) do not bear the high level of portfolio risk. The Japanese, Swiss, and Germans have generally had little competition in fund management (Davis 1994a), and suffer from inappropriate accounting standards. But as shown by the results for Germany, good economic performance (or international diversification) can overcome a number of handicaps. Comparison of the results with (nominally) risk-free yields suggests that the funds generally outperformed government bonds, albeit only narrowly in Denmark (Table 6). However, in Canada and Sweden the portfolio return is below that on market paper (it is open to doubt whether the markets were deep enough to absorb pension funds' size, of course). Returns are generally below those on equities, but at a benefit of much lower risk.

The most crucial test is the ability of a fund to outperform real average earnings, given that liabilities of defined benefit plans are basically indexed to them. Similarly the replacement ratio a defined contribution fund can offer will depend on asset returns relative to earnings growth. Following the discussion in the first section, it also indicates whether in practice the return to funding (the asset return) exceeds that on pay-as-you-go in

TABLE 7   Local Government and Private Pension Fund Returns (1967–90[1]): Mean (and Standard Deviation) of Annual Real Total Returns (domestic currency)

Country	Mean	Std. Dev.
United Kingdom		
Local authority funds	4.9	(13.4)
Private funds	5.6	(13.0)
United States		
State and local funds	1.2	(12.6)
Private funds	2.7	(11.7)

Source: Davis (1994a).
Note: [1] 1967–1988 for the United Kingdom.

a steady state (the growth rate of average earnings). The margin is sizable (over 2 percent per year) in the United States and United Kingdom, and between one percent and 2 percent in Germany and the Netherlands. Except for Germany, all these countries have "prudent man" rules. The margin remains positive in Denmark and (barely) in Australia. But in Sweden, Japan, Canada, and Switzerland, it is actually negative, implying that the returns on assets need to be constantly topped up to meet their target. It was noted above that this may relate to inefficient asset allocations, often arising from portfolio restrictions. Taking the results at face value, and disregarding demographic issues, pay-as-you-go would have offered a higher rate of return than funding over this time period in these countries.

Risk, measured crudely as the standard deviation of the annual real return, should not be disregarded; as noted, it is quite high in a number of countries. But defined benefit pension funds are well placed to accept a degree of volatility, as there can be risk sharing between worker and company as well as between younger and older members. Risk is more important for defined contribution funds as there is no back-up from the sponsor and pensions must typically be taken in a lump sum (to buy an annuity) at the precise point of retirement. In contrast, annuities from defined benefit funds typically come from the fund itself, or at least the rate is guaranteed. In the light of this, the high levels of risk in Denmark and Australia, where funds are mainly defined contribution, are of potential concern.[36]

The data for the United Kingdom and United States allow a further comparison of effects of ownership and management methods to be made, this time in the same markets, in that portfolios of public (local government) fund data can be identified separately from those of private sector funds. Estimates of the respective returns are shown in Table 7. In

TABLE 8   Targeted Replacement Rates with Indexed Pensions (percent)

Country	Replacement Ratio Assuming Indexation of Pensions to Prices	Percentage Contribution Rate for 40% Replacement Rate	Replacement Ratio Assuming Indexation of Pensions to Wages
United States	37	10.8	37
United Kingdom	60	6.7	50
Germany	39	10.3	27
Japan	29	13.8	20
Canada	25	16.0	20
Netherlands	44	9.1	37
Sweden	14	28.6	11
Switzerland	25	16.0	20
Denmark	36	11.1	27
Australia	30	13.3	27

Source: Vittas (1992) and estimates of average earnings, inflation, and real returns on pension funds shown in Table 9.

each case, local government funds obtain lower returns than private funds. This can be related to more conservative portfolio distributions and in some cases portfolio regulations. United Kingdom local authority funds held an average of 52 percent equity over the sample, while private funds held 56 percent. For United States funds the difference is more dramatic: 25 percent and 53 percent, according to the Federal Reserve flow-of-funds data. Interestingly, the risks in real terms were higher for the local government funds, partly as a consequence of the volatility of real returns on bonds (Table 6). In this context, Mitchell (1994) analyzed returns and funding ratios on a sample of United States state and local government pension funds and found, consistent with the discussion of risk aversion and of portfolio regulations above, that both returns and funding were lower when retirees and employees were on the board, and when "social investment" was required (i.e., a proportion of the portfolio invested in local companies).

In order to estimate the benefits/contributions trade-off, Table 8 shows the results of illustrative calculations on the relation between costs of providing pensions, average earnings, and real returns (Vittas 1992). The table shows the replacement rate that would be attainable given the real returns attained by funds in each country and the corresponding growth rates of wages shown in Table 6, assuming indexed pensions, a 10 percent "defined" contribution rate, 40 years of contributions, and 20 years of retirement. Abstracting from risk, the table illustrates clearly the benefits of a higher return relative to real earnings; assuming pensions are indexed to prices, United Kingdom funds can obtain a replacement ratio of 60 percent, Canadians only 25 percent. Conversely, to obtain a pension equal to 40 percent of average earnings, United Kingdom funds need a contribution rate of 6.7 percent, and Swiss funds of 16 percent.

Of course, in practice contribution rates are sometimes higher than 10 percent, implying higher potential benefits; for example the Australian government mandates a minimum of 12 percent beginning in 2000. Danish contributions tend to be around 10 to 15 percent, despite there being no ceiling imposed by taxation. Such ceilings are standard practice elsewhere, for example, in the United Kingdom, total contributions are limited to 17.5 percent of the employee's salary, and the maximum employee contribution is 15 percent of salary. Typically, employees contribute 5.5 percent and employers the remainder. However, in the United Kingdom, employers do not contribute on behalf of those opting out of company plans in favor of personal pensions, which reduces typical contributions to 6 percent. United States employers typically do contribute to employees' 401(k) plans, although these have many of the characteristics of United Kingdom personal pensions. In Sweden, contributions are 13 percent. In countries such as Germany, where private pension plans have limited "supplementary" objectives, contributions are typically much lower, around 3.5 percent of salary. In Japan, contributions to funds remaining in social security (TQPPs) are limited to 3.2 percent of salary regardless of the condition of the fund. Funds replacing social security (EPFs) are more flexible, in that contributions are set to obtain the promised benefit given an assumed nominal return of 5.5 percent. The distribution of contributions between employer and employee varies widely, although it need not have significant economic implications if employers reduce salaries to offset their contributions. The proportion paid by the employer is around 100 percent in Japan and Sweden, 89 percent in Germany, 87 percent in the United States (100 percent for most private defined benefit funds), 70 to 75 percent in the United Kingdom, Canada, and the Netherlands, 66 percent in Denmark, and 58 percent in Switzerland.[37]

As a further experiment, Table 9 shows the returns on artificial diversified portfolios holding 50 percent equity and 50 percent bonds between 1967 and 1990, implicitly assuming quantitative portfolio restrictions are replaced by "prudent man" rules. As noted, equity holdings are generally below 50 percent (Table 5). Compared with Table 6, the results confirm that returns may be boosted by raising the share of equity, at some cost in terms of risk, although the estimates suggest that risk is mitigated by international diversification.[38] Only for the United Kingdom are returns consistently below those actually obtained; for the United States there is little difference, since the portfolio approximates that actually held by United States funds (Table 6). Several of the countries that fall below a

TABLE 9 Artificial Diversified Portfolios: Mean (and Standard Deviation) of Real Total Return, 1967–90 (percent — domestic currency)

Country	Domestic[1]		Domestic — Estimated Portfolio Return[2]	Domestic and International[3]		Domestic and International — Estimated Portfolio Return[2]	Domestic and International — Average Earnings
United States	2.1	(12.9)	−0.1	2.8	(12.5)	+0.6	+2.6
United Kingdom	3.8	(14.8)	−2.0	3.7	(14.1)	−2.1	+1.1
Germany	6.1	(15.2)	+1.0	6.2	(13.4)	+1.1	+2.2
Japan	5.5	(15.5)	+1.5	5.3	(14.3)	+1.3	+1.1
Canada	2.2	(11.2)	+0.6	2.2	(10.8)	+0.6	+0.5
Netherlands	4.5	(17.0)	+0.5	4.2	(15.2)	+0.2	+1.6
Sweden	3.8	(13.5)	+3.6	3.7	(15.2)	+3.5	+2.2
Switzerland	2.0	(15.4)	+0.5	2.0	(12.3)	+0.5	+0.1
Denmark	5.3	(18.9)	+1.7	4.6	(13.4)	+1.0	+1.8
Australia	2.7	(16.1)	−1.1	2.8	(15.1)	+1.2	+2.1
France	5.2	(18.0)	—	4.9	(15.9)	—	+0.9
Italy	1.9	(22.1)	—	2.0	(18.7)	—	−1.1

Source: Davis (1994a).
Note: [1] 50% domestic equity, 50% domestic bonds.
[2] From Table 7.
[3] 40% domestic equity, 40% domestic bonds, 10% foreign equity, 10% foreign bonds.

satisfactory return on assets relative to average earnings (such as Japan, Australia, Denmark, and Sweden) would have found providing funded pensions less costly (absolutely and relative to pay-as-you-go) if they had followed such a rule. German funds would also have boosted their headroom considerably.

In summary, this section suggests that support be given to a "prudent man" rule, backed by flexible accounting and funding standards (perhaps, as in the United Kingdom, focusing on income rather than market value) to permit holding of a proportion, varying with the maturity of the fund, of high return but volatile assets. (It is not, of course, implied that a 100 percent equity portfolio would be anything but *prudent*). Since foreign investment is shown invariably to reduce risk, albeit often with a slight reduction in return, limits on such holding are suggested to be particularly counterproductive. Meanwhile, decentralized fund management may be superior to centralized, if the poor performance of the Swedish ATP fund can be generalized.

Conclusion

The diversity of experience in the external funding of private pensions has been shown to be influenced particularly strongly by social security and fiscal regulations, as well as by funding regulations per se. A generous and compulsory social security system across a broad range of incomes can effectively "crowd out" private pensions, while discriminatory tax treatment can discourage external funding. Such structures would seem to be counterproductive in the light of the higher return to funding relative to pay-as-you-go both in a steady state and given the aging of the population and the more adverse side effects of pay-as-you-go on economic efficiency, as well as the greater risk and danger of inefficient investment from "booking." An optimal system would probably include only a minimal pay-as-you-go sector catering for basic needs and for alleviation of poverty, with the bulk of earnings replacement being provided by private externally-funded plans. Only Australia (and Chile) approximate this at present.

Meanwhile the efficiency with which pension funds provide pensions is influenced by regulations such as those of minimum funding and of portfolios, as well as features such as taxation, accounting standards, and the competitiveness of fund management. In effect, these prevent the fund from reaching an optimal trade-off between risk and return. I would suggest that streamlining such regulations so as to allow "prudent man" rules and flexible funding limits may increase coverage of private pensions by increasing their attractiveness to the sponsor or member or, in the case of compulsory provision, reduce the cost of providing a given level of private pensions in terms of competitiveness. Other issues that arise in this context include the appropriate degree of risk for defined contribution funds as opposed to defined benefit funds, and conversely, the potential for excessively conservative investment strategies when employees are influential in fund management. Given the existing size and importance of pension funds in the countries studied, as well as buoyant prospects for development of occupational funded pensions in both European Union and developing countries, these issues are of considerable importance.

I would like to thank Zvi Bodie, Olivia Mitchell, and participants at the 1994 Pension Research Council conference for helpful comments. The views expressed are my own and not those of the Bank of England, the Financial Markets Group, or the EMI.

Notes

[1]This chapter draws on Davis (1994a).

[2]In effect, younger members may accept occasional shortfalls in the coverage of their pension rights while older workers continue to receive their pensions.

[3]The implicit assumption is that workers receive "actuarially fair" pensions proportionate to their contributions; in practice redistribution is common under pay-as-you-go.

[4]This discussion abstracts from distributional considerations. As noted below, private funding tends to benefit those who have a sufficiently high income to save during their working lives, whereas pay-as-you-go lends itself more readily to redistribution.

[5]Conceptually, the discussion in this section applies to benefits obtainable for "defined contributions," but for defined benefit schemes the reasoning is similar. "Defined benefit" contribution rates under pay-as-you-go for a given population, replacement rate (i.e., pension relative to final salary), and a pension indexed to wages depend only on the dependency ratio. Under full funding, the contribution rate to obtain a similar replacement rate depends on the difference between the growth rate of wages (which determines the pension needed for a given replacement rate) and the return on assets, as well as the passivity ratio. For a given population and population distribution, if the dependency ratio equals the passivity ratio, the schemes will be equivalent if the growth rate of wages equals the return on assets.

[6]An interest rate in excess of the economic growth rate is a prediction of most theories of economic growth, given a positive rate of time preference (i.e., that consumers require compensation for postponing consumption).

[7]In practice, average earnings growth may increase and the rate of return to capital fall during the process of population aging, thus constituting a partial offset.

[8]That is, the United States, the United Kingdom, Canada, France, Italy, Germany, and Japan.

[9]This risk is less important for defined benefit funds, as long as profitability of firms is unaffected. Investment risk *plus* a collapse of profitability are needed to threaten occupational defined benefit funds.

[10]In line with this suggestion, Blanchard (1993) has observed a decline in the premium on equity relative to debt, and attributes this to institutionalization. There remains a possibility that a switch to funding at a global scale could depress the world rate of return.

[11]Even in a closed economy, this point should not be exaggerated. At least ownership of the capital stock may be a more secure basis for retirement than the willingness of existing workers to pay pensions as in pay-as-you-go schemes. If, as suggested, funding raises saving relative to pay-as-you-go, then capital formation and growth will be higher with funding and the national income from which pensions must be paid correspondingly boosted.

[12]In the model of Merton (1983), all uncertainty regarding a worker's marginal product derives from the aggregate production function, with no individual-specific effects. Labor income is assumed to be perfectly correlated across individuals. Workers save for retirement via individual saving (or defined contribution pension funds). Since human capital cannot be traded, there is economic inefficiency, as individuals hold too much human capital early in their lives relative to physical capital, while at retirement all wealth is invested in physical capital. These rigidities prevent optimal sharing of factor share risk (i.e., relating to the division of GDP between wages and profits), which might, for example, derive from unforeseeable long-term secular trends related to the degree of union militancy or technological developments. Merton shows that a pay-as-you-go social security scheme is welfare-improving in this framework.

[13]This, in practice, depends on the benefit formula; it is not the case if benefits are based on career-average revalued earnings.

[14]However, note that the trust fund invests solely in government bonds, which has ambiguous consequences for benefit security.

[15]Adequate provision of unfunded pensions is likely to be particularly difficult for declining industries, as the worker/pensioner ratio falls.

[16]Projections of inflation will be needed when benefit indexation is a contractual or legal obligation.

[17]This is guaranteed in the United Kingdom and the Netherlands.

[18]This is a legal obligation in Germany and Sweden and will soon be in the United Kingdom; it is generally provided in Switzerland and the Netherlands.

[19]The facility with which funds of declining industries in the United Kingdom funded on a PBO/IBO basis (such as coal mining and railways) coped with maturity are a case in point.

[20]Given the cost of this measure, a decline of the company pension fund sector is predicted, but there is little evidence of this to date.

[21]Note that only long-maturity bonds will increase in price so as precisely to offset the increase in liabilities.

[22]These limits do not, of course, apply to reserve funding systems such as those common in Germany and Japan.

[23]Technically, portfolio restrictions are likely to prevent managers from reaching the frontier of efficient portfolios, which indicates where return is maximized for a given risk.

[24]For example, by closing down all alternative investment strategies such as international diversification.

[25]One way to avoid the regulations on equities and foreign investment is reportedly to invest via special security funds, whose investments are not subject to restriction.

[26]The precise wording is that fund money must be invested "for the sole benefit of the beneficiaries" and investments must be made with "the care, skill, prudence and diligence under the circumstances then prevailing that a prudent man acting in a like capacity and familiar with such matters would use in the conduct of an enterprise of a like character and with like aims."

[27]There is no explicit prudent man rule, but the duty of prudence to trustees can be interpreted as requiring diversification.

[28]Their analysis has been criticized for assuming that individuals realize capital gains on equities each year, which seems unlikely to be the case.

[29]This approach, while being fully consistent with a prudent man rule, highlights the high risk nature of book reserve or pay-as-you-go provision for private firms.

[30]Whether holding equities does help in this sense is a matter of some controversy in the literature. As noted by Tepper (1992), if equity returns are independent from one period to the next, there remains a risk that a series of returns at the tail of the distribution will occur, generating returns far lower than would be possible with bonds. But if returns tend to revert to a mean level, for example due to macroeconomic policy or even self-correcting tendencies in the economy, they will act to prevent longer-term shortfall risk.

Such insights are formalized in so-called asset-liability modeling exercises — an actuarial technique that involves comparing forecasts of liabilities in coming years with asset returns under various scenarios; this shows both risks to the employer and possible changes to portfolio strategy that may be warranted (Blake 1992).

[31]Also according to Wyatt (1993) there are unofficial tolerance limits for equity exposure of 30 percent, imposed by the supervisors.

[32]This point indicates the inflexibility of company-based defined contribution plans seeking to cater both for risk-seeking young workers and risk-averse older

ones. Some funds in Australia overcome this by offering four separate funds at different levels of risk.

[33]Research by Mitchell (1994) suggests that employees' representation reduces returns even for *defined benefit* funds, although in principle the employer is bearing the risk.

[34]Annual holding period returns on marketable fixed rate instruments are used, as in Table 7, instead of redemption yields. In my view, the holding period returns are the more relevant measure for an ongoing portfolio, since they take full account of losses or gains due to interest rate changes (although other assumptions regarding holding periods could also be made).

[35]The return in the United States and Canada is considerably higher if the sample begins in 1971 (4.0 percent and 2.7 percent respectively).

[36]Knox (1993) shows that returns on a fund based on 12 percent contributions with 45 years of payment invested, like current Australian pension funds, will obtain an average replacement rate of 61 percent, but the range of statistical probability of returns based on asset volatility in the past is between 35 percent and 96 percent.

[37]Employees may not contribute to book reserves or support funds.

[38]The table only shows international diversification up to 20 percent of the portfolio, holding bonds and equities for the "rest of the world" in proportion to global portfolio weights in the 1980s. A full "global portfolio," where domestic holdings are reduced to their weight in the global index, would imply 95 percent international investment for the small countries and over 50 percent even for the United States. Similar calculations for such a strategy (not shown in detail), with again 50 percent bonds and 50 percent equities, again shows lower risk, although the change in return may be in either direction.

References

Aaron, Harry J. "The Social Insurance Paradox." *Canadian Journal of Economic and Political Science* 32 (1966): 371–77.

Ambachtsheer, Keith. "Integrating Business Planning with Pension Fund Planning." In R. Arnott and F. Fabozzi, eds., *Asset Allocation: A Handbook.* Chicago: Probus, 1988.

Black, Fischer. "The Tax Consequences of Long-Run Pension Policy." *Financial Analysts Journal* (September–October 1980): 17–23.

Blake, David. *Issues in Pension Funding.* London: Routledge, 1992.

———. "Pension Schemes as Options on Pension Fund Assets: Implications for Pension Fund Asset Management." London: Birkbeck College, mimeo, 1994.

Blanchard, Olivier J. "The Vanishing Equity Premium." In Richard O'Brien, ed., *Finance and the International Economy: The Amex Book Review Prize Essays,* vol. 7. Oxford: Oxford University Press, 1993.

Bodie, Zvi. "Pensions as Retirement Income Insurance." *Journal of Economic Literature* 28 (1990): 28–49.

———. "Shortfall Risk and Pension Fund Asset Management." *Financial Analysts Journal* (May/June 1991): 57–61.

Bodie, Zvi and Robert C. Merton. "Pension Benefit Guarantees in the United States: A Functional Analysis." In Ray Schmitt, ed., *The Future of Pensions in the United States.* Philadelphia: Pension Research Council and University of Pennsylvania Press, 1993: 194–246.

Chen, Andrew H. and William Reichenstein. "Taxes and Pension Fund Asset Allocation." *Journal of Portfolio Management* (Summer 1992): 24–27.

Davis, E. Philip. "Financial Market Activity of Life Insurance Companies and Pension Funds." Basle: Bank for International Settlements Economic Paper 21, 1988.

——. *Pension Funds, Retirement-Income Insurance and Capital Markets, An International Perspective.* Cambridge: Oxford University Press, 1994 (1994a).

——. "International Investment of Pension Funds in Europe; Scope and Implications for International Financial Stability." Santiago: Pensions Privatization Conference, January 26–27, 1994 (1994b).

Deutsche Bundesbank. "Company Pension Schemes in the Federal Republic of Germany." *Deutsche Bundesbank Monthly Report* (August 1984): 30–37.

Feldstein, Martin and Ragnar Morck. "Pension Funding Decisions, Interest Rate Assumptions and Share Prices." In Zvi Bodie and John Shoven, eds., *Financial Aspects of the US Pension System.* Chicago: University of Chicago Press, 1983: 177–210.

Frijns, Jan and Carel Petersen. "Financing, Administration and Portfolio Management; How Secure is the Pension Promise?" In *Private Pensions and Public Policy.* Paris: Organization for Economic Cooperation and Development, 1992.

Hepp, Stefan. *The Swiss Pension Funds.* Berne: Paul-Haupt, 1990.

——. "Comparison of Investment Behavior of Pension Plans in Europe - Implications for Europe's Capital Markets." In Jurgen Mortensen, ed., *The Future of Pensions in the European Community.* London: Brassey's, for the Center for European Policy Studies, Brussels, 1992: 151–70.

James, Estelle. *Income Security in Old Age.* Washington, DC: World Bank, 1994.

Knox, David M. "An Analysis of the Equity Investments of Australian Superannuation Funds." University of Melbourne Center for Actuarial Studies Research Paper 6, 1993.

Kotlikoff, Laurence J. "Social Security." *New Palgrave Dictionary of Money and Finance.* London: Macmillan, 1992: 479–484.

Mehra, R. and Ed C. Prescott. "The Equity Premium: A Puzzle." *Journal of Monetary Economics* 15 (1985): 145–61.

Meier, Peter. "Aus der Praxis: Anlagestrategien für Pensionskassen - Auswirkungen der Neuen Anlagerichtlinien." *Finanzmarkt und Portfolio Management* 7 (1993): 365–72.

Merton, Robert C. "On the Role of Social Security as a Means for Efficient Risk Sharing in an Economy Where Human Capital Is Not Tradable." In Zvi Bodie, John Shoven, and David Wise, eds., *Financial Aspects of the U.S. Pension System.* Chicago: University of Chicago Press, 1983: 325–58.

Mitchell, Olivia S. and Ping Lung Hsin. "Public Pension Governance and Performance." NBER Working Paper 4632, January 1994.

OECD. "Pension Liabilities in the Seven Major Industrial Countries." Paris: Organization for Economic Cooperation and Development Working Paper 1, mimeo, 1993.

Pestieau, Pierre. "The Distribution of Private Pension Benefits: How Fair Is It?" In *Private Pensions and Public Policy.* Paris: Organization for Economic Cooperation and Development, 1992: 31–50.

Rappaport, Anna M. "Comment on Pensions and Labor Market Activity." In Zvi Bodie and Alicia H. Munnell, eds., *Pensions and the Economy: Sources, Uses, and Limitations of Data.* Philadelphia: Pension Research Council and University of Pennsylvania Press, 1992: 88–108.

Riley, Barry. "Why Pension Funds Are Glum at the Bull Market." *Financial Times,* June 12, 1993.

Romer, Paul. "Increasing Returns and Long Run Growth." *Journal of Political Economy* 94, 5 (1986): 1002–37.

Tamura, Matsuhiro. "Improving Japan's Employee Pension Fund System." *Nomura Research Institute Quarterly* (Summer 1992): 66–83.

Tepper, Irwin. "Comments." In Zvi Bodie and Alicia Munnell, eds., *Pensions and the Economy: Sources, Uses, and Limitations of Data.* Philadelphia: Pension Research Council and University of Pennsylvania Press, 1992: 173–79.

Thompson, Lawrence H. "Social Security Surpluses." *New Palgrave Dictionary of Money and Finance.* London: Macmillan, 1992: 484–86.

Van Loo, Peter D. "Portfolio Management of Dutch Pension Funds." De Nederlandsche Bank Reprint 197, 1988.

Vittas, Dimitri. "The Simple(r) Algebra of Pension Plans." Washington, DC: World Bank, mimeo, 1992.

Wyatt Data Services. *1993 Benefits Report Europe USA.* Brussels: Wyatt Company, 1993.

Comments by Marshall E. Blume

E. Philip Davis's chapter has two major themes. First, funded pension plans are generally to be preferred to pay-as-you-go plans. Second, state-supported pension plans, generally pay-as-you-go plans, "crowd out" privately funded pension plans. A related theme is that the investment strategies of private pension funds are often less than optimal to obtain the best possible returns due in part to restrictive government regulations and excessive risk aversion on the part of those making the investment decisions.

The chapter begins with Davis's reasoning for preferring funded pension plans over pay-as-you-go plans. The rest of the chapter contains comparisons across a number of countries of the relative sizes of funded pension plans and social security programs, the taxation and regulation of pension plans, and the asset allocations and returns of the portfolios of funded pension plans. The data presented in these comparisons are extremely interesting, and I recommend that they be carefully examined.

Let us now turn to the first major theme, that funded pension plans are generally preferable to pay-as-you-go plans. The arguments that the author puts forward read almost like an apology, in the classical sense of an explanation or a justification. Davis gives an extensive listing of favorable features of funded pension plans and a shorter listing of favorable features of pay-as-you-go plans. On the basis of these listings, he concludes that "an optimal [pension] system would probably include only a minimal pay-as-you-go sector catering for basic needs and for alleviation of poverty, with the bulk of earnings replacement being provided by private externally funded plans."

Davis may well be right in reaching this conclusion, but at least to this commentator, the arguments put forward in reaching the conclusion are not always persuasive and not as precise as they could be.

Davis's first reason for funding is that funding can generally provide the same level of benefits to retirees with lesser outlays than pay-as-you-go plans. Let us examine this reason in a very simple agrarian world contain-

TABLE 1   Comparing Pay-as-You-Go and Funded Plans: The Effect on the First and Succeeding Generations

Status	Period		
	1	*2*	*3*
Work Status			
Original Farmer	Works	Retires	
Son		Works	Retires
Grandson			Works
Income			
Original Farmer	1,000		
Son		1,000	
Grandson			1,000
Pay-as-you-go Plan Pension Contributions			
Original Farmer	0		
Son		300	
Grandson			300
Consumption			
Original Farmer	1,000	300	
Son		700	300
Grandson			700
Funded Plan Pension Contributions			
Original Farmer	200		
Son		200	
Grandson			200
Funded Plan Consumption			
Original Farmer	800	300	
Son		800	300
Grandson			800

ing only a farmer and his son, who will take over the land when the father retires. The father will die when his son retires, and his grandson will then take over the farm. After the first generation, there will as a consequence always be one person working the farm and one retired person. As to finances, the farmer makes US$ 1,000 a year from farming the land, and this income will remain unchanged into the future. There is a foreign bank that will accept deposits and that pays a positive interest rate.

The original farmer decides to set up a pension plan to provide 30 percent of his yearly income as a retirement benefit, or US$ 300, and is considering a pay-as-you-go plan or a funded plan. If he chose a pay-as-you-go plan, he will be able to consume US$ 1,000 a year during his working life and at retirement will receive US$ 300 from his son, leaving his son and all future generations with US$ 700 for consumption (Table 1).

If he chose a funded plan instead, he will have to save a portion of his income each year. Because he can invest these savings with a bank, he may have to save only US$ 200 to be able to have a retirement benefit of US$ 300 a year, which leaves during his working life US$ 800 a year for consumption. Under this plan, succeeding generations will have US$ 800 for consumption during their working career and US$ 300 for retirement.

It is true that in this example, the funded plan, not taking into account the time value of money, has a lower total outlay than does the pay-as-you-go plan. But does this mean that the funded plan is better? It depends upon the original farmer's trade-off between his utility of consumption and his concern for the utility of future generations. Thus the comparison of total benefits to total outlays under the two plans is not adequate to determine which plan is preferable.

Davis then turns to a political argument to justify funded plans over pay-as-you-go plans. He points out correctly that, if the G-7 countries maintain the same benefits for their pay-as-you-go plans in the future as today, these plans will require a very much greater proportion of GDP than they do today. This greater demand on GDP could lead to "political risks." But the author has not established that substituting funded plans for pay-as-you-go plans is the correct policy response to this political issue; perhaps, the benefits should be reduced.

Davis then raises but does not fully develop the notion that current savings rates are too low. He suggests that, under certain "plausible" conditions, the substitution of funded plans for pay-as-you-go plans will increase savings rates and, if savings are invested properly, future economic growth. Again, underlying this argument is a trade-off between the utility of the current generation and future generations. But even if policymakers thought that the current savings rates were too low, there are other ways of increasing savings, such as reducing the corporate tax rate.

The second major premise of the chapter is that pay-as-you-go pension plans "crowd out" funded plans. There are some good theoretical reasons for this contention, and the author presents them. The empirical evidence supporting this argument is weak. Table 3 presents the replacement rates of social security by country, and Table 2 contains measures of pension assets to GDP by country. These series should be inversely related following the author's theory, but there does not appear to be such a relation at least from a visual examination of the data.

A secondary thesis of the chapter is that pension funds should put more money into equities. This is a very commonly held view, popularized by McGeorge Bundy of the Ford Foundation in the mid-1960s, and is based upon the empirical observation that in the last 50 or so years the return on equities has exceeded the return of other commonly held financial assets. Fifty years is a long time, and expectations should be borne out. This is almost like a stochastic dominance argument—something that was addressed in detail in the seventies by researchers such as Robert

Merton and Paul Samuelson. What happens is that the probability of doing worse with equities decreases with time, but for any finite horizon is not zero. Thus, risk aversion comes into play.

Over even long horizons, the returns realized on the more risky assets can be less than on less risky assets; that is what makes them risky. Indeed, Jeremy Siegel (1992) found that in 16.9 percent of the decades over the 1926 to 1990 period, the returns on long-term governments bonds exceeded the returns on stocks, and there were even 20-year periods when returns on long-term governments exceeded the returns on stocks. Thus, Davis has not demonstrated that every pension fund should necessarily accept more risk and the corresponding greater expected returns. In recent history, accepting this greater risk would have been a good strategy, but there is no guarantee that the strategy will work over the next 10 or even 20 years.

Despite these objections, however, overall I found the chapter provocative. The comparison of pension plans across countries contains a wealth of interesting data.

Chapter 9
The Government's Role in Insuring Pensions

James E. Pesando

In the event of bankruptcy of the sponsoring firm, a defined pension plan may be terminated when pension assets are less than accrued pension benefits. If so, governments may elect to provide, either explicitly or implicitly, plan termination insurance designed to mitigate the corresponding loss in pension benefits suffered by plan members.

There are two distinct aspects to the study of the government's role in insuring pensions. The first, which is analytical, is to examine whether governments *should* provide plan termination insurance and, if so, what steps should be taken so as to ensure the financial soundness of the insurance fund. The second, which is descriptive, is to document the international experience with plan termination insurance, to highlight the similarities and differences in the public policy response to the risk of bankruptcy.

In the United States, plan termination insurance is provided through the Pension Benefit Guaranty Corporation (PBGC). In spite of an ongoing series of reforms, the long-term financial soundness of the PBGC remains a major concern. Against this background, this chapter reviews the experience with plan termination insurance of five countries: the United States, Canada, the United Kingdom, Germany, and Japan.

The fact that opinion is divided as to whether termination insurance is required is most apparent in Canada. Of the 11 jurisdictions (10 provinces and the government of Canada) that regulate private pension plans, only one, the Province of Ontario, has introduced plan termination insurance. Further, within a decade of introducing plan termination insurance in 1980, Ontario was considering its removal. The level of insured benefits is far more modest in Ontario than in the United States. Yet there is a parallel concern regarding the long-run solvency of the insurance system, in light of the risks posed by a relatively small number of poorly funded plans and the opportunities for strategic behavior.

This chapter is organized into three sections. The first briefly reviews the arguments for and against the public provision of plan termination insurance. The second examines the risks borne by plan members in the event of bankruptcy for the United States, Canada, the United Kingdom, Germany, and Japan. The third reviews the principal lessons to be learned from the international experience, using concerns expressed regarding the PBGC in the United States as a benchmark. This section includes an overview of the findings together with some implications for public policy.

The Public Provision of Plan Termination Insurance: An Overview of the Issues and the Policy Debate

To some policy analysts, the need for plan termination insurance is self-apparent. In its absence, workers in underfunded plans will not receive their promised pension benefits in the event of the bankruptcy of the sponsoring firm. Corporate bankruptcies are highly correlated due to the systematic risk inherent in macroeconomic fluctuations. So, too, are the returns to pension fund assets. For this reason, private markets may not be able to provide plan termination insurance, even if demand for this insurance exists at premium rates that are commensurate with risk. This "market failure," in the view of many, provides the fundamental rationale for the public provision of plan termination insurance.[1]

To economists, however, the argument is less clear. Even if the difficulties — political as well as economic — in designing a financially sound system of termination insurance are ignored, the fundamental rationale for its provision merits critical scrutiny.

Virtually all pension analysts, whether economists or not, now accept the proposition that pension benefits represent deferred wages. In other words, it is widely recognized that workers "pay" for their accruing pension benefits, either by reduced wages or by concessions elsewhere in their compensation package. Yet, in a competitive labor market with well-informed workers, wages will internalize the degree of risk posed by underfunded pension plans (Pesando 1982). Other things being equal, firms with fully funded plans or firms with very low probabilities of bankruptcy will extract greater wage concessions for a given level of promised pension benefits. In the limiting case, workers in poorly funded plans with a near-bankrupt employer will grant few or no wage concessions in return for enhanced pension benefits (for example, a retroactive enrichment to a severely underfunded flat benefit plan).

Those who conduct public policy are inclined to evaluate pension plans solely in terms of their ability to deliver retirement incomes. Even if workers have willingly borne the risks associated with plan termination, policy analysts may find this outcome to be unacceptable. If workers understand the risks associated with underfunded pension promises, the economic rationale for the public provision of plan termination insurance may reduce loss of pension benefits, such as increased burden on public assistance (Mitchell 1993). If so, the rationale for the public provision of plan termination insurance can be linked to this type of market failure.

The policy analyst may deem as unrealistic the assumption that workers (or their agents) understand fully the risks to which they are exposed, and hence that the appropriate adjustments have taken place elsewhere in the compensation package.[2] This point is reinforced by the recognition, emphasized by Bodie and Merton (1993), that workers (unlike, for example, shareholders) typically do not have well-diversified investment portfolios, and thus may not be well suited to bearing the additional risk of the loss of pension benefits in the event of the bankruptcy of their employer. However, if the government's primary concern is that workers misperceive the security of their contractual benefits, the preferred policy response is to require the disclosure of relevant information. Firms could be required, for example, to report to each worker the value of the worker's accrued benefit in the event of plan termination, with the presumption that this information would be used in formal or informal bargaining.[3] If policymakers view the market outcome as unacceptable, there remains the question of whether a substitute intervention is preferred to termination insurance. There are several obvious candidates. First and foremost, the government could impose tighter funding requirements. Reduced amortization periods for both experience deficiencies (i.e., actuarial shortfalls due to a divergence between assumptions and experience) and initial unfunded liabilities would reduce the scope for underfunding in the event of the sponsor's insolvency. This observation is especially relevant for Canada and the United States, where retroactive (and thus unfunded) enrichments to flat benefit plans in the union sector represent a major source of underfunding in the private pension system. A second alternative, for example, would be to elevate the legal status of unfunded pension benefits in the event of corporate bankruptcy.

If plan termination insurance is provided by the government, there is a strong economic argument for setting the insurance premiums so as to reflect the true risk posed to the insurance fund (Ippolito 1986; Pesando 1982; Turner 1993). Yet, as noted later in this chapter, no government that provides plan termination insurance has set premiums to reflect the true level of risk exposure. No observed premium structure, for example, incorporates the risk of corporate bankruptcy, although *universal* capital markets assess this risk on a daily basis in the process of rating corporate debt. The absence of market-based insurance premiums raises fundamental concerns. First, as is readily apparent in the United States, well-known moral hazard problems and the strategic behavior of firms will place the long-run financial soundness of the insurance fund at risk. Second, in the absence of true risk-based premiums, there is no evidence that the demand for plan termination insurance exists *at market-determined rates.*[4] This observation merits emphasis, since, as noted, many proponents of the public provision of termination insurance implicitly assume that demand for insurance coverage exists at a price commensurate with risk.

Finally, one should note that the success of plan termination insurance in the political arena is not necessarily linked to efficiency concerns. Rather, its introduction may reflect the response by governments to political interests. Some analysts, for example, see the introduction and the subsequent evolution of the Pension Benefit Guaranty Corporation (PBGC) in the United States in light of the political objective of forestalling industrial decline. The cost of the pension benefits provided by firms in declining industries is shifted, in the first instance, to the third party insurer. Ultimately, this cost is shifted to prosperous firms through their inappropriately high insurance premiums, or, in the event of catastrophe, to taxpayers at large. This cross-subsidization, one should emphasize, is endemic to existing termination insurance schemes. In Ontario, the catalyst to the introduction of plan termination insurance in December 1980 (which was made retroactive) was a series of threatened plant shutdowns. Not surprisingly, there was no attempt to levy insurance premiums commensurate with the risks posed by these distressed firms. To levy such premiums might, in and of itself, force these firms into bankruptcy.[5]

The preceding review of the arguments for and against the public provision of termination insurance is, of necessity, brief.[6] In my opinion, four points stand out. First, there is as yet no persuasive evidence that demand for termination insurance exists at premiums commensurate with risk. Thus the "market failure" argument is, as yet, untested. Second, compensating wage differentials will, in a competitive labor market, internalize the risk associated with underfunded pension promises. Third, there are other policy initiatives — tighter funding requirements, improved disclosure, bankruptcy reform — that could serve as substitutes for termination insurance. The potential attractiveness of these alternatives is enhanced by the political and economic obstacles to designing a financially-sound insurance system in which premiums reflect the true level of risk posed to the insurer. Fourth, the success of plan termination insurance in the political arena may reflect redistributive, rather than efficiency, considerations.

International Experience with Plan Termination Insurance

In this section, I briefly review the policies of governments in the United States, Canada, the United Kingdom, Germany, and Japan with regard to the provision and operation of plan termination insurance. The operation of the PBGC in the United States, reviewed first, identifies the issues to be addressed in the discussion of the other four countries.[7]

United States

If plans are fully funded (or nearly so), the potential loss of pension benefits in the event of bankruptcy is small, and the need for plan termination insurance is obviated. Further, the stated intent of United States government policy is to ensure that, ultimately, most defined benefit pensions (nominal) are fully funded. It is thus instructive to understand why, in fact, substantial underfunding of defined benefit pension plans does exist. As noted by Turner (1993), the degree of underfunding for some plans is dramatic. In 1988, there were US\$ 1.9 billion in unfunded liabilities in plans with termination funding ratios of 10 percent or less, and additional unfunded liabilities of US\$ 8.1 billion in plans with terminal funding ratios of 50 percent or less.[8] The typical claim on the PBGC, when valued using the PBGC's actuarial assumptions, arises from a plan that is 40 percent funded (Turner 1993).

There are several reasons for this degree of underfunding, including strategic underfunding by firms that are in financial distress. Of particular note, however, is the concentration of large claims against the PBGC among the flat benefit plans that predominate in the union sector. A flat benefit plan pays a fixed periodic amount (such as US\$ 20 per month) for each year of service. To offset the impact of inflation, and to provide real increases in pension benefits, flat benefit formulas are renegotiated upward on a periodic basis. Since these enrichments are always retroactive, new — and often quite substantial — unfunded liabilities are periodically created. United States tax law prevents these enrichments from being pre-funded. (It is not clear, if allowed, that firms would choose to pre-fund anticipated enrichments since this might weaken their position in future bargaining over the level of pension benefits.) In effect, flat benefit plans operate as "surrogate" final earnings plans, but without the pre-funding that accompanies the latter. Based on experience in the United States, one would expect that the amount of underfunding — and hence the risk borne by the public provider of plan termination insurance — would be less if there were no flat benefit plans in the universe of defined benefit plans.

The premiums charged each plan for PBGC insurance (which are set through legislation, not by the PBGC) do not reflect the true risk posed for the insurance fund. Since 1987, underfunded plans do pay higher premiums than fully funded plans, although there is a cap on the premium surcharge.[9] There is, however, no allowance for the risk of insolvency of the plan sponsor, nor for the degree of investment risk in the pension fund. As a result, firms with a low probability of bankruptcy subsidize firms that are less stable.

Because the insurance premiums are not market-based, there exist opportunities for strategic behavior; that is, for plan sponsors to "game" against the interest of the PBGC. As its financial situation deteriorates, a firm may reduce its plan contributions (through, for example, revising certain of its actuarial assumptions or requesting a funding waiver from the Internal Revenue Service), grant enriched pension benefits, and/or assume more risk in its pension fund. The incentives created by non-market insurance premiums, together with the relatively low priority of the PBGC's claim on a sponsor's non-pension assets under current United States bankruptcy law, invite behavior that threatens the long-run solvency of the PBGC.

There is a limit on the maximum pension benefit that is insured by the PBGC. In 1993, the maximum insured pension was US$ 2,420 per month, which is US$ 29,250 per year. There are other ways in which plan members coinsure the risk of default. Unvested benefits and special supplements for early retirement benefits are not insured, and guaranteed benefits that are created by plan amendments less than five years old are phased in at a rate of 20 percent for each year subsequent to the plan amendment. Because of the "backloading" of pension benefits in most defined benefit plans (i.e., the tendency for pension accruals to rise sharply with age and years of service), there is substantial coinsurance by virtue of the fact that members' benefits are frozen at the date of termination. Thus, in spite of the existence of termination insurance, plan members do risk a loss of pension benefits in the event of a plan windup due to the insolvency of the sponsor.[10] There is thus *some* market discipline on this account.

Canada

The most revealing observation from the Canadian experience is that only one of 11 jurisdictions (Ontario, in 1980) has introduced plan termination insurance. Nine other provinces and the federal government have chosen *not* to introduce such insurance. (The federal government has jurisdiction over certain designated industries, such as banking and telecommunications.) Like the PBGC, the Guarantee Fund was designed as a self-funding program financed by premiums paid by the sponsors of defined benefit plans. The Guarantee Fund was established six years after the PBGC, and was designed to preempt some of the more difficult problems that plagued the PBGC.[11] Nonetheless, by the end of the decade, the government of Ontario was considering abandoning the scheme (accompanied by tighter funding requirements, especially for flat benefit plans) as the result of concerns regarding financial soundness.

In Canada, as in the United States, flat benefit plans are typically less well funded than earnings-based plans. Thus the exposure of the Guarantee Fund, as revealed by unfunded liabilities measured on a termination basis, is largest in the flat benefit plans that predominate in the union sector. As in the United States, it is the periodic and retroactive enrichments of these plans that generate significant unfunded liabilities.

The premium structure for the Guarantee Fund resembles that of the PBGC. There is a flat premium per member plus a premium surcharge related to the degree of underfunding measured on a termination basis. As in the United States, insurance premiums do *not* reflect the probability of bankruptcy of the corporate sponsor, and thus are *not* set at market levels on this account.

There is a limit on the maximum pension insured by the Guarantee Fund. At present, the maximum insured pension is US$ 750 per month, or US$ 9,000 per year. This maximum insured pension is nominal, and has not been increased since the Guarantee Fund was introduced in 1980. The maximum pension insured by Ontario's Guarantee Fund is less than one-third of the maximum pension insured by the PBGC. To protect the integrity of the Fund, and to limit strategic behavior, certain enriched early retirement benefits and any benefit enrichment in effect for less than three years are excluded. Unlike the United States, there is no provision whereby a financially distressed firm can request a funding waiver from Revenue Canada, the equivalent to the IRS in the United States.

The most significant departure from the United States experience is the absence of plan termination insurance for all plan members in Canada except those subject to Ontario's jurisdiction. This result occurs in spite of the fact that pension law and regulations are very similar on all other accounts across the different jurisdictions.

To provide an economic rationale for this disparity is difficult. It seems unlikely, for example, that policymakers in Ontario reject the "rational worker" assumption implicit in the analysis of competitive labor markets, while policymakers in other jurisdictions accept this assumption. If there is an unexpected reduction in pension benefits due to a plan insolvency, there may be an increased claim on Canada's income-tested public pension programs. Yet the most important of these programs, the Guaranteed Income Supplement, is operated by the federal government and is available to Canadian residents in all the provinces. There is no reason why Ontario, alone, should respond to this potential externality.

Interestingly, Ontario has always been considered Canada's "industrial heartland," and the existence of termination insurance *only* in this province is entirely consistent with a political explanation that is frequently cited in the United States: that is, that an important, although unstated, goal for plan termination insurance is to subsidize the cost of pension benefits (and thus employee compensation) in declining industries.

United Kingdom

State Retirement Pensions in the United Kingdom have two parts. The first is a fixed benefit component, with a maximum value for a single person in 1994–1995 of US\$ 86 per week, which is US\$ 4,472 per year. The second part is linked to the worker's earnings, and is known as the State Earnings Related Pension scheme (SERPs). If an employer-sponsored plan meets specified criteria, the employer may contract out of SERPs. In this event, both the employer's and the employees' National Insurance contributions are reduced between the lower (about 18 percent of national average earnings) and upper earnings limits (7½ times the lower limit). Salary-based (defined benefit) plans that contract out are required to provide the additional earnings-related pension known as the Guaranteed Minimum Pension. The Occupational Pensions Board, a statutory body, has the responsibility for monitoring plans that have contracted out, and issues the contracting out certificate. At present, about 50 percent of workers in the United Kingdom are covered by an occupational pension plan, and 90 percent of these members have contracted out of SERPs. In the private sector, 78 percent of members of occupational pension plans have contracted out.

In the United Kingdom, there is, at least for the present, no formal system of plan termination insurance. In the event of the insolvency of the plan sponsor, any deficiency in plan assets relative to accrued benefits is treated as a debt of the employer. *If* this debt is not repaid, the trustees of the plan must reduce benefits, according to the priorities established in the trust deed. The protection of plan members thus relies on the fiduciary responsibility of the plan's trustees, to ensure that pension assets are sufficient to meet accrued pension benefits.

The absence of a formal system of plan termination insurance, however, is potentially misleading. If the sponsor of a contracted out plan goes bankrupt, the Guaranteed Minimum Pensions of its members will be restored upon transfer of the corresponding plan assets to the state scheme, even if plan assets are inadequate for this purpose. In effect, there is *implicit* termination insurance for Guaranteed Minimum Pensions, but not for benefits in excess of these amounts. No premiums are levied for this implicit insurance, implying (for example) that there is a potential cross-subsidy from the employers and employees of financially sound firms to their counterparts in less stable firms.

Occupational pension plans that contract out of SERPs usually provide benefits in excess of the Guaranteed Minimum Pension. Thus, in spite of the implicit termination insurance described above, most members of contracted-out defined benefit plans are at risk in the event of their employer's insolvency if pension assets are less than accrued pension liabilities. The trustees of the plan, in order to serve the interests of the beneficiaries of the trust (i.e., the members of the plan), have an obligation after each actuarial valuation to ensure that steps are taken to eliminate any shortfall of assets relative to accrued liabilities.

For perspective, it would appear that the *effective* level of termination insurance in the United Kingdom is close to that provided in Ontario, but well beneath the level that exists in the United States. Christopher Daykin (Chapter 2, this volume) notes that the target replacement rate for SERPs is 25 percent of average earnings in the range between the lower and upper earnings limits. The lower limit is (about) 18 percent of national average earnings, and the upper limit is 135 percent of national average earnings. The Guaranteed Minimum Pension, which is protected by implicit plan termination insurance, is thus equal to (about) 30 percent of national average earnings.[12]

If the sponsor of a contracted-out plan goes bankrupt, then those pensions that replace social security pensions are treated as if bought back into SERPs, even if the plan's assets are insufficient to do so. To protect the integrity of SERPs, the Occupational Pensions Board has the statutory responsibility to ensure that employers fully fund the accrued liabilities in respect to Guaranteed Minimum Pensions. If a plan fails to demonstrate that it has adequate resources, the Occupational Pensions Board may withdraw the right to contract out of SERPs. At present, the only funding requirement set out in regulations is that the pension plan have assets at least equal to the Guaranteed Minimum Pensions of its members. No statutory requirement is imposed, in general, if the funding level of the plan is less than 100 percent as established by its actuarial valuation. Further, the actuarial valuation, which must be made at least every three and a half years, need not provide the details of the method *or* the assumptions used in the calculation.

Following the highly publicized shortfalls in the Maxwell pension plans, policy analysts in the United Kingdom have recently revisited the question of plan termination insurance. The Pension Law Review Committee has recommended that a compensation fund be established, to cover shortfalls (*only*) if there has been fraud or theft of assets. The Committee has made a number of other recommendations designed to enhance the security of promised pension benefits.

From a North American perspective, two additional observations merit note. First, the problem of underfunding, so evident among distressed firms in the United States, does not appear to be a major problem in the United Kingdom.[13] This may reflect the fact that the members of defined benefit plans are in plans in which pensions are linked to salary at or near retirement. There are, apparently, no flat benefit plans whose periodic (and retroactive) enrichments are the primary source of underfunding in Canada and the United States. Second, at least for benefits in excess of Guaranteed Minimum Pensions, statutory funding and monitoring requirements appear to be less stringent than in either Canada or the United States.

Germany

In Germany, the book reserve method is the primary system for financing employer-sponsored pension plans.[14] Unlike the United States, Canada, and the United Kingdom, pension liabilities are *not* secured by pension assets held in a separate trust. In Germany, the employer has a direct liability to pay promised pension benefits, and these benefits are paid out of company, not pension, assets. Financing takes the form of the accrual of book reserves.[15] To protect the promised pension benefits in the event of the employer's bankruptcy, the book reserve system is accompanied, since 1974, by mandatory insolvency insurance. Insolvency insurance is provided by the Pensions-Sicherungs-Verein (PSVaG), a mutual insurance corporation.

In the event of bankruptcy, the PSVaG is required to pay all the pension benefits due under the terms of the employer's plan. These include pensions that are currently in pay, together with the pension benefits that are legally vested at the time of the bankruptcy. The PSVaG is not required to pay a monthly pension in excess of three times the Social Security Contribution Ceiling. However, this is a very large amount, equal to US$ 165,000 per year. Certain pension benefits — such as enrichments granted in the last year prior to insolvency that exceed the benefits granted in the prior year — are excluded from coverage. This is analogous to steps taken by the PBGC in the United States and the Guarantee Fund in Ontario to limit the scope for strategic behavior against the interests of the public provider of termination insurance. Insured benefits are paid in full even if the bankruptcy involves criminal behavior on the part of management, and even if the firm is not current in its required contributions to the PSVaG.

Employers are required by law to make contributions sufficient to finance the insolvency insurance on a pay-as-you-go basis.[16] Required contributions are based on the size of the employer's pension liabilities, including pensions in pay to retired workers. The contribution rate, like its counterparts in North America, is *not* linked to a measure of the likelihood of the firm's insolvency. For this reason, the insurance premiums levied by the PSVaG are not market-determined rates; that is, the true risks of a claim on the insurance fund are not internalized into insurance premiums. There is thus a cross-subsidy, as in North America, from stable to less financially secure firms. The annual contribution rate is set equal to the ratio of the capital required in the year by the PSVaG to the total amount of employers' liabilities for pension benefits. In 1975, the contribution rate was set equal to 0.15 percent. Since then, it has fluctuated from year to year. To date, the highest contribution rate occurred in 1982, at 0.69 percent; the lowest, in 1990, was at 0.03 percent (Peter Ahrend, Chapter 3, this volume). The high contribution rate in 1982 reflects the claim arising from a major company in the electronics industry.

In the United States, the PBGC levies premiums based, in part, on the amount by which pension assets fall short of pension liabilities. In Germany, there are no pension assets if the employer uses the book reserve system. From this perspective, the fact that the PSVaG levies premiums on the full amount of the employer's pension liabilities is a parallel policy, since this is the amount by which pension liabilities exceed pension assets. Ironically, there is nothing analogous in Germany to the major concern of policy analysts in the United States: the apparent success of firms in financial distress to underfund their pension liabilities, to the detriment of the PBGC.

From the perspective of North America, the apparent lack of concern regarding the financial soundness of the PSVaG is surprising. In large part, this may reflect the relatively favorable experience of the PSVaG, at least to date. From 1988 to 1992, for example, the required contribution rate averaged 0.07 percent. This is one-half the average contribution rate (0.14 percent) required during the five years (1975–1979) immediately following the creation of the PSVaG.

Yet, if a small number of large firms were to experience financial distress, the required contribution rate could rise sharply. (In 1982, the contribution rate rose to 0.69 percent, more than triple the contribution rate in 1981.) Further, adverse selection would appear to present more of a problem than in the United States, since the cross-subsidy from secure to less stable firms appears to be more pronounced. Perhaps, the tax-subsidized self-financing available to secure firms who use the book reserve method provides a strong enough incentive to prevent their seeking to exit the system by adopting a different type of financing arrangement for their pension plans (such as setting up a pension fund). In Germany, benefit enrichments in the year immediately preceding bankruptcy that exceed those granted in the previous year are excluded from insurance coverage. Yet this response to the moral hazard problem seems to be less onerous, and thus less of a constraint on strategic behavior, than does the five-year phase-in rule imposed by the PBGC.[17]

Japan

Historically, a distinguishing feature of the Japanese pension system has been the Lump Sum Retirement Benefit plan, financed on a book reserve basis. Tax Qualified Pension Plans (TQP) were introduced in 1962 and Employees' Pension Fund (EPF) plans were introduced in 1966. As a result, there are a number of possible financing arrangements for defined benefit pension plans in Japan. This fact, together with continued changes in the retirement income system, complicate the task of assessing the role of termination insurance in Japan.

A TQP plan must be funded through a financial institution, such as a life insurance company. An EPF is a contracted-out plan — more specifically, a plan that is a substitute for the earnings-related component of the Employees' Pension Insurance. The latter is the earnings-related public pension plan that covers the majority of workers in the private sector. To qualify for contracting out, the employer must establish the EPF as a legal entity separate from the plan sponsor, and provide a pension benefit that is at least 30 percent more generous than the social security benefits that are being replaced. An EPF, unlike a lump sum plan, is advance-funded. Like TQP plans, most EPF plans are managed by life insurance companies or trust banking companies. Firms that provide a book reserve plan may also provide a TQP or EPF.

The risk borne by plan members in the event of insolvency varies with the type of plan to which the member belongs. Since 1976, employers who sponsor book reserve plans have been required to guarantee this amount with a financial institution. In fact, Noriyasu Watanabe (Chapter 4, this volume) reports that the majority of employers do not guarantee their book-reserve plans, as the regulations are laxly enforced. As a result, it would appear that the lump sum payments due plan members remain at risk in the event of the insolvency of their employer.

There is no termination insurance for TQP plans, so members remain at risk in the event of the bankruptcy of their employer. For these plans, however, this risk is mitigated by the requirement of advance funding.

In 1989 the Pension Guarantee Program was established to provide plan termination insurance to members of EPF plans. EPF plans are required to make contributions to the insurance program. Noriyasu Watanabe (Chapter 4, this volume) indicates that the contributions required of plan sponsors reflect the statistical likelihood of termination as well as the unfunded liability if the plan is terminated. As previously noted, insurance premiums in the United States, Canada, and Germany do *not* attempt to distinguish among firms on the basis of their differing probabilities of bankruptcy. It would appear that the proxy for financial soundness in Japan is simply the size of the employer, as the required contribution per participant declines gradually as the number of participants increases. As of 1994, there had been only one plan termination under the Pension Guarantee Program, and this plan was sufficiently well funded that there was no claim on the insolvency insurance program. Consequently, unlike the case in Canada and the United States, there is no apparent concern regarding the solvency of the insurance fund.

An Overview of the International Experience

In spite of an ongoing series of reforms, the long-term financial soundness of the PBGC remains a major concern in the United States. Indeed, many analysts (Bodie 1992; Smalhout 1993) draw attention to the potential parallel with the Federal Savings and Loan Insurance Corporation (FSLIC), which ultimately failed at tremendous cost to the United States taxpayer. Common concerns include, for example, the lack of market discipline, the opportunities for strategic behavior by the insureds, and regulator forbearance.

The purpose of this chapter is to provide a comparison of international experience with plan termination insurance, with particular attention to common problems and attempts at their solution. In this context, the PBGC provides a useful benchmark against which the experience of other countries can be compared. The most salient observations are summarized below.

With the exception of Germany, the level of benefits insured by the PBGC (a maximum of US$ 2,420 per month or US$ 29,040 per year in 1993) is high by international standards. The higher the level of the insured benefit, the higher is the value of the protection afforded to plan members, other things being equal. On the other hand, the higher, too, is the potential exposure of the public provider of termination insurance.

The risk exposure of the PBGC is concentrated among collectively bargained flat benefit benefits, where retroactive benefit enrichments generate new unfunded liabilities on a periodic basis. The experience in Ontario is similar. In the United Kingdom, the Guaranteed Minimum Pensions in contracted-out plans are earnings-related and, as a result, less likely to be underfunded. In Germany, the type of defined benefit formula is not an issue, since there is no advance funding with the book reserve system.

A major concern in the United States is the apparent ability of financially distressed firms to underfund their pension plans, thereby increasing the risk borne by the PBGC. There is no advance funding by those firms in Germany that adopt the book reserve method of financing their pension plans, so this dimension of strategic behavior is simply not relevant. Yet, as of 1994, there appears to be no public policy concern in Germany regarding the financial soundness of the PSVaG.

In Ontario and Germany, as well as in the United States, there is no attempt to incorporate the probability of bankruptcy into the setting of insurance premiums. As a result, there is a potentially large cross-subsidy from financially secure to less secure firms. In the United Kingdom, an analogous situation exists with regard to the implicit insurance provided to Guaranteed Minimum Pensions in contracted-out plans. In Japan, there appears to be an attempt to incorporate the likelihood of bankruptcy into the setting of insurance premiums, but only to the extent that the size of the firm (as measured by the number of plan participants) is used as a proxy for the firm's financial soundness.

To contain the evident moral hazard problem, recently granted enrichments to pension plans are not immediately covered by plan termination insurance. It would appear that Germany has the least demanding requirement. Yet, as previously noted, there seems to be little public concern about the financial soundness of PSVaG.

The problem of adverse selection is relatively unimportant in the United States, Ontario, and the United Kingdom, where participation is compulsory. In Germany, firms may choose *not* to use the book reserve method. By setting up a pension fund, the firm can avoid participation in the PSVaG. Presumably, other things being equal, financially sound firms have the strongest incentive to avoid participating in the PSVaG.

In those countries where explicit termination insurance exists (i.e., all countries except for the United Kingdom), there is no distinction between insurance claims that do or those that do not arise from fraud or other employer malfeasance. In the United Kingdom, the Pension Law Review Committee has recommended that a compensation fund be established to protect promised pensions *only* in the event that there has been fraud or theft of assets.

The "big" question regarding plan termination insurance is whether, in fact, it is needed. In a competitive labor market with well-informed agents, the wages paid to workers will internalize the risk of promised pension benefits. This seems to be a persuasive argument in the case of collectively bargained plans, where underfunding in North America is concentrated. The apparent willingness of younger workers to accept the risks associated with underfunded flat benefit plans should be seen in the context of other objectives — in particular, the goal of encouraging and facilitating the retirement of older workers in order to enhance job security.[18] In the alternative, policy makers might deem the loss of pension benefits to be an unacceptable outcome, even if this possibility has been appropriately internalized into the compensation packages of affected workers. In this event, there remains the policy option of using tighter funding requirements as a means of reducing the risks that workers can, in fact, choose to bear. This could be accomplished, for example, by requiring very rapid amortization of any unfunded liabilities created by retroactive enrichments to flat benefit plans.[19]

As noted, Ontario began to consider the abandonment of plan termination insurance within a decade of its introduction. As the Ministry of Financial Institutions writes:

There is a risk that the PBGF will lack sufficient funds to meet current and future liabilities and that its potential liabilities cannot be known with certainty. As a result, the government is considering whether to maintain the Pension Benefits Guarantee Fund, possibly on a restructured basis designed to balance the potential liabilities and Fund assets, or whether to eliminate the Fund and strengthen the responsibilities of plan sponsors and plan members to provide for protection of benefits. (1989)

If the Guarantee Fund were eliminated, Ontario would take additional steps to improve the funding position of poorly funded plans.[20] In this context, the Ontario government highlights the special concern with underfunded flat benefit plan (Ministry of Financial Institutions): "The Superintendent of Pensions could be given the authority to deny approval of benefit enhancements which increase plan liabilities where the plan is funded at less than a prescribed level. This would not include statutory benefit improvements, but would require that supplementary benefits be adequately funded. It is recognized that such a restriction might be opposed as undue interference in the collective bargaining process and in some cases could impose limitations on negotiated benefits. However, for poorly funded plans it would represent an important safeguard to protect the benefits of both active and retired plan members."

With the change of government in Ontario in 1990, the question of whether the Guarantee Fund should be terminated is no longer under active consideration. However, the maximum insured benefit has remained at US\$ 750 per month since the creation of the Guarantee Fund. The *real* value of this ceiling has declined sharply, by 49 percent since 1980 and by 13 percent since 1989. In the United States, by contrast, the maximum insured benefit rises by the same factor used to escalate social security benefits. From this perspective, the importance of plan termination insurance in Ontario has effectively declined through a policy of benign neglect.

Conclusion

The "market failure" argument for the public provision of plan termination insurance is, at least superficially, appealing. In the absence of termination insurance, members of underfunded plans will suffer a loss of pension benefits if their employer goes bankrupt. Further, the public provision of plan termination insurance *has* met with considerable success in the political arena.

Economic analysis, however, suggests that the fundamental rationale for insurance is less clear. Equally important, no country has, as of 1994, sought to levy insurance premiums commensurate with the level of risk. In the United States, this fact underlies the continuing concern about the long-run financial soundness of the PBGC. The fact that market-based insurance premiums have never been levied indicates that the "market failure" argument has not been tested: there is as yet no evidence that the demand for insurance exists at premiums commensurate with risk. Since bankruptcy risk is not incorporated into the premium structure, profitable firms effectively subsidize unprofitable firms. This fact, in turn, invites the interpretation that the success of termination insurance in the political arena is due to redistributive, rather than to efficiency, considerations.

I am indebted to John Turner, Olivia Mitchell, Carolyn Weaver, and Dallas Salisbury for useful suggestions.

Notes

[1]Ippolito (1986, 1989) discusses possible efficiency arguments in support of introducing plan termination insurance (the PBGC) in the United States. He discusses, as well, the possibility that the PBGC was designed to benefit unprofitable firms with poorly funded plans at the expense of profitable firms with well-funded plans.

[2]Inman (1982) provides evidence that some public sector workers in the United States, whose benefits are not insured by the PBGC, receive higher wages in poorly funded plans.

[3]In light of a topical concern in the United Kingdom, one should note that

there is no suggestion in this formal analysis that wages will internalize the risk of funding shortfalls due to fraud perpetrated by the employer. While information on the funded status of the pension plan is readily disclosed, such is not the case for information regarding the likelihood of employer malfeasance. This does not, however, necessarily provide a rationale for government intervention. Ippolito (1986), for example, points out that private markets can and do insure against fraud or incompetence among pension fund managers.

[4]As noted by Ippolito (1986) and others, plan sponsors could be required to obtain insurance for their pension liabilities in private markets. This requirement would ensure that insurance premiums are set at market levels. The role of the government in this system would be to provide reinsurance in the event of system-wide adverse experience. Weaver (1993) proposes that the insurance function, as distinct from the transfer functions, of the PBGC be shifted to the private sector. In the absence of market-based pricing of insurance, and again as emphasized by Weaver (1993), the financially secure firms that subsidize their less healthy counterparts face a continuing incentive to opt out of the system by (for example) terminating their defined benefit plans and replacing them with defined contribution plans. Finally, the difficulties of the public insurer in setting risk-related insurance premiums merit emphasis. It is well known, for example, that the financial strength of the plan sponsor and the degree of underfunding should both be reflected in the premium structure. As emphasized by Bodie (1994), the mismatch between the degree of risk of the insured benefits, akin to (nominal) long-term debt, and the degree of risk of the pension assets is an important determinant of the long-run exposure of the public insurer. This factor, too, should be reflected in the insurance premium.

[5]The unwillingness of Ontario to levy risk-based insurance premiums eliminates the alternative strategy of mandating insurance coverage and inviting private insurers to enter the market. Ontario's insurance was made retroactive, for ongoing plans, to 1965. This is the year in which the Pensions Benefit Act of Ontario came into effect.

[6]Additional issues include, for example, the complications posed by the fact that termination insurance may cover only nominal (i.e., not real) pension benefits, together with the possibility that underfunding per se may provide efficiency gains by ensuring that workers have an important stake in the financial solvency of their employers (Ippolito 1985, 1986). To the extent that plan termination insurance subsidizes the compensation of older workers in declining industries, the public provision of this insurance may entail significant intergenerational transfers. The transfer of resources across generations, whether planned or not, has received increased attention by economists in recent years. Finally, an argument in support of pension insurance pertains to the market for "lemons." There are some "lemons" in the pension market, but workers have difficulty distinguishing them from reputable pension promises. As a result, workers give up smaller wage concessions to good firms than they would if they were assured that there is little or no risk to the pension promises of those firms. For good firms, the "unfair" pension insurance is the price they pay to assure their workers that their pension promises are reliable. For risks taken while young, individuals can offset losses through their labor market behavior as well as through their consumption. For risks taken later in life, however, individuals must absorb losses through reductions in consumption. Because they are less able to bear risk while old, workers are more likely to favor low risk retirement assets. For this reason, workers may prefer pension benefit insurance even though they are willing to accept other risks.

[7]For the United Kingdom, Germany, and Japan, the discussion draws heavily on Daykin (Chapter 2, this volume), Ahrend (Chapter 3, this volume), and Watanabe (Chapter 4, this volume). See also Clark (1991) for additional details regarding the retirement system in Japan. Other countries with plan termination insurance include Sweden, Finland, and Chile.

[8]These statistics are based on single employer plans with 100 or more members.

[9]In 1992 the premiums for fully funded plans were equal to US$ 19 per participant; for underfunded plans, US$ 19 per participant plus US$ nine for each US$ 1,000 of unfunded vested benefits per participant, to a maximum of an additional US$ 72 per participant. A plan with a large unfunded liability could thus be charged an insurance premium up to US$ 91 per participant. See Turner (1993) for further details. See Munnell (1982) for a discussion of the PBGC as structured at the time of its introduction.

[10]In a widely discussed and controversial case, LTV Corporation established, in 1987, follow-on plans that provided its workers with substantially the same benefits as in the underfunded plans that LTV wound up in 1986, transferring significant unfunded liabilities to the PBGC in the process.

[11]In Ontario, for example, the insured event has always been the *insolvency* of the plan sponsor. Further, the Guarantee Fund in Ontario has a lien on employer assets equal to the *full* amount of the insured shortfall of pension assets. There is no provision, unlike the United States, for funding waivers if the employer is experiencing financial difficulties. In spite of these steps, the potential for a financial crisis is both real and acknowledged. For the year ending March 31, 1993, the Guarantee Fund reports that there were 37 potential claims relating to the closure of 31 companies, with a potential liability to the Fund of US$ 27 million.

[12]This figure is equal to 25 percent, the target replacement rate, times 117 (i.e., 135 less 18) percent of national average earnings.

[13]This observation is, of necessity, tentative. Daykin (1991) reports that there is no centrally gathered information on the funded status of private sector plans.

[14]Ahrend (Chapter 3, this volume) reports that book reserves presently account for about 70 percent of the funds set aside to provide for employer-sponsored pension benefits.

[15]The book reserve appropriations made by the employer are tax-deductible. When pension benefits are paid, book reserves are reduced and the firm's taxable profits rise accordingly.

[16]The PSVaG does not pay insured benefits directly. Rather, the PSVaG buys the requisite annuities from a consortium of life insurance companies. For pensions in pay at the time of bankruptcy, the PSVaG purchases the necessary annuity contracts immediately from the consortium of life insurance companies.

[17]In theory, a firm facing imminent bankruptcy in the United States might grant benefit enrichments far in excess of those that it would grant if it were solvent. In spite of the five-year phase-in rule, the firm could succeed in enriching its workers at the expense of the PBGC.

[18]There remains, of course, the question of whether young workers (in particular) understand the nature of their employer's pensions (Mitchell 1988). As noted, Ippolito (1986) has argued that the underfunding of flat benefit plans serves to make union members resemble bondholders of the firm, thereby providing union members with a strong incentive to ensure the firm's solvency.

[19]If tighter funding requirements were to replace the public provision of termination insurance as a means of reducing the risk of employer-sponsored pen-

sions, the nature of the public policy debate might shift in new directions. For example, the government might consider issuing indexed bonds as a means of facilitating the preservation of real pension benefits during retirement. (In the United Kingdom, and more recently in Canada, government index bonds already exist.) In this context, it is worth emphasizing, for example, that the PBGC in the United States insures nominal, not real, pension benefits.

[20]There is, of course, no reason to view such initiatives solely as a *substitute* for plan termination insurance. Such initiatives could, evidently, *complement* a system of plan termination insurance.

References

Ahrend, Peter. "Pension Financial Security in Germany." This volume.

Birmingham, William. "Occupational and Personal Pension Provisions in the United Kingdom." In John A. Turner and Lorna Dailey, eds., *Pension Policy: An International Perspective*. Washington, DC: U.S. GPO, 1991: 211–227.

Bodie, Zvi. "The Pension Benefit Guaranty Corporation: Is the PBGC the FSLIC of the Nineties?" *Contingencies* (March/April 1992): 28–37.

——. "What the Pension Benefit Guarantee Corporation Can Learn from the Federal Savings and Loan Insurance Corporation." Working Paper 94-070. Cambridge, MA: Harvard Business School, 1994.

Bodie, Zvi and Robert C. Merton. "Pension Benefit Guarantees in the United States: A Functional Analysis." In Ray Schmitt, ed., *The Future of Pensions in the United States*. Philadelphia: Pension Research Council and University of Pennsylvania Press, 1993: 194–246.

Clark, Robert L. *Retirement Systems in Japan*. Homewood, IL: Pension Research Council and R. D. Irwin, 1991.

Daykin, Christopher D. "Occupational Pension Provision in the United Kingdom." This volume.

——. "United Kingdom Pension Statistics." In *Pension Policy: An International Perspective*. Washington, DC: U.S. GPO, 1991: 229–244.

Inman, Robert. "Public Employee Pensions and the Local Labor Budget." *Journal of Public Economics* 19 (1982): 49–71.

Ippolito, Richard. "The Economic Function of Underfunded Pension Plans." *Journal of Law and Economics* 28, 3 (1985): 611–52.

——. *Pensions, Economics, and Public Policy*. Homewood, Il: Pension Research Council and Dow Jones-Irwin, 1986.

——. *The Economics of Pension Insurance*. Homewood, Il: Pension Research Council and Dow Jones-Irwin, 1989.

Ministry of Financial Institutions, Province of Ontario. *Building on Reform: Choices for Tomorrow's Pensions*. March, 1989.

Mitchell, Olivia S. "Worker Knowledge of Pension Provisions." *Journal of Labor Economics* 6 (1988): 21–39.

——. "Retirement Systems in Developed and Developing Countries: Institutional Features, Economic Effects, and Lessons for Economies in Transition." Cambridge, MA: NBER Working Paper 4424, August 1993.

Munnell, Alicia H. *The Economics of Private Pensions*. Washington, DC: Brookings Institution, 1982.

Pesando, James E. "Investment Risk, Bankruptcy Risk and Pension Reform in Canada." *Journal of Finance* 37, 3 (1982): 341–49.

Smalhout, James H. "Avoiding the Next Guaranteed Bailout: Reforms for the Pension Insurance Program." *Brookings Review* (Spring 1993): 12–15.

Turner, John A. "U.S. Pension Benefit Insurance." *Benefits Quarterly* 9, 1 (1993): 77–85.

Watanabe, Noriyasu. "Private Pension Plans in Japan." This volume.

Weaver, Carolyn L. "Government Guarantees of Private Pension Benefits: Current Problems and Likely Future Prospects." Mimeo. Washington, DC: Center for Economic Policy Research Conference, 1993.

Comments by Carolyn L. Weaver

In light of the growing concern over the solvency of the United States pension insurance system, and the potential for a savings-and-loan-style taxpayer bailout of the Pension Benefit Guaranty Corporation, James Pesando has written a timely and important chapter on how five major nations have chosen to deal with securing employer pension promises. He provides a wealth of information on, and documents a fairly significant degree of variation in, pension insurance arrangements in other countries. This variation in arrangements suggests some fruitful avenues of future research.

In the United States, there is a formal system of pension insurance operated on a monopoly basis by the federal government and based only loosely on insurance principles. By contrast, most of Canada operates without pension insurance; the United Kingdom relies on an implicit system in which the government guarantees a minimum pension (with no explicit pricing of that guarantee or financing of the implied debt), requires full funding of that pension, and imposes on employers liability for any pension fund shortfalls in the event of bankruptcy; and Japan operates a system that is a hybrid of the United States and the Canadian systems, with some pensions uninsured and some pensions insured by the government with (apparently) some attempt to risk-relate premiums. This variation would lead any good economist to long to see the next study — the one that attempts to quantify, empirically, the effects of these institutional differences on underfunded plan terminations and on the solvency (or implicit debt) of pension insurance systems. It leads a political economist like myself to long to see the study that attempts to explain the variation in institutions across countries.

Given the more limited purpose of this chapter, which is to compare and contrast institutions, some critical details about the design of pension insurance systems warrant further elaboration. For example, what precisely is the event against which countries are attempting to insure, referred to loosely as the "insolvency" of insured plan sponsors, and how much discretion do sponsors retain over the timing of that event? Is it financial distress (how much distress?), negative net worth, or bankruptcy and liquidation, and how much pension debt can the company pile up as that event approaches? What kind of claims do workers (or the government insurer) have on the non-pension assets of plan sponsors, and what is the status of these claims in bankruptcy proceedings? How are minimum funding requirements monitored and enforced? What are the restrictions, if any, on investment practices? More generally, since all countries (with the possible exception of Japan) reject risk-based pricing, how precisely is moral hazard controlled other than by limiting benefit guarantees? While Pesando addresses some of these issues for some of the countries, a more thorough exposition would be helpful.

As a related point, I would have found it helpful to see some concrete data on the actual and expected future claims experience in other countries. In the United States, for example, the concentration of large claims in unionized firms offering flat benefit plans tells us a great deal about the efficacy of our funding rules and premium structure as well as the probable political purpose of pension insurance.

Were we to try to draw inferences from a study such as this about the effects of public pension insurance on, say, the retirement income choices open to workers, the ability of firms to respond flexibly to changing market conditions, the security of retirement incomes, or, more generally, economic efficiency, we would need to know still more. In particular, what is the tax, legal, regulatory, and labor market environment within which private pensions exist? How important are defined benefit pensions to retirement income saving? Are close substitutes available for insured pensions?

In the United States, for example, we have an enormous, well-developed private pension system, a variety of tax-preferred means of saving for retirement, competitive labor markets, and a mobile workforce.[1] These factors tend to limit the costs that can be imposed on the private sector through a poorly designed public program, while simultaneously creating a potentially large adverse selection problem for the government insurer.

While these latter questions go well beyond those that Pesando attempts to address, they are critical to evaluating the likely costs and benefits of pension insurance.

This brings me to Pesando's discussion of the economic rationale for pension insurance. Although he makes clear that his purpose is *not* to evaluate why governments *should* adopt pension insurance, he nevertheless touches on this subject and, in so doing, leaves unresolved a number of important issues.

Pesando presents three economic rationales or so-called "market failure" arguments for pension insurance:

- Imperfect information in labor markets, whereby workers (or their agents) can not properly perceive the risks of an underfunded termination and thus wages do not fully internalize these risks;
- Paternalism, whereby workers properly perceive the risks and wages adjust, but we (somebody!) nevertheless wish to protect them from the loss of pension wealth; and
- An externality for taxpayers, whereby losses of pension wealth from unanticipated, underfunded terminations result in increased public assistance expenditures.

As a student of public finance and public economics, these rationales raise three questions in my mind:

- Are they sound market failure arguments, worthy of attention in this chapter?
- If so, what specific public policies would they suggest?
- Are the benefits of government action likely to outweigh the costs? In other words, as James Buchanan has taught me to ask, how does the supposed market failure stack up against the potential for government failure, recognizing that public policies emerge from imperfect political institutions?

From this perspective, it is quite a stretch to get from any of these supposed market failures to a compulsory system of pension insurance organized around a monopoly public supplier, such as was created in the United States and to a greater or lesser degree in Ontario and the other countries studied.

As Pesando notes, the imperfect information argument (weak on its face in competitive labor markets) suggests policies designed to improve the information available to workers. For example, firms might be required to disclose workers' accrued benefits in the event of bankruptcy and the proportion of benefits that could be met with pension fund (or other) assets on hand. Pension insurance, by contrast, which shields workers from the loss of pension wealth, tends to weaken incentives to become informed about the ability of employers to back up their pension promises.

The second rationale, paternalism, is very nearly illogical on its face as a market failure argument. It implies that there is an identifiable group of people (i.e., paternalists) who cares about and is willing to pay some price to protect workers from pension losses even though these workers have already been compensated for the risk of loss through the wage premiums they extract from companies offering riskier pensions. While it is clear who comprises the recipient group, presumably the millions of workers who are or may one day be covered by pensions, who are the paternalists? Taxpayers other than workers? If so, it is not clear how pension insurance would be financed so that the true costs would be borne by paternalists rather than by the intended recipients. It is also not clear why the concerns of paternalists would not extend to workers covered by defined contribution plans who knowingly expose themselves to more investment risk than participants in defined benefit plans.

It would probably be more constructive to think in terms of the gains that might accrue to self-interested workers seeking to reduce the variability of pension outcomes. As Zvi Bodie and Robert Merton (1993) have explained, even if wages adjust to reflect the riskiness of pensions, workers may still prefer less pension risk because of the large, non-diversifiable stake they typically have in the firms in which they work. Since, in their view, the primary function of defined benefit pensions is to offer a specified benefit at retirement, it follows that "the function is less efficiently performed if the contract . . . calls for the benefit to be paid in the joint event that the employee retirees *and* the firm is still solvent."[2]

From this perspective, no paternalists are required to generate a demand for institutions to reduce the risk of default, and there are market-based responses or, at least, less costly government responses. For example, plan sponsors could reduce default risk by contracting with life insurance companies to provide pension annuities. Alternatively, pension claims could be given priority over the claims of other creditors in bankruptcy proceedings (Keating 1991; Lindeman 1993; Bodie and Merton 1993), or firms could be required to demonstrate their ability to meet promised benefits by purchasing a guarantee from a private financial institution (Weaver forthcoming; Smalhout 1993).

Finally, the externality rationale cannot properly be described as a *market* failure since the underlying problem is a pre-existing government program — public assistance. There is a fiscal externality, but it is created by government. As the history of the Pension Benefit Guaranty Corporation amply demonstrates, much justification for government intervention derives from trying to fix problems created by earlier interventions. This fiscal externality, moreover, has been used to justify everything from mandatory private pensions to social security and thus provides little guidance as to the appropriate policy response.

As some measure of the importance, empirically, of this rationale, Pesando makes the interesting observation that in Canada, where the major public assistance program is national in scope, neither the national government, nor nine out of ten provinces, have been moved to control this potential fiscal externality through pension insurance.

In sum, even if a market failure existed and it were demonstrated to be empirically important, a government-run pension insurance program that hews to insurance principles in name only — which is the only model we have of explicit pension insurance in any of the major countries studied — is probably the least appropriate policy response. Apart from the economic inefficiencies that are likely to result, such a program will (through mispricing and other problems) tend to discourage new companies from adopting defined benefit plans and encourage healthy companies with well-funded plans to discontinue them, thereby undermining rather than securing the defined benefit pension system. Information disclosure requirements, superpriority status for pensions in bankruptcy proceedings, and requirements that employers guarantee their pension promises through private financial institutions all appear to be policies that would address the same basic problems with fewer economic distortions. That we do not see much political demand for policies like these underscores the fact that *rationales* for government policy rarely constitute *explanations*.

Pesando's discussion of pension insurance in Ontario, Canada's "industrial heartland" makes clear that he is aware of this important distinction.

Pension economists would do well to move beyond the normative question of why we *should* have pension insurance to how we can bring about constructive reform of existing programs that redistribute wealth in predictable ways to entrenched political interests (Ippolito 1989; Weaver forthcoming). The political interests I have in mind are workers and shareholders in unionized firms in declining industries. Few pension analysts today would dispute the fact that, at least in the United States (and apparently in Ontario), pension insurance is a form of industrial policy — a system of cheap pension guarantees (to use a phrase coined by Bodie and Merton) designed to prop up unionized firms in declining industries.

Elsewhere I have argued for moving toward a system of private, competitively supplied pension insurance for all new companies and for existing companies that are commercially insurable (Weaver forthcoming). Companies with poorly funded plans and an unusual risk of default would continue to receive subsidized "insurance" from the government, only the subsidies would be financed from the general fund of the Treasury (rather than from workers and shareholders in other companies) and limited by strict standards that precluded any deliberate increases in exposure. For most companies, this new arrangement would amount to privatizing the supply of pension insurance subject to a government mandate.

Canada offers yet another model of privatization — apparently pure privatization — where workers in most provinces are compensated for pension default risks through the wage offers they accept (and may be protected by employers in other ad hoc ways) but are not formally insured in the event of pension losses. Unfortunately, none of the countries of the world offers an example of how to structure a transition back to a private system or to one explicitly disciplined by market forces once having taken the path of government-administered insurance.

Notes

[1]As noted in Ippolito (forthcoming), the most important of these, in terms of providing a close substitute for defined benefit plans, may be the 401(k) plan, a type of defined contribution plan into which employers can shift compensation and yet retain some of the bonding (or tenure) effects of defined benefit plans.

[2]See Bodie and Merton (1993). For an alternative view of pensions, see Ippolito (1987, 1988), who argues that workers and shareholders both stand to gain from some degree of default risk arising from underfunding. In his view, underfunding gives workers a stake in the long-term viability of firms and thus tends to align the interests of workers and shareholders.

References

Bodie, Zvi and Robert C. Merton. "Pension Benefit Guarantees in the United States: A Functional Analysis." In Ray Schmitt, ed., *The Future of Pensions in the United States.* Philadelphia: Pension Research Council and University of Pennsylvania Press, 1993: 194–246.

Richard A. Ippolito. "Pension Security: Has ERISA Had Any Effect?" *Regulation* 2 (1987): 15–22.

——. "A Study of the Regulatory Effects of ERISA." *Journal of Law and Economics* 31, 1 (1988): 85–125.

——. *The Economics of Pension Insurance.* Homewood, IL: Irwin, 1989.

——. "Toward Explaining the Growth of Defined Contribution Plans." *Industrial Relations* 34, 1 (1995): 1–20.

Keating, Daniel. "Pension Insurance, Bankruptcy and Moral Hazard." *Wisconsin Law Review* 65 (1991): 56–108.

Lindeman, David C. "Pension Plagues and the PBGC." *American Enterprise* 4, 2 (1993): 70–79.

Smalhout, James H. "Avoiding the Next Guaranteed Bailout." *Brookings Review* 11, 2 (1993): 16–21.

Weaver, Carolyn L. "Government Guarantees of Private Pension Benefits: Current Problems and Future Prospects." In Sylvester J. Schieber and John B. Shoven, eds., *Public Policy Toward Pensions.* New York: Twentieth Century Fund, forthcoming.

Comments by Dallas L. Salisbury

The discussion of PBGC and the guaranty programs it administers has at times been heated. The more normative the commentator the more oriented he or she will be toward a casualty insurance model that is more critical of the program.

Agree or not, Congress intended a social insurance model—that is, explicit subsidy within the defined benefit system. The original bill included far more than present law. The Contingent Employer Liability Insurance (CELI) called for by the original statute, and amended out of the law in the 1980s, would have raised far larger issues had it been implemented.

The original multi-employer program carried risks. It was changed with two initial results: protection of PBGC and no new multi-employer pension plans. Now that many of those plans are fully funded, employers are leaving. PBGC was protected; benefits promised will be paid but the system froze. Is that in the public interest? Is there no room for risk? Should we seek the same type of "stability" in the single employer defined benefit area? I do not claim to have the answers, but I do think we sometimes rush to judgments that are not in the long-term interests of economic security.

Much is said about PBGC and incentives. The existence of the program raises some interesting questions:

- Has government interest in having plans well funded to protect the PBGC in any way balanced desires to reduce tax incentives?
- Does the program in effect place some break on benefit increases and better funding to avoid higher premiums?
- Does the program encourage strong employers to care more about the practices of others and to pay more attention to pensions when mergers, acquisitions and spinoffs are being discussed?
- Does the program serve to enhance confidence in the economy and the pension system, thus leading to a stronger economy?

- Does the program make elected officials and citizens feel better?
- Given that public policy is at base paternalistic, do PBGC and defined benefit plans serve to hold down other government spending?

I would also harken back to the issue of privatization of the PBGC program. I served on groups that looked into this issue. They were created by advocates who concluded it would not work. Why? Because the underwriting standards the insurers said they would need went too far. The conclusion was that the strong would drop plans and the weak would not be able to obtain insurance at a price they could afford and would "leave" also. A short field day in the courts and for the servers, but an ultimate loss for participants, beneficiaries, and the public interest in economic security.

Against this backdrop, I suggest that the chapter by James Pesando provides a good summary overview of the pension termination guaranty programs in major industrial nations.

Pesando aptly points out that many policy analysts concerned about pension security see the need for such programs as self-evident. Without such programs, as the author notes, benefits might be lost. As critical to advocates of defined benefit pension arrangements is the relative public policy stability that such a program makes possible. The United States program resulted from public upheaval over the bankruptcy of the Studebaker auto company in 1954. Workers and employers were able to compromise on the concept of "social insurance" as a price for having defined benefit pension plans.

Economists question the need for a pension guaranty program, Pesando states, because of a belief that pensions are deferred wages. As such, the loss of a pension is the worker/retiree's problem. It may be true that "virtually all pension analysts . . . now accept the proposition that pension benefits represent deferred wages." As for "non-" analysts, I think many of them accept the proposition in theory in bargained situations, but in many other situations its acceptance is far less clear in the case of defined benefit plans, which may go many years with no new contributions, than with defined contribution plans, which make regular contributions. Present cash compensation practices pay little attention to the benefits promised in assessing the cash necessary to meet the competition. Discussion of "total compensation" continues, but few actually practice it, even though "in the long run" it may work its way through the labor market as deferred wages.

Pesando suggests that the program may simply be a form of paternalism. I would suggest it is both that and a kind of political necessity, a means of maintaining social peace. Employer surveys for decades have shown that younger workers have little appreciation of the defined benefit plan. They look for a market wage and possibly health benefits. They are unlikely to have knowingly accepted a lower wage for the pension promise. Disclosure would do little good at a practical level since other research indicates that little of the distributed material is read until the worker feels a problem. As we have seen in the area of retiree medical insurance in the United States, disclosure of the employer's right to take the plan away does not make workers accept an employer's doing it.

Pesando cites a number of areas where design of the program allows abuses to arise. Several legislative efforts have sought to correct these areas, and relative to the original 1974 statute much progress has been made in the United States. The author could not be more correct in suggesting that efficiency concerns are not linked to public policy and the program. I do agree with the tie to industrial decline, as the program allows smoother economic transitions and less political and social upheaval as a result. The creation last year of a new guaranty program for the retiree medical benefits of retired miners is further evidence of this line of argument.

Having been involved in the earliest studies in 1976 of the premium structure of the U.S. program, I note that the history of the program is a series of compromises aimed at maintaining a defined benefit pension system. The objective has been a PBGC that is solvent in the long run, not one made insolvent overnight by policy change that drives any employer with a well-funded plan to drop it. This desire for balance can be seen in the PBGC reform debates of the last 20 years.

Pesando states in his review of the United States' system that the stated intent is to ensure that ultimately pension benefits are fully funded. His review of ways in which this occurs is accurate. They also reveal why the law is what it is. The objective is retirement income and funding to pay the benefit when due, not a fully funded plan every day. Investment policy that emphasizes equities with high volatility suggest that it is assumed that at times the market will be down and unfunded liabilities will exist. Advocates of full funding have argued for all bond "immunized" portfolios for this reason. The sponsors of plans have rejected this logic. The original law contemplated the cross-subsidies the author identifies and each amendment of the law has reinforced that intent. At the same time, each amendment has sought to adjust the abuse potential he identifies.

Canada sought advice early from the PBGC on the advantages and disadvantages of such a program. Ontario was the leader in interest, and, as Pesando notes, the only province to take action. I agree with him that the union influence was significant, as it was in creation of the PBGC.

The unique characteristics of the system in the United Kingdom were the price to be paid for the concept of contracting out and the creation of individual pensions. The absence of flat dollar plans is a reasonable explanation for well-funded plans in the United Kingdom. Another, which may not last, has been tax laws that have given sponsors more flexibility than in the United States to fund as much as they wish in profitable years. These laws have taken on a more American restrictiveness in recent years, which may show up in poorer funding in the future.

German employers have been willing to finance a system with annual assessments. Therefore, the system is always funded on a current basis but does not require projections of future economic health. Because the event for payment by the agency is insolvency of the enterprise, there is limited incentive to game the system. I would argue that insolvency in Germany is a far more effective moral hazard protection than the system in the United States. And German firms do prefer putting capital to work inside their firms, rather than in the broader economy. If they cannot generate higher internal returns, why remain in business?

I would speculate that if the United States changed to a system of an annual accounting and an insolvency basis, much of the present angst would go away. There is not a general taxpayer guarantee to the PBGC, yet it is the "fear" of possible taxpayer liability that seems to drive much of the United States concern.

Discussion of the PBGC in comparison with the Federal Savings and Loan Insurance Corporation is fundamentally flawed since the promises, and the payment method for those promises, are so different (as is the underlying investment base of the pension system versus the dominance of real estate). Those with the greatest stated concerns do not find comfort in the social insurance aspect of the PBGC that was intended by Congress. "Reform" of the PBGC would happen quickly if many others did not find the social component a critical part of the program. This social factor is also the major reason that the program would be favored by many even if employees had been offered explicit cash compensation reductions in exchange for the pension promise. PBGC represents a balance of economic and social logic. One circumstance under which PBGC might go away or change fundamentally would be a decision by unions to drop defined plans in favor of defined contributions plans rather than maintaining a continued clear preference for the former.

Conclusion

The future of the PBGC can only be determined after Congress articulates its goals for the program. Many of the proposals put forth by analysts today advocate a mission and goals different from those set forth in ERISA (as amended).

The program was legislatively established with social insurance goals. A move to the casualty insurance model may well be justified, but it carries with it a fundamental change of mission. Too many analysts fail to begin their work with an articulation of why Congress was wrong and why they should change the mission. Instead, they analyze the program against a casualty model and declare the program in need of reform. By so doing, they confuse rather than enlighten. The time for clearer presentations is long overdue. Those who want change should be clear that they are advocates as well as analysts — advocates for a change of mission, not for more effective implementation of the present mission. The present mission is social insurance. Against that mission the PBGC has been a very successful agency.

References

Employee Benefit Research Institute. *Pension Plan Termination Insurance: Does the Foreign Experience Have Relevance in the United States?* Washington, DC: EBRI Policy Forum, June, 1979.

——. "PBGC and Pension Plan Termination Policy." Washington, DC: EBRI Issue Brief No. 54, May, 1986.

——. *What is the Future of Defined Benefit Pension Plans?* Washington, DC: EBRI/ERF Roundtable, 1989.

Korczyk, Sophie M. "Private Pensions and the PBGC: Strength for the Future." Washington, DC: EBRI Testimony No. 7, 1982.

Salisbury, Dallas L. "The Current Health and Future Prospects for Defined Benefit Pension Plans." Washington, DC: EBRI Testimony No. 10, 1983.

——. "The Single Employer Pension Plan Amendments Act of 1983 HR 3930." Washington, DC: EBRI Testimony No. 24, 1983.

——. "Financial Status of the Pension Benefit Guaranty Corporation's Single Employer Insurance Program." Washington, DC: EBRI Testimony No. 28, 1984.

——. "The Financial Strength of the Pension Benefit Guaranty Corporation." Washington, DC: EBRI Testimony No. 86, 1992.

——. "The Financial Status of the Pension Benefit Guaranty Corporation." Washington, DC: EBRI Testimony No. 89, 1993.

Salisbury, Dallas L., Frank McArdle, and Man-Bing Sze. Washington, DC: EBRI Testimony No. 52, 1986.

Salisbury, Dallas L., Paul Yakoboski, and Celia Silverman. "The Financial Condition of the Pension Benefit Guaranty Corporation." Washington, DC: EBRI Testimony No. 85, 1992.

Smith, Harry G. "Defined Benefit Plans and Individual Retirement Accounts (IRAs)." Washington, DC: EBRI Testimony No. 45, 1985.

Yakoboski, Paul, Celia Silverman, and Jack VanDerhei. "PBGC Solvency: Balancing Social and Casualty Insurance Perspectives." Washington, DC: EBRI Issue Brief No. 126, 1992.

Contributors

PETER AHREND is Managing Director and a shareholder of Beratungs-GmbH Dr. Dr. Ernst Heissmann, Wiesbaden, a leading firm of national and international pension consultants in Germany. Mr. Ahrend is an attorney-at-law and a specialist tax lawyer who at an early stage in his professional career worked for a leading German life office. He serves as Deputy Chairman of the Board of ABA (the German Association of Pension Consultants) and head of its tax committee, and as a board member of the International Pension and Employee Benefits Lawyers Association. He is a member of the German Society of Insurance Sciences, the Examination Committee of the German Actuarial Society, the European Committee of the International Foundation of Employee Benefit Plans, and the working group on pensions of AIDA, the International Society for Insurance Law. He is the author of numerous German and international publications on pension matters, including several standard texts. He is a visiting lecturer at the University of Karlsruhe.

LUCY APROBERTS is a researcher specializing in the economics of social welfare at the Institut de Recherches Economiques et Sociales (IRES) in Paris. Ms. apRoberts is co-author, along with Emmanuel Reynaud, of *Les systèmes de retraite à l'étranger: Etats-Unis, Allemagne, Royaume-Uni* (Retirement Systems Abroad: The United States, Germany, the United Kingdom) (Paris: IRES, 1992). She has done field work on company benefit plans in France. Her research focuses on the links between state-run social insurance and occupational benefit plans in the United States and in France.

ALAN J. AUERBACH is Professor of Economics at the University of California at Berkeley and formerly taught at the University of Pennsylvania. He is the author of *The Taxation of Capital Income,* and coauthor with Laurence Kotlikoff of *Dynamic Fiscal Policy.* Dr. Auerbach served as a Deputy Chief of Staff of the United States Joint Committee on Taxation during 1992, and he speaks frequently before committees of the House and Senate. He has been a consultant to the United States Treasury, the Swedish Ministry of Finance, the Organization for Economic Cooperation and Development, the International Monetary Fund, and the World Bank. He is a Research Associate of the National Bureau of Economic Research and a Fellow of the Econometric Society. He is a member of the Executive Committee of the American Economic Association and of the editorial boards of the *American Economic Review* and the *Journal of Economic Literature*. He received his BA from Yale University and his PhD from Harvard University.

MARSHALL E. BLUME is Howard Butcher III Professor of Finance and Director of the Rodney L. White Center for Financial Research at The Wharton School of the University of Pennsylvania. Dr. Blume has conducted extensive research into investments, the financial markets, and investor behavior. His most recent book is *Revolution on Wall Street: The Rise and Decline of the New York Stock Exchange,* coauthored with Jeremy Siegel and Dan Rottenberg. Dr. Blume is a Director of the Pennsylvania Economy League and a trustee of Rosemont School. He served on the United States Government Accounting Office advisory committee that investigated the October 1987 market crash and was a commissioner on the Knoll/Shaffer Bi-Partisan Commission on Pennsylvania Pension Fund Investments that examined the state pension funds. He is a past Managing Editor of the *Journal of Finance* and is currently an editor of the *Journal of Fixed Income*. Dr. Blume received his MBA and PhD from the University of Chicago.

ZVI BODIE is the Thomas Henry Carroll Ford Foundation Visiting Professor of Business Administration at Harvard University and Professor of Finance at Boston University School of Management. Dr. Bodie is a member of the Financial Accounting Standards Board Task Force on Interest Methods and of the Pension Research Council. He coedited *Pensions and the Economy: Sources, Uses, and Limitations of Data* and textbook, *Investments,* is used as the main finance text in the certification program of the Institute of Chartered Financial Analysts. He has consulted on pension policy for the United States Department of Labor, the State of Israel, and Bankers Trust Company. Dr. Bodie holds a PhD in economics from the Massachusetts Institute of Technology and has served on the finance faculty at MIT's Sloan School of Management.

ANGELA E. CHANG is an Economist in the Banking Studies Department at the Federal Reserve Bank of New York, where she has analyzed issues in discrimination in home mortgage lending. Dr. Chang has previously done research on the trend away from defined benefit pension plans and the effect of tax policies on the pension decisions of workers and employers, and she is a contributor to the Pension Research Council conference volume *The Future of Pensions in the United States.* She received an AB from Princeton University and a PhD from the Massachusetts Institute of Technology.

ROBERT L. CLARK is Professor of Economics and Business at North Carolina State University and Visiting Professor, Fuqua School of Business, Duke University. Dr. Clark serves as Senior Fellow at the Center for the Study of Aging and Human Development and as Senior Research Fellow at the Center for Demographic Studies, both at Duke University. He has published extensively on retirement and pension policies, economic responses to population aging, the economic well-being of the elderly, and international pensions. He is a member of the American Economic Association, the Gerontological Society of America, the International Union for Scientific Study of Population, and the National Academy of Social Insurance. Dr. Clark earned a BA from Millsaps College and MA and PhD degrees from Duke University.

E. PHILIP DAVIS is a Senior Economist at the Bank of England and research associate of the Financial Markets Group, London School of Economics. Mr. Davis currently is seconded to the European Monetary Institute in Basle, Switzerland. He has published widely in the fields of institutional investors, banking, financial regulation, corporate finance, and financial instability. He has written commissioned articles on pension funds for the World Bank, the Bank for International Settlements, the Commissariat Generale du Plan (Paris), and the Centre for European Policy Studies (Brussels), as well as the Bank of England. His first book, *Debt, Financial Fragility and Systemic Risk,* was followed by *Pension Funds, Old Age Security and the Development of Financial Systems.*

CHRISTOPHER D. DAYKIN is the Government Actuary of the United Kingdom. Mr. Daykin has been a member of the Council of the Institute of Actuaries since 1985, Honorary Secretary of the Institute from 1988 to 1990, and Vice-President from 1993. He has served as Chairman of the Solvency Working Party of the Institute of Actuaries General Insurance Study Group and Chairman of the Institute's Working Party on AIDS. Mr. Daykin currently is Chairman of the Continuing Professional Development Joint Committee for the Institute and the Faculty of Actuaries, and Deputy Chairman of the Education Joint Committee. He is the United Kingdom representative on the Pensions Observatory established by the Commission of the European Communities and the Chairman of the Permanent Committee for Statistical, Actuarial and Financial Studies of the International Social Security Association. In 1991, he was awarded a Finlaison Medal by the Institute of Actuaries. He graduated from the University of Cambridge (United Kingdom) with a degree in mathematics.

ANDREW DILNOT is Director of the Institute for Fiscal Studies, a post he has held since February 1991. His main research interests lie in taxation and social security and government economic policy, and he has published widely in these areas. Mr. Dilnot has taught at London School of Economics, Oxford University, and University College London, as well as overseas. He is a member of the Social Security Advisory Committee; the Councils of Queen Mary and Westfield Colleges, University of London; and the Council of the Royal Economic Society. Mr. Dilnot serves on the Fiscal Studies Task Force of the Office of Science and Technology on the Effect of the Tax System on Innovative Activity. He has been a Special Adviser to the subcommittees on social security systems and taxation of investment income of the House of Lords Select Committee on the European Communities. Mr. Dilnot is a regular contributor to the printed and broadcast media. He received a BA from Oxford University.

DONALD S. GRUBBS, JR. was President of Grubbs and Company, Inc. in Silver Spring, Maryland until his recent retirement. Mr. Grubbs is a Fellow of the Society of Actuaries and of the Conference of Consulting Actuaries. He served as member of the Pension Research Council and frequent contributor at its conferences. Mr. Grubbs co-authored the sixth edition of *Fundamentals of Private Pensions* with Dan M. McGill and *The Variable Annuity* with George B. Johnson. He was the first Director of the Actuarial Division of the Internal Revenue Service and Chairman of the Joint Board for the Enrollment of Actuaries. Prior to joining the IRS, Mr. Grubbs was Vice-President and Chief Actuary for the National Health and Welfare Retirement Association. He has been a member of the Department of Labor Advisory Council on Employee Welfare and Pension Benefit Plans and has served as a consultant to numerous governmental bodies. Mr. Grubbs graduated from Texas A&M University and Georgetown University Law Center. He is admitted to the Bar of the District of Columbia.

ESTELLE JAMES is Senior Economist at the World Bank, in which capacity she served as the lead author and team coordinator of the 1994 study of old age security arrangements around the world. In addition, she is the author of *The Nonprofit Sector in International Perspective, The Nonprofit Enterprise in Market Economies, Public Policy and Private Education in Japan,* and *Hoffa and the Teamsters: A Study of Union Power.* Dr. James has written numerous articles on the economic behavior of public and private educational institutions, on the role of the non-profit sector in developed and developing countries, and other applied economics issues. Dr. James received her PhD from Massachusetts Institute of Technology in 1961.

OLIVIA S. MITCHELL is the International Foundation of Employee Benefit Plans Professor of Insurance and Risk Management and Executive

Director of the Pension Research Council at The Wharton School of the University of Pennsylvania. Concurrently, Dr. Mitchell is a Research Associate at the National Bureau of Economic Research, serves on the Steering Committee for the Health and Retirement Survey for the University of Michigan, is an Associate Editor of the *Journal of Risk and Insurance,* and sits on a National Academy of Sciences panel on retirement income modeling. She has consulted with numerous private and public organizations including the World Bank, the United States Department of Labor, the United States Department of Health and Human Services, Mobil Corporation, the Association of Flight Attendants, IBM and the United States General Accounting Office. Dr. Mitchell has published three books and numerous articles on private and social insurance, and teaches in the areas of employee benefits in the United States and overseas, private and social insurance, the aging workforce, and pensions. She previously taught labor economics at Cornell University, was a Visiting Scholar to Harvard University's Department of Economics, and served on the ERISA Advisory Council to the United States Department of Labor. She received her MA and PhD in economics from the University of Wisconsin-Madison.

JAMES E. PESANDO is Professor of Economics and Director of the Institute for Policy Analysis at the University of Toronto. Dr. Pesando has published extensively in the areas of finance and financial economics, and he researches and serves as a consultant on pension issues. He is a coauthor of *Public and Private Pensions in Canada: An Economic Analysis.* He has served as an Associate Editor of the *Journal of Finance* and as a member of the Pension Research Council. He received a BA from Harvard University, a MA from the University of California (Berkeley), and a PhD from the University of Toronto.

DAVID M. RAJNES is a doctoral candidate at the Johns Hopkins University in the Department of Geography and Environmental Engineering. His dissertation is on old age pension arrangements in central and eastern Europe, especially Hungary.

DALLAS L. SALISBURY is President of the Employee Benefit Research Institute (EBRI). Mr. Salisbury has served on the staff of the Washington State Legislature, at the United States Department of Justice, as Assistant Executive Director for Policy and Research at the Pension Benefit Guaranty Corporation (PBGC), and as Assistant Administrator for Policy and Research of the Pension and Welfare Benefits Administration, United States Department of Labor. He also has served on the ERISA Advisory Council and PBGC Advisory Committee. Mr. Salisbury is a member of the National Academy of Social Insurance Board of Directors, the Board of Directors of The Health Project, the National Academy on Aging's National Advisory Board, and the National

Coordinating Committee on Worksite Health Promotion; and is a fellow of the National Academy of Human Resources. He is on the Editorial Advisory Boards of *Employee Benefit News, American Compensation Association Journal, Benefits Quarterly,* and *Employee Benefits Journal.* Mr. Salisbury attended the University of Washington and the Maxwell Graduate School of Syracuse University.

ANTHONY M. SANTOMERO is Deputy Dean and Richard K. Mellon Professor of Finance at The Wharton School of the University of Pennsylvania. Dr. Santomero has advised the Federal Reserve Board of Governors, the Federal Deposit Insurance Corporation, and the United States General Accounting Office. Internationally, he has been a consultant to the European Economic Community in Brussels, the Kingdom of Sweden, the Ministry of Finance of Japan, the Treasury of New Zealand, the Bank of Israel, the National Housing Bank of India, and the Capital Markets Board of Turkey. He currently serves as a permanent Advisor to the Swedish Central Bank and has also served as United States representative on the steering committee of the European Finance Association. Dr. Santomero is associate editor of seven academic journals, including the *Journal of Money, Credit and Banking, Journal of Financial Services Research,* and *Journal of Banking and Finance.* Dr. Santomero received his AB from Fordham University, his PhD from Brown University, and an honorary doctorate from the Stockholm School of Economics.

SYLVESTER J. SCHIEBER is a Vice President of The Wyatt Company and the Director of the Research and Information Center in Washington, DC. During his professional career, Dr. Schieber has specialized in the analysis of public and private retirement policy and health policy issues and has been responsible for the development of a number of special ongoing survey programs focusing on these issues. He is a member of the Pension Research Council and a coeditor of its 1993 conference volume, *Providing Health Care Benefits in Retirement.* Prior to joining The Wyatt Company in 1983, he served as the first Research Director of the Employee Benefit Research Institute in Washington, DC. Before that, he served as the Deputy Director, Office of Policy Analysis, Social Security Administration, and Deputy Research Director, Universal Social Security Coverage Study, Department of Health and Human Services. He received a PhD in economics from the University of Notre Dame.

JOHN A. TURNER is Deputy Director of the Office of Research and Economic Analysis, Pension and Welfare Benefits Administration, United States Department of Labor, and Adjunct Professor of Economics at George Washington University. Dr. Turner formerly worked in the research office of the Social Security Administration. He received a Fulbright Senior Scholar award to do pension research at the Institut de Recherches Economiques et Sociales in Paris in 1994. He has written or edited six books on pensions and employer-provided health benefits, one of which has been translated into Japanese. His most recent book is *Pension Policy for a Mobile Labor Force,* and he has published numerous articles on pension and social security policy. He has a PhD in economics from the University of Chicago.

MARC M. TWINNEY recently retired from a position as Director of the Pension Department of the Ford Motor Company. Mr. Twinney is a Fellow of the Society of Actuaries, and he has been a member of many professional groups, including the Conference of Actuaries in Public Practice, the Washington Pension Report Group, and Enrolled Actuaries, a consultant to the United States Civil Service system, and a member of the Committee on Pension Actuarial Principles and Practices, and of the Board of Directors, American Academy of Actuaries. He is a member of the Pension Research Council and a contributor to its conference volume, *The Future of Pensions in the United States.* He holds a BA in mathematics from Yale University and a MBA in finance from Harvard University.

DIMITRI VITTAS is Principal Financial Specialist in the Department of Financial Sector Development at the World Bank and served as a core team member for the 1989 *World Development Report.* Previously, Mr. Vittas was a Senior Consultant in the Policy and Research Group of the British Bankers Association and a Senior Economist in the Public Policy Group of the Inter-Bank Research Organization. He also has been an Economist and Loan Officer in Shipping Finance for Citibank in Piraeus, Greece, and an Economist for Doxiadis Associates, Athens. Mr. Vittas received a BSc from Athens School of Economics and a MSc from the University College London.

NORIYASU WATANABE is a Lecturer in Social Security Law at the Tokai University Law Faculty, a Lecturer in Insurance and Pensions at the Musashi University Economics Faculty in Tokyo, and the President of the International Pension Research Institute, which is a non-profit public policy research organization. He has written or coauthored eight books and numerous articles on pensions and social security policy. Mr. Watanabe has translated into Japanese many articles on pensions and social security policy in the United States, Germany, and England. He studied law and politics at the Tokyo University of Education.

CAROLYN L. WEAVER is Director of Social Security and Pension Studies at the American Enterprise Institute. Dr. Weaver is the editor of two recent AEI books, *Social Security's Looming Surpluses: Prospects and Implications* and *Disability and Work: Incentives, Rights, and Opportunities.* Before joining AEI, she was a Senior Research Fellow at the Hoover Institution at Stanford University. Dr. Weaver has served as Chief Professional Staff Member on social security for the United States Senate Committee on Finance and as Senior Advisor to the National Commission on Social Security Reform. She is Senior Editor of *The American Enterprise* magazine and the former Editor of *Regulation*. Dr. Weaver has been a member of the economics faculties of Tulane University and Virginia Polytechnic Institute and State University, where she received her PhD.

Index

Aaron, Henry, 245
Accounting for pensions, 19–20, 136–37; and standards, 115–16, 130
Accrual of pension obligation, 46–47, 87–88, 251–52; ABO, PBO, IBO, 258–59. *See also* actuarial; liability; retirement age; vesting
Actuary, 35–39, 47, 63, 67
Actuarial: assumptions, 87, 101–2, 115–16, 127–28; entry age normal, 87–88; neutrality and risk of insolvency, 13; projected unit credit method, 54; valuation, 44–47, 52–56
Acuna, R., 164, 174, 180
Adequacy of retirement benefits, 1–2, 59–63, 76–77, 112, 241–44. *See also* poverty
Administrative costs in pension plans, 65, 114, 154–55, 164–65, 173–75, 307. *See also* disclosure; insurance; mandatory pension plan
Adverse selection: as rationale for government regulation of retirement system, 5–6; in contracting out system, 70–72. *See also* contracting out
Africa, 20; pensions in, 151, 153, 162
Age discrimination, 130
Aging of the population, xi, 1, 73, 96, 123, 144–45, 147, 151; and costs of financing retirement, 73–74, 123–24, 129; international comparisons, 20–21. *See also* pensions; retirement age; social security
Ahrend, Peter, 12, 18, 73, 103 n.2, 105–7, 303 n.7, 14
Andrews, William, 230 n.1
Ambachtsheer, Keith, 263
Annuity: and life insurance, 5–6; and market failures, 5–6; and pension benefits, 9–10, 14–15, 119, 133–34, 156, 167, 173–75
apRoberts, Lucy, 19, 105
Argentina, 153, 156, 173
Armed forces. *See* military; public employee
Arthur, Terry G., 67 n.3
Asia, 20, 58; pensions in, 153. *See also* Japan; India; Malaysia; provident funds; Singapore
Asociacion de Fondos de Pension (AFP). *See* Chile
Asset: allocation in pension plans, 4, 15–17, 42, 91–95, 103 n.3, 106–7, 172, 250, 260–70; and diversification, 65–67, 95, 172–173; and liquidity, 95; managers, 65; matching with liabilities, 15–17, 263, 278 n.30, 314; pension as, 37; performance, 21–22, 95, 245–85; segregation of pension from employer portfolio, 39–40, 91–94, 116–17. *See also* bond; book reserve; equities; indexed bond; insurance; investment, money market; performance; portfolio; real estate; return; risk; stock markets
Assumptions. *See* actuarial
Atkinson, Anthony, 180
Auerbach, Alan J., 20
Australian pension system, 2–3, 21, 216–19, 222, 227, 229, 244–85

Baby boomers. *See* demography; elderly
Bankruptcy: and retirement benefits, 13–15, 25, 50–55, 92–93, 107, 139, 286–315; economic and legal framework, 50–55,

Bankruptcy (*cont.*)
286–315. *See also* employer; insurance; insolvency; prudent investment; trust
Banks, 71–72, 164
Barbados, 162
Belgium, 101
Beller, Daniel, 166
Benefits: tradeoff with contributions, 273, 287, 313; security, 24. *See also* accounting; funding; pensions; poverty; replacement rate; tax
Black, Fischer, 263
Blake, David, 263, 278 n.30
Blanchard, Olivier J., 277 n.10
Blume, Marshall E., 22, 282
Bodie, Zvi, 1, 12, 17, 25 n.2, 3, 5, 6, 8, 26 n.11, 12, 249, 251, 256, 264, 269, 288, 298, 309, 311 n.2
Bondholders, 13
Bonds: and investment strategies, 115; domestic holdings, 42; government, 163–64; international holdings, 42; in pensions, 42, 103 n.3, 116, 262–70. *See also* assets; investments; liability; prudent investments; returns; risks
Bonilla, Alejandro, 177, 180
Book reserve systems, 18–19, 82–95, 106–20, 139–40, 218, 253–54, 261, 295–96. *See also* German pension system; insolvency; insurance; investment
Bovenberg, Alans, 223
Britain. *See* United Kingdom
Buchanan, James, 308

Canada, xi
Canadian pension system, 2, 11, 22–23, 216–22, 244–85, 286–315
Capital: accumulation, 151–53, 178–79; human, 161, 277 n.12
Capital market, 8, 58, 111, 116, 158–60, 214; and pension funds, 116, 213; and rates of return, 119–20. *See also* assets; bonds, equities; financial institutions; investments; multinational firms; real estate; return; risk
Carribean Islands, 153
Carroll, Chris, 222
Carter Commission, 231 n.1
Cash in pension plans, 42, 116
Cash-balance pension plan, 9, 24
Chang, Angela E., 21, 232–33

Chen, Andrew H., 263
Chile: and minimum pension, 168; and pension funds (AFP), 16, 20, 153–80; and pension privatization, 152–53; and regulation, 169–78
Cifuentes, Rudrigo, 166
Civil Service employees. *See* public sector
Clark, Robert L., 13, 19, 143, 303 n.7
Collins, Andrew, 67 n.3
Colombia, 156
Compensation. *See* wage-benefit tradeoff
Competition: between asset managers, 65–66, 174–75, 271–72; international, and impact on pensions, 70–72, 118–20
Consumption, 3–5, 218–19
Contracting out, 22; in Japan, 128–29; in the United Kingdom, 35–55, 69–72; and transition problems, 70–72. *See also* Chile; United Kingdom pension system
Contributions to pensions: defined benefit versus defined contribution, 8–10; targets, 154–55; taxes and, 214–43. *See also* actuaries; funding; insurance; pensions; taxation
Corporate finance: and links to pension funding in Germany, 88, 108–9; and links to pension funding in the United States, 115. *See also* asset; insurance; prudent investment; return; risk
Corporate governance, 164–65
Cost of capital. *See* corporate finance
Cost-of-living adjustment for pensions, 12–13
Costs, of pensions. *See* administrative costs
Coverage by retirement systems, 2, 252–53. *See also* French pension system; German pension system; Japanese pension system; United Kingdom pension system; United States pension system
Credit ratings, 19
Cross-border: employment, 102–3; membership, in pensions, 65–67. *See also* European Community; global; labor market; mobility
Cross-cultural comparisons, 105, 108
Czech Republic, 20

Dailey, 25 n.6
Danish pension system, 2, 217, 244–85
Davies, Bryn, 67 n.3

Davis, E. Phillip, 2–3, 22, 244, 250, 257, 264–67, 276 n.1, 282, 284

Daykin, Christopher D., 11, 13, 17–18, 25 n.6, 67 n.2, 3, 69, 72, 263, 294, 303 n.7, 9, 13

Death benefit, in pensions, 46–47. *See also* survivors' benefits

Debt, pensions as employer, 48–49

Default risk, in pensions, 13–15

Deficit, government, 124

Defined benefit plan, 29, 43, 45, 163, 244–45, 251; and comparison with defined contribution plan, 8–10; in Japan, 126–27; in the United Kingdom, 36–55; in the United States, 114–20. *See also* funding; investment; public sector; tax policy; unions

Defined contribution plan, 29, 244–45, 251; and comparison with defined benefit plan, 8–10, 114–20; and 401(k) plans, 233; in Europe, 71–72; in Japan, 126–27; in the United Kingdom, 36–55. *See also* investment; public sector; tax policy

Demographic factors: and the dependency ratio, 245; and the passivity ratio, 245. *See also* aging; baby boomers; elderly

Department of Social Security, 67 n.3

Deutsche Bundesbank, 259

Development, 2; of financial markets, 157–60; and pensions, 20–21, 151–92

Diamond, Peter, 16, 25 n.3, 177, 180

Dilnot, Andrew, 6, 11, 21–22, 67 n.2, 222, 229, 232, 234

Disclosure of pension information, 53, 62–63, 164–65, 170

Disability pensions, 46–47, 75, 83, 122, 155, 168, 175. *See also* survivor

Discrimination. *See* age; women and pensions

Diversification: in pension assets, 14–15, 152, 239, 266–67, 274–75. *See also* asset allocation; investment; prudent investment; return; risk

Divorce and pensions, 52. *See also* women and pensions

Downsizing. *See* competitiveness

Early retirement. *See* retirement ages

Earnings-related pension plan, 33–67, 112, 122. *See also* French pension system; German pension system; Japanese pension

system; United Kingdom pension system; United States pension system

Economically targeted investment. *See* investment

Economic security. *See* adequacy

Efficiency issues in pension systems, 5–6, 157–58, 213, 219, 247, 249. *See also* administrative costs; evasion; tax policy

Equity concerns in pension systems, 112, 151–52, 155, 249. *See also* adequacy; poverty; replacement rate

Elderly. *See* aging; retirement

Equities in pensions, 42, 116–120, 164, 262–70, 263. *See also* asset; investment; portfolio; return; risk

Emerging economies and pensions, 151–209

Employee benefits. *See* pensions

Employee Retirement Income Security Act of 1974 (ERISA), 116–17

Employers: and costs of pensions, 65, 224–25; and decision to insure pension, 49–55; and employment of older workers, 147, 165; and occupational pensions, 33–67, 250–51; and pensions in Germany, 75–80, 116–17; and pensions in Japan, 138; and pensions in the United Kingdom, 37–55; and relationship with employees, 75, 289; and trends in pension plans, 116–17; as insurer for employees, 70–72; as multinational firms, 103; rationale for offering pensions, 5–8. *See also* competitiveness; international; labor contract; off-shore; plan sponsor; unions

Equities: in corporate finance, 108–9; in pension funds, 22, 58–59, 103 n.3. *See also* asset; investment; return; risk; portfolio

Europe, 16–23; Central and Eastern, 20, 160; labor markets, 71–72; and pension trends, 96–97, 99–103

European Commission, 64–65

European Community (EC), 18; and equal treatment of men and women in pensions, 63–64, 101–2; and labor mobility, 58–66, 102–3; Pension Funds Directive, 64–67, 99–100; transferability, 71–72, 99–101. *See also* mobility; women, and pensions

European Court of Justice, 19, 46, 64, 101–2

Evasion. *See* tax

Expatriate employees, 66–67; and tax status of pensions, 104 n.6. *See also* labor market; global

Federal Savings and Loan Insurance Corporation, 315

Feenberg, Daniel, 223, 233

Feldstein, Martin, 223, 233, 260

401(k) plans, 233. *See also* defined contribution plans

Fiduciary responsibility in pensions, 44, 137–38, 140–41, 168. *See also* trustees

Fiji, 156, 162

Financial Accounting Standards Board (FASB). *See* accounting

Financial: institutions, 136, 151, 221–22; market development and pensions, 151–80. *See also* banks; capital markets; insurance company; money managers; pensions; trusts

Financing retirement systems, 22–23, 86–91, 154–55. *See also* asset; defined benefit and defined contribution; funding; tax; German pension system; Japan pension system; United Kingdom pension system; United States pension system

Finland, 79

Farms, 283–85

Firms. *See* employers

Fiscal status of pensions: alternative regimes, 108–9, 213–43; economic issues raised by mandatory saving plan, 166, tax policy, 214–43. *See also* French pension system; German pension system; Japanese pension system; tax policy; United Kingdom pension system; United States pension system

Fisher effect, 258

Fixed income securities. *See* bonds

Flat pension, 9; in the United Kingdom, 34–35

Flat tax. *See* tax policy

Ford Foundation, 284

Foerster, Wolfgang, 103 n.2

Free rider problems, as rationale for government regulation of retirement system, 6

France, French pension system, 19, 79, 105–13, 244–85; complementary retirement plans (régimes complémentaires),

66, 105, 109–12; coverage, 2; fiscal treatment in, 216–19; for cadres, 109–10; historical development of, 109–10; performance of, 244–85; structure, 22–23, 105–13

Fraud, 299

Friedman, Benjamin, 25 n.4

Friedman, Milton, 25 n.25

Frijns, Jan, 258, 268

Friot, Bernard, 109

Funding status; and taxes, 214–43; of pension plans, 10–17, 22–25, 29, 40–45, 54–57, 114–20, 244–85, 282–85; of multiple-pillar system, 151–52, 164–65; of social security system, 16. *See also* assets; liabilities; social security; pay-as-you-go; pension

Fund management. *See* asset, investment, portfolio, prudent investment, return, risk

G-7 Countries, 284

The Gambia, 156

Germany, xi, 18–19, 244

German pension system, 19, 73–120, 105–11, 114–20, 244–85; benefits and replacement rates, 74–85, 82–83; closed plans, 96; coverage, 2; and book reserve system, 66, 75–76, 82–89, 105–9, 114–20, 218–19, 295–96; fiscal treatment in, 12, 79–80, 89–91, 216–22; future issues in, 95–103; historical development, 75–86; and inflation, 82; legal framework, 79–86; and insolvency protection, 81–83, 91–99, 107–9, 286–315; and the New Federal States, 98–99; occupational pensions, 73–104; Occupational Pensions Act (BetrAVG), 80–81; and performance, 244–85; retirement ages, 81; role of union in, 79–80; social security, 78–79; structure, 22–23, 75–86; support funds, 83, 88–89, 106–9; vesting, 80–81

Ghana, 155, 162

Gillion, Colin, 177, 180

Global: labor market, xi, 64–65; portfolio, 279 n.38. *See also* asset; European Commission; European Community; international competitiveness; labor market

Glossary of Terms, 29–30

Goode Report, 50–55. *See also* United Kingdom pension plan

Governance, corporate, 164–65
Government: Actuary, 35, 67, 67 n.2, 3;
  bonds in pension portfolio, 42; em-
  ployees, 15–17; insurance of pension
  promise, 11–25, 25 n.13; regulation of
  pensions, 25. *See also* Pension Benefit
  Guaranty Corporation; public sector
Gravelle, Jane, 223
Greek pensions system, 217
Growth, economic, and pensions, 157–58
Grubbs, Donald S. Jr., 20
Guarantee funds, 95, 114–20. *See also* insol-
  vency; insurance; social security
Gustman, Alan, 13, 25 n.5

Harwick, P., 228
Hepp, Stefan, 259, 269
HMSO, 230 n.2
Hsin, Ping-Lung, 180
Hungary, 20
Hutchens, Robert, 25 n.7
Hybrid plan. *See* cash-balance plan

Iglesias, Augusto, 163–64, 174, 180
Incentives, 165; and pension plan design,
  24
Incidence of pension system costs
Income tax. *See* tax policy
Indexed bonds in pension portfolio, 42, 58,
  172, 264
Indexation of pensions, 18–19, 30, 34–35,
  47–48. *See also* inflation
India, 153, 156, 159, 162
Individual accounts, 8–10, 75
Individual Retirement Accounts (IRAs),
  232–33
Indonesia, 153, 156, 162
Industrial Revolution, 2
Industry-wide pensions, 41. *See also* occupa-
  tional pension plans
Inflation, 21–22, 55; and pension assets,
  155–57, 172; and pension benefits, 75,
  82, 156–57, 263; and pension taxes, 236–
  39. *See also* indexed bonds
Information: and inefficiencies as rationale
  for regulation of pensions, 5–6, 308; and
  pensions in Chile, 174–75. *See also* disclosure
Inman, Robert, 310 n.1
Insolvency: and pensions in Chile, 174–75;
  and pensions in Germany, 81–82, 91–99;

and pensions in Japan, 138–39; and pensions in the United Kingdom, 11–13, 48–
  53, 58–59. *See also* bankruptcy; default;
  insurance; prudent investment; return;
  risk
Insurance: broker, 7; company role in pensions, 9, 58–59, 164, 167, 175, 249, 262,
  289, 297–98; contract in pension portfolio, 103; for longevity, 8; for other risks,
  24–25, 58–59; of pension benefits, 13–
  15, 39–55, 48–53, 83–86, 138–39, 249–
  50, 286–316; premiums, 288–91; regulatory framework, 49–53, 58–59, 288–90;
  social, 312–15. *See also* annuity; French
  pension system; German pension system;
  Japanese pension system; United Kingdom pension system; United States pension system
Integration of pensions, 6–7
Interest: rates, 155, 163–64, 258–59; taxable, 104 n.5. *See also* asset; inflation; insurance; investment; return; risk
International: investments, 51–58, 267,
  161, 279 n.38; mobility of labor, 64–67;
  pension funding, 116–19; trends, 1,
  114–15. *See also* European Community;
  global; labor market
Investment: choices, 9–10, 118–20, 152;
  competition, 65–66; earnings, 10–11,
  226–27, 249; economically or socially targeted, 167; international diversification
  of, 64–67, 114–20; managers, 54–55, 65;
  performance, 10–11, 226–27, 249; policy
  in pension plans, 15–17, 42, 51–55, 57–
  58, 129–30, 137–38; regulation, 169–78,
  257–70; risk, 13–25, 168. *See also* asset; insurance; prudent investment; return;
  risk; tax policy
Ippolito, Richard, 11, 26 n.9, 288, 301 n.1,
  302 n.4, 6, 303 n.18, 310, 311 n.1, 2
Ireland pension system, 216–19, 227
Italy pension system, 2, 244–85

James, Estelle, 2, 5, 20, 151, 180, 247
Japan, xi, 130–31; companies exposed to
  global competition, 71
Japanese pension system, 19, 22–23, 58,
  121–47, 244–85; accounting system, 130;
  benefits, 121–24, 138, 145; book reserves
  in, 126–27; contracted-out plan, 128–29,
  131–32; contributions, 123–24, 132–35;

Japanese pension system (*cont.*)
    coverage, 2, 122, 131; defined contribu-
    tion and defined benefit plans, 127–29;
    earnings-related plan, 122; Employees'
    Pension Insurance, 128–29, 131–32, 146;
    fiscal treatment in, 123–24, 127–29,
    131–34, 216–22, 227; funding, 127–28;
    historical development of, 121–23, 125–
    29; individual savings plans, 129; insur-
    ance in, 138–41, 286–315; investment,
    129, 135–38; lump sum in, 124–25, 127,
    143; Mutual Aid plans, 126–29; National
    Insurance Contributions, 34–35; Na-
    tional Pension Plan, 121–23, Pension
    Council, 124, 129; performance, 244–85;
    structure, 19, 22–23, 121–29, 131–32;
    Trust Fund Bureau, 123
Johnson, Paul, 222, 229
Joint ventures, 169–70
Jumpertz, Bettina, 102 n.2

Kaldor, Nicholas, 230 n.1
Katz, Lawrence, 25 n.7
Keating, Daniel, 309
Kenya, 156, 159, 162
Kiribati, 156
Knox, David M., 279 n.36
Kotlikoff, Lawrence, 25 n.3, 257
Kurozami, Akira, 125

Labor contracts; and pensions' role, 5–6,
    24–25, 70–71. *See also* unions
Labor markets: and demand for workers,
    130–32, 146–47, 287; and lifetime em-
    ployment, 145; and mandatory retire-
    ment, 146; and mobility, 65–67, 152, 165;
    and retirement, 155; and supply of
    workers, 130–32, 146, 165, 247; and
    unions, 70–71. *See also* cross-border; mo-
    bility; retirement age
Labor, organized. *See* unions
Latin America, 152
Liability: accrual, 35–36, 278 n.19; and in-
    surance, 48–49; and interest rate used in
    determining, legal definitions, 10–11; in
    a pension plan, 12, 15–17, 86–87, 264–
    65; matching with assets, 15–17, 263, 278
    n.30; projected unit credit method, 54
Life cycle model, 3–5
Life expectancy, 5–6; and assumptions in
    pension plans, 87. *See also* actuarial

Lifetime employment system. *See* Japan; la-
    bor market
Life insurance, 88, 168, 297. *See also* an-
    nuity; insurance; insurance company
Lindeman, David, 309
Liquidity, 267. *See also* assets; corporate
    finance
Longevity: insurance, 167; risk, 5–6. *See also*
    annuity; insurance; life expectancy
Long-term contract. *See* labor market
Lump sum, 9–10, 19–22, 45–47, 56, 167,
    233; and equal treatment of men and
    women, 63–64, and taxation, 227–28. *See
    also* annuity; insurance
Luzadis, Rebecca, 25 n.7
Lynes, Tony, 110

Malaysia, 151, 153–57, 159, 162, 167, 174,
    179
Management of pensions. *See* pension
    management
Mandatory pension, 5, 151–92; *see also* de-
    fined benefit and defined contribution;
    pension reform
Mandatory retirement. *See* retirement ages
Market failure, 301, 307–11
McGill, Dan, 25 n.3
McLeish, David J. D., 67 n.4
Maxwell company pensions, 49–50, 63,
    260, 294. *See also* United Kingdom pen-
    sion plans
Mehra, R., 264
Men and pensions. *See* women and pensions
Membership in pension plans. *See* coverage
Merton, Robert, 17, 25 n.2, 3, 8, 249, 277
    n.12, 285, 288, 309
Mexico, pensions in, 153
Migrant workers. *See* mobility
Military pensions: in the United Kingdom,
    40. *See also* public employees
Minimum pension, 9
Mitchell, Olivia S., 1, 11, 16, 25 n.7, 16 n.13,
    180, 268, 279 n.33, 288, 303 n.18
Mitsui Company, 124–25
Mobility, labor: and pensions, 24–25, 46–
    47, 64–67, 102–3, 125–26, 152, 165;
    taxes as obstacle to, 66–67. *See also* cross-
    border; European Community; expatri-
    ate employees; labor market; portability;
    vesting
Modigliani, Franco, 25 n.1

Money: managers, 57–58; market instruments, 119–20. *See also* assets; investment; stock brokers

Money purchase plans, 53. *See also* defined contribution plan

Moral hazard, 151; and effect on pension insurance, 23, 307

Morck, Randall, 260

Mortgages: in pension funds, 22–23

Mortality. *See also* life expectancy

Multi-employer pensions, 110, 131, 312

Multinational firms, 103 n.3; and pension issues, 115–19. *See also* employers; off-shore

Multiple-tier (or pillar) plan, 9, 17–19, 23–24, 33–36, 111, 121, 151–92. *See also* James; mandatory pension; three-legged stool

Munnell, Alicia, 26 n.11, 223–24, 303 n.9

Murphy, Kevin, 25 n.6

Myers, Robert, 16–17

Myopia, in retirement saving, 152, 247

National Audit Office, 222

National: retirement policy, 240; saving, 222. *See also* retirement; saving, tax policy

Netherlands pension system, 2, 217, 244–85

Nepal, 156, 162

New Zealand pension system, 21, 217–27, 229, 241–43

Nigeria, 156, 162

North America, 19, 295

Occupational pension plans; compared to mandatory pensions, 152–53; international comparisons, 65–67; in Germany, 73–104; in the United Kingdom, 25–72

Off-shore pension arrangements, 66. *See also* expatriate employees; multinationals

Ohzi Papermaking Company, 125

Ontario insurance plan, 286–315

Organization of Economic Cooperation and Development (OECD), 19, 22–23, 123, 224, 247; and pension comparisons, 2, 157, 213, 214–19; and pension taxation, 227, 228, 234

Overseas. *See* international; multinational

Pacific region, 58, 153. *See also* Asia

Palacios, Robert, 180

Paternalism, in pension systems, 308–9, 313–14

Pay-as-you-go system, 66–67, 73, 92–93, 105, 163, 246; and taxes, 214–17; versus funding, 157, 244–85. *See also* funding; tax policy

Payroll tax. *See* tax policy

Pechman, Joseph, 230 n.1

Pension: assets and liabilities of, 22–23, 64–67, 314; benefits, 12–13, 178, 227–28; costs, 65; coverage, 2; defined benefit and defined contribution, 1–25; funding of, 20–25, 112 n.1; guarantees, 176; management of, 157–92; solvency and insurance of, 22–23, 50–55; taxation of, 214–43; trusts and trustees, 41–44, 268–69; security, 1. *See also* asset; French pension plan; German pension plan; investment; Japanese pension plan; return; risk; portfolio; prudent investment; tax policy; United Kingdom pension plan; United States pension plan

Pension Benefit Guaranty Corporation (PBGC), 11, 258, 286–315. *See also* funding; insurance; pension; United States pension system

Pension Research Council, xi–xii

Performance of pension assets, 22–23, 270–75. *See also* portfolio; return; risk

Personal pension plan, 55. *See also* defined contribution plan; 401(k); IRA; United Kingdom pension plan

Peru, 153, 156

Pesando, James E., 11, 14, 22–23, 25 n.8, 285, 287–88, 306–9, 313–14

Pestieau, Pierre, 248

Petersen, Carel, 258, 268

Pillars of retirement income. *See* multiple pillar system; three-legged stool

Plan sponsor, 9. *See also* employer; occupational pension; insurance company

Political risk to pensions, 158–60, 247–48

Portability of pensions, 46–47, 71–72, 128–29. *See also* cross-border membership; European Community; global; labor market; mobility; vesting

Portfolio holdings in pensions, 42, 116, 262–70; diversification of, 116, 255–57; insurance contracts, 103 n.3; regulation of, 116; target allocation, 59. *See also* asset; bonds; cash; equities; investment; prudent investment; real estate; return; risk

Portugal pension system, 217

Poterba, James, 223, 233
Poverty, 240; and pensions' effects on, 167–68
Preferences, 151
Prescott, Ed C., 264
Principal-agent problems; and pensions, 7–8
Privatization of pensions, 151–92; in the United Kingdom, 69–72. *See also* adverse selection; Chile; contracting out; employer pensions; insurance; mandatory pension
Productivity, 155
Profitability: of companies, 70–72; of pension providers, 170–78. *See also* competitiveness; international
Provident funds, 151–92. *See also* Malaysia; Singapore
Prudent investments, 44–45, 51, 58–59, 179, 250, 256–70, 275
Public policy toward pensions, 214–43. *See also* multiple-tier systems; tax policy
Public sector: employees, 15–17, 301 n.1; pension plans, 15–18, 25 n.13, 40, 121–22

Qualified plans. *See* tax policy
Queisser, Moniker, 166

Rajnes, David M., 16, 20, 128
Rappaport, Anna, 168
Rate of return, 246; in mandatory pension system, 154–56, 246; on pension assets, 10–13, 119–20, 224, 245–85. *See also* assets; portfolio; prudent investment; risk
Real estate, in pensions, 22–23, 42, 58–59, 116, 118, 164, 176, 266–67. *See also* asset; investment; mortgages; return; risk; portfolio
Redistributive effect of pensions. *See* poverty
Reform of pensions, 151–92. *See also* development; mandatory pension; social security
Reform of social security. *See* development; mandatory pension
Redistribution of income in pensions. *See* adequacy
Regulation of pensions, 256–62, 264–65, 268–70, 307–11. *See also* tax policy; retirement income policy
Reichenstein, William, 263

Reid, Gary, 180
Reinsurance and pensions, 104 n.4
Replacement rate, 2, 59–60, 78–79, 273; target, 3–5, 154–55. *See also* Chilean; German pension system; Japanese pension system; United States pension system; United Kingdom pension system
Retention, labor, 24. *See also* carry-over pensions; labor markets; mobility
Retirement income policy, 1, 20–21. *See also* multiple-tier plan
Retirement ages, 9, 13, 45–46, 64, 81, 121–22, 124, 130–31, 155. *See also* German pension system; Japanese pension system; United States pension system; United Kingdom pension system
Return on pension portfolios, 13–25, 118–20, 159–61, 266–67. *See also* assets; investment; portfolio; risk
Revenue. *See* tax policy
Reynaud, Emmanuel, 108–9, 113
Riley, Barry, 259
Risk: aversion, 163, 268; diversification, 152, 170; in investments, 13–25, 137–38, 154–56, 245–47; of default, 13–15; pooling, 8; in retirement plan, 23–25, 59, 137–38, 270–74; and return, 21–22, 270–72. *See also* asset; bankruptcy; default; inflation; insurance; investment; return; risk
Roessler, Norbert, 103 n.2
Romer, Paul, 248
Rothschild, Michael, 25 n.4

Safety net, 5–6
Salisbury, Dallas L., 23, 312
Samuelson, Paul, 285
Santomero, Anthony M., 69
Saving: crowded out, 276, 284; inducements for, 158–60, 220–22; and life-cycle model, 3–4; and pensions, 151–92; and pay-as-you-go-social security, 22; rationales for, and pensions, 220–22; and tax policy, 214–43
Schieber, Sylvester J., 21–22, 235
Schwartz, Anita, 155
Security of promised pensions, 11–25
Securities: in pension plans, 116; regulation, 260–70. *See also* assets; bankruptcy; diversification; equities; investments; portfolio; return; risk

Securities and Exchange Commission (SEC), 260
Self-administered private plans, in the United Kingdom, 38–50. *See also* contracting out
Self-directed pension investments, 152. *See also* Chile; 401(k); investments
Self-employed workers, 25, 34–35, 121
Sex-neutrality of pensions. *See* women and pensions
Shareholders, 10–11
Siegel, Jeremy, 285
Simplification of pension regulation, 51
Singapore, 151, 153–59, 162–67, 174, 177
Skinner, Jonathan, 223, 233
Skully, Michael, 180
Slovakia, 20–21
Smalhout, James, 298, 309
Smith, Robert S., 11, 16, 25 n.13
Social Security Administration, 156
Social security system: benefits, 2–3; costs, 147; funding, 151–80; indexation, 12; integration with private pensions, 33–67; international comparisons, 65–67, 112, 151–80; in France, 111–12; in Germany, 73–104; in the United States, 16–17; in the United Kingdom, 33–67; replacement rates, 2. *See also* French pension system; German pension system; Japanese pension system; United Kingdom pension system; United States pension system
Solomon Islands, 156, 162
Solvency of pension plans, 50–55, 258, 286–315. *See also* funding; insurance
Soviet pension system. *See* development
Sri Lanka, 155–56, 162
State Earnings Related Pension Plan (SERPs), 11, 33–67. *See also* United Kingdom pension plan
State government pension systems. *See* public sector
Steinmeier, Thomas, 13, 25 n.5
Stewart, Colin M., 67 n.4
Stock: brokers, 7–8, 57–58; holders, 33–67; market, 137. *See also* asset; capital market; financial institution; portfolio
Stocks. *See* equities
Subsidiaries: *See* multinational employers
Summers, Lawrence, 222
Sunden, Annika, 180

Surrey, Stanley S., 228
Survivors' benefits, 46–47, 83, 122, 155, 175
Swaziland, 156, 162
Swedish pension system, 2, 22–23, 79, 217, 244–85
Swiss pension system, 2, 79, 244–85

Tamura, Matsuhiro, 269
Tax revenue for public pension plans, 15–17
Taxpayer, 11
Tax: expenditures, 228–43; sensitivity of pension contributions, 232–43. *See also* tax policy
Tax policy: and evasion, 166, 177; and funded plans, 248; and retirement systems, 6–7, 11–12, 21–22, 45, 65–67, 89–91, 107–9, 116–17, 127–29, 134–37, 165, 214–43; flat tax, 214–43, 225; income tax, 214–43; objectives for, 219–24, 236–41; payroll tax, 214–43. *See also* fiscal status of pensions; French pension system; German pension system; Japanese pension system; United Kingdom pension system; United States pension system
Tax shelter, 12
Teachers. *See* public sector
Tepper, Irwin, 264, 278 n.30
Termination. *See* bankruptcy; insurance; solvency
Thompson, Lawrence H., 248
Three-legged stool, 2, 17, 23. *See also* multiple-tier plan
Transferability, for pensions, 69–71. *See also* cross-border membership; global, mobility
Transition, from social security to private pension plan, 71–73, 151–92. *See also* Chile; contracting out
Trust: for pension funds, 41–44, 48–53, 117–20; Fund Bureau, in Japan, 123. *See also* asset; pension manager; portfolio; prudent investment; return; risk
Turner, John A., 16, 20, 25 n.6, 128, 166, 288, 303 n.9
Turnover and pensions, 24–25
Twinney, Marc M., 19, 114

Underfunded pensions. *See* funding
Uganda, 156

United Kingdom, xi, 244
United Kingdom pension system, 33–72; assets, 39–42, 58–59; benefit accruals and payments, 30, 34–49, 59–63; and contracting out, 22, 33–67, 69–72; contributions, 33–67; coverage, 2, 38–43; defined contribution, 54–55; disability pensions, 46–47; disclosure, 53–55; fiscal treatment in, 11–12, 39–40, 49–55, 216–19, 227, 229; funding, 35–45, 50–57; and insurance, 11–13, 34–36, 48–53, 58–59; and mobility, 30, 46–47, 65–67; and performance, 244–85; and savings rates, 222; and insurance, 28–315; investment of assets, 57–59; legal framework, 39–67, 49, 54, 61–63; Maxwell company pensions, 49–50, 260; Parliament, 36, 52; personal pensions, 36, 55, 61; private pensions, 61; privatization, 61; retirement age, 34–35; occupational pensions, 25–72; role of Ombudsman, 56; self-employed, 60; solvency, 50–55; State Earnings Related Pension Plan (SERPs), 33–67, 293–94; and social security, 25–36, 60–63; structure, 33–67, 69–72; survivors' benefits, 46–47; trustees, 51–55
Unions: and pensions, 6, 14–15, 22–23, 26 n.9, 42, 62, 79–82, 108–10, 125, 144–45, 314; prefer defined benefit plans, 70
United Auto Workers, 108
United States, xi, 235, 240; budgets, 241; capital markets, 244; Congress, 16, 315; Department of Labor, xi, 20; companies exposed to global competition, 71
United States pension system, 58, 105–13; and savings rates, 222; coverage, 2; fiscal treatment in, 11, 21, 117–18, 166, 216–22; funding, 104 n.3, 107–8, 114–20, 255–85; indexation, 30 and insolvency insurance, 11–14, 107–8, 176, 286–315;

management, 19; pension trends, 9, 114–20; performance, 244–85; portability, 30; qualification, 117–18; structure, 58, 105–13, 244–85
United States social security system, 16–17
United States Treasury, 230 n.1
Utgoff, Kathleen, 11

Valdes, Prieto, Salvador, 166, 177, 180
Van Loo, Peter D., 268
Venti, Stephen, 222–23, 233
Vesting and portability of pensions, 29, 46–47. *See also* coverage; portability
Vittas, Dimitri, 2, 5, 20, 151, 155, 163, 180, 247–48, 273
Voluntary pensions, 111

Wachter, Susan, 25
Wagner, Gert, 177
Walker, Ian, 67 n.2
Wall Street Journal, 115–16
Warshawsky, Mark, 25 n.4
Watanabe, Noriyasu, 19, 26 n.10, 121, 128–29, 136, 139, 144–46, 255, 297–98, 303 n.7
Weaver, Carolyn L., 23, 302 n.4, 306, 309–10
Welfare system, 5. *See also* poverty
Western Samoa, 156
Wharton School, xi
Willis, J., 228
Wise, David, 222–23, 233
World War II, 19, 75–76, 108–9, 125–26
Women and men in pensions, 19, 34–35, 46, 63–64, 101–2, 167
Workforce. *See* labor market
World Bank, xi, 20, 154, 156, 159, 162, 180
Wyatt, 278 n.31

Zambia, 156, 159, 162, 174

Pension Research Council Publications

Corporate Book Reserving for Postretirement Healthcare Benefits. Dwight K. Bartlett, III, ed. 1990.

Demography and Retirement: The Twenty-First Century. Anna M. Rappaport and Sylvester J. Schieber, eds. 1993.

An Economic Appraisal of Pension Tax Policy in the United States. Richard A. Ippolito. 1990.

Economics of Pension Insurance. Richard A. Ippolito. 1989.

Fundamentals of Private Pensions. Dan M. McGill and Donald S. Grubbs, Jr. Sixth edition. 1988.

Future of Pensions in the United States. Raymond Schmitt, ed. 1993.

Inflation and Pensions. Susan M. Wachter. 1987.

It's My Retirement Money, Take Good Care of It: The TIAA-CREF Story. William C. Greenough. 1990.

Joint Trust Pension Plans: Understanding and Administering Collectively Bargained Multiemployer Plans Under ERISA. Daniel F. McGinn. 1977.

Pension Asset Management: An International Perspective. Leslie Hannah, ed. 1988.

Pension Mathematics with Numerical Illustrations. Howard E. Winklevoss. Second edition. 1993.

Pensions and the Economy: Sources, Uses, and Limitations of Data. Zvi Bodie and Alicia H. Munnell, eds. 1992.

Pensions, Economics and Public Policy. Richard A. Ippolito. 1985.

Providing Health Care Benefits in Retirement. Judith F. Mazo, Anna M. Rappaport, and Sylvester J. Schieber, eds. 1994.

Proxy Voting of Pension Plan Equity Securities. Dan M. McGill, ed. 1989.

Retirement Systems for Public Employees. Thomas P. Bleakney. 1972.

Retirement Systems in Japan. Robert L. Clark. 1990.

Search for a National Retirement Income Policy. Jack L. VanDerhei, ed. 1987.

Social Investing. Dan M. McGill, ed. 1984.

Social Security. Robert J. Myers. Fourth edition. 1993.

This book was set in Baskerville and Eras typefaces. Baskerville was designed by John Baskerville at his private press in Birmingham, England, in the eighteenth century. The first typeface to depart from oldstyle typeface design, Baskerville has more variation between thick and thin strokes. In an effort to insure that the thick and thin strokes of his typeface reproduced well on paper, John Baskerville developed the first wove paper, the surface of which was much smoother than the laid paper of the time. The development of wove paper was partly responsible for the introduction of typefaces classified as modern, which have even more contrast between thick and thin strokes.

Eras was designed in 1969 by Studio Hollenstein in Paris for the Wagner Typefoundry. A contemporary script-like version of a sans-serif typeface, the letters of Eras have a monotone stroke and are slightly inclined.

Printed on acid-free paper.